Contents

Foreword by Sander Kristel, Chief Operating Officer, UCAS   vii

Introduction   1
The job of UCAS   1
Using this guide   2
Timetable for advanced-level students   3

Part I. In the think tank   7

1| **Is higher education right for you?**   8
Overview of higher education today   8
All about you   8
Chapter summary   10

2| **Looking to the future: career routes**   12
Developing a career plan   12
The graduate skill set   14
Work experience   16
Chapter summary   22

3| **A matter of money**   23
Tuition fees   23
Living expenses   24
Funding your studies   25
Additional support   27
Other sources of cash   30
Chapter summary   31

4| **Choosing what to study**   32
Which subject area?   32
Which qualification?   34
Which mode of study?   37
Which courses?   39
Chapter summary   40

5| **Choosing where to study**   41
Working out your priorities   41
Staying close to home?   42
Researching your shortlist   43
Selecting the final five   45
Chapter summary   45

6| **Academic requirements**   47
What might the entry requirements be?   47
How are entry requirements expressed?   50
Targeting the right courses   58
Chapter summary   59

Part II. The admissions procedure: applications, interviews, offers and beyond   **61**

7| **Applications and offers**   **62**
Making your application   62
Decisions and offers   64
What if you don't get any offers?   67

8| **Non-standard applications**   **69**
Oxford and Cambridge   69
Applying to study at a conservatoire   70
Medicine, dentistry and veterinary science/veterinary
   medicine courses   72
Mature students   73
Deferred entry   74
Making a late application   76
International students   76

9| **Interviews and selection**   **78**
Interviews   78
Auditions and portfolios   82
Aptitude tests   83
Other entrance tests   86

10| **Exam results and afterwards**   **87**
Before results day   87
Results day   88
Retakes   93

Part III. Your UCAS application   **95**

11| **Getting started**   **96**
Register with UCAS   96
Looking for apprenticeships?   97
Starting your application   97
Your written reference   98
Navigating your application   99
Checking the progress of your application   100
Security tips   102
How the rest of this book works   102
Stop and think!   103

12| **Personal details**   **104**
Personal information   104

13| **Nationality details**   **105**
UK nationals   105
International   106
Visa and passport details   107

14| **Where you live**   **108**
Home address   108
Residential category   108

15| **Contact details**   **111**
   Postal address   111
   Nominee access   111

16| **Supporting information**   **112**
   Living or working in the EU, EEA or Switzerland   112

17| **Finance and funding**   **113**
   Sponsorship   114

18| **Diversity and inclusion**   **115**
   Ethnic origin   115
   Religion or belief   117
   Sexual orientation   117
   Transgender   118
   Care support information   118
   Parental education   118
   Occupational background   118

19| **More about you**   **120**
   Students with a physical and/or mental health condition,
      long-term illness, or learning difference   120
   Estranged students   121
   Students with caring responsibilities   121
   Students with parenting responsibilities   123
   Refugees, asylum seekers and students with limited
      leave to remain   123
   Students with a parent or carer who serves in the
      UK Armed Forces, or has done in the past   123
   Students who have served in the UK Armed Forces   124
   Students receiving free school meals   124

20| **Education**   **125**
   Unique Learner Number   125
   Places of education   125
   Add qualifications   127
   Which qualifications should I add?   130

21| **Employment**   **132**
   Add your employment   132

22| **Extra activities**   **134**

23| **Personal statement**   **136**
   What are admissions tutors looking for?   136
   Top tips   139
   Creating a winning personal statement   141
   Mature students   147

24| **Adding a choice**   **149**
   Add your university or college and your course   149
   Start date   149
   Further details   150
   Point of entry   151

	Living at home while studying?	151
	Criminal convictions	151
	Confirm choices	154
	Admissions tests and assessments	154
25|	**Finishing your application**	**156**
	Declaration	156
	Submitting your application	157
	Payment	158
	What happens next?	158
26|	**Troubleshooting**	**159**
	Some common problems	159
	Need help?	160
	And finally …	160
	Further information	**161**
	Glossary	**165**
	Appendix: A note for staff on becoming a UCAS centre	**167**

Foreword

First decision: where to begin?

Congratulations! You've made an important decision to consider your options and potentially apply to a university or college course, or for an apprenticeship. With so many choices to make you might need some help in deciding what is best for you or what and where to study. This book will help you turn that decision into a reality.

We at UCAS believe giving you access to as much information as possible is vital in helping you to make a good decision about your future studies.

The research you do and the advice you get can provide a valuable insight into which method of study or which course is right for you. The UCAS Hub on ucas.com should be your starting point – register now to explore, research or chat to current students. After registration there is no obligation to apply, and you can explore a wide range of options. The UCAS Careers Quiz in the Hub, for instance, has already supported over a million people, just like you, to make their choices.

When you're ready to begin your search for courses or apprenticeships, the UCAS search tool and UCAS's apprenticeship search are the definitive sources of information on your options. We advise you to look closely at this information and, if possible, make a visit to the universities and colleges you're interested in. Remember, you could potentially be spending three or four years there, so it needs to feel like the right place for you. At the same time as looking at full-time university courses, you can also consider an apprenticeship, which is a great way to get a degree while you work.

This guide will tell you what you need to know about applying, and make sure you also head to ucas.com where we've got tips and blogs from students, parents and advisers. Have a look around – and if you have a question that remains unanswered, get in touch.

Best of luck with your research and application!

Sander Kristel
Chief Operating Officer, UCAS

Introduction

This book is intended to be a guide for anyone wanting to gain a place on a UK higher education course. In the 2022/23 application cycle, 752,025 people applied for undergraduate courses, a decrease of 1.3% on the previous year. Of these, 554,465 were accepted through UCAS to start an undergraduate course in 2023. All of these students had to complete UCAS applications to try to gain their university or college place.

The job of UCAS

With very few exceptions, every application to a full-time higher education course must be made through UCAS – whether a degree, a course leading to a degree, a Foundation degree, Higher National Diploma (HND) or Diploma of Higher Education (DipHE). UCAS manages and monitors the flow of applications to universities and colleges and their decisions to applicants. UCAS acts as the intermediary between students and their chosen universities and colleges, providing lists of available courses and the means by which prospective students can apply for them.

As well as handling initial applications, UCAS offers Clearing as a way for students to find a place when the summer exam results come out. Find out more about Clearing in Chapter 10.

UCAS supports students to explore all their options – entering higher education, apprenticeships and employment – and provides information and advice to help you make the right choice. On ucas.com, you can:

- register for the UCAS Hub – allowing you to explore and research your options, and even chat to current students based at universities and colleges around the UK
- take the UCAS Careers Quiz to find your ideal career and see what courses previous students studied to get there from your UCAS Hub, virtually experience university and the world of work before you apply, through Subject Spotlights. You'll have access to interactive university taster courses and immersive and information virtual work experiences with leading employers (from spring 2024)
- use the UCAS search tool to research the courses offered by different universities and colleges – using a number of variables, such as qualification (degree, HND, etc.), subject, university or college, or geographical area

- use UCAS's apprenticeship and graduate job search tool to search for apprenticeships, filter by subject area, industry, role type, location and level, and sign up for alerts to keep you posted on the latest opportunities
- explore jobs and careers, industry guides and employer profiles
- use UCAS's CV builder to quickly and easily create a CV to support your apprenticeship applications, using the details you entered when you registered for the UCAS Hub (available from summer 2024)
- use the accommodation search tool for university-owned and private options
- find out the entry requirements for courses, including grades and Tariff* points and any additional requirements
- find out more about each course, including its content, teaching methods and method of assessment
- make an application to your chosen university courses and/or apprenticeship
- follow the progress of your application
- find an additional course to apply to if you've used all your choices and you aren't holding any offers (through our Extra* service)
- get information about financing your studies
- go through Clearing* if you have your results but no offers.

* All these terms are explained in the Glossary (see page 165).

Of course, applying through UCAS is no guarantee of a place on a higher education course. Every year, a number of people apply but aren't offered places.

Using this guide

This book is divided into three parts. A brief outline of the content and purpose of each part is given below.

Part I. In the think tank

Before you make a UCAS application, research all your higher education options thoroughly. The first part of this guide gives you a number of ideas about the areas you need to consider carefully before you can be confident of making the right higher education course choices. These six chapters guide you through the decision-making process, helping you to find answers to key questions, such as:

- is higher education the right option for me? (Chapter 1)
- how will a degree or higher diploma fit in with my career plans? (Chapter 2)
- how will I afford it? (Chapter 3)

- how do I choose what and where to study? (Chapters 4 and 5)
- will I meet the entry requirements? (Chapter 6)

You need to be ready to explain and justify your decision. Admissions tutors read your UCAS application and may interview you – they'll want to know why you've applied for a place on their particular course. At the end of this book there's a 'Further information' section suggesting points of reference you can access in your school or college library, or your local careers centre. Ask advisers for help in finding the most up-to-date materials.

Part II. The admissions procedure: applications, interviews, offers and beyond

Once you've decided which courses to apply for, Part II provides an overview of the entire admissions procedure. It works through the whole process, answering key questions such as:

- when do I submit my application? (Chapter 7)
- how do universities and colleges communicate their offers to me? (Chapter 7)
- how do I accept or decline offers? (Chapter 7)
- what about non-standard applications? (Chapter 8)
- how can I maximise my chances if I'm called for interview? (Chapter 9)
- what happens on exam results day? (Chapter 10)
- how do I use Clearing? (Chapter 10)

Part III. Your UCAS application

Part III covers the technicalities of filling in and submitting your UCAS application online, taking you through the process step by step and offering helpful advice and tips.

Timetable for advanced-level students

If you stick to the timetable, the whole process of applying to higher education is straightforward. The application timetable below gives you an idea of what to do and when.

Please note: the term advanced-level students doesn't mean simply A level students – it's for all students doing any advanced or level 3 course.

First year of advanced-level course

Autumn term
- Start to explore the range of possible options beyond your advanced-level courses at school or college. (Chapters 1 and 2)

- Consider your GCSE or equivalent qualifications – the range and grades achieved – and review any A level, Scottish Higher, International Baccalaureate (IB), Irish Leaving Certificate (ILC) or BTEC National subjects you're taking. (Chapter 6)
- Will your qualifications help you to achieve your future plans? Discuss this with your careers adviser.

Spring term
- Work through a skills, aptitudes and interests guide like MyUniChoices (www.myunichoices.com) or Morrisby Profile (www.morrisby.com/morrisby-profile), Indigo (https://indigo.careers) or Unifrog (www.unifrog.org) and/or complete a career development profiling exercise. (Chapter 2)
- Start to research your higher education options in the light of these results. Prepare for and attend a UCAS higher education exhibition. From 30 April 2024, UCAS's search tool will display 2025 courses. (Chapters 4 and 5)
- Explore the financial implications of attending a higher education course. (Chapter 3)

Summer term
- Prepare for and attend a UCAS exhibition, if you missed out on this in the spring. (Chapters 4 and 5)
- Attend university and college open days.
- Continue to research your higher education options, and check UCAS course entry requirements.
- Draw up a shortlist of possible universities and/or colleges.
- Make decisions on courses and modules to take next year.
- Arrange to do work experience during the summer. This is important for entry to some courses, for example medicine, those leading to healthcare professions (such as occupational therapy, physiotherapy, radiography and speech therapy), veterinary science and veterinary medicine, social work, the land-based industries and teaching degree courses. (Chapter 2)
- Try to obtain sponsorship for courses – write to possible organisations you have researched. (Chapter 3)
- Start to organise your year out if you plan to take a gap year.
- Gather up material evidence from which to draft a personal statement for your UCAS application. (Chapter 23)
- Research details for sitting the University Clinical Aptitude Test (UCAT), which is required for entry to medicine and dentistry at some universities. You can register from 14 May 2024, book your test between 18 June and midday on 19 September 2024, and take the test between 8 July and 26 September 2024. (Chapter 9)

Summer holidays

- Undertake the work experience you arranged during the summer term. Keep a diary of what you did so that you can refer back to it when you write your personal statement. (Chapter 23)
- Possibly attend a taster course (which can be arranged by many universities). (Chapter 4)

Second year of advanced-level course

Autumn term

- Between 3 September 2024 and the equal-consideration date (which is either 15 October 2024 or 29 January 2025 depending on your course), submit your completed UCAS application. 'Equal consideration' means that your application will be considered inthe same way whether it is received by UCAS on in early September or on 15 October 2024 or 29 January 2025 depending on your course. (Chapter 7 and Part III)
- Registration and booking for the Law National Aptitude Test (LNAT) for 2025 entry opens on 1 August 2024; testing starts on 1 September 2024; the standard closing date for booking a test is 20 January 2025; and the last date for sitting the LNAT is 31 January 2025. (NB: Some universities have an earlier closing date.) (Chapter 9)
- Before 26 September 2024 (last available date) take the UCAT test if necessary.
- Before 18.00 (UK time) on 15 October, submit your UCAS application for the universities of Oxford and Cambridge. The University of Oxford requires some extra information for some international interviews and for choral or organ awards. (Chapter 8 and Part III)
- Before 18.00 (UK time) on 15 October, submit all UCAS applications for entry to medicine, dentistry, veterinary science and veterinary medicine.

Spring term

- 29 January 2025 at 18.00 (UK time) is the equal-consideration date for UCAS to receive applications for all courses except those with a 15 October deadline. Use the UCAS search tool at www.ucas.com to check your course deadline.
- Apply for bursaries, sponsorship or scholarships as appropriate.
- Prepare for possible interviews with admissions tutors; a mock interview if your school/college offers them is useful at this point.
- If you live in England, Wales and Northern Ireland, you should make your application for financial assessment through the Student Loans Company, whatever your particular circumstances. Applicants from Scotland make their application for financial assessment to the Student Awards Agency for Scotland (SAAS).
- If you used all five choices in your application but aren't holding an offer of a place, you can use the Extra option. Extra applications can be made from 26 February 2025.

Summer term

- By 14 May 2025, decisions should have been received from all universities and colleges if you applied by 29 January.
- Once you have received all your university and college decisions, you need to reply to the offers by 4 June 2025.
- 30 June 2025 at 18:00 (UK time) is the last date for receipt of applications before Clearing.
- Until 4 July, further applications can be made using UCAS Extra (if you applied for five courses originally and are not holding an offer).

Summer holidays

- 5 July 2024 is IB results day (the date for 2025 is still to be confirmed).
- 15 August 2024 is A level results day (the date for 2025 is still to be confirmed).
- 6 August 2024 is Scottish Highers results day (the date for 2025 is still to be confirmed).
- From 5 July 2025, UCAS Clearing vacancy information is available. If you don't get the results you were hoping for, you may need additional support through Clearing to find an alternative higher education option or further information and guidance from your local careers service.
- 24 September 2025 is the last date for new Clearing applications for 2025 entry. You have until 20 October 2025 to add a Clearing choice to an existing application.

Part I
In the think tank

1 | Is higher education right for you?

Overview of higher education today

Applying for entry to higher education may well be the most important step that you've taken up to now. It's one that will certainly affect the next three or more years of your life and in the long term will affect your career choices and prospects, which in turn will impact on your future lifestyle.

There are plenty of people who can help you choose your higher education course and place of study – your careers adviser, your careers and subject teachers, your present employer and your family and friends. The decision is ultimately yours though, and you'll need to be confident about the suitability of your chosen higher education course.

Every year, people take up places only to find that the course content, teaching style or institution isn't what they expected – and they subsequently leave their courses. The average non-continuation rate during the first year of study on a full-time first degree course is 5.3% for the UK as a whole, but the rate at individual universities and colleges varies considerably (source: Higher Education Statistics Agency).

This can be difficult, not just for the student but also for the university or college, so it is worth taking the time at this stage to make sure that your application choices are right for you.

All about you

Before considering higher education courses have a think about the following questions.

Are you happy to continue in education?

Going on to higher education is a big step to take. Put simply, you've got to be committed and enthusiastic. If you don't enjoy your chosen course, you will find your time in higher education very difficult.

Advanced-level study – for example GCE, A level, Scottish Higher, Irish Leaving Certificate (ILC), International Baccalaureate (IB), BTEC National Award and so on – is an essential preparation for many aspects of higher education, not just in terms of subject-specific knowledge but also in terms of analytical skills. On your higher education course, you'll be further developing your powers of deduction, reasoning, critical analysis and evaluation – just as much as you'll be learning new facts about your chosen subject. Are you ready for this?

There are literally thousands of courses, and many include opportunities for practical learning, work experience and studying abroad. Do you like the sound of this?

Have you seriously explored your aptitudes, interests and career aspirations?

Do you want to learn more because you have strong ability in a particular area and because you find the subject matter interesting? If so, you are in a good starting position and you're likely to enjoy your studies.

Some degree-level courses explore one particular subject area in great depth, with no direct link to employment or a career structure (for example history, anthropology, geography, physics, English, American studies and French). Have you thought about what you'll do once you graduate? How will your degree link with your long-term career plan? (See Chapter 2 for more on this.) A degree may only be a stepping stone to the start of a professional career – once you're in employment, it is often necessary to continue studying to gain professional qualifications. So you'll need commitment to reach your goals.

Some people are influenced by promotional publicity or by the enthusiasm of other people, and don't consider the possible long-term impact of their choice on themselves. You need to think carefully about this. Step back and try a number of aptitude and interest guides that are available online and in careers centres (see the 'Further information' section at the end of the book).

Are you ready to be a student?

Student life is likely to offer you all of the social and extracurricular opportunities you ever dreamed of. Are you confident you can balance your social life with your studies – especially if you apply for a course with fewer scheduled contact hours, such as English or history? Remember, there's a big change from the guided learning you've experienced at school or college to the self-management of study in higher education.

You'll have to develop your own study skills and become an independent, self-motivated learner. Your subject teachers or tutors can offer helpful guidance on this point.

Don't be surprised if you feel confused and uncertain about applying to courses a long way from home. You're taking an important decision that may result in you striking out on your own, seemingly leaving behind everything you find familiar. It's natural to feel apprehensive about this – many people do experience insecurity and can feel isolated and disorientated at first, but most find they adapt very quickly.

If you're feeling very worried about the prospect of leaving home, talk to a friendly careers adviser, student adviser, personal tutor, or a friend or relative, and focus on the positive aspects of your higher education intentions. It's important to make sure you're clear about your plans and the changes these will mean for your day-to-day life.

Lastly – money. How you're going to finance your higher education course is likely to be a major consideration. You'll need to give careful thought to the financial implications of going through higher education. For example, some people decide to live at home rather than go away in order to save money. Some choose universities and colleges that offer cheaper accommodation. Others look carefully at the scholarships and bursaries on offer at different places. This subject is discussed in depth in Chapter 3.

Chapter summary

The decision to pursue a higher education course isn't one to take lightly. However, if you have read through the questions and points above and still feel confident that higher education is the right choice for you, read on. The rest of Part I will help you focus your research so you can narrow down the huge number of courses on offer to the ones you'll enter on your UCAS application (you can add between one and five courses).

As you work through the following chapters, keep testing yourself by asking the following questions.

- Have I given enough consideration to each point?
- Which resources proved useful in my research?
- Have I talked to people with knowledge or experience in this area?
- Will I feel the same in two or three years?
- Should I do more research?

Essential research

- Talk to subject teachers, tutors or form teachers and careers advisers.
- Check to see whether your local careers service gives information on higher education opportunities on its website.
- Use the timetable on pages 3 to 6 to draw up your own calendar of important dates and deadlines. You will need to make decisions about courses to apply to in the autumn term of 2024, and then you'll need to meet all subsequent UCAS deadlines.
- Register for your UCAS Hub on ucas.com to start your research and chat to current students.

2 | Looking to the future: career routes

Since you'll be committing a lot of time and money to study a higher education course, it's vital to research possible graduate career routes. This is the moment for in-depth careers exploration and planning, looking at where a particular subject area might take you and what previous graduates have gone on to do.

This may seem tricky. How can you possibly know what you want to do in four years' time? How can you narrow down the options when you are having enough trouble just choosing which courses to apply for? While some people do have firm career ideas. For others, the idea of planning for the future can be difficult – because there's simply too much choice. It may also seem time consuming when you are busy working for exams.

In most cases, investigating possible careers doesn't mean committing yourself to one particular career at this stage. Remember, any decisions you make or ideas you have at this stage aren't set in stone. You can change and adapt your plans as you go. It's good to have some career ideas though, not least because admissions tutors want to see that you're looking ahead, and that you'll be an interested and motivated student with career plans beyond your time at university or college. Plus, thinking about your plans now will prepare you for career-related questions if you're invited to an interview (see Chapter 9).

There are many people who can help you form some ideas about a future career, but ideally your first port of call should be your school or college's careers department or a chat with a careers adviser. Unfortunately, availability varies in different areas, but there are other people you can ask for help, too – like parents, friends, former students from your school or college – and there are useful online tools which your school or college might have. (These are listed in the 'Further information' section at the end of the book.)

Developing a career plan

If you already have a career plan

Now's the time to research it in as much depth as possible. Find out which courses are the most relevant and which get you professional accreditation in the career you have chosen (if applicable). For many careers, a degree is only the first step – you'll have to undertake further training, often in employment, in order to qualify (e.g. accountancy and engineering). Also, find out which courses have the best record of placing graduates in their chosen career area. (For more on this, see Chapters 4 and 5.)

If you already know what subject interests you, but you don't know what you want to do next

This is the time to do some broad research. Take a look at a careers directory or website (see the 'Further information' section at the end of this book) to find out what's out there, and focus on the jobs that seem to relate to your chosen subject. Research possible progression routes and projected salaries in different careers.

If you're interested in a career that requires postgraduate training in order to qualify with a professional association, look on the organisation's website to find out what will be required after your degree. You could also investigate future job opportunities and likely salaries.

If you're interested in a subject that doesn't lead directly to a specific career (e.g. history or sociology), a good starting point is to find out which careers have been entered by graduates in these subjects. This information is usually available on university and college websites. Find the subject department and look up destinations of recent graduates. It will also be useful to find out how many of last year's graduates are in full-time professional occupations that draw on their particular skills and abilities.

In addition to looking at university and college websites, you could consult the latest edition of *What do graduates do?* which is jointly produced by Jisc and the Association of Graduate Careers Advisory Services (AGCAS). The report, which gives the destinations of students who graduated in 2020 15 months after graduation, is available at https://luminate.prospects.ac.uk/what-do-graduates-do.

Better still, try to find information on graduates' destinations one or two years on, if universities and colleges are able to provide this. Again, university and college websites could be useful here – take a look at the individual subject departments. If they have former students who are in particularly interesting jobs, you can be sure they'll want to show where their courses can lead.

If you have no idea at all

If you're not sure what subject area interests you and you don't have a particular career in mind, it may be worth reconsidering whether higher education is right for you. On the other hand, if you're simply feeling bewildered by the number of options available to you, there are plenty of books (Trotman's *Getting into* series can give some useful insights into career pathways), websites and online tools that can help you to assess your interests. Try a range of them, and take it from there.

TIP!

Remember – your careers adviser is always a good starting point.

The graduate skill set

Some courses lead naturally into a recognised career or occupational area (e.g. engineering, hospitality management, law and medicine), but most don't. So, for many, the benefit of higher education in terms of career prospects is to develop a 'graduate skill set', because study of any subject at this level should develop your abilities in some of the areas employers value, while practical opportunities can help you to develop other valuable skills.

Employers recruit graduates as they value the skills they have developed during their studies, such as:

- planning and organising their work
- time management
- researching facts and broader issues
- understanding and analysing information
- problem solving, critical and logical thinking
- writing well-structured reports, essays, etc.
- giving presentations
- putting forward arguments to support a case in a debate.

These skills are transferable and relevant to a wide range of jobs. Employers also look for other skills and qualities such as motivation and enthusiasm, self-reliance, adaptability, computer literacy, communication (speaking and listening), teamworking and leadership skills. Such skills may be developed during your time at university – either through your course or other activities.

The *Education and Skills Survey*, published by the CBI (Confederation of British Industry) and Pearson Education, reports views from employers on which skills are important to possess for people leaving school, college or university.

The factor that was ranked most important by top employers was attitude and aptitude for work. 64% of employers selected this among their top three factors when recruiting graduates and 78% when recruiting school and college leavers.

Attitude and aptitude for work: what are these skills?

They are often known as non-technical, soft, transferable or employability skills. They have different names in different organisations, but generally come under the following headings:

- business and customer awareness
- communication and literacy
- critical thinking
- entrepreneurship/enterprise
- IT
- managing complex information
- numeracy
- positive attitude
- problem solving
- research skills
- self-management
- team working.

Many degree and diploma programmes help you to develop these skills. Use the UCAS search tool to check your chosen course at several different universities and colleges, or look at apprenticeship opportunities in UCAS's apprenticeship search, to learn about the skills they could help you develop. The careers advisory services may also be able to assist. They are there to help students in all years, and making early contact can be very useful.

Many universities and colleges include relevant modules in all their courses and issue students with a logbook or certificate that shows how they gained each skill – for example:

- analysis and solving problems
- team working and interpersonal skills
- verbal communication
- written communication
- personal planning and organising
- initiative
- numerical reasoning
- information literacy and IT.

Plus, many careers services or employability centres run separate employability and personal development courses, which you can follow while working for your academic qualifications. These are well worth exploring when you arrive at university or college – you'll normally receive an award valued by many graduate employers.

Many careers advisory services also run special sessions for students to help them understand which transferable skills are most in demand by employers, and how to acquire them. Some workshops are run by major employers in conjunction with careers advisory services, while others are run independently by careers advisers and focus on subjects such as:

- assessment centres
- commercial awareness
- numbers for the world of work (designed to give confidence in numeracy)
- how to raise your profile when networking online
- industry insights
- successful meetings
- perfect presentations
- realising your strengths
- interview skills
- preparing for psychometric assessment
- project management
- putting your skills to work
- success in business
- team and leadership development.

Having high-level skills in these areas will increase your appeal to prospective employers. With severe competition for the best graduate jobs, employers are able to pick and choose whom they hire. So you might like to see what's offered in the way of employability skills training before you make your final choice of course and university or college.

However, some university and college admissions tutors – and some graduate employers – will require you to have demonstrated your interest in your chosen career area through work experience or work placements **before you apply for a higher education place through UCAS**. This is a major reason why it's important to think hard about your career aspirations as early as possible.

Work experience

For many courses, being able to write about suitable work experience on your UCAS form will boost your application. Many courses (especially those linked with health or social care and with careers in the land-based industries, for example) nearly always expect applicants to have arranged some experience – even for a short period – in a relevant job. Maybe your school or college is already onto this and has arranged some form of work experience or shadowing for you? If not, you could try to arrange something yourself to take place in the holidays.

Even one or two days spent in gaining relevant experience or in work shadowing can be helpful.

What is work shadowing?

This term refers to observing someone at work – normally in a highly skilled job. A solicitor, dentist or surgeon for instance might let a student spend some time with them (though wouldn't have the knowledge yet to try out the job!). A good shadowing period would though allow you to learn by watching and asking questions.

Try some or all of the following:

- look for the type of business you'd like to work for (for example, solicitors, hospitals, etc.)
- make a list of the companies you'd like to work for
- make a note of their contact details – you can usually get these details online
- ask if they have any work experience opportunities by email; it's a good idea to phone first and ask whom to contact.

If they don't have any opportunities at the time, you could ask if they could contact you when something comes up next – and offer to send them a copy of your CV (a document that lists your personal information, education and experience; this is sometimes also known as a résumé, though this is primarily a North American term).

Writing a CV

A CV should include:

- your full name
- your address
- contact details – phone number and email address
- education – schools/colleges, qualifications, beginning with the most recent
- skills – e.g. knowledge of computer/software packages, driving licence
- previous work experience, giving name of employers
- positions of responsibility in or out of school or college
- interests/hobbies
- names of two or three referees – it is essential you gain permission from the people you list as able to provide a reference.

A CV should be no longer than two sides in length. Use a clear font, like Calibri or Arial, at a minimum font size of 11pt.

Recent research has found that employers spend around 10 seconds reading a CV. So, be concise with language – avoid lengthy sentences or paragraphs and make use of bullet points, e.g. when listing key skills.

And always send an accompanying 'cover letter'. See opposite for a sample CV.

Finding work experience

Finding work experience isn't always possible. Some professionals, such as doctors, vets, accountants and lawyers, are often flooded with requests from students. Plus, they have the problem of contacting patients or clients to ask if they'll agree to have a student present.

Since the Covid-19 pandemic, there has been a significant growth of virtual internships where people can work with employers from home. Online work experience is open to all, and for the majority of opportunities all you need to get involved is access to a computer and a stable internet connection. Virtual internships are in many ways similar to in-person internships, but their online nature enables participants to work with organisations across the UK and abroad. The Prospects UK website is a useful source of information on virtual internships and includes a vacancy search facility.

If you can't get any experience in the profession you are hoping to enter, there are alternatives. You could, for example, visit law courts and observe different trials. If you can't arrange work experience in a hospital or with a GP, you could try to observe what goes on at a typical doctor's practice. You could ask if it's possible to spend some time with a practice nurse or healthcare assistant.

If you can't find any opportunities in a relevant profession, you could still demonstrate that you have the right sort of personal skills by doing paid or voluntary work in a caring environment where you'll learn to work with people directly, for example:

- in a children's nursery if you're interested in teaching
- in a day centre for people with disabilities if you're interested in nursing, physiotherapy or social work
- with a volunteer agency such as a drug rehabilitation centre or a night shelter for homeless people if you hope to study social work or psychology
- on a local conservation project if you're hoping to do a course connected with the environment.

While you should not do voluntary work just to make your UCAS application look good, it can certainly help to strengthen an application. It can also give you the satisfaction of helping other people and help you to find out a bit more about careers that might interest you. A good place to start is your local volunteer centre, which will have a list of opportunities, or through online databases such as www.doit.life, where you can search for over one million volunteering opportunities by interest, activity or location and apply online.

CHLOE ADAMS

4 The Pines, Anytown, Hampshire, HR51 3DF
07987 123456; ca2005@zmail.com

PERSONAL PROFILE

*An A level student of biology, psychology and English literature,
looking to make a career as a speech and language therapist.
Currently gaining experience supporting primary school pupils with
reading skills, including working with a school SEN Co-ordinator.
Patient, empathic, approachable, and highly conscientious.
Looking for experience in a health setting to enhance my prospects
for entry to a degree in speech and language therapy at university.*

KEY SKILLS, QUALITIES & EXPERIENCE

- Sensitive to and understanding of others
- Understanding and awareness of how people communicate, including recognising facial expressions and body language; able to adapt to communication needs of children worked with
- Strong attention to detail
- Patient and calm in stressful situations
- Computer literate, proficient in MS Word, Excel and PowerPoint
- Well-developed written and spoken communication skills

EDUCATION, TRAINING & QUALIFICATIONS

Sept 2023 to date: Anytown Sixth Form College, Hampshire
Studying for GCE A level: Biology, Psychology and English Literature.
GCSEs: English Language (7), English Literature (8), Mathematics (6), Biology (7), Chemistry (6), Physics (6), French (7), Design Technology (6). A member of the school council in Years 10 and 11. Represented the school at hockey from Years 7 to 11.

WORK EXPERIENCE

October 2023 to date: **Volunteer Support Assistant**, St Peter's Primary School, Anytown, Hampshire
I attend school for half a day per week to assist with reading and writing activities with Year 2 children; this involves one-to-one reading and listening with pupils, assisting with classroom set up and providing general support to teachers as required.
June 2021 to date: **Saturday Cafe Assistant**, The Coffee Shop, Anytown, Hampshire
The role involves taking orders, serving customers, taking payments (cash and card), and preparing refreshments and light meals to order. I gained my Level 2 Food Hygiene Certificate in June 2021.

SOCIAL ACTIVITIES & INTERESTS

Keeping fit and healthy through attendance at local gym, running and swimming.

REFERENCES

Available on request.

> **TIP!**
>
> Admissions tutors are impressed by applicants who have built up knowledge of a related work sector and whose plans include developing useful employment links while studying. If you tried hard to obtain work experience but were unsuccessful, explain this on your UCAS application and describe related activities that you have undertaken as an alternative.

While in higher education

The same points apply once you get to university or college. You may need to work during term time, so look first for relevant experience. Try to spend time in a job that will broaden your experience and give you insight into a potential employment area. If that's not possible, do your best to draw up a list of transferable skills applicable to any career from any kind of job, e.g. bar work, sales, whatever you can find.

Your university's careers advisory service or student services unit can usually help, and may run a job shop to help students find part-time opportunities. It can also provide details of vacation work placements – and may even be able to give you a grant to help with additional expenses you might incur on a placement.

> **Describing work experience on your UCAS application**
>
> *When describing work experience in your personal statement, it is important to explain how the things you did support your application, and also what you learned from the experience gained and, further, what you learned about yourself. This is particularly important for applications for degrees such as medicine or nursing, but can be applied to other areas of study as well. Here is an example:*
>
> 'During my work experience at a GP practice, I had the opportunity to engage in a variety of tasks and gain valuable insights into the medical field. One of the key responsibilities I had was assisting the medical staff in managing patient appointments and maintaining patient records. This involved organising and scheduling appointments, updating patient information, and ensuring confidentiality and accuracy of the records.
>
> 'I also had the chance to observe and learn from the medical professionals during patient consultations. This allowed me to understand the importance of effective communication and empathy in providing quality healthcare. I learned how to interact with patients, actively listen to their concerns, and provide reassurance and support.

'In addition, I was involved in administrative tasks such as filing documents, organising medical supplies, and managing inventory. This experience enhanced my organisational skills and attention to detail, as I had to ensure that everything was in order and easily accessible for the medical staff.

'Overall, my work experience at the GP practice allowed me to enhance my interpersonal skills, organisational abilities, and knowledge of the healthcare industry. It provided me with a valuable foundation for pursuing a career in the medical field and reinforced my passion for helping others.'

Admissions tutors are interested to see how you dealt with situations encountered during work experience placements with clear examples, not just claiming that you have particular qualities or skills.

Case study - Deb

At the time of writing, Deb is a second year student reading a sociology and criminology joint degree.

'I chose *what* to study at university based on my interest in sociology at A level. Right now, I don't have any set ideas about what my future career will be, although hopefully it will be connected to the criminal justice system – perhaps criminal rehabilitation or probation work. I loved sociology at A level, and I was hungry to learn more about why people commit crime and the effect it has on society.

'I chose *where* to study based on the enthusiasm of the lecturing staff I met at an open day. I found their talks about the research they were doing so interesting, and when I saw that the course involved visits from people who had experienced the criminal justice system themselves, as well as people who work in the system, I thought this course would be a great opportunity to get a real insight into the causes of criminal behaviour and how people manage to turn their lives around. I was also attracted to the small group sizes of seminar groups, as this allows for discussion of topics with other students and lecturers. We did lots of this on my A level sociology course too and I really enjoyed this way of learning. We were taught to challenge ideas, and I have learned how to analyse and not accept things at face value.

'Everyone is different and we all have our own priorities and preferences, but my advice to people choosing universities and courses is to get a good understanding of the course, how it is taught, how it is assessed and how comfortable you feel with the overall set up of the university. It really is important to visit the place if you possibly can.

Virtual events and websites can give a glossy picture of what universities are like; it's only by visiting them that you get a real idea of what they are like, as well as the surrounding area.

'I chose the university that was really helpful and quick to respond to my questions at all stages of my application journey. Other places were less helpful, and didn't feel right for me.

'This degree is equipping me with a lot of useful skills, including data analysis, report writing and effective listening, all of which can be used in all sorts of careers.'

Chapter summary

It's helpful to have a career path in mind, even if it might change later as you progress through your course and gain experience. The earlier you start your research, the better your chance of making an informed decision – with the added benefit that evidence of your long-term approach will strengthen your UCAS application and help you give a good interview.

3 | A matter of money

If you've come this far in the book, you're serious about applying to a higher education institution. Though, even before considering whether you're likely to achieve the entry grades for the course, you'll probably have asked yourself, 'Can I afford it?'

Certainly, you'll need to think through your finances very carefully and research all the types of assistance that's available to you. There is a lot of information available on government websites, on ucas.com, from universities and colleges and in books written specifically on this subject. A summary is given in this chapter, with details of where to look for more information in the 'Further information' section at the end of the book.

To help you consider whether higher education is right for you, this chapter looks at the two main costs in attending higher education: tuition fees and living expenses.

All figures given in this chapter were current in March 2024. You can expect increases in future years – you'll need to check for up-to-date rates.

Tuition fees

UK students

The tuition fee that you will have to pay for undergraduate courses will depend on where you live and where you intend to study. Universities are allowed to charge home undergraduate fees up to £9,250 per year, as part of the government's Teaching Excellence Framework (TEF), which assesses universities and colleges on the quality of their teaching. The tuition fee cap had been set at £9,000 in Wales, but in February 2024 the Welsh government announced that it was increasing to £9,250 for 2024 entry. Elsewhere in the UK, the tuition fee cap has been in place for a number of years and increases are expected in the future.

There are a number of variations between the systems in England, Scotland, Wales and Northern Ireland, which can result in significant differences between the fees that are ultimately paid by students. Currently (for 2024/2025 entry) the rules are as follows, although they may be subject to change in the future.

- Students from England and Wales are required to pay a maximum of £9,250 if they are studying in England, Wales, Scotland or Northern Ireland.
- Students from Scotland who study at Scottish universities are not required to pay tuition fees (or, rather, tuition fees of £1,820 for 2024 entry are covered the Student Awards Agency for Scotland (SAAS) for students who qualify for home student status). Scottish students have to pay fees of up to £9,250 if they study in England, Wales or Northern Ireland.
- Students living in Northern Ireland pay up to £4,750 if they attend university in Northern Ireland, up to £9,250 if they study in England, Wales or Scotland.

EU students

At present, EU students are charged the same fees as charged to non-EU international students, which are significantly higher than those charged to UK students and are determined by each university. Some students from the EU may be eligible for some support in terms of student loans from the UK government, but this is dependent on a number of factors, so it is best to check personal eligibility. Students from the Republic of Ireland are exempt from paying higher fees and are eligible for home fee status.

Living expenses

Your living expenses include the cost of your accommodation, food, clothes, travel and equipment, leisure and social activities – plus possible extras like field trips and study visits, if these aren't covered by the tuition fees.

Check university and college websites for information about possible living costs. Some offer more detailed advice than others and give breakdowns under various headings such as accommodation, food and daily travel. Others go even further and give typical weekly, monthly or annual spends.

If you're living away from home, accommodation will make up the largest proportion of your living costs. There is likely to be a range of accommodation options – from a standard room in university halls through to privately rented accommodation – with a range of price points. You'll probably be surprised when you do some research to find that the cheapest and most expensive towns are not as you might have expected; the cost of accommodation often depends on how much of it is available in a particular area.

When choosing accommodation, it is essential to consider its location and factor in the cost of travel to your university or college. It is also important to find out what's included in the accommodation costs (such as utilities, personal property insurance and Wi-Fi) and whether it is possible to pay for accommodation during term time only.

TIP!

Many universities have accommodation brochures online. In some towns a large amount of student accommodation is owned by private companies as opposed to the universities and colleges themselves. This option means you could potentially be sharing accommodation with students from other universities and colleges.

Funding your studies

How do you fund your time in higher education? Don't ignore this question and leave it until the last minute! You will need to think carefully about how to budget for several years' costs – and you need to know what help you might get from:

- the government
- your family or partner
- paid part-time work
- other sources, such as bursaries and scholarships.

This chapter gives a brief overview of a complicated funding situation, which can vary according to where you come from and where you plan to study. For more details about the different types of funding available and how to apply for them, check your regional student finance website:

- www.gov.uk/contact-student-finance-england
- www.saas.gov.uk
- www.studentfinanceni.co.uk
- www.studentfinancewales.co.uk

Tuition fee loans

For UK students, tuition fees can be covered by taking out a tuition fee loan, which will be paid directly to your university or college at the start of each year of your course. You are effectively given a loan by the government that you repay through your income tax from the April after you finish your course but only once your earnings reach a certain threshold. Currently, these income thresholds stand at:

- £25,000 per year for students from England
- £27,295 a year for students from Wales
- £27,660 for students from Scotland (who go to university outside of Scotland)
- £24,990 for students from Northern Ireland

(All figures apply to students starting their course after 1 August 2023.)

So, if you never reach this threshold, you will not have to repay the fees. In addition, any outstanding balance on your loan will be cancelled after a certain period of time if you have not already cleared it in full. The length of time depends on the rules at the time you took out the loan. For students in England who started their studies in September 2023, the repayment period was extended to 40 years (from 30 years), so it is recommended that students in other regions keep a close eye on any developments with respect to the length of the loan repayment period.

The current situation regarding repayments is that you repay 9% of anything you earn over the annual income threshold.

The interest rate charged on student loans depends on what repayment plan you are on, but for students in England who started their course after 1 August 2023 (Plan 5) it is set at the RPI (Retail Price Index) rate of inflation.

Maintenance loans

In addition to a tuition fee loan, all students can apply for a maintenance or living cost loan. All students are entitled to a maintenance loan; however, the amount you can borrow will be dependent on your household income – in other words, it is means tested. 'Household income' refers to your family's gross annual income (their income before tax). With the exception of loans available to Scottish students, the amount you can claim also varies depending on your living situation, with the maximum loan being available to students living away from home in London.

Each regional student finance website includes a finance calculator tool that will give an estimate of the finance you would be eligible for based on your family income and other factors, and it is well worth looking at this before planning your budget.

England (2024/2025)

The maximum annual maintenance loan in England:

- £8,610 for those living in the family home
- £10,227 for those living away from home (£13,348 in London).

Wales (2024/2025)

In Wales, students can get a combination of a maintenance grant, which they do not have to pay back, and a maintenance loan. Although the grants are means tested, most students will get a grant of at least £1,000.

The maximum amounts for maintenance loans and grants in Wales:

- £10,315 for those living in the family home
- £12,150 for those living away from home (£15,170 in London).

Scotland (2024/2025)

In Scotland, students can get a mix of maintenance loans and non-repayable bursaries (grants) to cover living expenses. These are as follows (all figures per year):

- household income up to £20,999: £2,000 bursary and £9,400 loan
- household income £21,000–£23,999: £1,125 bursary and £9,400 loan
- household income £24,000–£33,999: £500 bursary and £9,400 loan
- household income £34,000 and above: no bursary and £8,400 loan.

Unlike the rest of the UK, maintenance loans for Scottish students are means tested according to household income bands rather than exact household income.

Northern Ireland (2024/25)

The maximum annual maintenance loan in Northern Ireland:

- £5,250 for those living in the family home
- £6,776 for those living away from home (£9,492 in London).

In addition, you may be eligible for a non-repayable maintenance grant or special support grant if your household income is below £41,065 and it is paid to you. This is paid alongside any maintenance loan you qualify for and is up to £3,475.

> **TIP!**
> You're advised to apply to the appropriate authority for funding as soon as you have firmly accepted an offer of a place.

Additional support

Bursaries and scholarships

What's the difference? Bursaries are usually non-competitive and automatic, often based on financial need, while scholarships are competitive and you usually have to apply for them. However, many universities and colleges use the terms interchangeably.

As well as the funding described above, most universities and colleges offer tuition fee bursaries, mainly to students who receive the maximum maintenance loan. These bursaries cover part or all of the cost of the course and are awarded according to the universities' own criteria, but they are often worked out according to the level of parental income. Approximately one-third of students receive some kind of financial assistance in this way.

Some universities and colleges offer scholarships to students enrolling on certain courses **or** to students with the highest entry grades. Merit-based scholarships and prizes are also sometimes available once you have started university, for example, if you have performed particularly well in end-of-year examinations.

Students leaving care

Care leavers who are entering higher education for the first time and are under 25 are eligible to apply for a bursary of at least £2,000 from their local authority area; this may be paid to them as a lump sum or in instalments. Many universities and colleges offer further support and are often able to provide accommodation for the whole year – which means that students don't have to move out during vacations. Find out more at www.ucas.com/undergraduate/applying-university/individual-needs/ ucas-undergraduate-care-experienced-students.

Other help from universities and colleges

Not all help comes in the form of cash. Students may receive any of the following – again probably dependent on income:

- assistance with cost of compulsory field trips and visits
- help to purchase laboratory clothing
- free laptops.

Additional financial support may be available to students with disabilities, for those with dependants and for mature students with existing financial commitments. These regulations are subject to change so it is essential to check them.

Other bursaries and scholarships

Students on particular courses, with particular career aspirations or with particular personal circumstances may be eligible for extra financial help. It's worth checking the sources listed in the 'Further information' section at the end of the book to find out whether you might be eligible for a grant made by a particular professional organisation or charity.

Sponsorship

Students applying for particular courses – for example accountancy, business studies and engineering – can sometimes be sponsored by employers or related organisations. In return for a sum of money paid to you as a student you would normally be expected to work for your sponsor during some of your vacations. Naturally, if you were suitable they would expect you to work for them for a period after you graduated. (However, the number of sponsorships available to new students has declined. Many employers now prefer to sponsor students whom they select during the first or second year of their courses.)

Degree and Higher apprenticeships

Degree apprenticeships involve studying for a degree or postgraduate level qualification. Higher apprenticeships involve studying for a qualification such as a Foundation degree, Higher National Diploma or other professional qualification equivalent to these, although in some cases Higher apprenticeships can lead to the award of a degree.

Degree apprentices don't pay for training or tuition fees – these are covered by the employer and the government. You will be paid a wage throughout the course, which will help to cover your living costs. Degree apprentices aren't entitled to student loans.

NHS bursaries

Students on degree courses in medicine and dentistry are treated in the same way as students on other degree programmes for the first four years of their courses. Then, from the fifth year, there's NHS funding to assist with tuition and living expenses. These bursaries are income-related. The system is not the same for all parts of the UK, so check your national student finance websites. This link may contain useful information: www.nhsbsa.nhs.uk/sites/default/files/2023-01/NHS%20Bursary%20Funding%20for%20Medical%20and%20Dental%20Students%202022-23%20%28V5%29%2012.2022.pdf

> **TIP!**
>
> Make a note of any deadlines for loan or funding applications and ensure that you have completed all the forms in time.

Other sources of cash

Part-time work

Many students need to balance studies with part-time employment. One report showed that the annual average amount earned was £3,500. This is something to think about when you choose your universities and colleges. Some towns have many more opportunities than others. In an area of high unemployment, for instance, all the jobs may be taken by permanent workers. In more affluent areas there might be more hourly paid work available – especially at hours when students are willing to work. At the time of writing, employers in sectors such as retail, hospitality, warehousing and care are struggling to recruit staff in many areas of the country; depending on location, jobs are relatively plentiful. There are also more opportunities to work from home, so IT skills are useful to keep up to date. You can find free digital courses by using the National Careers Service website; see link: https://nationalcareers.service.gov.uk/find-a-course/the-skills-toolkit.

You can check out the local employment situation on university and college websites.

Here are some additional ideas to bear in mind.

- Many universities and colleges help by running their own jobs banks. Students can get work, for example, in the Students' Union, libraries or offices (secretarial and administrative work if they have the skills), or in catering, domestic or manual work.
- Other opportunities often include guiding visitors around the campus or acting as student guides on open days.
- Most universities and colleges also have a job shop provided by student services or the careers advisory service that advertises jobs in the town or city.
- A useful website with a number of part-time jobs is www.fish4.co.uk.

However, many higher education courses include practical coursework, field studies and/or time spent abroad, which leave little opportunity for employment during term time. Plus, it's often recommended that students spend no more than 15 hours a week in paid employment to make sure their studies don't suffer. Oxford and Cambridge don't encourage any of their students to work during term time.

If you are an international student, you'll need to check the wording on your visa regarding part-time work. It may say that you are not permitted to undertake paid work at all, or perhaps only for a certain number of hours each week or month.

> **TIP!**
>
> Check the cost of living and employment availability in the university towns you're interested in. This will help you estimate what your living costs are likely to be and the availability of part-time work.

Banking deals

Many students take advantage of the student banking deals available from a number of high street banks. These can include interest-free overdrafts (which are advisable as a last resort only because they do have to be repaid – and interest rates on late payments can be very high) as well as various other freebies like free driving lessons or rail-cards. Shop around carefully for the deal that best suits your priorities – and remember, the advice that banks give on their websites is unlikely to be wholly impartial.

Many universities and colleges have student financial advisers whom students can approach for help. A students' union is also a good source of information and advice on financial assistance.

> **TIP!**
>
> Try not to run up a large overdraft or credit card debts, as in the long run you can end up paying large sums of interest on the money owed.

Chapter summary

Money can be a major headache for students, so it is well worth taking the time to work out how you're going to fund yourself. It's also very important to be on top of all the administration required for loan applications because missed deadlines can mean that you start your course before your finance comes through.

4| Choosing what to study

You're probably already aware that there's a vast number of subjects on offer. You can get an idea of the full range by searching ucas.com and the other resources listed in the 'Further information' section at the end of the book.

You can enter up to five course choices on your UCAS application. However, if you are applying for medicine, dentistry or veterinary science you're limited to four courses in your chosen subject, although you can make one additional application to a course in another subject (see Chapter 8 for more information).

So how do you start to narrow it down? This chapter covers some of the questions you can ask yourself so that you can focus your research on the courses that suit your interests.

Which subject area?

You might already have an idea of what you'd like to pursue further. If not, here are a few questions to think about.

- Which of the subjects you are currently studying interests you most? Are you interested enough to want to study it for the next few years?
- Are you interested in one particular aspect of your advanced-level course? If so, some specialist higher education courses could allow you to focus on this particular aspect.
- What are your career plans? What are the entry requirements for that career? Which courses match this best?
- Are you prepared to potentially undertake more specific job-related training once you have graduated? If not, perhaps you should be looking for a vocational (career-related) course that leads directly into an occupation.

The following online tools can help you choose a course. They might be available for you to use at your school, college or local careers centre.

Indigo

Indigo is a digital platform that enables students to explore university and career choices, and includes a wide database and a variety of resources. See https://indigo.careers for further details.

The Morrisby Profile

This is an online activity comprising a range of psychometric aptitude tests and preference-based questions. These give an indication of your learning potential and the most effective ways that you are likely to use your skills. Some schools and colleges use the profile as a guidance tool for students age 15+.

As well as career recommendations, Morrisby also identifies A level and university course suggestions and has online careers materials you can use in your research. There are advisers who will provide a post-assessment guidance service to individual clients as well as institutions, on a fee-paying basis. See www.morrisby.com/morrisby-profile for further details.

MyUniChoices

Find courses that might appeal to you by completing an online question-naire – which is used to assess your interests, abilities and personal qualities. This assessment matches your replies with thousands of higher education courses in the UK, Ireland, Europe and Canada – at mainly degree, HND or Diploma levels.

MyUniChoices asks you:

- 150 questions about what you do and do not like
- what stage you are at with your current academic studies
- which courses and subjects you are taking now or planning to take.

You'll receive a list of courses to investigate and an action plan suggesting further research. It may challenge your existing ideas and point you towards courses you have not considered. If it's not available to use at school or college, the cost to access this site yourself is £68.

The UCAS Hub and Careers Quiz

Register for the UCAS Hub on ucas.com – your starting point to explore, research and chat to current students. After registration there is no obligation to apply and you can explore a wide range of options. The UCAS Careers Quiz will help you find your ideal job matched to your personality, and give you a list of courses previous students studied in order to get there at www.ucas.com/careers-quiz.

Unifrog

Unifrog is designed as a one-stop platform encompassing universities, apprenticeships, work-related learning and further education colleges in the UK, as well as US, Canadian, European, Asian and Australasian universities.

The 'Further information' section at the end of the book should give you some more ideas of where to start your research.

Which qualification?

It is important to know something about each of the different types of qualification on offer so that you can choose one that's right for you. For example, course lengths (and therefore expenses) vary widely. Here are some of the main options.

DipHEs

Some universities and colleges offer undergraduate courses leading to a DipHE (Diploma of Higher Education). Two-year full-time DipHE courses are normally equivalent to the first two years of a first or bachelor's degree, and can often be used for entry to the final year of a related degree course. They're mainly linked to performance or vocational areas such as animal studies, dance education, health and social care, and paramedic practice – although some universities and colleges offer them in humanities subjects, including English and history.

HNDs

A Higher National Diploma (HND) is a vocational qualification roughly equivalent to the first two years of a three-year degree course.

Many universities and colleges offer HND courses in the same subject areas as their degree courses, giving you the option to transfer between courses or to top up your HND to a degree through a further year's study. In fact the majority of students do this, either by taking a special one-year top-up course or by transferring to the second or third year of a degree course in a similar subject at their university or college. Keep this in mind when planning your application strategy.

HNDs often fall into two main subject areas: science, construction, engineering and technology, and business studies and related subjects. Although HNDs do exist in art and design, health and social care, performing arts and hospitality management.

Science, construction, engineering and technology

Courses at all levels in these categories attract comparatively fewer applications than business and finance courses. It's therefore likely that if you apply for a degree in, for example, mechanical engineering at an institution that also offers an HND in engineering, admissions tutors will make you an offer covering both the degree and the HND course, but with different entry conditions for each (normally lower for the HND).

Business studies and related subjects

The HND courses in this subject area usually attract a large number of applications in their own right: many students choose HND courses because they are shorter and often more specialised than the degrees. It's therefore less usual for universities and colleges to make dual offers for degrees and HNDs.

If you have doubts about your ability to reach the level required for degree entry, you could instead apply for the HND. Talk through the options with your teachers or careers adviser.

Foundation degrees

As with HNDs, these courses focus on a particular job or profession. They're available in England, Northern Ireland and Wales. Full-time courses last two years and, like HNDs (which in some subject areas Foundation degrees have replaced), can be converted into honours degrees with a subsequent year of full-time study. Designed by business and industry to meet their skills needs, Foundation degrees were originally developed to train employees in particular roles as higher technicians or associate professionals, but entry to full-time courses is now available to anyone.

Foundation degrees combine academic study with the development of work-related skills. Programmes are offered in areas such as digital media arts, business and management, horticulture, equine studies, hospitality, fashion design and a vast range of other subjects. Foundation degree courses lead to the awards of:

- FdA (arts)
- FdEng (engineering)
- FdSci (science).

Entrance requirements for Foundation degrees vary, but typically are very similar to those required for HNDs: a **minimum** of a pass grade in one A level or equivalent qualification and another subject studied to A level standard but not necessarily passed. However, in some cases entrance requirements can be higher, so please check individual institution entrance requirements carefully.

Degree courses

Bachelor's degrees

In England, Northern Ireland and Wales, first degree courses usually last three years, or four if a year abroad or work placement is included. They lead to the award of a bachelor's degree, with the title of the degree reflecting the subject studied. Some of the more common ones are:

- BA: Bachelor of Arts
- BCom: Bachelor of Commerce
- BEng: Bachelor of Engineering
- BMus: Bachelor of Music
- BSc: Bachelor of Science
- LLB: Bachelor of Law.

The exceptions to this are the universities of Oxford and Cambridge (Oxbridge), which award a BA regardless of the subject. (Oxbridge graduates are then able to upgrade to a master's degree, without further exams, about four years later.)

Entrance requirements for entry to degree courses vary considerably, ranging from two low grade to three top grade A levels or equivalent.

Master's degrees

In England, Northern Ireland and Wales, master's degrees are usually acquired via a completely different course that must be applied for separately and can't be taken until the bachelor's degree has been completed.

However, some first degree courses lead directly to the award of a master's degree (e.g. MEd, MEng, MPhys and MSc). These courses are usually extended or enhanced versions of the bachelor's course, lasting at least four years, and are likely to be in engineering or science disciplines.

Scottish universities and colleges

At Scottish universities and colleges standard bachelor's degrees normally last for four years rather than three, and students typically take a broad range of subjects in the first two years before going on to specialise in the final two years.

At some universities and colleges, students are awarded a master's as standard for a four-year degree in arts, humanities and social science subjects, while science students receive a BSc.

Single, joint or combined honours?

Most universities and colleges offer single, joint and combined honours degree courses. Combined honours courses enable you to combine several areas of interest and may lead you to an interesting programme or additional career opportunities (for example, studying biology with French may enable you to work in France).

It's important to check the weighting given to each subject in a combined course. Popular ones include 50/50 and 75/25. As a general rule you can assume that **Subject A AND Subject B** means equal time given to each whereas **Subject A WITH Subject B** means much less time spent on the second or minor subject. There are some exceptions though, and universities and colleges are able to decide on their own course titles. The best way to be sure you know what you'll be studying is to check course information very carefully.

If you intend to take a joint or combined honours course, you'll be kept busier than you would be on a single honours course. You may have to make your own connections between the modules of study, and the work may not be closely coordinated. Ask the admissions tutors for the subjects you're interested in about the possibilities and potential problems of combining courses.

Degree classification

Honours degrees are classified as:

- First Class
- Upper Second Class (2.i)
- Lower Second Class (2.ii)
- Third Class.

Otherwise, ordinary and pass degrees can be awarded – depending on the system – to students who aren't studying honours courses, or to students who narrowly fail an honours course.

Which mode of study?

While full-time study is the most popular choice, there are also the following options.

Part-time

Part-time undergraduate study has become less popular since a peak in 2008–2009. It can be popular with students for financial or personal reasons; on the other hand it can be difficult to balance the demands of a job and higher education. Make sure you research the practicality of your options before making your decision.

Distance learning

This option was once available only through the Open University, but is now offered by many universities and colleges. This mode of study is more realistic if your circumstances make full-time course attendance difficult, e.g. because of employment or childcare commitments.

A government tuition fee loan is available to some students who study with the Open University and other providers of distance learning, higher education-level qualifications. Repayment is on the same basis as applies to full-time university students.

Sandwich courses

Many degrees and HNDs offer periods of work experience from three to 12 months. The 12-month programmes add a year to your course duration.

Study abroad

The Turing Scheme is a study and work abroad programme, and applies to countries across the world. During the 2023/24 academic year, the Turing Scheme supported more than 40,000 students, including around 22,000 from disadvantaged backgrounds, to study and work around the world. For more details on the Turing Scheme, see www.turing-scheme. org.uk.

Sponsored study

Sponsorship is sometimes offered to students on certain courses. In some cases students apply for a degree or HND course through UCAS and the university or college helps to arrange their training placement. (Full sponsorship is becoming rarer however, since, increasingly, employers are offering sponsorship only from the second year of a course. It's important, therefore, to check which ones have links with particular universities and colleges.)

If a sponsor requires you to attend a particular university or college, the sponsor will inform you and the institution will sort out the UCAS arrangements.

Degree apprenticeships

Degree apprenticeships are organised differently from sponsorship programmes. They offer the opportunity to gain a full bachelor's degree (and in some cases postgraduate qualifications) through an arrange-ment between employers and higher education institutions. Part-time study takes place at a university or college, with the rest of your time learning on the job. They can take from three to six years to complete, depending on the course level, and are available in a wide range of sectors.

Degree apprenticeships work differently across the UK. England and Wales both offer degree apprenticeships, with the most options currently available in England. In Scotland, degree apprenticeships are known as Graduate Apprenticeships. Northern Ireland offers Higher Level Apprenticeships (HLAs) that offer you qualifications up to Level 7, which is the equivalent of a master's degree; however, the majority are at Level 5, which is equivalent to a Foundation degree.

From 2024, students will be able to apply for apprenticeships through UCAS alongside an undergraduate degree application. Almost half of people that register on UCAS say they would consider an apprenticeship, but currently there are not enough vacancies being advertised through the service to meet growing demand.

Use UCAS's apprenticeship search at www.ucas.com/explore/search/apprenticeships to:

- search for all apprenticeship roles
- filter by subject area, industry, role type, location and level of apprenticeship
- sign up for alerts so you don't miss new vacancies.

You can also take a look for vacancies at www.gov.uk/apply-apprenticeship or on job search websites like www.gov.uk/find-a-job, https://uk.indeed.com/jobs?q=degree+apprenticeships&l=uk&vjk=71099e6938e64ff5. Availability of degree apprenticeships varies according to locality.

An apprenticeship is a real job, so you'll also need to meet any criteria set out by the employer, such as specific grades. Entry requirements are different depending on the employer and the industry you're going into. The big attraction of degree apprenticeships is the prospect of getting a university qualification without any debt. However, universities themselves have said that it is hard work being employed and studying at the same time. You're very likely going to need to give up evenings and some weekends to keep up with study and assignment writing, so this should never be thought of as a soft or easy option.

If you're not sure what you want to do yet, there's nothing stopping you applying to university through UCAS, while also applying for apprenticeship vacancies.

Which courses?

This is, of course, the million-dollar question! Having thought about the above points, you should now have a clearer idea of the type of qualification and subject area you'd like to apply for. However, there may still be hundreds of courses available fitting your criteria – so this is the point where you can start to narrow down your options. The only way to do this is by further research. Take a look through directories, prospectuses and websites, as well as visiting specific departments at specific universities.

Here are some of the things you should take into account.

- **Course content**: there can be a whole world of difference between courses with exactly the same title, so take a detailed look at the content and see how it relates to your particular interests. How much do you want to specialise? How much freedom do you want in selecting your options?
- **Teaching and assessment methods**: again, these can vary widely. For example, some courses may be very practical, with workshops and case studies, while others may be centred on essays and tutorials. If you don't perform well in exams, you can search for courses assessed via modules and projects.
- **Professional accreditation**: if you're planning to enter a specific career which you need professional accreditation for (e.g. law, engineering or accountancy), it is well worth checking out which courses offer full or partial exemption from the exams required to gain this accreditation.
- **Links with industry**: some courses and departments have strong links with industry, which can help graduates secure jobs.
- **Graduate destinations**: these are often listed on university and

---

TIP!

The UCAS search tool enables you to search courses by a wide range of features – including subject, region and town. You can also filter searches by qualification level, study mode, and single or combined subjects. You'll find entry requirements and tuition fees for each course and links to university and college websites.

---

college websites and can help you assess whether the course will give you the skills you'll need in the workplace.

Chapter summary

You should now be able to begin to develop a clear idea of the kind of course you'd like to apply for. However, there are two aspects of the decision-making process yet to be discussed: your choice of university or college and entry requirements. These factors are examined in detail in the following chapters.

5 | Choosing where to study

The previous chapter hopefully helped you build a picture of your ideal course and start to create a shortlist. However, it's still likely that a lot more than five courses will fit the bill, so you'll need to narrow the list down further. Now's the time to start thinking about which university or college you would like to study at.

Working out your priorities

There are over 380 institutions in the UCAS application scheme that offer higher education courses – including universities, colleges of higher education and further education colleges. Different considerations and priorities affect each person's choice of institution. To give you some idea of the range, current students say they were influenced by one or more of the following factors.

Academic factors

- The type of course you are looking for.
- The reputation for research in a particular department.
- Quality of teaching – check the Teaching Excellence and Student Outcomes Framework document at www.officeforstudents.org.uk/advice-and-guidance/teaching/about-the-tef.
- The status of the university/college as a whole – you can check league tables, which vary in reliability; however, the *Guardian*, *The Times* and *The Complete University Guide* are more impartial sources (or you could also seek advice from professional bodies and/or employers).
- Entry requirements – be positive but realistic about your potential results at advanced level, so you won't need to revise your plans months later.
- Number of student places on particular courses – the bigger the intake target, usually the better your chances; prospectuses and websites may give an indication of the size of intake.
- Employability of graduates.

Social factors

- Location – do you like the big city or countryside? Do you want to be on a campus or in the middle of a city? Are you trying to stay within easy reach of home, or get as far away as possible?
- Popularity of the university/college.
- Facilities for sport, leisure activities, music, etc.
- Cost of living.
- Accommodation – is there enough available? Does it suit your preferences, e.g. self-catering or with meals provided?
- Financial support available (e.g. bursaries and scholarships).
- Level of support and facilities for students with disabilities.

You may think of more factors, though you'll have to work out which are most important to you personally.

Once you've decided on your key priorities, where can you start to find out the answers to all your questions? The 'Further information' section at the end of the book lists publications and websites that collate this type of information. Using these as a first port of call can speed up your research no end, but there's no substitute for first-hand research at university/college open days and via their websites and prospectuses.

It is also well worth talking to former students from your school or college, family friends and older brothers and sisters about their experiences. More advice on this is given in the 'Researching your shortlist' section below.

> **TIP!**
>
> Don't forget to get university prospectuses (download or request a hard copy) and look at university/college websites.

Staying close to home?

A growing number of students only apply to universities and colleges that are within daily commuting distance – opting to save on living expenses while enjoying the support and comforts of home. With current tuition fees of up to £9,250, the choice of living in a hall of residence or in rented accommodation may not be affordable. But, don't forget, as mentioned in Chapter 3, in some towns where you might assume that living costs are high, rents can be lower than you think and it can be easy to find part-time jobs.

Studying from home could limit your 'student experience' though, as time spent travelling cuts down your opportunities for involvement in societies and social activities. You may also be less likely to network and make new friends, especially if you still have close friends from school living in the area.

You may decide on a compromise solution. A number of higher education courses – HNDs, Foundation degrees, even first degree courses – start with a year studying at a local, franchised further education college before transferring to the parent campus to complete your degree.

Researching your shortlist

As soon as you feel ready, draw up your shortlist of about 10 possible courses. From these you can select up to five final choices for your UCAS application. For each of your shortlist entries, make sure you've considered the following questions.

- What will I actually be studying on this course?
- Do I like the environment?
- Where's the course held? Many universities and colleges have several campuses. To avoid possible disappointment, research this now, as you wouldn't want to find yourself on a small satellite campus if you really wanted to be at the main site – or vice versa.
- Where will I live?
- Which options can I select on this course?
- How is progress assessed?
- Is there a tutorial system and how much support and advice on learning do students get?
- Can I achieve the qualifications needed for entry? (Chapter 6)

On the UCAS website you can find entries from individual universities and colleges. Most use the following format:

- Why study this course? Gives details on the topics studied and teaching and learning methods.
- Exchange possibilities with universities or colleges in other countries. Many institutions offer the opportunity to spend part of your course in another country – in Europe or much further afield – in the USA, Canada or Hong Kong for example. The list is almost endless.
- Location.
- Who is this course for?
- More about this course – description of individual modules, compulsory and optional, and any equipment needed.
- Modular structure.
- Skills and experience gained.
- After the course – information on careers entered by previous graduates.

It's important to attend open days and taster sessions at universities and colleges that really appeal to you, and to talk with student ambassadors who can answer your questions about university life. You can also arrange a visit to the department you're interested in; make sure to spend some time in the town or city as well in order to get some experience of the place where you might spend three or four years.

For students with disabilities, this is particularly important – you need to make sure the university or college will be able to meet your particular needs. Some campuses are better than others for wheelchairs, while some have special facilities for people who are visually impaired or deaf. Get in touch with the disability officers at your shortlisted universities or colleges. More information about access and facilities for students with disabilities is also available at ucas.com/disabled-students and, of course, from the prospectuses and websites of the universities and colleges themselves.

You should also attend UCAS events – real or virtual – to talk directly with representatives from higher education institutions about courses. They're free to attend but you'll need to book a place – either through school or college or individually. While virtual open events or tours can never properly replace a real visit, they can at least give some insight into the universities, their facilities and accommodation. Also, bear in mind that you could attend many more open events this way, allowing you to explore a wider range of institutions, courses and facilities more thoroughly. However, it's also important to get an experience of the locality, so it's wise to visit the area you intend studying in.

Read the details of the courses you're interested in and for which you think realistically that you can match the entry requirements. Highlight important points you may want to address in the personal statement part of your UCAS application, or refer to at interview.

TIPS!

Keep the prospectuses of places to which you're definitely applying!

Don't take anything as given. Email or phone departments directly and ask to speak to an admissions tutor if you want to ask specific questions, e.g. about the destinations of course graduates, possible career progression, admission details, or anything else. Tutors can be helpful and informative – they aren't there just to teach.

If you can't get to any open days, try watching the UCAS online virtual tours of different universities and colleges.

Selecting the final five

If there's one particular university or college you want to attend (perhaps because you're a mature student or can't move away from home), you can use your choices to apply for more than one course at the same institution (apart from at Oxford and Cambridge). On the other hand, at some universities or colleges it's not necessary to apply for more than one course because admission is to a faculty or group of related subjects.

The other major factor to consider in selecting your final five courses is the entry requirements. Most universities and colleges supply entry requirements for their courses at ucas.com. To maximise your chance of success, apply to courses that are likely to make you an offer – e.g. corresponding roughly with the grades you expect to achieve. This question is examined in greater detail in the next chapter.

Also, bear in mind you only get one UCAS personal statement, so if you choose to apply for different subjects be careful not to dilute the focus of your personal statement too much.

Chapter summary

University might well be your first experience of leaving home, so it is important to fully explore local amenities, availability of student accommodation, the student support available from the university or college, cost of living and the environment you will be living in, to ensure you'll feel happy in your new surroundings.

Case study - Josh

Josh decided to study mechanical engineering, but how did he decide which university to attend?

'I had always enjoyed and been good at physics and mathematics, so mechanical engineering was long in my sights as a university subject. The application of mathematics to solving real world solutions also attracted me to mechanical engineering; in that sense I had a head start in choosing what I was going to study at university.

'That said, I do think it is very important to choose the SUBJECT first, and then explore the universities where you could study. I wanted to do a degree that gave me the option of an industrial placement as part of the course, so a sandwich degree in which

I would spend my third year in a working environment was a big attraction. I used the discoveruni.gov.uk website to compare universities on employability of subjects, and my chosen university had a 95% success rate of mechanical engineering graduates being in graduate level employment within six months of completing their studies. This proved correct in my case, as I had two job offers with companies even before completing my degree, owing to the network of contacts I had built up while on placement.

'An important factor for me in my university choices was ease of transport between university sites as I have mobility difficulties. I wanted to be sure that the universities were either campus based, thereby offering most facilities and access to lectures, etc on one site, or that the transport facilities between sites were good and frequent. My first-choice university when I came to accepting offers was the one that clearly offered the best support for students with additional needs. They were really helpful and always came back to me with clear answers to any questions or concerns I had.

'It is also very important to visit the university and the surrounding area, as you will be spending several years living there; you need to feel comfortable with the accommodation and facilities available. Virtual events are okay, but they can hide a lot; it is only by visiting a place for real that you will be able to get the real experience of all that it has to offer and whether it is right for you.'

6| Academic requirements

You may have been thinking since Year 10 or 11 about whether you'll be able to meet higher education entry requirements, planning how your A levels, Scottish Highers, IB, ILC or BTEC Level 3 Awards will help you progress into higher education. Or you might not have given the matter any serious thought yet.

Either way, it's important to make sure you're realistic about the grades you hope to achieve, and that you target your applications to suitable universities and colleges.

This chapter will help you understand how they set their entry requirements and offers some basic dos and don'ts for choosing your final five courses.

What might the entry requirements be?

To enter higher education you normally need to achieve minimum qualifications equivalent to one of the following:

- two A levels
- one Double Award A level
- the Cambridge Pre-U
- one BTEC National Award
- two Advanced Highers
- one T level (equivalent to 3 A levels)
- an ILC
- an IB.

See pages 51–55 for a full list. Note that not all of the above may be accepted by all universities for all degrees – you must check course requirements carefully.

You'll also need:

- England – GCSEs at grades 9–4/5 or A*–C (including English language and Mathematics) depending on requirements at different institutions
- Scotland – National 5s at grades A*–C
- Wales and Northern Ireland – GCSEs at grades A*–C.

(Requirements vary for mature students and other groups – see page 73.)

In reality, most universities and colleges require more than the absolute minimum and many demand particular subjects for entry.

There are two main reasons for admission to some courses requiring higher than minimum grades.

1. **Coping with the course** – for the study of some subjects, a higher education department or faculty can decide their students need to achieve a particular qualification (say, B or C in A level Mathematics) in order to get through the course.
2. **Rationing places** – where there's high demand for a course the entry requirements will rise, because if a course asks for three Bs, fewer applicants will qualify for entry than if three Cs were requested (even though the three-C candidates might cope perfectly well with the course); these grade requirements help to prevent courses from becoming oversubscribed.

The second of these two reasons is the more common – so it's worth being aware that high grades are often an indication of popularity, and not always of quality. Some universities, colleges and courses are more popular than others and can therefore set high grades if they feel that the 'market' in a particular subject will bear them. It's worth knowing which courses are usually the most in demand.

On the equal-consideration deadline for applications, 31 January 2024 (for 2024 entry), the top ten subject groups chosen by applicants were:

1. subjects allied to medicine (down 3%)
2. business and management (up 1%)
3. social sciences (down 4%)
4. design and creative arts and performing arts (up 0.1%)
5. engineering and technology (up 10%)
6. computing (up 7%)
7. biological and sport sciences (down 0.3%)
8. law (up 4%)
9. psychology (down 6%)
10. medicine and dentistry (down 6%).

In addition, any course with a special feature (such as sponsorship or an exchange with a university or college overseas) can attract large numbers of applications and may therefore also require high grades.

Whatever course you apply for, your qualifications will be examined carefully by admissions tutors. They'll be looking at your advanced-level study and checking you have:

- the right subjects to satisfy entry requirements
- subjects they are prepared to include in an offer
- the types of qualification they want (e.g. A level, BTEC Extended Diploma)
- the right number of qualifications

- made an effort to fill any gaps in your record (e.g. by retaking GCSE mathematics at the same time as or before your advanced qualifications).

Admissions tutors will be on the lookout for students who are repeating advanced-level qualifications; your UCAS application must give full details of your results at the first attempt and include details of what you are repeating and when (see Chapter 15). Further explanations should be given in your personal statement.

Many admissions tutors will also attach a lot of importance to your results at GCSE or National 5 level. After all, these results, together with your predicted grades, will usually be the only evidence of your academic achievement to date. Tutors will be looking for:

- a reasonable spread of academic qualifications
- key subjects, like English language and mathematics (even if the university or college does not require them for your subject choice, most employers do)
- signs of academic capacity or potential.

Additional and alternative entry requirements

Applicants to music, art and design and other creative or performing arts courses often have to compile a portfolio of work, and may also have to attend an interview or audition (see Chapter 9).

If you'd like to train for work with young children or vulnerable adults (for example in teaching, social work or the healthcare professions), you'll need a criminal record check from one of the national disclosure and barring services, known as an Enhanced DBS check (see Chapter 24).

To study medicine, students are expected to complete a Health Declaration and Immunisation Form. It is essential that you consult the universities about specific details, but it is likely that vaccinations for the following are required: measles, mumps, rubella, tuberculosis, diphtheria, tetanus, polio, meningitis and haemophilus influenzae b. You will be asked to be screened for hepatitis B and advised to complete a full course of the hepatitis B vaccine.

To study nursing, all nurses, but particularly those who work with infants, need tetanus, diphtheria, and pertussis vaccines. Other important immunisations include hepatitis B, varicella, measles, mumps, and rubella. Check the immunisation requirements with the universities and colleges you've chosen.

If you're applying for career-related courses, such as law or veterinary science, work experience may be an essential prerequisite for entry. Check this well before applying to give you time to gain any experience you need.

Students with certain disabilities may also be offered different entry requirements – it's worth checking with admissions tutors for individual courses as the criteria for admission may be relaxed.

How are entry requirements expressed?

Entry requirements may be expressed as specific grades (e.g. ABC at A level or ABBB at Scottish Higher), as a target number of UCAS Tariff points (e.g. 120 points) or as a mixture of the two (e.g. 120 points, including at least grade B in A level Chemistry).

The UCAS Tariff

The UCAS Tariff is the system for allocating points to the qualifications used for entry to higher education.

As if the number of qualifications available weren't confusing enough, different qualifications can have different grading structures (alphabetical, numerical or a mixture of both). Finding out what qualifications are needed for different higher education courses can be very confusing – the Tariff allows students to use a range of different qualifications to help secure a place on an undergraduate course.

Admission to higher education courses generally depends on an individual's achievement in level 3 qualifications, e.g. A levels or Scottish Highers. The UCAS Tariff gives a points value to each of these. A wide range of Level 3 qualifications (SCQF Level 6 qualifications in Scotland) are included in the Tariff tables, and universities will accept Tariff points for multiple qualifications, providing the content of these qualifications is not too similar (in which case points for the highest qualifications will be counted). Universities also reserve the right not to count the points for a qualification if the qualification is not relevant to their degree course.

Tariff points allow universities to compare the wide range of qualifications they see on applications, although they will typically look at other factors too when making a decision. Entry details (available from UCAS and on the institutions' own websites) provide a fuller picture of what admissions tutors are seeking.

The tables on pages 51–55 show the points values for the most common qualifications covered by the UCAS Tariff. To see the points values for other qualifications you may hold or be studying for, you should visit www.ucas.com/tariff, and search for the qualification.

UCAS Tariff Points tables

A levels and AS

Grade					
A level Double Award	A level with additional AS	A level	AS Double Award	AS	Tariff points
A*A*					112
A*A					104
AA					96
AB					88
BB					80
	A*A				76
BC					72
	AA				68
CC	AB				64
CD	BB	A*			56
	BC				52
DD		A			48
	CC				44
	CD				42
DE		B	AA		40
			AB		36
	DD				34
EE		C	BB		32
	DE				30
			BC		28
		D	CC		24
	EE		CD		22
			DD	A	20
		E	DE	B	16
			EE	C	12
				D	10
				E	6

Scottish Highers/Advanced Highers

Grade	Higher	Advanced Higher
A	33	56
B	27	48
C	21	40
D	15	32

Advanced Welsh Baccalaureate – Skills Challenge Certificate

Grade	Tariff points
A*	56
A	48
B	40
C	32
D	24
E	16

T levels

Grade	Tariff points
Distinction* (D*)	168
Distinction (D)	144
Merit (M)	120
Pass (A*–C) (P)	96
Pass (D or E) (P)	72

Irish Leaving Certificate

Grade		Tariff points
Higher	Ordinary	
A1		36
A2		30
B1		30
B2		24
B3		24
C1		18
C2		18
C3	A1	12
D1		12
	A2	10
	B1	10
D2		9
D3		9
	B2	8
	B3	8
	C1	6
	C2	6

TIP!

Entry requirements are listed on each course listing in the UCAS search tool. Check these before you apply and keep an eye on them, as requirements are subject to change!

International Baccalaureate (IB) Diploma

While the IB Diploma does not attract UCAS Tariff points, the individual qualifications within the IB Diploma do, so the total Tariff points for an IB Diploma can be calculated by adding together each of the following four components:

IB Certificate in Higher Level

Grade	Tariff points
H7	56
H6	48
H5	32
H4	24
H3	12
H2	0
H1	0

Size band: 4; grade bands: 0–14.

IB Certificate in Standard Level

Grade	Tariff points
S7	28
S6	24
S5	16
S4	12
S3	6
S2	0
S1	0

Size band: 2; grade bands: 0–14.

IB Certificate in Extended Essay

Grade	Tariff points
A	12
B	10
C	8
D	6
E	4

Size band: 1; grade bands: 4–12.

IB Certificate in Theory of Knowledge

Grade	Tariff points
A	12
B	10
C	8
D	6
E	4

Size band: 1; grade bands: 4–12.

Certificates in Extended Essay and Theory of Knowledge are awarded Tariff points when the certificates have been taken individually.

Cambridge International Pre-U Certificate

Grade	Principal Subject	Global Perspective and Research	Short Course
D1	56	56	22
D2	56	56	20
D3	52	52	20
M1	44	44	18
M2	40	40	14
M3	36	36	12
P1	28	28	10
P2	24	24	8
P3	20	20	6

Progression Diploma

Grade	Tariff points
A*	168
A	144
B	120
C	96
D	72
E	48

Extended Project

Grade	Tariff points
A*	28
A	24
B	20
C	16
D	12
E	8

Music examinations

Performance			Theory			Tariff points
Grade 8	Grade 7	Grade 6	Grade 8	Grade 7	Grade 6	
D						30
M						24
P						18
	D					16
	M					14
	P	D				12
		M	D			10
			M			9
		P	P	D		8
				M		7
				P	D	6
					M	5
					P	4

Additional points will be awarded for music examinations from the Associated Board of the Royal Schools of Music (ABRSM), University of West London, Rockschool and Trinity Guildhall/Trinity College London (music examinations at grades 6, 7, 8 (D=Distinction; M=Merit; P=Pass)).

NB: Full acknowledgement is made to UCAS for this information. For further details of all qualifications awarded UCAS Tariff points see ucas.com/tariff. Note that new qualifications are introduced each year.

TIP!

If you have (or are likely to achieve) less than the minimum qualifications for entry to an honours degree course, your qualification level may be suitable for entry to an HND course or Foundation degree. You can then convert this additional qualification into a full degree with an additional year of study (see Chapter 4).

Further information on the Tariff

Although Tariff points can be accumulated in a variety of ways, not all of these will necessarily be acceptable for entry to a particular higher education course. So, the achievement of a points score doesn't give you an automatic right to a place, and admissions staff take many other factors into account when selecting students. The UCAS search tool at www.ucas.com is the best source of reference for which qualifications are acceptable for entry to specific courses.

How does the Tariff work?

- Students can collect Tariff points from a range of different qualifications.
- There's no ceiling to the number of points that can be accumulated.
- There's no double counting. Certain qualifications in the Tariff build on qualifications in the same subject that also attract Tariff points. Tariff points are generally only counted for the highest level of achievement in a subject. This means you can't usually count AS grades if you have an A level in the same subject and you can't count a BTEC Diploma if you have the Extended Diploma in the same subject.
- UCAS Tariff points are allocated to Level 3/SCQF Level 6 qualifications.
- All UK-regulated qualifications are eligible to receive points.

How does higher education use the Tariff?

Not all qualifications attract UCAS Tariff points. Universities or colleges can accept qualifications outside the Tariff if they are relevant for their degree course.

Not all institutions use the UCAS Tariff. Some prefer to express their entry requirements and make offers in terms of qualifications and grades rather than in Tariff points. Around one-third of course entry requirements make reference to the Tariff.

The courses that refer to UCAS Tariff points in their entry requirements do so in different ways:

- some list their entry requirements and make offers using only Tariff points, with no reference to specific qualifications or grades
- some ask for specific qualifications and a set number of Tariff points
- some link the Tariff points required to specific qualifications and grades. Examples include:
  - o 120 points to include a grade B in A level History
  - o 120 points including SQA Higher grade B in Mathematics
  - o 120 points. A levels, Scottish Highers and BTEC National Diplomas are acceptable qualifications
  - o 120 points. Points from General Studies A level, AS exams, key skills and COPE won't be considered
  - o 120 points gained from at least three A levels or equivalent 18 unit qualifications
  - o 120 points including A level Mathematics and Physics.

Use of the Tariff may also vary from department to department at any one university or college, and may in some cases depend on the programme being offered.

Unit grade information

There is space for you to fill in your unit grade scores on your UCAS application – but you don't have to do so. (See under **Which qualifications should I add?** in Chapter 20.) Unit grades may be specified as part of conditional offers, but this practice is not widespread.

You should look at individual university and college prospectuses and websites to check entry requirements and profiles to find out their individual policies on unit grade information.

Subjects

It's important to check the combination of advanced-level subjects that's acceptable for admission to particular courses. This can sometimes be quite specific! Some departments, particularly at some of the UK's older universities, prefer the more traditional A level, Scottish Higher and IB subjects for the minimum entry requirement to some courses.

The list below shows the most commonly approved subjects:

- biology
- business
- chemistry
- classical civilisation
- classical languages
- computing
- drama and theatre studies
- economics
- English (English language, English literature, and English language and literature)
- environmental science
- further mathematics
- geography
- geology
- history
- history of art
- law
- mathematics
- modern languages
- music
- philosophy
- physics
- politics
- psychology
- religious studies
- sociology
- statistics.

However, if you have taken subjects that aren't on the list on page 57, they may still be acceptable for university entry.

The Russell Group – a 24-strong group of research-intensive UK universities – runs the Informed Choices website (www.informedchoices. ac.uk), which allows students to explore various degrees and subject areas available at their institutions.

Generally speaking, if you're taking two or more of the following subjects (and related titles) at advanced level, even though each one may be approved individually, you should check that the combination will be acceptable for entry to the higher education courses you're considering:

- accounting
- art
- dance
- design and technology
- drama
- environmental science
- film studies
- media studies
- music technology
- photography
- sport science.

For some specialised career-related higher-education courses, two or more subjects from the upper above list would be useful. However, a common misconception among students, and for that matter, parents, is that all subjects should be relevant to the chosen university course. This isn't the case – universities are often more interested in the skillset students bring, e.g. a modern foreign language might be an advantage for entry to business-based degrees, as might be sciences or mathematics as they develop analytical skills, along with social science subjects such as geography as they develop written communication, evaluation and investigative skills.

So, it really is essential to check the exact entry requirements for any course you are considering. There are no standard university-wide lists available, so the only way to clarify this is by consulting the admissions requirements for the course you'd like to study.

Targeting the right courses

Here are a few dos and don'ts to make sure that your chosen final five courses give you the best chance of success.

Do ...

- Read course descriptions very carefully. Remember that courses with similar titles can have very different content, which can also affect the subjects required for entry.
- Carefully check the required entry grades and qualifications on the UCAS website, then confirm them by checking the university or college prospectuses or websites. If you are unsure on any point contact the institutions directly to make sure there's no chance you have misunderstood or to ask whether any changes have been made since the information was written.
- Check that the pre- and post-16 qualifications you've opted to take will give you the entry qualifications you need, and check with your subject teachers that you're on track to achieve the right grades.
- Be realistic about the grades you're likely to achieve. Make sure that you know what exam grades teachers are going to predict for you.
- As a safety net, make sure you apply to at least one course that's likely to give you a slightly lower offer. Even if you expect high grades, think very carefully before applying to five very popular universities for a very popular subject. Entry will be extremely competitive and, even with high predicted grades, you can't be sure of being accepted. However, if at all possible, only add a university/course that you'd genuinely be prepared to take.

Don't ...

- Apply for lots of different or unrelated subjects – you'll have a difficult job justifying this in your personal statement, and admissions tutors will question how genuine your interest is in each subject.

Chapter summary

Be positive, but realistic, in your higher education applications. And have a backup plan! As you'll see in Part II, you will have the opportunity to make a first (Firm) choice and a backup (Insurance) choice in response to university or college offers on your UCAS application – make sure your backup choice is on a course and in a place you'll genuinely enjoy.

Part II
The admissions procedure: applications, interviews, offers and beyond

7 | Applications and offers

Making your application

As the timetable on pages 3–6 shows, if you're on a two-year advanced course, ideally you should do all your higher education research work by September or October of the second year – more than a year before you start in higher education.

If you're on a one-year course, you won't have time to do all the activities suggested for the first year, but you'll be working to the same application deadlines so you still need to research all your options.

UCAS applicant journey

The UCAS applicant journey (see Figure 1, opposite) has been designed to guide you through the different steps you will take when making your application for higher education.

Deadlines

There are two deadlines for applications to courses through UCAS. They are 18:00 hours (UK time) on 15 October and 29 January.

The deadline for application to most courses is 18:00 hours (UK time), 29 January. (Remember, however, that you will have to submit your application to your referee well before this to make sure it reaches UCAS in time.) All applications submitted by 29 January are considered – however, it's advisable to apply as early as you can.

Aim to submit your UCAS application to your referee by late November or by any internal deadline given by your school or college. You're still able to apply after 29 January and universities and colleges may consider your application if they still have places – but they are not obliged to do so. Any applications received after 30 June will be referred to Clearing (see Chapter 10). However, if you are applying as an international student you may apply until 30 June without being regarded as a late applicant.

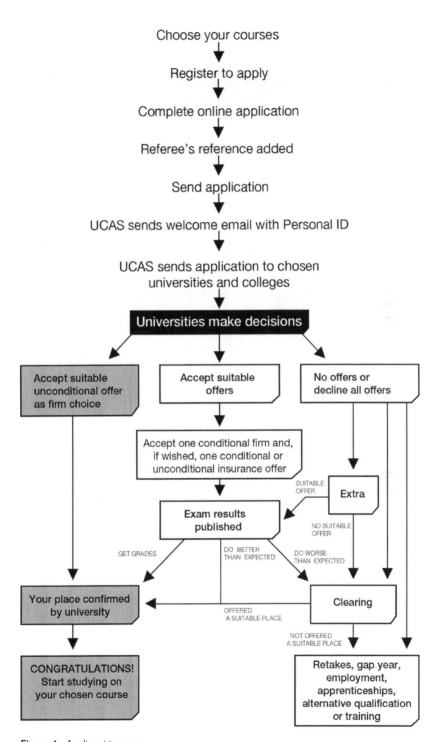

Figure 1: Applicant journey

Some courses have an earlier application deadline:

- applications for courses leading to professional qualifications in medicine, dentistry or veterinary science/medicine must be submitted by 18:00 hours (UK time) on 15 October
- applications for all courses at the universities of Oxford or Cambridge must be submitted by 18:00 hours (UK time) on 15 October.

What happens once you submit your application?

UCAS will send you a welcome email acknowledging receipt of your application and confirming your personal details and the courses you have applied for. You must check that this information is correct, and contact UCAS immediately if it isn't:

- www.ucas.com/contact-us.

UCAS will also provide you with your Personal ID and, along with the password you used for your application (see Chapter 11), this will enable you to log in and follow the progress of your application. Keep a careful note of your Personal ID and, if you contact UCAS, universities or colleges, be prepared to quote it.

Admissions tutors can now look at your application and decide whether to make you an offer.

Decisions and offers

Universities and colleges will inform UCAS of their decisions. You should log in to check the status of your application – although UCAS will email you to tell you when a change has been made to your application status. The message won't specify whether you have received an offer or a rejection, but will ask you to log in to find out.

Decisions will arrive in a random order, possibly beginning a few weeks after you apply. Decisions will be displayed as soon as UCAS receives them. If you have a long wait, it may mean that an admissions tutor is under great pressure due to a large number of applications. So, don't worry if people you know receive offers while you're still waiting to hear – it does not necessarily mean bad news.

There are three main categories of decision.

1. **Unconditional offer**: no further qualifications are required. If you accept this offer, and meet all non-academic requirements (DBS and health checks for example), you are in!
2. **Conditional offer**: you still have some work to do ... but if you accept the offer and achieve the conditions in the examinations you are about to take, a place will be guaranteed.

3. **Unsuccessful**: sorry – no luck. However, it may be that you receive an offer from one of your other choices. If all decisions are unsuccessful, you shouldn't feel discouraged, as there's still the option of applying to courses through UCAS Extra and, later in the application cycle, Clearing.

The following decisions may also appear:

*   withdrawn: you have withdrawn this choice
*   cancelled: you have asked UCAS to cancel this choice.

Universities and colleges have to decide by 14 May 2025 whether to offer you a place, provided you applied by the equal-consideration deadline of 29 January.

Interviews and open days

Before they make a decision, admissions tutors may invite you to an interview. Be prepared to travel to universities or colleges during the late autumn and winter – a 16–25 Railcard or a National Express Young Persons Coachcard might be a good investment! Since the Covid-19 pandemic, universities have increasingly been conducting interviews virtually using online platforms.

Some universities and colleges will contact you directly to invite you for interview. Others will inform you of interview details through your UCAS application. If you're invited for interview through UCAS, you'll receive an email asking you to look at the change to your application. You can accept the interview invitation, decline it or request an alternative date or time.

If you need to change the interview time or date, you should also contact the university or college direct. They can then update the invitation so that the revised details are shown on your UCAS application. You should try to attend interviews on the first date given, as it may be difficult for admissions tutors to offer an alternative date.

Advice on preparing for interviews is given in Chapter 9.

Alternatively, you may be offered a conditional or unconditional place and invited to attend an open day. You might also be asked to submit a portfolio or piece of written work.

Replying to offers

You will be asked to reply to any offers you receive – and you must do so – but you don't have to reply until you have received decisions from all the universities and colleges to which you applied. UCAS will give you a deadline for replying. This may be different from the deadlines received by your friends. Don't worry about this. There's no one single deadline – UCAS acts only after you have heard from all your choices.

Through your UCAS application, you must reply to each offer with one of three options.

1. **Firm acceptance**. If you firmly accept an offer (either as an unconditional offer or as a conditional offer), this means you're sure that this offer is your first preference of all the offers you've received through UCAS. If you get the grades, this will be the higher education course you take. You can make this reply only once – you won't be able to change or cancel your reply. There's also an equal commitment on the university's or college's part to accept you if you fulfil the conditions.

2. **Insurance acceptance**. If you've firmly accepted a conditional offer, you may also hold one additional offer (either conditional or unconditional) as an insurance acceptance. This is your fall-back, in case your grades are too low for your firm acceptance. It's worth knowing you're not obliged to make an insurance reply – if you do so and then your firm acceptance offer isn't confirmed, you'll be expected to attend your insurance choice if that's confirmed. If you don't feel 100% committed to your insurance choice, it would be better to wait and see what is available in Clearing. Please ask for advice before making this decision!

3. **Decline**. If you decline an offer, you're indicating that you definitely don't wish to accept it.

You must either accept or decline your offers. You can accept two offers (your firm and insurance choices) and must decline all your other offers, so your combination of replies will be one of the following:

- accept one offer firmly (unconditional firm or conditional firm) and decline any others
- accept one offer firmly (conditional firm) and one as an insurance (unconditional insurance or conditional insurance), and decline any others
- decline all offers.

If you firmly accept an **unconditional** offer of a place, you're not entitled to choose an insurance offer. If you firmly accept a **conditional** offer, you may accept an unconditional offer or another conditional offer as your insurance acceptance.

TIP!

Don't worry if people you know receive replies before you do. This does not mean that you are going to be rejected. Some admissions tutors, for various reasons, take longer to deal with applications than others.

Tips on making your replies

- Consider your replies very carefully. Ask for advice from your school/college tutor or careers adviser.
- Don't accept an offer (firm or insurance) unless you're sure that you will be happy to enrol on the course.
- It's advisable to choose an unconditional offer as your insurance acceptance or one with conditions that are easier for you to meet than those of your firm acceptance.
- Don't include as an insurance acceptance a course that you would be unwilling to take up. If you're not accepted for your firm choice and the insurance offer is confirmed, you're committed to going there. It would be better not to hold an insurance acceptance than to hold one you wouldn't be willing to take up.
- Bear in mind the precise requirements of the offer. For example, if a BCC offer requires a B in a subject you're not very confident about, but an offer requiring higher grades overall doesn't specify the B in that subject or perhaps counts general studies, then your firm/insurance decision needs to take these factors into account.

What if you don't get any offers?

If you're in this position, you may be able to make a further application in Extra between 26 February and 4 July. In 2023, 5,385 people were placed through Extra.

You'll be eligible to use Extra if you've used all five choices in your original application and you fulfil any one of the following criteria:

- you've had unsuccessful or withdrawn decisions for all your choices
- you've cancelled your outstanding choices and hold no offers
- you've received decisions from all five choices and have declined all offers made to you.

If you're eligible to use Extra, UCAS will let you know. When you log in to your UCAS application, you'll see the option to 'Add choice'. You'll still be able to search for courses that have vacancies in the UCAS search tool on the website. You can apply for several courses – but only one at a time.

> **TIP!**
>
> It is a good idea to contact the admissions tutors for the courses that interest you and ask whether they will consider you.

When you enter the Extra course details on your UCAS application, it is automatically sent online to the relevant university or college.

If you're made an offer, you can then choose whether to accept it. If you're currently studying for examinations, any offer that you receive is likely to be a conditional one and will contain the required exam grades. If you decide to accept a conditional offer, you won't be able to take any further part in Extra. (There are no insurance options in Extra.) If you already have your exam results, you may receive an unconditional offer. Once you accept an unconditional offer, you have that place.

If you're unsuccessful, decline an offer or do not receive an offer **within 21 days of choosing a course** through Extra, you can (time permitting) make a further application in Extra. The Extra button in your application will be reactivated.

Tips on using Extra

- Do some careful research and seek guidance from your school, college or careers adviser and from the universities and colleges themselves.
- Think very carefully before applying again for the types of course for which you have already been unsuccessful – it may simply result in another rejection.
- Be flexible – for example, if you applied to high-demand courses and universities and colleges in your original application and were unsuccessful, you could consider related or alternative subjects.
- If you're not offered a place in Extra, you may still find a place through Clearing (see Chapter 10).
- You can find out more about Extra on the UCAS website, at ucas. com/extra.

Case study - Freddie

Freddie originally applied to study English and received four offers, but then realised he wanted to study Ancient History instead.

'Firstly, I researched my options because once you applied to one university then you can't replace the initial choice for 21 days. Research done, I really liked the look of a course so I telephoned the University of Liverpool to see if they still had places for Ancient History and if they would consider me. They were positive, so I rang UCAS and asked them to decline all of my offers, so that the Extra option popped up on my UCAS Hub page. I then applied and got a place at Liverpool.'

8 | Non-standard applications

Applications for the majority of courses follow the pattern outlined in the previous chapters. However, there are some exceptions, specifically for:

- courses at the universities of Oxford and Cambridge
- music conservatoires
- medicine, dentistry and veterinary science or veterinary medicine courses
- mature students
- deferred entry
- late applications
- international students.

Oxford and Cambridge

If you intend to apply for any course at either Oxford or Cambridge, the deadline for submitting your application is 18:00 hours (UK time) on 15 October 2024. (Additional forms must be submitted at an earlier date if you want to be considered for a music or choral scholarship at either university. You can find details on their websites.)

All University of Cambridge colleges will accept mature students, but three are exclusively for mature students: Hughes Hall, St Edmund's College and Wolfson College.

Shortly after submitting your UCAS application, you'll be asked via email to complete an online My Cambridge Application form (MCA). You must submit your MCA by the deadline set. For 2025 entry, this deadline is 22 October at 18:00 hours (UK time) in the majority of cases.

The purpose of the MCA, Cambridge says, is to ensure that admissions tutors have consistent information about all applicants. It also permits them to collect information that is not part of the UCAS application such as the topics students have covered as part of A level (or equivalent) courses and helps the interviewers decide which questions to ask.

Cambridge interviews are typically conducted online for students living outside of the UK. If you want to take advantage of this scheme, rather than come to Cambridge, you must consult the list of dates on the website. However, applicants invited for interview for architecture, history of art, classics and music are advised to travel to Cambridge for interview.

Most applicants to the University of Oxford are not required to submit a separate form, but extra information is required for some international interviews, and choral and organ award applicants must submit an additional form online by 1 September 2024.

You can apply to only one course at *either* the University of Oxford *or* the University of Cambridge. *You cannot apply to both universities.* There is only one exception to this – if you'll be a graduate at the start of the course and you're applying for course code A101 (graduate medicine) at the University of Cambridge, you can also apply to medicine (course code A100) at Cambridge and graduate medicine (course code A101) at the University of Oxford. No other combinations are permitted. However, those applying for organ awards can audition at both universities.

Some applicants will need to complete an additional application form. For full information about applying to the universities of Oxford or Cambridge, please visit their websites at www.ox.ac.uk or www.study. cam.ac.uk. In-depth advice on making applications to these universities is also given in *Getting into Oxford & Cambridge* (Trotman).

Applying to study at a conservatoire

You can apply for performance-based music, dance, drama and musical theatre courses at nine of the UK conservatoires online using the UCAS Conservatoires scheme, which is run by UCAS and works in a similar way. You can select six courses rather than the five possible through the UCAS Undergraduate scheme. The application fee for UCAS Conservatoires is £28.50 and there are also assessment fees to pay.

The nine conservatoires are:

1. LAMDA (London Academy of Music and Dramatic Art)
2. Leeds Conservatoire (jazz and classical courses only via UCAS Conservatoires, all other undergraduate courses via UCAS)
3. Royal Academy of Music
4. Royal Birmingham Conservatoire
5. Royal College of Music
6. Royal Conservatoire of Scotland
7. Royal Northern College of Music
8. Royal Welsh College of Music and Drama
9. Trinity Laban Conservatoire of Music and Dance.

If you're applying for music courses, you can choose either a joint course (50/50) or a major/minor course (75/25), or choose both options providing you'd be happy to study either.

You can apply for music, dance, drama and musical theatre courses from 10 July 2024. For music courses the application deadline is 18:00 hours (UK time) on 2 October 2024, although late entries may be considered if there are vacancies.

For most undergraduate dance, drama and musical theatre courses the deadline is 29 January 2025. There are some exceptions though – particularly for certain assessment locations and for international applicants – so it's important to check the conservatoire websites for full details.

Applying to UCAS Conservatoires doesn't mean you're excluded from the UCAS Undergraduate system. The two systems run independently, so you can also make up to five choices through UCAS Undergraduate. However, you may only accept a place through one of the systems.

Some members of the organisation Conservatoires UK don't recruit through UCAS Conservatoires. They use either the standard UCAS scheme or run their own independent admissions systems. They include:

- some of the colleges that are part of the group Conservatoire for Dance and Drama
- Guildhall School of Music and Drama
- Royal Central School of Speech and Drama.

Conservatoire auditions preparation advice from Nicola Peacock of the Royal College of Music

Auditions are a busy time for conservatoire staff, but also exciting, as we get to meet the talented new students who will be joining us next year. We are very aware that auditioning at a conservatoire can seem a daunting prospect, but we really want applicants to have a positive experience and a lot of effort goes into ensuring we look after you on the day.

How to prepare
Each conservatoire will have information on its website about what you need to prepare and any particular requirements, so check these carefully when you know your audition date. If you don't understand something, please don't be afraid to contact us to ask.

Practical tips
Our top tip would be to allow plenty of time for your journey, so that you arrive on time feeling calm and prepared. There is no need to wear concert dress – we would recommend smart casual clothes that you feel comfortable in. Don't forget to bring along the music for both you and your accompanist (people really do forget!) and anything you may need for your instrument, like spare reeds, strings, or a mute.

When you arrive, there will be people on hand to direct you to your audition room and answer any last minute questions. Audition stewards are often current students, so take the opportunity to ask them what student life is like!

For performers auditioning in the UK, the conservatoire can usually provide an accompanist for you, and you will have time to warm up together before the audition.

The audition

The exact structure of your audition will depend on the conservatoire and your specialism, but for most instrumental and vocal performers, your audition will probably last around 15–20 minutes. There will normally be two or three panellists, who will be experts in your specialism. They may choose which of your pieces they want to hear, and don't worry if they don't ask you to play all the way to the end of what you prepared. There will probably also be a sight-reading test and some auditions may include some scales or aural work. It is possible you may also get asked to perform for a second panel or in a group workshop. For composers, your portfolio will have already been assessed, so the panel will want to talk to you about your ideas in more detail. There may be some different assessments too for students of dance and drama, such as dance classes or a group interview.

Ask questions

Most auditions will include a conversation about your experience and interests. Don't forget that this is a chance for you to get a feel for the conservatoire and ask us some questions! You might want to ask about performance opportunities on the programme, or which professors you could end up working with.

Good luck!

If you have any questions about your conservatoire application, check out our website – www.rcm.ac.uk – or send us a message on Facebook (www.facebook.com/royalcollegeofmusic) or X (formerly Twitter (@RCMLondon).

Medicine, dentistry and veterinary science/veterinary medicine courses

If you want to apply for a course leading to a professional qualification in medicine, dentistry or veterinary science/medicine, the deadline for submitting your application is 18:00 hours (UK time) on 15 October 2024. You're allowed to select a maximum of four courses in any one of these subjects – if you list more than four, your UCAS application (described fully in Part III) will ask you to reduce your number of choices. You can, if you'd like to, use the remaining space on your UCAS application for a course in another subject. There's strong competition for entry to these professional courses.

In-depth advice on making applications in these subject areas is given in the *Getting into* series (see the 'Further information' section at the end of the book).

Mature students

There's no single definition of a 'mature' applicant, but most universities and colleges now classify students as 'mature' if they are over 21 years of age at the date of entry to a course. The vast majority of departments welcome applications from mature students, and many, especially science departments, would like more.

As a mature student, you're more likely to be accepted with qualifications that wouldn't be good enough if they were presented by a student aged 18 in full-time education. That said, there's still fierce competition for places, and in most subjects places aren't set aside for mature students. If you're considered favourably, you're likely to be called for interview. It isn't usually advisable to rely only on qualifications gained several years ago at school; university and college departments will probably want to see recent evidence of your academic ability so that they can evaluate your application fairly. In addition, taking a course of study at the right level helps prepare you for full-time student life.

The Access to Higher Education Diploma, for example, is for students aged 19 or over who do not hold the formal qualifications required for university entry. It provides excellent preparation for study at higher education level. Access Diplomas vary in subject emphasis, and what is available depends on your locality. Access courses are often linked to particular higher education courses at certain institutions.

It's also very important to demonstrate relevant work experience if you're applying for courses leading to any of the caring professions or those related to medicine.

Admissions tutors for courses you're interested in will be able to advise you. If they do expect evidence of recent study they might suggest:

- attending a further education college to study for one of the usual post-16 qualifications (e.g. an A level, Higher or National Award)
- taking one of the Access to Higher Education or Foundation courses specially designed for mature students.

You may also find that, through what's known as **Accreditation of Prior Learning** (APL), you can gain acceptance of alternative qualifications or, through **Accreditation of Prior Experiential Learning** (APEL), acceptance of some of the skills you have developed in the workplace. You'll need to contact universities and colleges direct to find out what their policies are.

Definitions:

- Accreditation of Prior Learning (APL, also known as Recognition of Prior Learning) is essentially credit awarded for wider learning gained through self-directed study, work or training. It's a process used by many organisations around the world, including higher education institutions, to evaluate skills and knowledge acquired outside formal education. Methods of assessing prior learning are varied and include: evaluation of experience gained through volunteer work, previous paid or unpaid employment, or observation of actual workplace behaviour.
- Accreditation of Prior Experiential Learning (APEL) is an extension of APL that includes assessed learning gained from life and work experience. APEL is similar to APL in that it's recognition of prior learning but is broader as in theory it allows for learning from any prior experience. Often APEL and APL are used synonymously and the terms overlap.

For further information visit www.ucas.com/mature-students.

TIPS!

Evidence of relevant work experience will boost your application and show that you know what you're committing to.

Evidence of previous study will show that you'll be able to cope with the academic content of the course.

It's advisable for mature students to contact departments directly to ask about their admissions policies before applying to UCAS and to tailor their applications accordingly.

Deferred entry

Taking a gap year is an increasingly popular option for many students – offering a unique opportunity to broaden horizons, travel or work as a volunteer. And, as the cost of higher education continues to rise, it can be a good way to save some money while gaining valuable experience in the workplace. If you do plan, for whatever reason, to defer your entry into higher education until 2026, there are three options available to you – each is listed below with a few notes on the pros and cons.

Option 1: apply through UCAS for deferred entry

You can make your application this year and select a start date of 2026 in your UCAS application to show you want to defer your entry (see Chapter 24). The major advantage of this option is that you get the formalities out of the way while you're still at school or college and available for interview – then you can relax. It's important to note that you'll still have to meet the terms of offers made to you.

Generally speaking, applications for deferred entry are dealt with in the normal way, but for some subjects (such as medicine, certain science and mathematics subjects and professional subjects) admissions tutors may be a little cautious about offering you a place. (They may say they want to be sure that your skills and knowledge are really up to date.) So it's important you're sure you want to defer, and to check with the department you're applying to whether they would be happy to admit you a year later.

Remember, if you do apply for entry in 2026 but then find that you have no useful way of spending the gap year after all, the university or college is not obliged to take you a year earlier (i.e. in 2025). If you choose to defer, remember to mention your reasons and plans for your year out in the personal statement section of your UCAS application (see Chapter 23); this is much more likely to make admissions tutors willing to give you a deferred place.

Option 2: apply through UCAS for standard entry

If you're not confident enough of your decision to apply for deferred entry on your UCAS application, you can apply for the normal admission year and, later on, ask the university or college where you're accepted whether you can defer. This means you don't need to say anything on your UCAS application about deferred entry. However, the university or college is quite entitled to say that the place it has offered you is for 2025 entry only, and you could either take it up or start a new application for entry in 2026.

Option 3: don't apply through UCAS until the following year

It's possible to delay applying to UCAS until after you've received your results – making your UCAS application during your gap year. This can be a good option in some instances, especially if your exam results turn out to be significantly different from those that were predicted. Your grades are also guaranteed, and if you accept an offer it will be a firm decision, so universities and colleges may consider you a better bet than a candidate who is only predicted those grades. The disadvantage, though, is that you must find time during your gap year to get your research up to date, fill in your UCAS application and (possibly) attend open days and interviews. This can limit your gap year options as you'll need to be contactable at all times. Flying back from Australia (or anywhere you might decide to spend your gap year) to attend an interview could put a serious dent in your finances!

Making a late application

If at all possible, avoid applying late. Many popular courses fill up quickly, and getting a place will be more difficult, if not impossible. However, if you decide you'd like to apply to higher education late, you still can. Up to 30 June, UCAS will send your application to your named institutions, but the universities and colleges will only consider you at their discretion. If they do choose to consider you, the same procedures are followed as for a normal application, and you'll reply to offers in the usual way. Applications for 2025 entry received between 1 July and 24 September will be processed through the Clearing scheme, which operates from 5 July to 20 October 2025.

International students

If you're an international student, the general information given in this chapter and Chapter 7 applies to you. However, UCAS has some specific additional advice for you.

● Make sure you add all the qualifications you have or are currently working for. Visit ucas.com/fillinginyourapplication for advice on entering qualifications on your application.
● Give as much information as possible – without it, admissions tutors will struggle to make a decision.
● You may have to send proof of your results in certificates or transcripts to the universities or colleges. They all have different policies on how they want to receive them. While some of them ask you to send everything straight away, others will do their initial assessment of your application before asking to see proof of your results.
● Although UCAS can send some results from the awarding bodies to your chosen universities and colleges – including the International Baccalaureate – for most international qualifications you'll have to send them direct to universities and colleges yourself.
● Follow the advice in Chapter 23 for your personal statement, but also say why you want to study in the UK and describe your English language skills (mentioning any English courses or tests you have taken). Also explain why you want to be an international student rather than studying in your own country.

As mentioned in Chapter 7, your application deadline is 29 January, but for courses listed on page 64 you must observe the same (earlier) deadlines as UK students. You'll find a lot of useful information on ucas.com on costs of study here, visas and student life in the UK.

Visa requirements

Since 5 October 2020, students from outside the UK who need a visa to study at UK universities and colleges will apply for a Student visa. All international students applying for degree courses, including those from EU and EEA countries, need to apply through the Student visa route.

To obtain a visa, the university that has made you an offer will need to act as a sponsor for your visa application. Once you have accepted the offer, the university will then give you a Confirmation of Acceptance for Studies (CAS) letter, after which you can apply for the visa.

You can apply for a Student visa either online at the www.gov.uk website or at a visa application centre local to you.

You need to show that you have:

- an offer of a place at a university or college
- the right level of English to join that course (see below)
- finances to pay for your first year of tuition fees and living expenses.

You can apply for a student visa from three months before the start date of your course if you are already in the UK, and from six months if you are outside the UK.

If you are already in the UK and eligible to apply for your student visa without returning to your home country, you must make sure there are no more than 28 days between the end of your previous course of study and the start of your new course. A standard Student visa application costs £490 if you apply from outside the UK, and £490 to extend or switch to a Student visa when you are already in the UK.

For full guidance on the requirements of student visa applications in relation to your circumstances, visit www.gov.uk/study-uk-student-visa and www.ukcisa.org.uk.

9 | Interviews and selection

In many cases, the decision to offer you a place will be made using the information you supplied on your application, but admissions tutors for several courses often require more detailed information about applicants. So you may be asked to attend an interview or audition, or to take a written test.

Interviews

Many universities and colleges (especially the popular ones, running competitive courses) want to meet applicants and find out whether they would cope with the demands of the course before making an offer.

Admissions tutors are seeking able students with academic potential in sufficient numbers to fill the places on their courses.

In deciding which applicants to accept, they are looking for the following.

- **Intellectual ability** – can you cope with the academic and professional demands of the subject and course?
- **Competition** – how well do you compare with other applicants for the course?
- **Applicants who are likely to accept** – if offered a place, is there a good chance that you will accept it?
- **Students who will make a contribution** – will you get involved in the life of the university or college and contribute in lectures, practicals and tutorials?
- **Applicants who are likely to get the grades** – are you expected to achieve the level of grades in your exams that this course generally requires?

And, very importantly!

- **Motivation**: a real and enthusiastic interest in the subject.

They may be able to find much of this information in your personal statement (see Chapter 23), but some will also use interviews to help them decide which applicants to make an offer to. There's usually no standard policy for each institution. In most cases admissions tutors themselves decide whom to interview.

In general, interviews are still used:

- for applicants with mitigating circumstances, or whose background would merit further consideration; also, mature students or those taking non-standard qualifications may be interviewed by some universities to assess their suitability for a course
- for borderline candidates – give it your best shot, because many admissions tutors like to give all applicants a chance
- for applicants who haven't studied the subject before – tutors need to know that you have researched it and know what's involved
- to distinguish between large numbers of similar, very able, applicants – particularly if you're applying for very competitive courses
- for vocational courses – those that lead to a particular career, e.g.:
  - agriculture
  - dentistry
  - health and social care
  - medicine
  - nursing
  - healthcare professions, e.g. physiotherapy, radiography, dietetics or occupational therapy
  - social work
  - teaching
  - veterinary science.

The majority of the above courses lead to work in a caring profession, which is why admissions tutors particularly need to be able to assess a student's suitability for the career. However, it's not unusual for applicants to courses in architecture or engineering to be interviewed, and they may also be asked to take examples of work or to talk about a project.

Universities and colleges that have a policy of calling applicants for interviews may arrange to conduct them by telephone or video conferencing (e.g. Microsoft teams or Zoom).

Your interview invite could come by letter or email or through your UCAS application. In all cases, you'll be offered a date and time. Instructions will be given on how to change these if they are inconvenient.

What will you be asked?

Interviews can take different forms. You could find yourself in front of just one person or an interview panel; or in a group, being observed as you discuss a topic or carry out a particular task. You may even be asked to take a written test.

Interview questions can be wide ranging and unpredictable – but, on the other hand, there are a few that tend to come up over and over again. Think about how you might respond to the following questions.

- Why do you want to study this subject?
- What aspects of your current studies have you found most interesting and why?
- Why have you applied to this department or faculty?
- Why have you chosen this university or college?
- What are your spare-time interests?
- Why should we offer you a place? (Don't be modest.)
- Tell me about an achievement you are proud of.
- What have you read outside your syllabus?
- What skills have you gained from your part-time job?
- Tell me more about the sports team/voluntary work/drama group you described on your application.
- Why are you taking a gap year and what are your plans? (If you're applying for deferred entry.)
- What have you learned about yourself from any work experience/ volunteering you have done?
- Have you any questions to ask? (This is a good way to demonstrate enthusiasm.)

You should also be prepared to talk about the following:

- your advanced-level study – what particularly interests you and what additional reading and research have you done?
- topical issues relating to your chosen subject
- anything you have mentioned in your personal statement.

For vocational courses, you can expect to discuss anything you've done to gain useful experience, such as work experience in a hospital, care setting, architectural practice, engineering company, accountant's or solicitor's office. Be prepared to describe what you did, what you learned and how the experience helped you to decide on your higher education course.

You may be asked about your understanding of the career you're thinking of, e.g. for medicine, what personal qualities do you believe a doctor should have? It's very important to keep up to date with developments in the career area you are exploring, especially if you're applying for subjects such as medicine or primary teaching. Websites such as www.gmc-uk.org (the General Medical Council) or www.tes.com (Times Education Supplement) are worth looking at, as interview questions are likely to ask about a particular issue relevant to that career.

Preparing yourself

Prepare as much as you can. Don't memorise or recite answers to any of the questions above – but think through the kind of things you would like to say. Taking the question 'Why should we give you a place?' as an example, you could:

- talk about your strengths, interests and ambitions, particularly with reference to courses you are interested in
- mention anything a bit individual or a little different that you can bring to share with others: for example, you may have debating experience, great rugby skills, extensive experience in charity fundraising or orienteering expertise; or you may have developed mentoring skills through your work as a sixth-form or college ambassador to 11–16-year-olds.

Ask your school or college to give you a mock interview – preferably with a member of staff who does not know you. This can be an excellent way of preparing yourself to think on your feet and answer unexpected questions, and you should get some helpful feedback.

Start thinking about interviews as early as possible. As you consider your course choices and compile a shortlist of universities and colleges to apply to, you should research answers to the questions admissions tutors might ask. If the admissions tutor asks 'Why have you chosen this university or college?', you'll then remember their particularly strong facilities or the unique angle of the course.

Try to keep interviews in mind as you write your personal statement (see Chapter 23). It is very likely that interviewers will use this as a basis for their questions, so don't mention anything you can't talk about and expand on. And, if you have a particular passion or area of interest in your chosen subject that you'd love to talk about, make sure you mention it in your statement.

Top tips for interviews

- Dress should be 'smart casual'. There's no need for it to be very formal. The interviewer probably won't be dressed formally either. As a general rule avoid jeans, and go for a skirt or smart trousers with a shirt, rather than a t-shirt. This holds true for virtual interviews using digital platforms too.
- Make eye contact with the interviewer. If there's more than one interviewer always reply to the person who asked the question – but look at the other/s from time to time to include them in your answer.
- Do not read from pre-prepared notes; the interviewer would like you to respond organically and not be overly rehearsed.
- Do your best to show you're thoughtful, committed and genuinely interested in your chosen subject.
- Always have one or two prepared questions of your own about the course, opportunities after you graduate or a relevant academic topic. (Don't ask questions only on topics covered in the material already published and sent to you by the university or college.)
- Make sure that you know exactly what you wrote in your personal statement.

- Don't bluff. If you don't know the answer to a question, ask the interviewer to repeat it or put it in a different way. If you still don't know, admit it!
- Most important – be sure you know exactly how to get to the interview. Check your travel arrangements. Make sure you're going to the correct site if the university or college has more than one. Allow plenty of time for your transport to be late and to find the right building and room when you get there.
- Take the interviewer's name and phone number with you so that you can call and explain if you're unavoidably delayed.

There are further useful tips on preparing for interviews and on what to expect on the UCAS website, www.ucas.com/invitations.

More detailed advice on interview technique and possible interview questions is given in the *Getting into* series (see the 'Further information' section at the end of the book).

Auditions and portfolios

Your subject teachers will be able to offer more specific advice, but here are a few general points. If you're applying for a performance-based course in drama, music, dance or musical theatre, you will have to attend an audition – usually before an interview. (Some applicants are weeded out at the audition stage.) Policies vary at different institutions, but drama applicants might be asked to:

- perform one or more pieces
- deliver a monologue
- do some improvisation
- do some movement work
- work in a group.

You'll be sent detailed instructions on what to prepare for your audition.

Music students might be asked to:

- perform at least two (contrasting) pieces – often from a set list – sent to you in advance – but sometimes of your own choice
- sight read
- improvise
- do technical tests (scales and arpeggios).

Dance students might be asked to:

- participate in one or more dance classes, observed by teaching staff
- improvise
- perform a short piece choreographed by themselves
- participate in a group interview
- have an interview that focuses on their future ambitions.

Sometimes a physical examination is included.

Music, drama, dance and musical theatre applicants can benefit from performing for a small audience before attending an audition. Your teachers may organise this automatically and arrange for you to perform in front of them and other students. You should then receive some feedback and constructive criticism.

Art students normally have to take a portfolio of work with them – and will be expected to talk about it. You might be asked questions by one or two individual interviewers or you might be expected to display your pieces like a mini exhibition and explain how you developed and changed a piece as you worked on it. The usual advice is to:

- include some work that you have done on your own, i.e. not as part of coursework
- include notebooks and sketches as well as finished work
- bring photographs of three-dimensional work that is too heavy to take with you.

You'll be told what size your portfolio should be and how many pieces of work it should contain. However, some admissions tutors prefer to see portfolios in advance and assess them at the same time as they read the UCAS application. If so, you'll receive a request (usually by email) for your portfolio. The email you receive will tell you how to submit your portfolio – and full instructions will be given if you're expected to do so online.

It's a good idea to ask your art teacher to give you a mock interview and ask you questions on your portfolio.

Applicants for film-making and screen courses are expected to submit a different type of portfolio. You may normally include still work – photographs and art work – but the major element will be a short film lasting just a few minutes. (Timing is very important. Films that overrun aren't accepted.) You will be told whether you should use a set theme or one of your own, how many actors the film should include and whether to use an indoor or outdoor location. You'll be invited to explain your film and what you were aiming to achieve to the interview panel.

Aptitude tests

Many students now get top A level (or equivalent) grades, so admissions tutors for oversubscribed courses have no way of distinguishing between them. As such, several admissions tests have been devised to provide additional information that is relevant to their subjects. The most common tests are for medicine and law, usually the UCAT and the LNAT.

UCAT (University Clinical Aptitude Test): used by UK and overseas universities for entry to medicine and dentistry

UCAT is an online test consisting of the following sections.

- **Verbal Reasoning:** designed to assess ability to think logically about written information and to arrive at a reasoned conclusion. 21 minutes, 44 questions.
- **Decision Making:** assesses ability to deal with various forms of information, to infer relationships, to make informed judgements, and to decide on an appropriate response to situations given. 31 minutes, 29 questions.
- **Quantitative Reasoning:** assesses ability to solve numerical problems. 25 minutes, 36 questions.
- **Abstract Reasoning:** assesses ability to infer relationships from information by convergent and divergent thinking. 12 minutes, 50 questions.
- **Situational Judgement:** measures capacity to understand real-world situations and to identify critical factors and appropriate behaviour in dealing with them. 26 minutes, 66 questions.

All answers are multiple-choice.

The test must be taken online at an approved test centre. There are centres in many countries around the world, as well as numerous centres within the UK, so you should be able to find one within convenient travelling distance.

At the time of writing, UCAT registration opens on 14 May 2024, booking opens on 18 June 2024 (and closes on 19 September) for those wanting to start courses in 2025, with testing taking place between 8 July and 26 September 2024. These dates could be subject to change, so always check at www.ucat.ac.uk. As of January 2024, the fee for taking the UCAT in the UK is £70, and for taking it outside the UK it is £115.

If you plan to sit the test outside the UK, you should enquire whether the test centre you will attend uses QWERTY, AZERTY or other keyboards.

If you have any disabilities or additional needs that require you to have extra time in exams, make sure you register for the UCATSEN rather than the regular test. If you need special access arrangements for examinations, contact Pearson VUE customer services directly to discuss your personal requirements before booking the test.

Full information, including a guide to what to expect at a test centre, is given at www.ucat.ac.uk.

Law National Aptitude Test (LNAT): used by nine UK universities for entry to law

LNAT is a two-part online test that takes two and a quarter hours. It's designed to test the skills required to study law, but doesn't require any previous knowledge.

Section A consists of 42 multiple-choice questions based on argumentative passages. Candidates are given 95 minutes to answer all of the questions. For Section B, candidates have 40 minutes to answer one of five essay questions on a range of subjects and demonstrate their ability to argue economically to a conclusion, displaying a good command of written English.

You must take the LNAT assessment in whichever academic year you are applying to university (e.g. if you intend to start university in September 2025, you need to take it before January 2025). You can only sit the test once in the year, and results cannot be carried over from one year to the next. Registration for LNAT tests opens every August, with testing beginning in September; see https://lnat.ac.uk/registration/dates-and-deadlines.

Tests are offered at 500 centres around the world, including 150 in the UK. As of December 2023, the fee for taking the LNAT is £75 in the UK and £120 elsewhere. If you are going to sit the LNAT test outside the UK you should enquire whether test centres use QWERTY, AZERTY or other keyboards.

There is much more information on the LNAT website, www.lnat.ac.uk, where you can find out more about the different parts of the test and read some tips on both tackling multiple-choice questions and writing the kind of essay that will impress. You can access practice LNAT tests at https://lnat.ac.uk/how-to-prepare/practice-test; sample essays can be found at https://lnat.ac.uk/how-to-prepare/sample-essays.

Can you prepare for UCAT and LNAT?

You can't learn or revise anything for these tests. However, you can certainly prepare for them by finding out what to expect and practising, using practice papers, which are freely available online. You should also familiarise yourself with the type of equipment in the case of computer-based tests.

> **TIP!**
>
> Bursaries are available for applicants who would have difficulty in meeting the cost. Read full details on the test websites.

Other entrance tests

If you apply to either Oxford or Cambridge, you'll find that for many courses you'll be required to take an additional test. Cambridge has introduced common-format written assessments for all subjects except mathematics and music. You can very quickly find a list on the two universities' individual websites.

Many other universities and colleges also use entry tests for particular courses. You can find a full list of those that have been declared to UCAS, with details of how and where you can take them, on the UCAS website.

10 | Exam results and afterwards

This chapter looks at what might happen when you have your exam results. However, please don't skip the chapter and think 'I don't need to read this yet!' You might not need any of the information, but then again you might – and panic stations can set in in the summer. A lot of people whose exam results aren't what they hoped for make rushed decisions, leaping at the first option that presents itself. They can live to regret doing so.

This chapter discusses what happens at exam results time and the options you might have if you need or decide to change your plans. These include:

- Clearing
- rethinking your higher education plans, perhaps retaking certain subjects or taking different ones
- deciding not to do a higher education course at all.

Before results day

Most applicants are accepted conditionally before their exam results are known, so the results of exams taken or assessments completed in May/June are very important.

After you have taken your exams, you deserve to relax; but it is worth giving some thought to what you'll do if you don't get the grades needed for your higher education place – a sort of 'Plan B'. Will you try to secure a place through Clearing (see page 88)? Would you rather retake and apply again next year for the course you really want to do? Or are you having any doubts about whether higher education is really for you?

If you're ill or have some other problem at exam time that you think may adversely affect your results, tell the universities and colleges whose offers you're holding, or ask your school or college to contact them on your behalf. You may need to get a doctor's certificate to support your case. Admissions tutors will do their best to take such circumstances into account, but they'll need to know about them before your results come out. If you leave it until after you have disappointing results, it may be too late.

Results day

You will not see your results in your UCAS application. Your school, college or exam board will give your results to you.

Clearing vacancies will be available on www.ucas.com from 5 July.

IB results day for 2025 is yet to be confirmed at the time of writing, but is usually early July. Unless you plan to go to your school or college in person you will need to access them online via the 'candidate results website' a day later. You'll need the PIN and personal code that your IB programme coordinator will have given you earlier in the year. Remember to find out what time your results are released, as this is done at different times in different time zones; usually the UK receives them around 12 noon.

SQA results will be released in early August 2025. Your results will be sent to you to arrive in the post on results day. If you've signed up to MySQA and activated your account you can request to have these sent via email or text.

A level results are published in mid-August. You should be able to check your UCAS application from the morning onwards to see whether your place has been confirmed. But you won't see your results. You'll have to contact your school or college for them – usually by going in at a time you've been given. If admissions tutors are still considering whether to give you a place then your UCAS application won't be updated yet. Remember, that if you meet or exceed the exact terms of your offer your place is guaranteed. It's only people who have not done so who may need to wait.

UCAS receives most results from the exam boards. After checking they match the information on your application, UCAS sends them to the universities and colleges where you're holding any offers of a place. You can check at ucas.com/undergraduate/clearing-and-results-day/results-day/sending-exam-results to see the full list of qualifications UCAS do this for.

If your exams aren't listed, you'll have to send your results to your universities or colleges yourself. If you've taken any other exams, such as Nationals 4 and 5, GCSE or international qualifications, you must send your results as soon as you receive them to those universities and colleges where you are holding offers. (IB results may or may not be received by UCAS as schools and colleges need to give permission for this.)

When your results are released and have been received by the admissions tutors, they'll compare your results with the conditions they set and make a decision on whether to accept you.

If you get the grades

Congratulations! Your place will be confirmed – a university or college can't reject you if you have met the conditions of your offer by 3 September 2025.

> **TIP!**
>
> Arrange your holidays so you're at home when the results are published. Even if all goes well and your grades are acceptable, you may need to confirm your place and deal with your registration, accommodation and loan. And, if things haven't gone according to plan, you may need to take advice, find out about course vacancies and make some quick decisions about possible offers in the Clearing system (see below).

> **TIP!**
>
> You can check university and college decisions on results day.

If you missed out ...

Don't panic! You should contact admissions offices immediately to find out whether they'll accept you anyway. Admissions tutors may decide to confirm your offer even if you failed to meet some of the conditions. It has been known for applicants to be accepted with much lower grades if there are places available, there's good school or college support and, perhaps, a good interview record – although this varies greatly from course to course. (But don't count on this!) Alternatively, you may be offered a place on a different course, but you don't have to accept this if you don't want to.

UCAS will send you an official notification of the outcome of your application. If you have been offered a place on an alternative course, you'll have a choice of actions. These will be listed in the notification letter.

If your place isn't confirmed, you can find a place through Clearing (see below); alternatively, you can retake your exams and apply again the following year.

Clearing

If you don't get the grades you had hoped for and your offer isn't confirmed, don't worry. If you're flexible and have reasonable exam results, there's still a good chance you could find another course through Clearing. In 2023, a record 74,990 students found places using this service.

You're eligible for Clearing if you haven't withdrawn from the UCAS system and:

- you're not holding any offers (either because you didn't receive any, or because you declined the offers you did receive), or
- your offers haven't been confirmed because you haven't met the conditions (such as not achieving the required grades), or
- you made your UCAS application too late for it to be considered in the normal way (after 30 June), or
- you've declined your firm place using the 'decline my place' button in your application.

Your Clearing matches

Available alongside Clearing is a tool designed to help you find your perfect course.

To speed things up, UCAS takes what they know about you and what they know about the types of students universities and colleges are looking for, to suggest some courses you might like. If you express an interest in a course, the university or college can contact you. Find out more at www.ucas.com/clearing-matches.

Holding an offer, but changed your mind?

From 5 July, if you're holding a confirmed place and decide you no longer want it, you can use self-release into Clearing, by using the 'decline your place' button in your UCAS application. You should only use this button if you no longer want to take up your place at your firm choice, and you've spoken to your university or college and/or an adviser at your school/centre.

What do I have to do?

You need to find a course you're interested in that has vacancies. In your UCAS application, you'll be able to click through to a list of suggested course matches based on your qualifications and the courses you applied for previously. Here, you can follow the on-screen advice to connect with universities and colleges you're interested in.

Official course vacancies are also published in the UCAS search tool from early July until October.

The national Exam Results Helpline on 0800 100 900, which is staffed by trained advisers, is also a useful source of information and advice. You'll also see many advertisements for universities and colleges with vacant places in the national press.

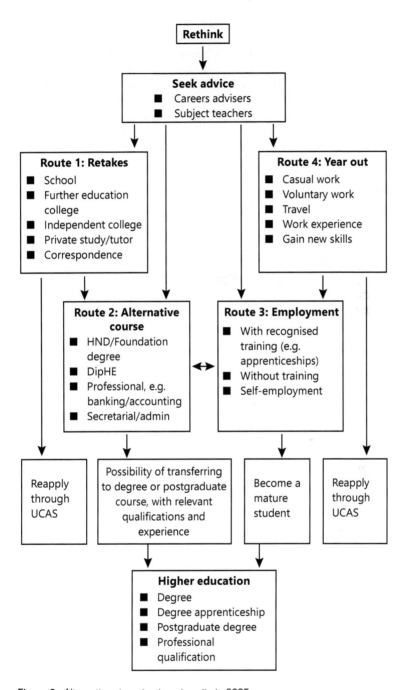

Figure 2: Alternatives to going to university in 2025

Make a list of the courses you're interested in, and contact the institutions, in order of your preference, to ask whether they'll accept you. It's recommended that you telephone, email or visit in person because the admissions tutor will want to speak to you personally, not to your parent or teacher. Keep your Clearing number (given in your UCAS application) to hand as you'll probably be asked for it. If you're not convinced that a course is right for you, remember you don't have to commit yourself. You just need to contact universities or colleges direct about any vacancies you're interested in.

If one agrees to give you a place on the course you want, you enter the institution and course details in your UCAS application and they'll then be able to accept you. Only accept an offer of a place when you're certain you have found the right course for you. Once you've accepted, you won't be able to take any further part in Clearing and you'll be committed to taking up your place. Figure 2 (page 91) gives tips on what you might do if you don't get a place through Clearing.

Top tips on Clearing

- Talk to your careers adviser about which courses and subjects would be most suitable for you, particularly if your original UCAS application was unsuccessful.
- Remember that you can apply for any course that has places left – you don't need to keep to the same subjects you first applied for. If you do decide to apply for courses that are quite different from the ones you originally selected, make sure you do your research thoroughly, referring back to prospectuses and websites. Remember, though, you won't be able to change your personal statement.
- Although you'll have to act quickly, don't make any hasty decisions – only accept an offer if you're sure the course is right for you.
- One way of making sure you're happy with your choice of course is to visit the university or college. Most universities and colleges are happy to make arrangements to meet applicants and show them around, and many will have Clearing open days. They know that you could be spending the next three or four years there, and will be reassured that you want to be sure you're making the right choice.
- If you're applying for art and design courses, you may need to supply a portfolio of work as well as your Clearing number.
- Remember that universities and colleges are likely to refer back to your UCAS application when deciding whether to make you an offer. So, it's a good idea to have another look at what you wrote on your personal statement to make sure you're familiar with it, just in case an admissions tutor wants to ask you about it.

When you've secured a place through Clearing

Make sure you get from your new choice of university or college the information you'll need about:

- accommodation
- term dates
- introductory arrangements.

Retakes

Remember, disappointing results don't have to mean the end of your ambitions. If low grades mean that you haven't been accepted on a course of your choice, you could consider retaking your exams, or you could change to a new subject if you think that would give you a better chance of improving your grades.

- Retakes of A levels and Scottish Highers are available only once each year – usually in June.
- IB retakes are available in both November and May. There are some restrictions, so you'll need to contact the centre where you might want to do your retakes.

While most university and college departments consider retake candidates – and some welcome the greater maturity and commitment to hard work that retaking demonstrates – be aware that you may be asked for higher grades. It's always worth checking with the relevant admissions tutor that your proposed retake programme is acceptable. It's very rare for Oxford or Cambridge to accept applicants who have retaken their exams, for example.

Part III
Your UCAS application

11 | Getting started

You can register for your UCAS Hub on ucas.com and complete your application online. It's easy to use, accessible from any online device and:

- speeds up the processing of applying to higher education courses
- incorporates checks that prevent you from making simple errors
- is supported by the very latest UCAS course data and relevant additional information.

This chapter provides a brief outline of the application process. The following chapters explain each section of your online application.

Register with UCAS

The first thing you have to do is register in the UCAS Hub.

- Click 'Sign in' on ucas.com.
- Click 'Register'.

Once you've registered you'll be asked a few questions about:

- when you want to start studying
- what level of study you're interested in, e.g. undergraduate if you're still at school or college; plus additional information on apprenticeships and conservatoires if you'd like
- where you live – so UCAS can direct you to the right information
- your preferences – the information you can receive by email
- what you're interested in – three initial subjects you'd like to know more about.

> **TIP!**
>
> If you forget your password, you can use the 'Forgot your password?' service on the login page.

Looking for apprenticeships?

From your UCAS Hub, you can sign up to get the latest apprenticeship opportunities straight to your inbox. Smart Alerts is an email service that can match you to apprenticeship opportunities where employers are looking for specific candidates.

Just share some basic information about yourself and your apprenticeship aspirations, and UCAS will match you to potential employers who have opportunities that fit your future goals.

Starting your application

When you log in to your account, you'll be able to mark as 'favourite' the courses you're interested in and view them in your Hub anytime.

From 14 May 2024, you can start your applications to study in 2025.

Applying via a school or college

Each year, all schools, colleges and careers centres registered with UCAS set up a unique password or 'buzzword', made up of at least six letters and numerals. This is used by you and all other UCAS applicants at your centre so that your application can be identified with that centre.

When you start your application you'll be asked if you're applying from a school, college or centre.

- Select 'Yes'.
- Enter the buzzword.
- Confirm the details are correct.

This links your application to your school, college or centre so they can support your application and add your reference.

You'll complete all the sections of your application – although you won't be able to see the reference on your application homepage, as this gets added by your school or college separately. The referee is likely to be one of your teachers, personal tutor or head of sixth form.

> **TIP!**
>
> The buzzword allows you to start your application, and lets UCAS see which centre you're from. Some centres are also set up as a **group**, which you can select for your type of application – your centre should let you know if that's the case.

Applying as an individual

If you want to apply, but you aren't attached to a school or college, you can easily make an application through ucas.com.

When you start your application you'll be asked if you're applying through a school, college or centre – just select 'No'.

From here, the only difference between making an application as an individual and making it via a school or college is how you provide a reference. You could ask your old school to supply your reference if you've left recently; you'll need to supply their buzzword in your application. When they've added the reference, they'll return your application to you to forward to UCAS.

You can enter an independent referee's details in the Reference section of your application; they'll receive an email from UCAS asking them to provide a reference directly onto your application through a secure website.

Your reference must be written by a responsible person who knows you well enough to comment on your suitability for the courses you've applied to. This could be an employer, a senior colleague in employment or voluntary work, a trainer, a careers adviser or the teacher of a relevant further education course you have recently attended. Your referee can't be a member of your family, a friend, partner or ex-partner.

TIP!

Make sure that you allow plenty of time for the person writing your reference to complete it before the UCAS application deadline. They may receive several requests at the same time. If you're a student at a school or college you'll probably be given an internal deadline.

Your written reference

The good news is, you're not allowed to write your own reference, so there's relatively little for you to do here. Your referee (usually a teacher if you're applying via a school or college) will write it and then attach it to your application, through their UCAS coordinator or administrator.

Having said this, it's important not to disregard your reference entirely. In some ways it's the most important item in the selection process. It's only your referee who can tell the admissions tutors about your attitude and motivation, and who can comment on your ability – so that admissions tutors aren't reliant solely on exam results and predicted grades.

Admissions tutors will be interested in any information about your circumstances that may affect your performance in exams or other assessments.

Referees are asked to estimate your level of performance in forthcoming exams, and these predictions of likely grades are important to your chances of acceptance. The best advice in this respect is to work hard and impress your referee!

Under the 2018 General Data Protection Regulations, you have the right to see your reference. Contact UCAS if you want to see all the information UCAS holds about you, including what your referee has written about you. There's now no such thing as a confidential reference.

Your reference will normally come from your current school or college, or the school or college you attended most recently. If you choose anyone else, make sure it's someone who can provide the kind of assessment higher education institutions need. Be aware, if you're attending a school or college, it will look very odd if you choose someone from outside as your referee.

If you have any difficulties at any stage, there's help within your application and on the UCAS website, or you can contact UCAS on 0371 4680 468 between 08:30 and 18:00 hours (UK time) on weekdays.

Navigating your application

From your application you can select English or Welsh, and choose to receive correspondence in your preferred language. You can change your preference back at any point.

The help text in your application is available in Welsh too. It is not possible to apply in any language other than English or Welsh.

Your application homepage

Your Personal ID will be displayed on the screen – make a note of this as you'll need it in future communications with UCAS and with universities and colleges.

Your homepage is where you'll see the sections that need to be completed. You don't need to complete the application all at once – you can log in and out at any time until you're finished.

As you add information to each tile, the 'Percentage complete' dial should increase each time you mark a section as complete.

See Figure 3, Application status, page 100.

These are the different sections of your application:

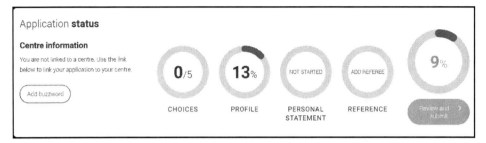

Figure 3: Application status

- personal details
- contact details
- where you live
- employment
- education
- nationality details
- supporting information
- finance and funding
- diversity and inclusion (UK students only)
- more about you
- extra activities (UK students only)
- your personal statement
- choices.

See Figure 4, Application sections, opposite.

You can access each section by clicking on its tile. There are on-screen instructions in every section, guiding you through what you have to do. If you get stuck at any point, you can access help text by clicking on the question mark in each section.

You're free to move between sections as you like, leaving them partially completed and returning to them later. When you've completed a section, just tick 'Mark this section as complete'.

Checking the progress of your application

As well as percentages of completion at the top of your application, each section will turn green when completed – with the confirmation 'Section complete'.

The tiles will give you an overview of whether a section is complete, in progress or needs to be started.

All sections must be marked as complete to send to UCAS. You must complete all mandatory questions – identified with an asterisk * – to mark a section as complete.

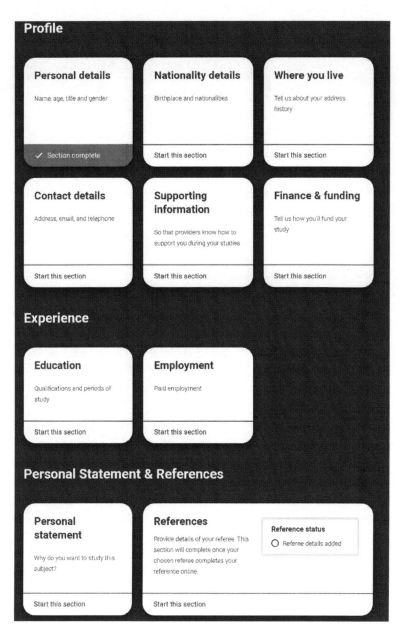

Figure 4: Application sections

TIP!

Remember to save all your changes.

Once you've finished your application (and it's showing 100%), there are four steps to the submission process:

1. check your application – double check the details and download a PDF copy
2. update your preferences – e.g. what information about universities and student life you'd like to receive
3. confirm you've read and understood the terms and conditions
4. pay and submit – if you're applying through a school, college or centre they'll complete this (you'll just need to submit).

Once you've submitted your application to UCAS and received your welcome email, you can log in to your application to keep up to date with your progress and reply to your offers.

Security tips

To apply through ucas.com, it's recommended that you use the latest version of your chosen browser – as older versions may be less secure.

For data protection reasons, your application is in a secure area of the UCAS website. More recent web browsers have a built-in feature allowing you to save your password so that you don't have to remember or retype it later. However, if you use this facility it will allow anyone using that particular computer to log in to your account and change the details of your application. For this reason, it's strongly advised that you don't use this feature.

When you've finished a session in your application, it's strongly recommended that you log out properly by using the 'Log out' button (not by simply closing the window you are in). Once you've logged out, you should close your web browser down completely.

How the rest of this book works

The remaining chapters of this book will take you step-by-step through each section of your application, giving you general advice on the nature of the information you are asked for and the basic principles of getting it right.

Chapter 25 deals with finishing off your application, including information on:

- your declaration – your agreement with UCAS and higher education institutions
- submitting your application

- fee payment
- your reference.

At the end of the book you'll find a chapter on troubleshooting (Chapter 26), which will help you solve some of the most frequently encountered problems. Further help is available through the 'question mark' link on each section of your application.

Stop and think!

Before you start your application, here are some final tips and reminders.

- Make sure you've done all your research thoroughly and you're happy with your choices. If in doubt, take another look at Part I of this book, 'In the think tank'.
- Collect together:
  - o   your personal details
  - o   all school or college attendance dates
  - o   exam results slips and entry forms
  - o   any employment details (a copy of your CV is useful to have at hand)
  - o   details of the higher education courses you want to apply for, including institution and course codes (you can find these in the search tool on the UCAS website).
- Carefully read through the guidance available within your application.
- Be honest and truthful – you must be able to back up all your statements.
- Don't try to make more than one application in the same year.
- Remember, once your application reaches UCAS, you can't amend it or add anything to it. So, get someone – preferably someone who is well informed about higher education, such as a tutor – to check your personal statement.

You should now be ready to start your application – read on, and good luck!

12 | Personal details

Obviously, UCAS and the universities and colleges you're applying to need to know who you are and how they can contact you. They'll also need to know about a number of other aspects of your life. This can be for important financial reasons (e.g. in deciding who assesses your eligibility for funding), or to check whether you need any additional support while studying, for example if you have a disability.

Your application will, therefore, contain quite a lot of information about you, which we'll go through step by step in the upcoming chapters.

Personal information

The name you entered when you registered will have been drawn through into the personal details section of your application. You'll also be asked to provide your:

- title
- previous name(s) – including by marriage or deed poll
- preferred name – what you would like to be called, e.g. Matthew or Matt
- date of birth – required for UCAS's and institutions' records
- gender – select the gender you most identify with at this time. You can tell the university or college directly if you'd feel more comfortable identifying in another way, or if this changes.

> **TIP!**
>
> Don't provide nicknames. It is important that you enter the same names that appear on official documents such as exam certificates.

The list on the left of each section will show which sections are completed (with a tick), which are in progress (with a half moon), and which haven't been started yet (no icon).

If you'd like more information about a section, click on the question mark link for help text to provide advice about what to put.

13 | Nationality details

UK nationals

You're asked to confirm your country of birth and nationality – this information is for statistical purposes only, to find out where applicants come from. It won't be used for selection purposes.

If you were born in the UK, you should select 'United Kingdom' for your country of birth and 'UK national' for your nationality – i.e. you can't select 'Scotland', 'English'.

See Figure 5, UK nationality questions, below.

What is your country of birth? *

For the purpose of this question the UK includes the Channel Islands and the Isle of Man.

[⌄]

What is your nationality? *

If you're applying from outside the UK choose your nationality as it appears in your passport. If you have dual nationality and you need a visa to enter the UK, enter your first nationality as it is shown on the passport you intend to use when travelling to the UK for your course.

[⌄]

Dual nationality

If you have dual nationality, select your first nationality in the previous field and your second nationality here.

[⌄]

Figure 5: UK nationality questions

International

If you were born in the UK but have a different nationality, you'll be asked additional questions. The information you provide will help universities and colleges to determine your eligibility – and allow them to assist you with the visa application process if needed.

If you weren't born in the UK, you're asked for the date of first entry to the UK. If you're not in the UK yet, put the date you plan to arrive.

See Figure 6, International nationality details, below.

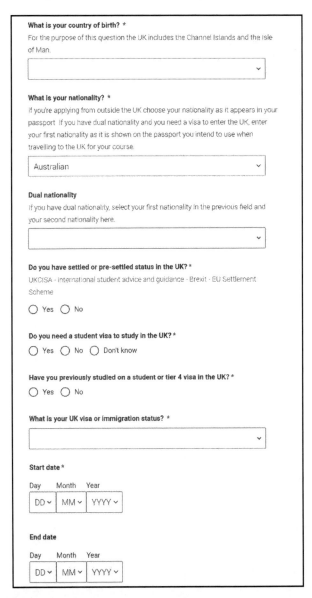

Figure 6: International nationality details

Visa and passport details

If you select 'Yes' when asked if you will need a visa, you'll also be asked for your passport details. If you don't have a passport yet, you can provide these details to your university or college when you receive an offer.

See Figure 7, Passport details, below.

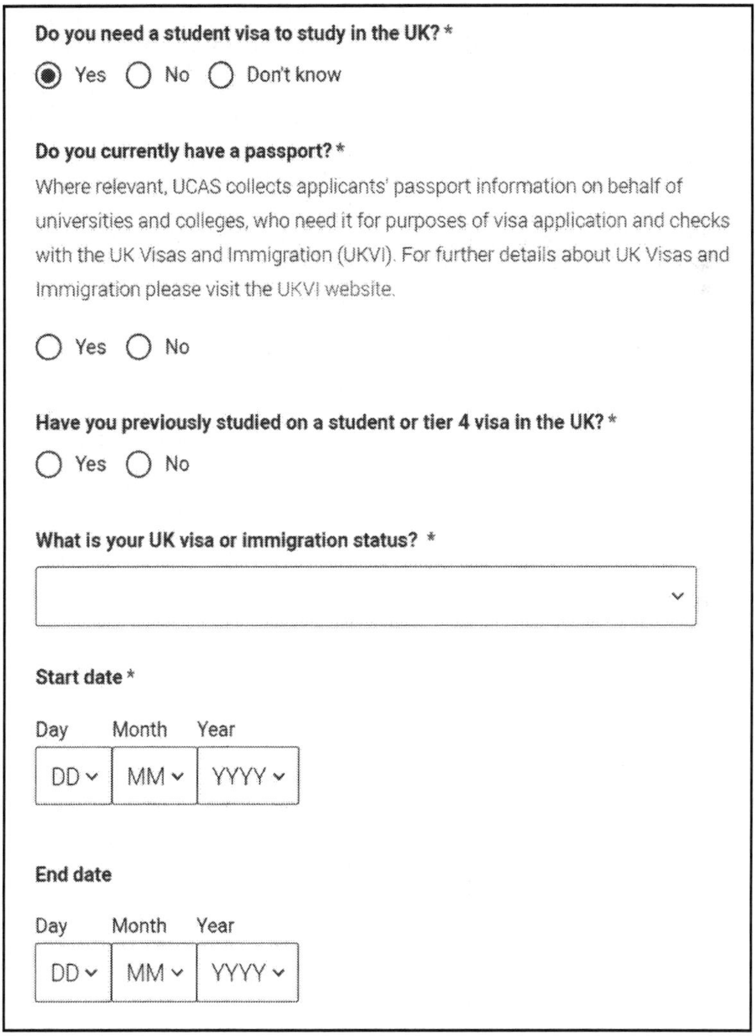

Do you need a student visa to study in the UK? *

◉ Yes   ○ No   ○ Don't know

Do you currently have a passport? *

Where relevant, UCAS collects applicants' passport information on behalf of universities and colleges, who need it for purposes of visa application and checks with the UK Visas and Immigration (UKVI). For further details about UK Visas and Immigration please visit the UKVI website.

○ Yes   ○ No

Have you previously studied on a student or tier 4 visa in the UK? *

○ Yes   ○ No

What is your UK visa or immigration status? *

[⌄]

Start date *

Day   Month   Year

[DD ⌄] [MM ⌄] [YYYY ⌄]

End date

Day   Month   Year

[DD ⌄] [MM ⌄] [YYYY ⌄]

Figure 7: Passport details

14| Where you live

In this section you'll be asked to provide:

- the address(es) you've lived at for the last three years, when you started living there, and for what purpose. This is because universities and colleges need to know if you're living there permanently or for a temporary reason
- your residential details – choose the option that most closely applies to you.

See Figure 8, Add current address, opposite.

Home address

If your home address is different to your postal address, you can add that here.

Residential category

Residential category can be complicated, but it's particularly important because what you enter here will be the point from which universities and colleges will start to classify you as 'home' or 'overseas' for the purpose of tuition fees. Those classified as overseas students pay a much higher annual tuition fee. (Your tuition fee status has no direct connection with your nationality – it depends on your place of ordinary residence and the length of time you have been ordinarily resident there.) You must choose from a list of residential category options (as defined by UCAS), summarised below.

UK citizen – England, Northern Ireland, Scotland, Wales, Channel Islands and Isle of Man, and British Overseas Territories

You're a UK citizen, or the child or grandchild, or the spouse or civil partner of a UK citizen and have lived in England, Northern Ireland, Scotland, Wales, the Channel Islands and Isle of Man, or British Overseas Territories for the past three years, but not just for full-time education. If you've been living in any of these regions for three years partly for full-time education, you also lived in any of these regions prior to that three-year period.

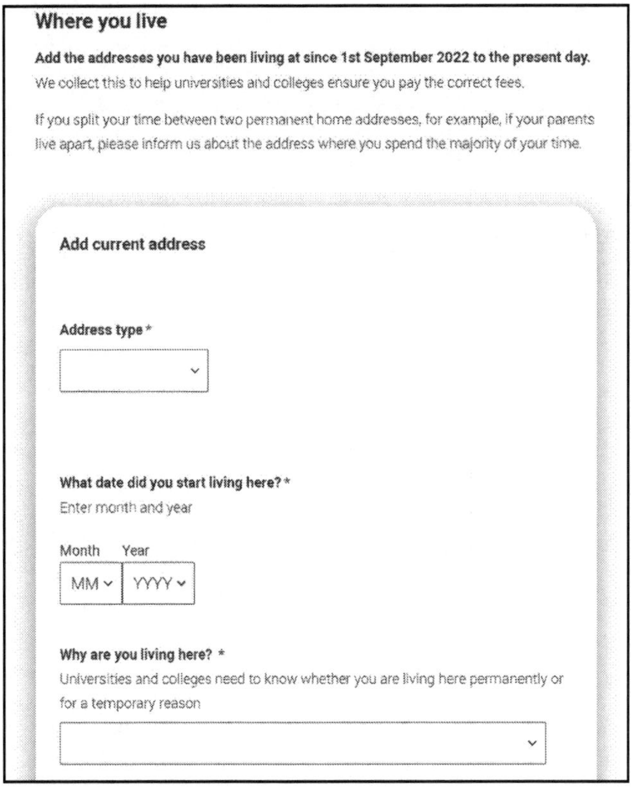

Where you live

Add the addresses you have been living at since 1st September 2022 to the present day.
We collect this to help universities and colleges ensure you pay the correct fees.

If you split your time between two permanent home addresses, for example, if your parents live apart, please inform us about the address where you spend the majority of your time.

Add current address

Address type *

[⌄]

What date did you start living here? *
Enter month and year

Month   Year

[MM ⌄] [YYYY ⌄]

Why are you living here? *
Universities and colleges need to know whether you are living here permanently or for a temporary reason

[⌄]

Figure 8: Add current address

EU national (non-UK citizen)

You're an EU national, or are the child or grandchild, or the spouse or civil partner of an EU national, and have lived in the European Economic Area (EEA) or Switzerland or European Overseas Territories (OT) for the past three years, but not just for full-time education. If you've been living in the EEA or Switzerland or OT for three years partly for full-time education, you also lived in the EEA or Switzerland or OT prior to that three-year period.

EEA or Swiss national

Either: You're an EEA or Swiss national working in the UK, or you're the child, spouse or civil partner of such a person or you're the parent or grandparent of an EEA national working in the UK. You've lived in the EEA or Switzerland or OT for the past three years, but not just for full-time education. If you've been living in the EEA, Switzerland or OT for three years partly for full-time education, you also lived in the EEA, Switzerland or OT prior to that three-year period.

Or: You're the child of a Swiss national and have lived in the EEA or Switzerland or OT for the past three years, but not just for full-time education. If you've been living in the EEA, Switzerland or OT for three years partly for full-time education, you also lived in the EEA, Switzerland or OT prior to that three-year period.

Child of a Turkish worker

You're the child of a Turkish national who has lawfully worked in the UK, and you've lived in the EEA, Switzerland or Turkey for the past three years.

Refugee

You've been recognised as a refugee by the British government or you're the spouse, civil partner or child under 18 of such a person at the time of the asylum application.

Humanitarian Protection or similar

You've been granted Exceptional Leave to Enter or Remain, Humanitarian Protection or Discretionary Leave or you're the spouse, civil partner or child under 18 of such a person at the time of the asylum application.

Settled in the UK

You have Indefinite Leave to Enter or Remain in the UK or the Right of Abode in the UK and have lived in the UK, the Channel Islands or the Isle of Man (or more than one of these) for three years, but not just for full-time education. (However, this does not apply if you're exempt from immigration control, for example, as a diplomat, a member of visiting armed forces or an employee of an international organisation or the family or staff member of such a person; in this situation your residential category is Other.)

Other

If you don't fit any of the above categories then answer 'Other'. Universities and colleges will try to be fair to you, but they do have a duty to apply the regulations equitably to all their students. Before applying, you could write to universities and colleges outlining your circumstances. Some overseas companies have standard letters for employees to use. It sometimes happens that different universities and colleges will classify the same student in different ways, depending on their reading of the rules.

> **TIP!**
>
> If you cannot find your area on the list, you need to look through the existing options to find one that matches your circumstances.

15| Contact details

In this section you'll be asked to provide:

- a contact phone number
- your postal address
- whether you want to nominate anyone else to act or speak on your behalf about your application

Postal address

You can provide both a postal and a home address (in the **Where you live** section) if you want to.

Your postal address is the one where written correspondence about your application will be sent. This doesn't have to be your home address.

If you decide to give your school address, you'll need to provide your home address as well.

Nominee access

You'll have the option of naming one person who can act on your behalf regarding your application. It's a good idea to do so, in case of illness or injury, for example. You just need to fill in their name and their relationship to you.

16 | Supporting information

These questions are mandatory, but you have the option to answer 'I don't know' or 'Prefer not to say'.

Living or working in the EU, EEA or Switzerland

These questions ask if you've lived or worked – or have parents from – the EU (excluding the UK), EEA or Switzerland.

See Figure 9, Supporting information questions, below.

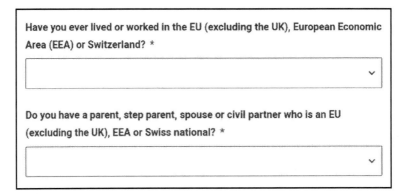

Figure 9: Supporting information questions

17| Finance and funding

You'll only be asked further questions on finance and funding if you select 'UK, ChI, IoM or EU Student Finance Services' (United Kingdom, Channel Islands, Isle of Man, European Union).

You'll also be asked for the name of your local authority under 'Student support arrangements'.

For more information on funding and other financial concerns see Chapter 3 or ucas.com/finance.

See Figure 10, Finance and funding, below.

What will be your main source of funding for your studies? *

Select an option from the drop-down list to tell us how you expect to pay for your tuition fees. Most applicants from the UK, Channel Islands, Isle of Man, and those eligible EU students under the EU Settlement Scheme will be in the category UK, ChI, IoM, or EU student finance.

This guidance has been created based on eligibility advice from the Student Loans Company, and you should give your answer as guided. Universities and colleges are aware that EU applicants will be selecting the UK, ChI, IoM or EU student finance option.

If you require additional guidance, we recommend contacting the UK Council for International Student Affairs.

| UK, ChI, IoM or EU student finance services ∨ |

Student support arrangements

Tell us who will assess you for tuition fees, or how you will pay for your course. Please select the option which best describes your situation.

| Bristol ∨ |

Figure 10: Finance and funding

Sponsorship

If you're applying for sponsorship you can give the name of your first-choice sponsor in the personal statement section of your application (see Chapter 23). You can find out more about company sponsorship from a careers adviser.

Also make a note in your personal statement if you plan to defer to 2026 if your application for sponsorship is unsuccessful this year.

18 | Diversity and inclusion

You'll only see this section if you have a UK home or postal address. It covers:

- equality monitoring:
  - ethnic origin
  - religion or belief
  - sexual orientation
  - identifying as transgender
- whether you've been in care
- parental education
- whether you would like to receive correspondence in Welsh
- occupational background.

Don't worry about the equality monitoring

Universities and colleges have a legal obligation to make sure applicants are not discriminated against or disadvantaged. They only see this information after you've secured a place or at the end of the application cycle – so it doesn't influence any decision making. It's used to ensure applications are treated fairly.

There are two mandatory fields, but you have the option to respond with 'I prefer not to say'.

See Figure 11, Diversity and inclusion, page 116.

Ethnic origin

You're asked to select your ethnic origin, or the category that most closely describes it. The options are:

- white
- gypsy, traveller or Irish traveller
- black – Caribbean
- black – African
- black – other background
- Asian – Indian
- Asian – Pakistani

- Asian – Bangladeshi
- Asian – Chinese
- Asian – other background
- mixed – white and black Caribbean
- mixed – white and black African
- mixed – white and Asian
- mixed – other background
- Arab
- other ethnic background
- I prefer not to say.

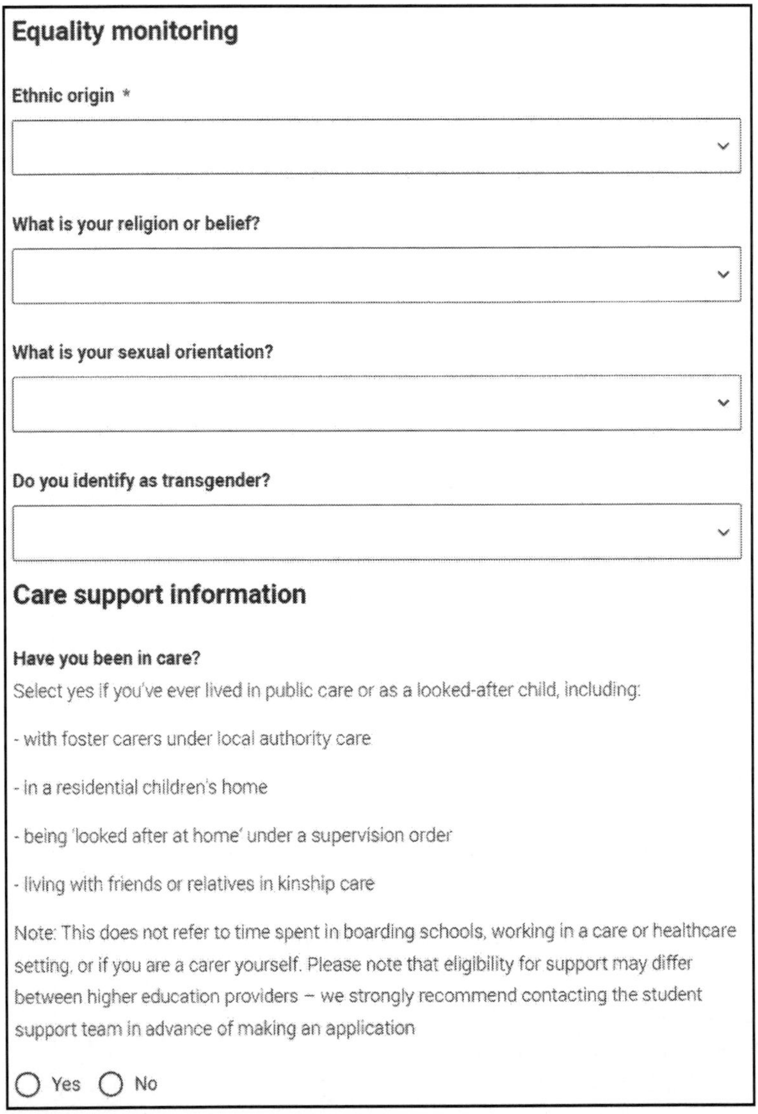

Equality monitoring

Ethnic origin *

[∨]

What is your religion or belief?

[∨]

What is your sexual orientation?

[∨]

Do you identify as transgender?

[∨]

Care support information

Have you been in care?

Select yes if you've ever lived in public care or as a looked-after child, including:

- with foster carers under local authority care

- in a residential children's home

- being 'looked after at home' under a supervision order

- living with friends or relatives in kinship care

Note: This does not refer to time spent in boarding schools, working in a care or healthcare setting, or if you are a carer yourself. Please note that eligibility for support may differ between higher education providers – we strongly recommend contacting the student support team in advance of making an application

○ Yes ○ No

Figure 11: Diversity and inclusion

Religion or belief

You're asked to select your religion or belief from a drop-down list:

- No religion or belief
- Buddhist
- Christian
- Hindu
- Jewish
- Muslim
- Sikh
- Spiritual
- Any other religion or belief
- I prefer not to say.

Responding to this question is optional and won't be considered as part of your application. If you decide to disclose this information, your response will be treated in the strictest confidence. Your school or college, adviser and referee won't have access to it – and during the application process it won't be seen by the universities or colleges you're applying to. The university or college where you secure a place will have access to this information once your place has been confirmed. All data disclosed will be stored in compliance with data protection legislation.

Sexual orientation

You're asked to select your sexual orientation from a drop-down list:

- Bisexual
- Gay man
- Gay woman/lesbian
- Heterosexual
- Other
- I prefer not to say.

> **TIP!**
>
> You must enter one of the options listed – even if it is 'I prefer not to say' – to complete the section.

As with the 'Religion or belief' section, responding to this question is optional, and won't be considered as part of your application.

Transgender

You'll be asked if you identify as transgender, and to select from a drop-down list:

- Yes
- No
- I prefer not to say.

As with the 'Religion or belief' section, responding to this question is optional, and won't be considered as part of your application.

Care support information

Growing up in care means you are entitled to a range of practical support. This can include support during your application (e.g. events to help you with your transition to university), financial assistance, year-round accommodation, or help with managing your health and well-being.

When you give this information, you are letting the university know that you may need additional support during your studies. They may get in touch to tell you more about the benefits and options available, if you want it.

The availability of support will vary between providers, so always speak to the university or college directly to discuss your circumstances and understand what help you may be eligible for.

Parental education

You'll be asked whether or not either of your parents, or your step-parents or guardians, have any higher education qualifications – such as degrees, diplomas or certificates of higher education. If you're unsure, select 'Don't know' from the drop-down list. If you don't want to disclose this information, you can select 'I prefer not to say'.

See Figure 12, Parental education and occupational background, opposite.

Occupational background

If you're aged under 21, you should give the occupation of your parent, step-parent or guardian who earns the most. If they're retired, give their most recent occupation. If you're 21 or over, you should give your own occupation. Enter at least three characters of the job title in the search box and select the job title you want. If you prefer not to give this information, please enter: 'I prefer not to say'.

This information is converted into occupational classifications based on those used by the Office for National Statistics, and is used to help monitor participation in higher education across all parts of society. NB: This information won't be released to your chosen universities or colleges until after a decision has been made regarding your application.

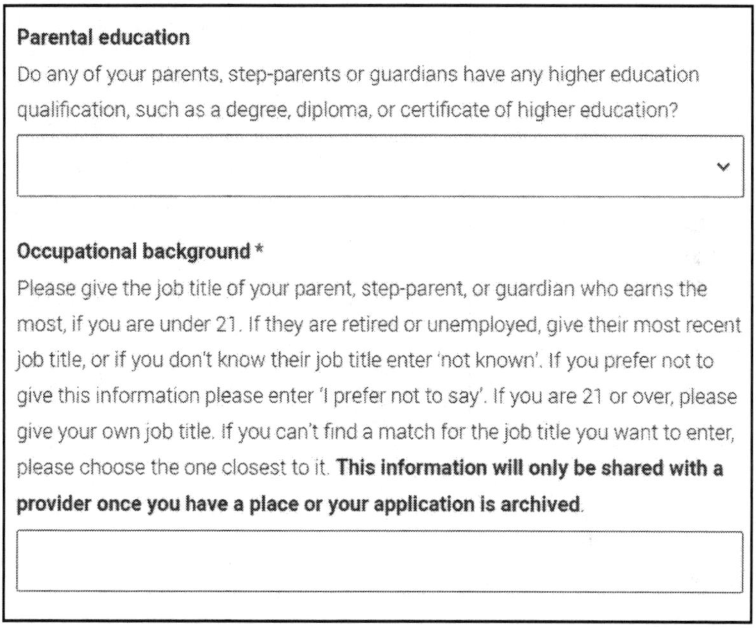

Parental education

Do any of your parents, step-parents or guardians have any higher education qualification, such as a degree, diploma, or certificate of higher education?

Occupational background *

Please give the job title of your parent, step-parent, or guardian who earns the most, if you are under 21. If they are retired or unemployed, give their most recent job title, or if you don't know their job title enter 'not known'. If you prefer not to give this information please enter 'I prefer not to say'. If you are 21 or over, please give your own job title. If you can't find a match for the job title you want to enter, please choose the one closest to it. **This information will only be shared with a provider once you have a place or your application is archived**.

Figure 12: Parental education and occupational background

19 | More about you

If you have a home or postal address outside the UK, you will only see the question asking if you have a physical and/or mental health condition, long-term illness, or learning difference. The other questions are for UK residents only.

This section gives you the option to highlight your individual circumstances. Universities and colleges can make more informed decisions about your circumstances and make sure supportive measures are in place for you.

See Figure 13, More about you, page 122.

Students with a physical and/or mental health condition, long-term illness, or learning difference

In 2023, 128,525 students with a physical and/or mental health condition, long-term illness, or learning difference applied through UCAS to study at a university or college in the UK, and accessed a range of support available to help with their studies, day-to-day activities, travel, or lifestyle. The information you give in your application will help your university or college to do this.

Telling a course provider about a health condition or impairment early means they can work to make the arrangements or adjustments ready for your arrival. However, if you decide not to give this information now, you can do so after you have sent your application, by contacting them directly.

The information you provide here may also be used (anonymously) for monitoring purposes to inform and improve support for future students.

Select the option(s) you feel best describe(s) any physical and/or mental health condition, long-term illness or learning difference you may live with. If you have no impairment or condition, select 'None'. If you want to give details of more than one option, you can do this in the further text box.

You'll be asked if you consider yourself as living with any of the following:

- a learning difference (e.g. dyslexia, dyspraxia, or AD(H)D)
- a visual impairment uncorrected by glasses (e.g. blindness or partial sight)
- a hearing impairment (e.g. deafness or partial hearing)
- a physical impairment or challenges with mobility (e.g. climbing stairs or uneven surfaces), or dexterity (e.g. using a keyboard or laboratory equipment)
- a mental health condition, challenge or disorder (e.g. anxiety or depression)
- a social, behavioural or communication impairment (e.g. an autistic spectrum condition or Tourette's syndrome)
- a long-term illness or health condition which may involve pain or cause fatigue, loss of concentration or breathing difficulties – including any effects from taking associated medication
- a condition or impairment not listed above (you will be asked to give further details)
- two or more impairments or conditions (you will be asked to give further details)
- none.

Estranged students

An estranged person is someone who no longer has the support of their parents, and often also other family members (e.g. biological, step or adoptive parents or wider family members who have been responsible for supporting you in the past), due to a permanent breakdown in their relationship which has led to a cessation of contact.

Select 'Yes' if you feel this description applies to you.

If you select 'Yes', your information will be treated in confidence, to help the university or college provide support for you. It may also be used for monitoring purposes to inform and improve support for future students who are estranged from their parents.

Students with caring responsibilities

Select 'Yes' if you're responsible for providing unpaid care to someone who has, for example:

- a long-term illness
- a disability
- a mental health condition
- an addiction
- temporary care needs following, e.g., an accident or operation.

Would you consider yourself estranged from your parents (i.e. you're not in contact with and supported by your parents)?

○ Yes   ○ No

Do you have any unpaid caring responsibilities (not including parenting)?

○ Yes   ○ No

Are you a parent or do you have parenting responsibilities for a child aged 17 or under?

○ Yes   ○ No

Do you have official refugee status or limited leave to remain, or are you seeking asylum?

○ No

○ The UK government has granted me refugee status or humanitarian protection in the UK

○ I have limited or discretionary leave to remain in the UK

○ I'm currently seeking asylum in the UK

Do you have a parent or carer who currently serves in the UK Armed Forces, or who has done so in the past?

○ Yes   ○ No

Have you ever served in the UK Armed Forces?

○ Yes   ○ No

Are you currently receiving free school meals, or were you in receipt of free school meals between the ages of 11 to 18?

○ Yes   ○ No   ○ Don't know

Figure 13: More about you

If you select 'Yes', your information will be treated in confidence, to help the university or college provide the right support for you. It may also be used for monitoring purposes to inform and improve support for future students who have care responsibilities.

Students with parenting responsibilities

Select 'Yes' if you're a parent, or responsible for the care and wellbeing of a child aged 17 or under. This can include being:

- a biological parent
- a step-parent
- an adoptive or legal parent
- a legally appointed guardian
- a foster carer
- someone who provides kinship or other parental care to the child of a family member or friend.

If you select 'Yes', your information will be treated in confidence, to help the university or college provide the right support for you. It may also be used for monitoring purposes to inform and improve support for future students who have parenting responsibilities.

Refugees, asylum seekers and students with limited leave to remain

Select the option that most closely represents your circumstances. Don't worry if your choice doesn't exactly match your residency status – the university or college will discuss your circumstances with you in more detail to decide if you qualify as a 'home' or 'international' student.

Your information will be treated in confidence, to help the university or college provide support for you. It may also be used for monitoring purposes to inform and improve support for future students who are refugees or asylum seekers, or with limited leave to remain in the UK.

Students with a parent or carer who serves in the UK Armed Forces, or has done in the past

Select 'Yes' if you have a parent who currently serves in the regular UK Armed Forces or as a reservist, or has done so at any point during the first 25 years of your life.

If you select 'Yes', your information will be treated in confidence, to help the university or college provide support for you. It may also be used for monitoring purposes to inform and improve support for future students who are from Armed Forces families.

Students who have served in the UK Armed Forces

Select 'Yes' if you have served as a Regular or Reservist in the UK Armed Forces (including: the Royal Navy, Royal Marines, British Army, Royal Air Force, or Merchant Mariners who have seen duty on military operations).

If you select 'Yes', your information will be treated in confidence, to help the university or college provide support for you. It may also be used for monitoring purposes to inform and improve support for future students who have a Service background.

Students receiving free school meals

Young people in the UK are usually eligible for free school meals if their parents or carers are on a low income or in receipt of certain benefits. If you're not sure, ask your school – they will be able to confirm this for you.

You may also be eligible if you're paid qualifying benefits directly, instead of through your parent or carer.

20| Education

It's essential to include information about your education to date in your application. This helps to give universities and colleges a better idea of who you are, as well as providing them with evidence of your academic achievements and potential. They'll use the information you give here to put together conditional offers.

This chapter covers:

● the places of education you've attended
● your qualifications – both those you've already completed and those you're studying for now.

Unique Learner Number

You'll be asked for a Unique Learner Number (ULN). You probably won't have one of these – if so, just leave the question blank. Though you may have a ULN if you started studying for a UK qualification from 2008 onwards. If so, enter it in the box provided – it should be ten digits long (i.e. only numbers).

International students: if you've registered for, or already hold, Test of English as a Foreign Language (TOEFL) or International English Language Testing System (IELTS) tests, enter your registration number in the relevant field.

See Figure 14, Unique Learner Number (ULN), page 126.

Places of education

You need to add details of where you've studied, or are studying – including any schools or colleges overseas.

● If you're applying through a school, college or centre, your place of education will be pre-populated.
● If you're not applying through a centre, start by clicking 'Add place of education'.
● Type the name of where you studied. Once you find your centre, click on the name and the Exam centre number will automatically

Unique Learner Number (ULN)

UK Students ONLY - This is a 10-digit number connected to a UK Student's Personal learning record. You can find this on a qualification certificate or results slip. If you don't have one or don't know yours, please leave this blank.

English language certificates

English language certificates are often needed for international students as an entry requirement for the course.

Not everyone will need an English language certificate. If you're unsure whether you need one, check the entry requirements for the course on the search tool.

If you have a language certificate that is not listed here, ie Pearson, Cambridge you can add these as a qualification in the section above.

Test of English as a Foreign Language (TOEFL) Number

International English Language Testing System (IELTS) TRF Number

Figure 14: Unique Learner Number (ULN)

populate if the centre has one (many don't, so don't worry if this remains blank).

- Add when you started and finished, and if you're still studying there add the month you're due to finish.

Enter all the secondary schools, colleges and universities you've attended (up to a maximum of ten). If you've attended more than this, enter the ten most recent. If you've spent any time at a higher education institution you need to say so – and be prepared for questions about it if you're invited to an interview.

If, after typing the school name, a result does not appear, you can add this manually by clicking 'add' underneath. You can then type the name of the school into the box, or type 'home-school' if your secondary education has all been home-based.

You'll be asked whether you attended an education provider in person or online.

> **TIP!**
>
> There are warning messages to help you – e.g. you can't say you attended two or more places of study full-time during the same date range. Red text means something is wrong and blue text is information you need to be aware of.

Add qualifications

As outlined in Chapter 6, this part of the application is crucial, as it's bound to be scrutinised by admissions tutors to ensure you meet their entry requirements. There are so many different kinds of qualification that you might already have, or may be planning to take.

For each place of education you've attended, you'll add details of the qualifications you achieved there, and those you're still studying towards, e.g.:

- A level
- BTEC Diploma
- European Baccalaureate
- GCSE
- T level
- Irish Leaving Certificate
- SQA Scottish Higher.

Click the 'Add qualification' button and search for your qualification. You'll see a list of popular qualifications, or search for yours.

See Figure 15, Add qualification, page 128.

> **TIP!**
>
> Enter into the 'Search' box the country where you took a qualification, and you will find a list all the qualifications for that country.

Enter the details for each qualification

The qualification dates you can select are based on those you entered when you added your place of education.

If you know which awarding organisation it is, enter it here – speak to your teacher or tutor if you're not sure.

If you haven't finished the qualification or had your result yet, then select 'Pending'.

See Figure 16, Search for your qualifications, page 129.

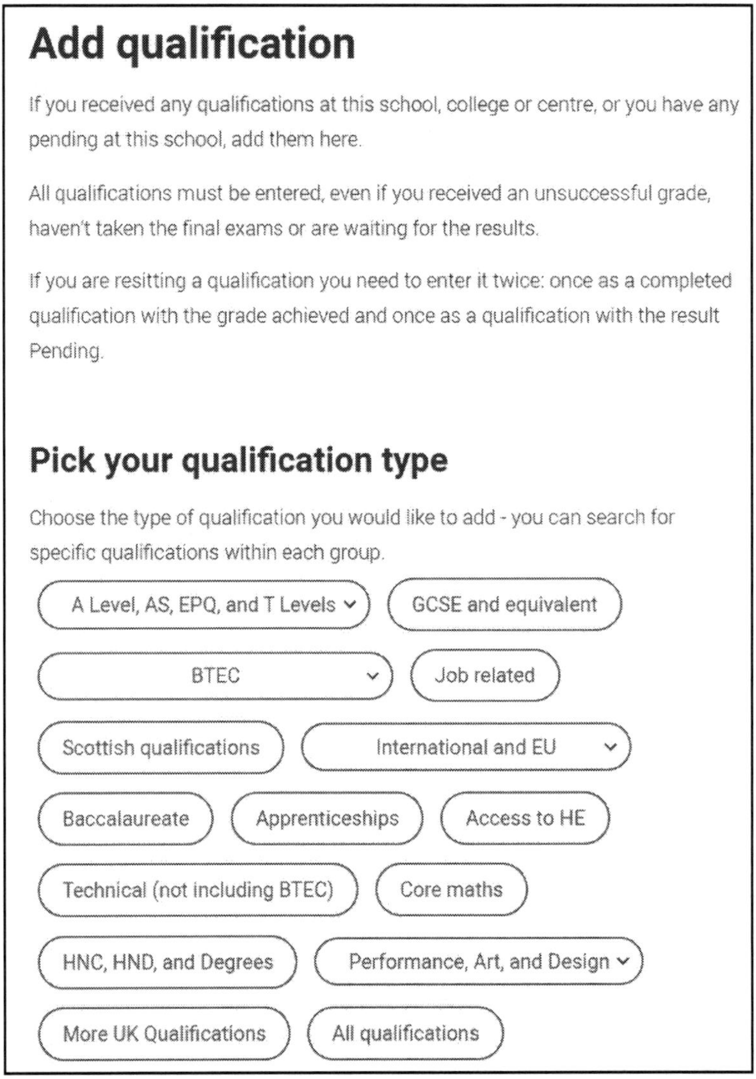

Add qualification

If you received any qualifications at this school, college or centre, or you have any pending at this school, add them here.

All qualifications must be entered, even if you received an unsuccessful grade, haven't taken the final exams or are waiting for the results.

If you are resitting a qualification you need to enter it twice: once as a completed qualification with the grade achieved and once as a qualification with the result Pending.

Pick your qualification type

Choose the type of qualification you would like to add - you can search for specific qualifications within each group.

- A Level, AS, EPQ, and T Levels ⌄
- GCSE and equivalent
- BTEC ⌄
- Job related
- Scottish qualifications
- International and EU ⌄
- Baccalaureate
- Apprenticeships
- Access to HE
- Technical (not including BTEC)
- Core maths
- HNC, HND, and Degrees
- Performance, Art, and Design ⌄
- More UK Qualifications
- All qualifications

Figure 15: Add qualification

You'll also be asked to enter information about the modules or units you've taken, and the unit grades you've achieved in qualifications that have been completed and certificated (e.g. GCE AS exams). Entering unit details is optional, but could be worth doing if you had exceptional results or completed a highly relevant module to the courses you're applying to.

If you entered a Scottish qualification, you'll be prompted to enter your Scottish Candidate Number. If you don't know your number, ask your college or check your exam certificate.

Search for your qualifications

If you cannot find your qualification, select the "All qualifications" filter and search there, if you still can't find your qualification you can select the "All qualifications" filter and search "Other".

We also found these qualifications (Showing 50 of 1024)

2013 qual

A Level (9 units)

A Level Double Award (GCE - 2005 onwards)

A Level Double Award (VCE - 2002-2006)

A Level Examination-Hong Kong

A Level Examination-Hong Kong

A Level copy practical deleletion test

AAT Level 3 Diploma in Accounting (QCF)

AAT NVQ level 3 in Accounting

AAT level 3 NVQ in Accounting

ABC Awards Diploma in Fashion Retail

ACT (American College Testing Program - USA)

ACT Year 12 Certificate-Australia-Capital Territory

AQA Baccalaureate

AQA Certificate in Use of Mathematics

AS Level (first award 2001)

AS Level (first award 2001)

AS Level (last award 2001)

Figure 16: Search for your qualifications

Some BTEC qualifications will also ask for your BTEC Registration Number – ask your school or college if you're not sure what this is.

Putting the right information on your UCAS application is important. Incorrect or incomplete information can cause problems for your university or college and could result in inaccurate or delayed decisions.

Once you've entered all the qualifications you've completed or are yet to complete, click 'Save this section'.

> **TIP!**
>
> You can return to the education area of your application, to edit or add to the entries already made, up to the point when you submit your application through your UCAS coordinator.

Which qualifications should I add?

Qualifications you've already received

You should list all qualifications for which you've received certification from the awarding body (this will usually include GCSEs, Scottish Nationals 4 and 5, and other GCSE-equivalent qualifications). Include all the qualifications you've taken, even if you didn't pass them. You mustn't conceal anything because you'll have to declare at a later stage that you've entered complete and accurate information.

You may be asked to supply original certificates to support the qualifications listed in your application at any time during the application process. You must include details of these qualifications even if you're planning to retake, whether completely or only in part. (You can explain your reasons for retaking in your personal statement.)

If you're a mature student with no formal qualifications, enter 'No formal qualifications'. (See page 147 for advice on how you can address this issue in your personal statement.) If you're hoping to enter university or college via APL or APEL, you should contact your chosen institution before applying to UCAS. Mature students should complete this section as fully as possible – many forget to list their present college.

If you're an international student, you need to give full details of all your qualifications in the original language. Do not try to provide a UK equivalent. If your first language is not English but your qualifications were completely or partly assessed in English, make this clear. You should also provide details of any English language tests you have taken or plan to take, giving dates, titles and any syllabus codes.

Send a copy of all transcripts, certificates or other proof of your qualifications direct to each university or college you apply to, quoting the title and code number of the course and your UCAS Personal ID once you have submitted your application to UCAS. Do not, however, send anything of this sort to UCAS.

> **TIP!**
>
> If you feel there are genuine reasons why some of your grades were lower than expected, make sure the person who's going to write your reference is aware of this and can explain the reason.

Qualifications you're currently studying for

You must also enter details of all qualifications that you're studying for now and those for which you're awaiting results. These may include A levels, Scottish Highers and Advanced Highers, BTEC qualifications, NVQs, Access courses and so on.

> **TIP!**
>
> If you have one, take your full Progress File (a record of your personal development, skills development and achievements) with you if invited for interview. You could even send a brief summary direct to the institution, quoting your Personal ID. You can then discuss and explain what your file comprises, and how it was developed.

21 | Employment

It's very useful for admissions tutors to know if you've had a job, particularly if you've worked in an area relevant to your application or chosen career. Include paid full-time and part-time roles – even weekend jobs – but only if you worked in them for a reasonable period. Even if the jobs were just to earn pocket money, an admissions tutor will see this as a broadening of your experience. (Note that institutions won't contact previous employers for a reference without your permission.)

> 'Work experience, whether paid or unpaid is useful to write about on a personal statement. If, for example, someone is applying for nursing, if they have done jobs in areas such as retail they will have gained some useful experience. Jobs such as these involve working in teams and helping customers, both of which require people-handling skills that are necessary for nursing. Also, being a nurse involves being in a position of considerable trust, and so anything that applicants have done that requires them to be honest and trustworthy is also very good to write about on the personal statement, e.g. handling money or being responsible for others in some way. I like to see what the applicant is like as a whole person, as having the right personal qualities is essential for a career in healthcare.'
>
> Admissions tutor for Nursing

Add your employment

- Click 'Add employment'.
- Fill in the employer's name (i.e. the company/organisation name) and address, your role title, start and end dates, and whether it is/was full- or part-time. If the job you are entering is where you are employed currently, you don't need to enter a finish date.
- If you add more than one instance of employment experience, they'll appear in chronological order, with the most recent at the top.
- Remember to mark the section as complete, even if you haven't created an employment record.

See Figure 17, Employment, opposite.

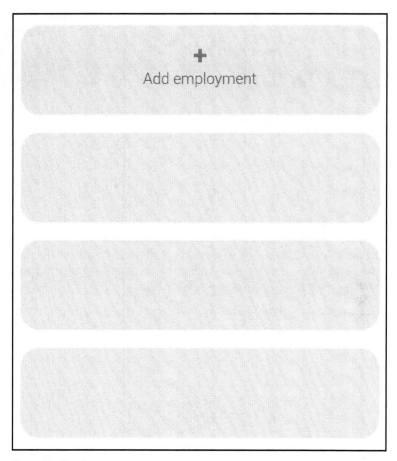

Figure 17: Employment

22 | Extra activities

You'll only see this section if you have a UK home or postal address.

If you've participated in an activity to prepare you for higher education you can give details of it here. You can select the activity from a drop-down list. For example: national or regional schemes, university-run programmes, summer schools, campus days, taster courses and booster courses. You can also use your personal statement to include more details about the activities you took part in, the skills you learned, and how this prepared you for higher education.

NB: Open days are not relevant to this question.

If you haven't attended any such activity, please leave this section blank.

If this section is relevant to you, you'll be asked to give the following details:

- the type of activity [drop-down list]
- the activity provider [drop-down list]
- the name of the activity/programme [free text box – optional]
- the start and end date of the activity.

See Figure 18, Add activity, opposite.

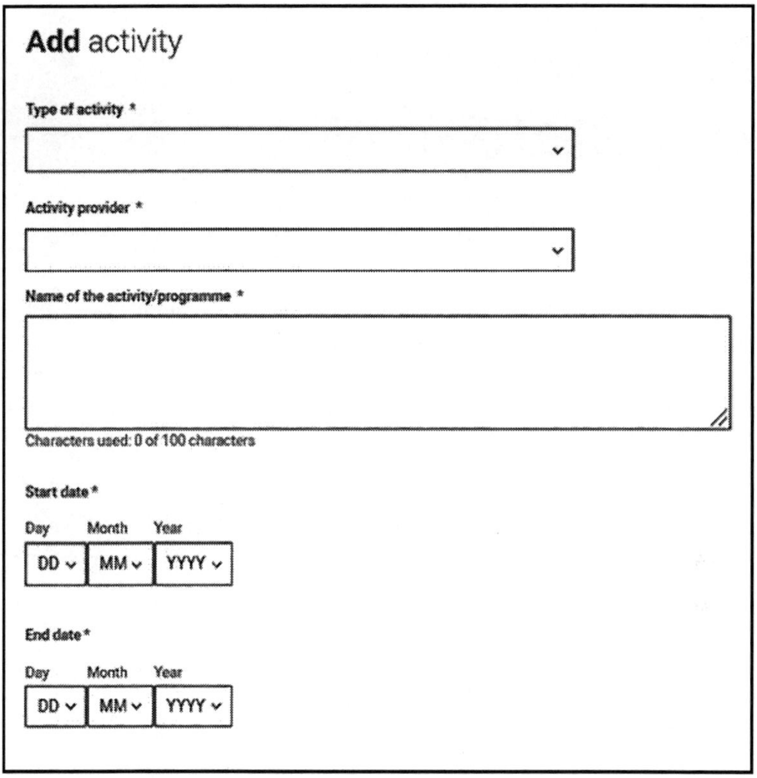

Add activity

Type of activity *

⌄

Activity provider *

⌄

Name of the activity/programme *

Characters used: 0 of 100 characters

Start date *

Day   Month   Year

DD ⌄ | MM ⌄ | YYYY ⌄

End date *

Day   Month   Year

DD ⌄ | MM ⌄ | YYYY ⌄

Figure 18: Add activity

23 | Personal statement

This section is crucial because it's the only part of the application where you have the chance to select and emphasise points about yourself – and to explain to admissions tutors why you're interested in your chosen subject(s). It's your chance to impress and convince admissions tutors to offer you a place.

Personal statements have a maximum length of 4,000 characters (47 lines) and a minimum of 1,000 characters – so you need to think very carefully about exactly what you want to say in the limited space provided. You can click on 'Save' at any time to update the line and character count.

You can save and edit this section as many times as you need to. If you try to navigate away without saving your work, you'll be reminded with a pop-up warning.

The personal statement builder in the UCAS Hub is designed to help you think about what to include and how to lay it out. It also counts the characters you've used, so it's easy to see when you're close to the 4,000 limit.

See Figure 19, Personal statement, opposite.

> **TIP!**
>
> Note: 'foreign characters' e.g. pound signs are converted to ASCII/ Unicode – so '£' will convert to 'GBP'. University and college admissions tutors will be expecting this, so it's nothing to worry about.

What are admissions tutors looking for?

Factual information

The admissions tutors will want to know about:

- your career aspirations – many higher education courses aren't job-related, so don't worry if you don't have a clear idea of your future career direction, unless of course you're applying for a vocational course

Our guide to writing your personal statement (opens in a new window) should help you complete this section.

We strongly recommend you write the statement using a word-processor and paste it in to your application.

You can type your statement directly into the box or edit a statement you have pasted in.

Personal statement *

Characters used: 0 of 4000 characters

Figure 19: Personal statement

- your reasons for choosing the course(s) – wherever possible these should be backed up by evidence of particular reading or additional things you've done that have reinforced your commitment to your chosen subject
- relevant background or experience – which could include work experience/work shadowing, practical activity in music or theatre, attendance on courses, time abroad, etc. (evidence of practical experience may be vital to the success of an application to a medical or veterinary school, and may also significantly help your application if you're applying for some management and engineering courses)

- any interests you may have (e.g. Duke of Edinburgh's Award, charity fundraising, painting, potholing, positions of responsibility) – these may not seem strictly relevant to the course, but they help to give an impression of you as a person
- the name of any sponsor you may have – relatively few students are sponsored through their course and you will not be at a disadvantage if you have nothing to mention; but if you have applied for sponsorship, universities and colleges are keen to know whether you've been successful, or to where you've applied.

Reading between the lines

Your statement will convey more about you than just the bare facts. The way you present the facts will give valuable clues about other qualities such as critical thinking and communication skills.

Analytical skills

Admissions tutors are usually looking for students who can analyse their current experience. A common weakness is that applicants tend to describe what they're doing now, rather than analysing their current experiences and relating them to what they hope to get from higher education and their future career prospects.

Alongside the descriptive approach tends to be a listing of data already entered in the application (e.g. present studies) or details of apparently unrelated hobbies. Hobbies are an important part of your statement, but they need to be analysed in the context of how they have contributed to your skills or personal development in a way that would be an indicator of success on the courses you've applied for.

Communication skills

The text and presentation of your statement provide the admissions tutor with an indication of your communication skills – from grammar and spelling to your ability to express information and ideas clearly.

Maturity

A good statement provides evidence of maturity of thought and a sense of responsibility. If you intend to study away from home, it's important to show that you have these attributes, as they indicate that you'll be likely to adapt well to your new environment.

TIP!

It's difficult for an applicant who has selected a wide range of disparate courses to give plausible reasons for having done so, which is why this approach isn't recommended.

> **TIP!**
>
> Save your work regularly to keep the line count updated – and click to preview your statement.

Top tips

Impression. Think about the impression you want to give – try to show you're interested and interesting, bright, mature and eager to learn.

Structure. Organise what you want to say into a logical structure and make sure that everything you say is clear and concise. Use subheadings if you think it will help.

Length. Do not try to pack too much in – it can get confusing. Deliver your main points well, rather than saying a little bit of everything.

Relevance. Explain why each point you mention is relevant. Do not unnecessarily repeat anything that appears elsewhere on your application.

Honesty. It's so important to be honest and specific. If necessary, be selective – claiming too much is not always a good idea.

Accuracy. Check your spelling. The UCAS application doesn't have a spell-check facility, so it's worth typing your statement in something like a Microsoft Word document so you can spell-check it first, then copy and paste it into the personal statement section of the application. Get someone else to read it through, too – it's sometimes hard to spot your own mistakes, and computer spell-checkers aren't infallible.

Placing 'leads'. Admissions tutors are likely to use your statement as inspiration for interview questions. So, only mention things you're prepared to talk about at an interview. If there's something you would particularly like to be asked to discuss, you can give the interviewer a lead by mentioning it in your statement.

And finally …

Check up on yourself. Read critically through everything you've written. Try to imagine you're the admissions tutor, trying to pick holes in what you've said. You may also find it useful to work with friends and read through each other's drafts – you'll be surprised how often a friend will say to you, 'But haven't you forgotten …?'

Advice on writing the personal statement

The personal statement is a very good opportunity for you to demonstrate your interest and motivation in the subject(s) you want to study.

- Be concise in your use of language – sentences should be kept short and to the point. Admissions tutors must read hundreds of personal statements and don't want to wade through clunky paragraphs, especially if they are not relevant.
- Avoid using vague, worn-out clichés, like 'I have good communication skills'. What does this mean to someone who doesn't know you? Better to say, 'In my role as a student mentor to younger pupils in school, I have developed my listening skills and how to communicate information to them effectively. I have needed to consider their level of vocabulary and understanding.'
- If you don't know where to start, look at some examples of personal statements written by previous applicants (see overleaf).
- Never plagiarise (this means copying work of others claiming it to be your own work). Generating (and then copying, pasting and submitting) all or a large part of your personal statement from an AI (artificial intelligence) tool, such as ChatGPT, and presenting it as your own words, could be considered cheating by universities and colleges and could affect your chances of an offer. UCAS's Verification Team runs checks to detect patterns of similarity, and you are also required to declare that your personal statement hasn't been copied or provided from another source.
- Wherever possible, give examples of things you've done, what you learned from the experiences, what you learned about yourself and how those learnings are relevant to your application.
- As you write the personal statement, read it aloud to yourself – that way you can see if it flows well, or repeats words and phrases.
- Avoid spelling and grammatical errors! These look particularly bad if you're applying for a degree such as English Literature!
- Demonstrate interest and enthusiasm for the subject(s) you want to study at university. Give examples of additional reading you've done, activities you have taken part in, e.g. summer schools or taster events.
- Have a beginning, middle and end. The opening sentences set the direction of the personal statement, the middle gives the evidence of your motivation and suitability, and the end draws the parts together with a summary and conclusion.
- Get someone else to read it! A sixth form or college tutor are obvious examples – preferably someone who is knowledgeable and up to date with applying to higher education.

Creating a winning personal statement

Amazingly, every year there are a few applicants who leave the statement section completely blank. Obviously this is inadvisable, to say the least! But many others do themselves no good simply as a result of the way they present information.

Good sample personal statements

Timmy - Computer Science (3,777 characters with spaces)

Technology is at the forefront of the world we live in today; it is rapidly developing and evolving. Artificial intelligence (AI) and software development are aspects of computer science that intrigue me the most. Questions around AI's future – such as, Will it outperform humans? – inspires me to gain a deeper understanding of it. Through further study of software development, I am keen to learn about developing scalable, secure and complex software.

I have a strong desire to gain a greater understanding of computer science to enable me to explore how current systems work and are maintained. The idea that after studying this subject I could contribute to real world issues, such as creating the perfect speech-to-text software and pushing the boundaries of what a machine can do, ignites a real passion within me. Due to the enthusiasm and ability I showed for ICT at school, I was nominated to attend a three-month computer science masterclass at the University of Birmingham. The course explored various topics, including security, AI and software development. We built programs using Python and gained an insight into robotics, which further developed my curiosity for AI.

My interest in software development was amplified when I began my own business venture. The projects I undertook ranged from creating websites for individuals to complex web applications for larger businesses. One project I completed was an integrated staff portal to assist an entrepreneur in managing all of his businesses and employees. It included a task manager, an integrated news section, customisable weekly reports, as well as various other features. I have also worked with smaller clients to help them build websites to boost their online presence. These sites ranged from a blog for a cosmetics company to an e-commerce site selling toys. These projects helped me develop my interpersonal skills when working with clients and built on my project management skills through handling issues such as scope creep. I used WordPress for most of the smaller projects and worked on creating custom themes for clients who wanted their site to be unique. To do this I used HTML, CSS, JavaScript as well as PHP, my language of choice when creating larger and more complex applications. I have used frameworks such as Laravel, as this helps me keep my code clean and optimised. I have learnt about how the internet works and best practices for securing applications against vulnerabilities such as MySQL injection.

In the summer of 2023, I was invited to undertake a summer internship with a home automation company. I helped program the systems, install equipment and setup networks which allowed me to learn about the scalability of networks. Through my internship I had great exposure to working in a team, as well as having the opportunity to communicate directly with clients. I was able to use my problem-solving skills to logically understand why a system was malfunctioning. At the end of this, I was offered a job at the company on a zero-hour contract to fit around my studies. Outside of school and work, I have a passion for football, and in 2023 I began captaining my local team. I also spend time coaching the Under-11s squad, and I am due to take this further in 2024 when I will take a course to become a Level 2 football coach. Following on from this, I will get the opportunity to manage one of our junior teams; this will give me great pride as I will be able to give something back to the club that mentored me from a young age.

I look forward to widening and developing my understanding of computer science at degree level and being able to combine my current practical and theoretical experience with the vast array of skills and techniques I will learn at university.

Jeffrey - Mathematics (3,987 characters)

Mathematics is a life-changing skill. Without it, individuals and organisations can struggle and fail to reach their potential. It plays a crucial role in society, evolving from basic tasks, such as managing finances or calculating expenses through to crucial advancements in engineering and medicine. My fascination with mathematics, I suspect, is inherited from my mother, a banker by profession. It was she who introduced me to the wonderful world of numbers through playful counting games with an abacus during my early childhood, and it was in those tender years that I developed an unyielding joy for the subject and an unrivalled passion to explore it further.

Whether I was engrossed in the challenge of a Sudoku puzzle in my spare time or assisting my grandmother with tax calculations for her company, I felt an indescribable happiness. This delight grew as I discovered the enchanting world of numbers and the intellectual challenges and satisfaction that mathematics and physics provided. My mother, recognising my interest, nurtured it by supplying me with a wealth of books on the subject, including a particularly fascinating one titled 'The Nine Chapters on the Mathematical Art'. I recall grappling with the intricacies of ancient Chinese mathematics within its pages, attempting to solve problems that had confounded scholars for centuries. Inspired by this, I researched other famous maths problems and discovered 'Fermat's Last Theorem', which remained unsolved for over 350 years, until Andrew Wiles, using complex principles such as elliptic curves and modular forms, found a solution.

Throughout my academic journey, I have always been the quickest to grasp new concepts and have consistently achieved the highest scores, most notably only dropping one mark across Pure Mathematics papers 1 and 2. Outside the classroom, I have taken my passion further by participating in various competitions; here I have mastered mathematical methods such as proof by contradiction, assumption, and reasoning to validate formulas or theorems. My extensive preparation for the TMUA deepened my understanding of mathematical logic and graph theory. I learned to deduce the correct answers by analysing the characteristics of functions and utilising logical reasoning to clarify the relationship between necessary and sufficient conditions.

As an individual, I strive to push myself to achieve excellence. This led to my involvement in mathematical competitions, such as the UKMT Senior Mathematical Challenge, where I won a Gold Medal. Alongside this, I achieved a distinction in the Canadian Senior Mathematics Contest for two consecutive years. This has not only boosted my confidence but also honed my problem-solving skills. Recently, I earned a Bronze in the British Physics Olympiad Senior Physics Challenge, and was comfortably in the top 25% of contestants in the Euclid Contest. These achievements validate my abilities and fuel my desire to tackle increasingly complex mathematical issues. I strongly believe that you can overcome any problem, whether it's an obscure calculation or a complex theorem if you engage, focus and work with passion. This joy extends beyond my own achievements to moments when my teachers guide me through challenging questions. These are not merely solutions on paper, they are life lessons in perseverance, flexibility and the sweet reward of intellectual curiosity.

While my love for numbers is profound, I also believe in a balanced life. To achieve this, I immerse myself in music and have representing my school in several musical events. In my leisure time, I enjoy listening to various genres of music, which provides excellent relaxation.

I see the world as a complex tapestry of calculations and variables intertwined in delicate balance. Moving forward, I aspire to contribute to ongoing academic discourse, addressing the philosophical implications and foundational questions that arise from mathematical advancements.

Roderick - Nursing (3,295 characters)

If you were to have asked me five years ago what my career aspirations were, nursing would not have been on my list. However, 2023 was the ultimate turning point for me, when my beloved sister lost her battle with pancreatic cancer. Witnessing first-hand the care, nurture and support both my sister and family received through the district nurses, sparked a fire within me that I could not quench. This led me to further investigate what it really takes to become a nurse.

The primary role of a nurse is to advocate and care for individuals and support them through health and illness. However, there are various other responsibilities under the umbrella of healthcare. Nursing requires one to passionately care for all types of patients, provide emotional support, ensure a high standard of care, and utilise exceptional communication skills to provide a calming bedside manner.

As every moment is experience, the past six months have been spent working at St Andrew's Healthcare as a healthcare assistant. This has given me a valuable insight into a working hospital environment, but also solidified my expectations of the professional standards of practice and behaviour that must be upheld, the importance of delivering efficient patient care while maintaining the patient's dignity, and patient confidentiality.

Being a nurse requires various skills. My past work experiences have contributed to my development, ranging from hospitality and events manager at Aston Villa Football Club where my leadership skills were honed, to volunteering in an outpatient physiotherapy department where I was able to successfully follow instructions and complete tasks given to me. Both experiences have taught me valuable lessons: the importance of communication, and the strength of teamwork while being able to effectively work independently within the scope of my competence.

I undertook the Science Foundation Year, which gave me an excellent academic grounding. I was able to develop my exam techniques, research skills, essay writing and language vocabulary. I have also studied a BTEC National Diploma in Applied Science. This course, which is essential in nursing, covers all the sciences and includes specific units such as Anatomy, Physiology of the Human Body Systems, Physiology of Human Regulation and Microbiological Techniques.

I have a great passion for sport, including athletics, badminton and basketball. I particularly enjoy travelling and experiencing new cultures. Alongside this, I have a keen interest in landscape photography. It is important to me to have a healthy balance of both physical and mental growth.

In line with the NMC code of practice, I am fully aware of my duty of care; this includes knowing my limitations. I am enthusiastic and confident within my scope of practice. I am a competent team player, always willing to seek the guiding hand of my senior colleagues. I take pride in my multifaceted career; I know that healthcare is not prescriptive, however I am able to transpose theory into practice. I have experience in being flexible in adapting to a changing work environment, and I can rise and meet the many challenges in the profession. I believe the attributes and skills I have gained, academically and in my work experience have given me an excellent foundation to pursue a career in nursing.

TIP!

If you want to supply more information than the statement space allows, once your application has been processed and you've received your welcome email, you can send information directly to your chosen universities or colleges, quoting your Personal ID. (Do not send it to UCAS.)

Subject-specific advice

The personal statement is especially important in subjects such as **creative and performing arts**. Say what you've done, seen or heard – do not be one of the music applicants who do not actually mention their chosen instrument!

Applicants for **teacher training**, **medicine**, **veterinary science**, **dentistry** or **physiotherapy** courses should be sure to give details of work experience (including locations and dates).

If you are currently studying for a **vocational or occupational qualification** that your admissions tutors may be unfamiliar with, explain the relevance of your studies to the course(s) you're applying for.

If you are an **international** student, explain why you want to study in the UK. Can you provide evidence that you will be able to complete a course run and taught in English?

If you're into **sport**, give details of your achievements, e.g. 'I play tennis for my county', showing you're committed to something you excel in.

It is wise to check with admissions staff at universities about how they feel about students taking gap years *before* you apply. Institutions will vary on this – some will be happy for you to take a year out, others may not be, and others may require (or at least prefer) you to do something during the year that will enhance your studies. Don't just assume they'll accept you taking a gap year. If you plan to take a gap year, it is advisable to cover your reasons for doing so in your personal statement. Remember that anything you say is likely to be used as a basis for questions if there's an interview. The two examples below show common pitfalls.

Example 1

'In my gap year I hope to work and travel.'

Comment

This statement is far too vague and would cause many admissions tutors to wonder whether you had really good reasons for deferring entry, or whether you were just postponing the decision to take up a place on their course.

Example 2

'In my gap year I hope to travel to gain work experience.'

Comment

This is likely to lead to questions such as: What kind of work experience? For how long? Is it relevant to your chosen course? How? Where? What will you do while you are there? Try to be as specific as possible. This candidate's statement would have been better if they had explained what sort of work experience they wanted and what drew them to their chosen country.

In contrast, the following gives a clear indication of a well-planned gap year.

Example 3

'For my gap year I have arranged a work experience placement in my local primary school. This will be for two days per week from September 2025 until July 2026 and will include helping children with reading, assisting class teachers in preparation of lessons and materials to be used in art and craft sessions, as well as accompanying staff and pupils on outside visits. This, I believe, will give me invaluable experience in the classroom which will support my intended degree in primary education. I will also be travelling to the USA for one month in the summer where I will stay with relatives for part of this time. This will give me experience of another society and culture as well as getting me accustomed to being away from home.'

You can find more subject-specific inspiration on writing your personal statement at www.ucas.com/personal-statement-guides

Mature students

You must say what you've done since leaving school. If, like many mature applicants, you've had a variety of occupations and experience, you may find the UCAS application too restrictive. So, you could summarise your career on the application and then send a full CV direct to your chosen universities or colleges. However, there is enough space for you to present your background and interests in a fair amount of detail.

As a mature student, your personal statement will still cover the same basic things as any personal statement: evidence of your interest in, understanding of, and enthusiasm for the chosen subject. You may also have a lot more life history to fit into your statement than the average school leaver. So, think carefully about which aspects of your past experiences best suit the course and type of university you want to apply to. You can find more advice at www.ucas.com/mature-students-personal-statement.

Everyone's circumstances are different, but the following example is the kind of thing that might attract favourable attention from an admissions tutor.

Example

- 1998–2003: Left school with GCSEs in four subjects at grade C, including mathematics and a grade B in English language.
- 2003–2006: Completed mechanical engineering apprenticeship.
- 2006–2019: Worked with two engineering companies until my redundancy.
- 2019–2022: While unemployed, I took a part-time pre-access course and also volunteered at a training centre for people with moderate learning difficulties and also befriending the elderly in a nursing home.
- September 2022–date: I have been studying on an Access to Higher Education Diploma in social sciences.

I had grown tired of working in engineering and took the opportunity to change career direction towards one where I could help and support people. My aim is to qualify as a professional social worker by taking a degree in social work at university. I have absolutely loved my access course which has made me all the more eager to learn.

TIP!

Make sure your statement is all your own work. UCAS will use similarity detection software to check your statement against other statements. If they detect similarity they will inform the universities and colleges you've applied to. They'll also let you know. Each of your universities and colleges will decide independently what action to take.

24| Adding a choice

This is one of the most important parts of your application – the outcome of all your research into higher education. It's often best to leave entering details of the courses you're applying to until you've completed all the factual information required and worked out your personal statement.

You're allowed a maximum of five course applications. You can apply to fewer than five if you want to, and can add further courses until the end of June as long as you haven't already accepted any offers. The application fee for all applications is £28.50 (see Chapter 25 for more information on payments).

Add your university or college and your course

- Start typing the name of the university or college into the 'Institution' field – select from the options displayed.
- Do the same for the course you have selected.
- Locations and start dates are also displayed according to the course – you'll be able to choose the right ones for you.
- For most courses you'll leave 'Point of entry' blank – unless the university or college has agreed that you can join the second or third year of the course (more below).

See Figure 20, Add a course choice, page 150.

Start date

You can select from a list of available start dates. If you want to apply at this stage for deferred entry (that is, starting your course in 2026 rather than 2025), choose the correct date from the list. More information on deferred entry is given in Chapter 8. Your personal statement (see Chapter 23) gives you the chance to explain why you want to defer entry.

It's no use applying for 2026 entry if some of your exams won't be taken until 2026, as a final decision on this application has to be taken by September 2025 (unless otherwise agreed by the university or college). Plus, you're not allowed to keep a deferred place at a university or college and then apply the following year to other institutions of the same kind. UCAS will intercept and cancel applications like these!

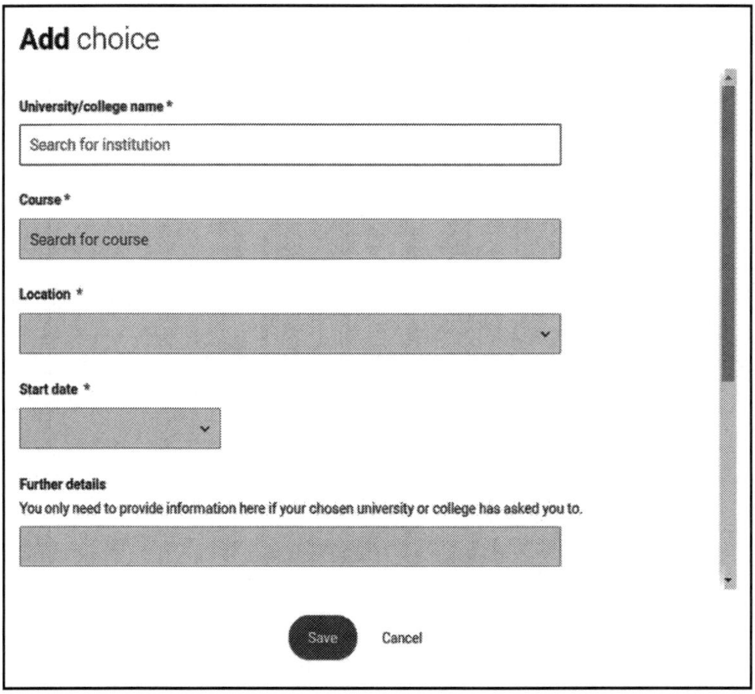

Figure 20: Add a course choice

Further details

On many UCAS applications this part is left blank, but in some cases further information can be requested by universities or colleges. Check the UCAS search tool on www.ucas.com or the university or college prospectus to find out whether this is the case. The sort of information you may need to give could include:

- duration of the course (three- or four-year course)
- minor, subsidiary or first-year course option choice
- specialisations within your chosen course
- Qualified Teacher Status
- previous applications
- if you're applying to Oxford and have selected a permanent private hall (rather than a college with a campus code), this section can be used to state which hall you have chosen.

Point of entry

If you plan to join the course at the beginning of the first year, leave this part blank. If you think you may qualify for credit transfer or entry with advanced standing (entry at second-year level or perhaps third-year level in Scotland), check this possibility with the institutions you want to apply to before completing your application. You may then indicate this to the universities and colleges by entering '2' or '3' (i.e. the year of proposed entry) on the relevant course.

Living at home while studying?

Choose 'Yes' if you're planning to live at home while attending university or college, or 'No' if you'll need accommodation information from the university or college.

Criminal convictions

UCAS only asks applicants who apply for certain courses – for example, those that involve work with children and vulnerable adults – to declare whether they have any criminal convictions, including spent convictions. This question only appears if you are applying for one of these courses.

See Figure 21, Criminal convictions, page 152.

Certain professions or occupations are exempt from the Rehabilitation of Offenders Act (1974) or involve regulated activities – such as (but not limited to) teaching, medicine, dentistry, law, accountancy, actuarial, insolvency, healthcare, social work, veterinary medicine, veterinary science, pharmacy, osteopathy, chiropractic, optometry and professions or occupations involving work with children or vulnerable adults, including the elderly or sick people.

Different rules apply to such professions or occupations with regard to disclosure of information about criminal convictions. You may be required to disclose information regarding any convictions even if they are spent.

Some courses in respect of such professions or occupations involve an integral work placement and you may not be able to undertake such placement and complete your studies if you have criminal convictions.

Further, while you may be permitted to study for one of the above professions or occupations, you may not be able to register and practise upon completion of your course.

You should not declare convictions, cautions, warnings or reprimands which are deemed 'protected' under the Rehabilitation of Offenders Act

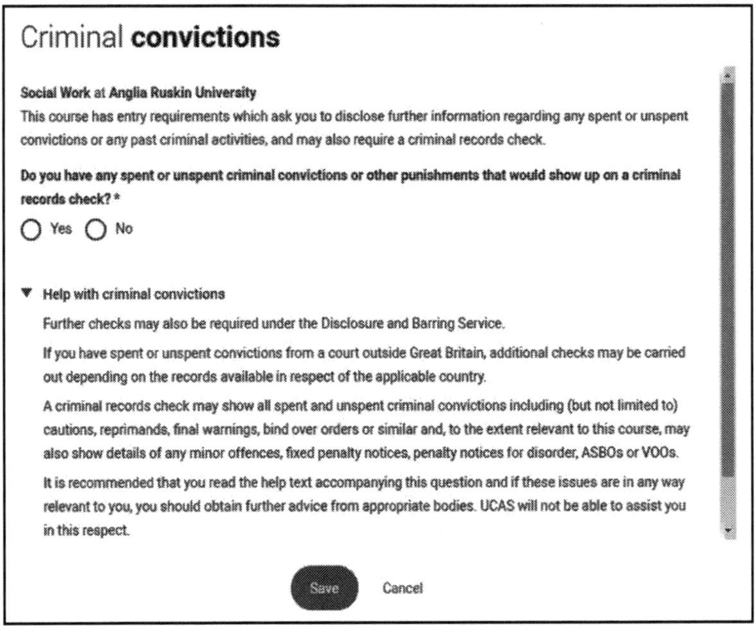

Criminal **convictions**

Social Work at **Anglia Ruskin University**
This course has entry requirements which ask you to disclose further information regarding any spent or unspent convictions or any past criminal activities, and may also require a criminal records check.

Do you have any spent or unspent criminal convictions or other punishments that would show up on a criminal records check? *

○ Yes ○ No

▼ Help with criminal convictions

Further checks may also be required under the Disclosure and Barring Service.

If you have spent or unspent convictions from a court outside Great Britain, additional checks may be carried out depending on the records available in respect of the applicable country.

A criminal records check may show all spent and unspent criminal convictions including (but not limited to) cautions, reprimands, final warnings, bind over orders or similar and, to the extent relevant to this course, may also show details of any minor offences, fixed penalty notices, penalty notices for disorder, ASBOs or VOOs.

It is recommended that you read the help text accompanying this question and if these issues are in any way relevant to you, you should obtain further advice from appropriate bodies. UCAS will not be able to assist you in this respect.

Save Cancel

Figure 21: Criminal convictions

1974 (Exceptions) Order 1975 (as amended in 2013). A conviction or caution can become 'protected' as a result of a filtering process. Guidance and criteria on the filtering of convictions and cautions can be found on the Disclosure and Barring Service (DBS) website. Further information on filtering can be found at: www.gov.uk/government/collections/dbs-filtering-guidance.

You should be aware that in respect of these courses:

1. The university or college may ask you to provide further information regarding any convictions (including spent convictions), and/or may ask you to agree to a Disclosure and Barring Service (DBS) check.
2. Where required, the university or college will send you instructions regarding how to provide the information they require. They may send you documents to fill in. Where such documents come from will depend on the location of the college or university that you are applying to. Please see the table on page 154 for further information.
3. Depending on the type of check, different levels of information will be revealed. The information revealed may include unspent convictions and spent convictions (including cautions, reprimands and final warnings or similar). Information about minor offences, penalty notices for disorder (PNDs), anti-social behaviour orders (ASBOs) or violent offender orders (VOOs) and other locally held police information may be revealed where it is appropriate to the course for a particular occupation or profession. The information may be disclosed irrespective of when it occurred (unless it is filtered).

4. This means that if you have a criminal conviction (spent or unspent) or, in certain circumstances, any minor offence, this information may be made known to the university or college (but not UCAS) as part of the check (unless it is filtered).

5. If the check reveals that you have had a conviction (including any caution, reprimand, final warning, bind over order or similar) or any other relevant information including (in certain circumstances) any minor offence, PND, ASBO or VOO, the university or college will need to assess your fitness to practise in the profession or occupation to which your course relates. Applicants to medicine, for instance, should be aware that the General Medical Council will not permit students deemed unfit to practise to be entered on the medical register and so they will not be able to practise as doctors. Similar restrictions may be imposed by other professional bodies including (but not limited to) those connected with law, teaching, accountancy, social work, healthcare, veterinary services, pharmacy, financial and insurance services and the armed forces.

6. You may also be subject to further checks (before and/or after you complete your course) by prospective employers who will make their own assessments regarding your fitness to practise in the relevant profession or undertake the relevant occupation.

7. If these issues are in any way relevant to you, you should obtain further advice from appropriate bodies.

8. In England and Wales you may also be required to complete documentation and maintain a registration with the Disclosure and Barring Service (DBS). The DBS scheme is designed to allow universities and colleges to identify any individual who is barred from working with children and vulnerable adults, including elderly or sick people.

How will the university or college handle my application if I declare a criminal conviction?

If you tick the box you will not be automatically excluded from the application process. The information concerning criminal convictions will be passed to appointed persons at the university or college. In line with best admissions practice, they will consider your application separately from your academic and achievement merits. During this consideration, they may ask you to provide further information about your conviction. If they are satisfied, your application will proceed in the normal way although they may add certain conditions to any offer they may make. Otherwise, they won't notify you of their decision.

It's important to note that a failure to declare a criminal conviction is taken very seriously, and could result in expulsion from your university or college. You should therefore seek advice before answering this question if you are unsure how to answer it.

All information concerning criminal convictions must be treated sensitively, confidentially and managed in accordance with data protection legislation.

You may find further details about how a criminal conviction declaration is handled (including the right to appeal a decision) on the university or college website.

In addition, you may also find the details in the following table useful.

Region	Agency	Website address
England and Wales	Disclosure and Barring Service (DBS)	www.gov.uk/government/organisations/disclosure-and-barring-service
Scotland	Disclosure Scotland	www.disclosurescotland.co.uk
Northern Ireland	Access Northern Ireland	www.nidirect.gov.uk/accessni

You'll be asked this question each time you add a course that requires an enhanced criminal conviction declaration.

Confirm choices

Once all choices are added select confirm choices There's a maximum of five choices and choice restrictions still apply (a maximum of four courses in any one of medicine, dentistry, veterinary medicine or veterinary science).

> **TIP!**
>
> Don't forget that you can make insurance subject choices as alternatives to your applications to medicine, dentistry or veterinary medicine or science (see Chapter 8).

Admissions tests and assessments

Some courses have extra admissions tests and assessments which are further conditions you need to meet to confirm your place. You'll be able to read about these when researching your courses.

Find out more about admissions tests and assessments in Chapter 9.

Clicking the three dots at the bottom right of a card enables you to see a summary of the details. Any choice combinations that aren't permitted will be flagged with red text on the right of each relevant card.

See Figure 22, Admissions tests and assessment details, opposite.

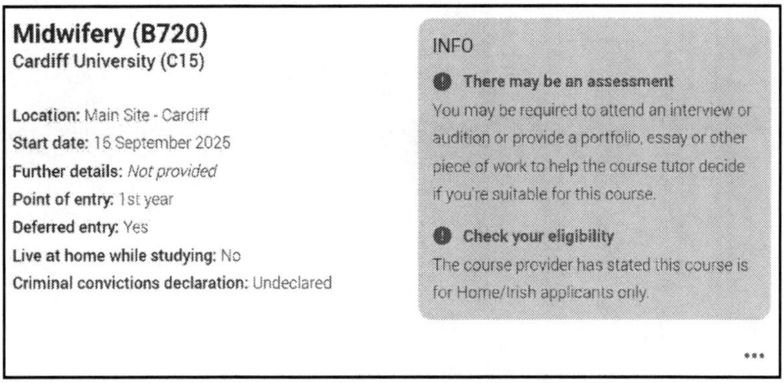

Midwifery (B720)
Cardiff University (C15)

Location: Main Site - Cardiff
Start date: 15 September 2025
Further details: *Not provided*
Point of entry: 1st year
Deferred entry: Yes
Live at home while studying: No
Criminal convictions declaration: Undeclared

INFO

🟠 **There may be an assessment**
You may be required to attend an interview or audition or provide a portfolio, essay or other piece of work to help the course tutor decide if you're suitable for this course.

🟠 **Check your eligibility**
The course provider has stated this course is for Home/Irish applicants only.

•••

Figure 22: Admissions tests and assessment details

25 | Finishing your application

There are four steps to the submission process.

The application must be complete (showing 100%) before pressing submit.

See Figure 23, Application status, below.

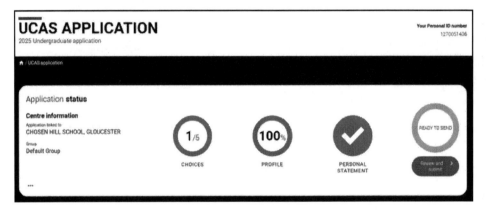

Figure 23: Application status

Declaration

Once you've completed all the sections, press 'Submit' and you'll be asked to read the declaration carefully, and only agree if you're absolutely sure that you're happy with its contents. UCAS can't process your application unless you confirm your agreement (with its terms and conditions), which legally binds you to make the required payment (see page 158).

When you submit your application, click 'Accept and proceed'.

Remember, by agreeing you're saying that the information you've provided is accurate, complete and all your own work and that you agree to abide by the rules of UCAS. You're also agreeing to your personal data being processed by UCAS and universities and colleges under the relevant data protection legislation. Any offer of a place you may receive is made on the understanding that, in accepting it, you also agree to abide by the rules and regulations of the institution.

To prevent and detect fraud of any nature, UCAS may have to give information about you to other organisations, including the police, the Home Office, the Foreign and Commonwealth Office, UK Visas and Immigration, the Student Loans Company, local authorities, the SAAS, examination boards or awarding bodies, the Department for Work and Pensions and its agencies, and other international admissions organisations.

If UCAS or an institution has reason to believe that you or any other person has omitted any mandatory information requested in the instructions on the application, has failed to include any additional material information, has made any misrepresentation or given false information, UCAS and/or the institution will take whatever steps it considers necessary to establish whether the information given in your application is correct.

UCAS and the institutions reserve the right at any time to request that you, your referee or your employer provide further information relating to any part of your application, e.g. proof of identity, status, academic qualifications or employment history. If such information is not provided within the time limit set by UCAS, UCAS reserves the right to cancel your application. Fees paid to UCAS in respect of applications that are cancelled as a result of failure to provide additional information as requested, or as a result of providing fraudulent information, are not refundable.

False information is defined as including any inaccurate or omitted examination results. Omission of material information will include failure to complete correctly the declaration on the application relating to criminal convictions and failure to declare any other information that might be significant to your ability to commence or complete a course of study.

Submitting your application

Once you've agreed to the terms of the declaration, you can pass your application on to your UCAS coordinator or administrator – usually a head of sixth form, form teacher or careers adviser. To do this, click 'submit application'; this then goes to your centre head for approval.

They'll check it over, add your written reference (see page 98), make arrangements for collecting your application fee and, finally, send it to UCAS.

If you find that you need to alter your application after you've submitted it, you should ask your UCAS coordinator or administrator to return it to you. You'll then be able to make the necessary changes before resubmitting it. If mistakes are spotted by the coordinator or administrator, they'll return it to you for amendments.

Payment

Application to higher education via UCAS costs £28.50.

Applying through your school or college

They'll let you know how they handle payments. Normally you'll pay by debit or credit card, but some schools and colleges prefer to collect applicant fees themselves and send UCAS a single payment covering everyone.

Applying as an individual

If you aren't making your application through a school or college, you'll need to make your payment online using a credit or debit card.

You don't need to make your payment until you've completed your application. Once you've agreed to the terms of use of the UCAS application in the declaration, you will be asked for your card details (if you're paying by this method). UCAS accepts UK and international Visa, Visa Electron, Delta, MasterCard, JCB and Maestro credit and debit cards. At the moment it does not accept American Express or Diners Club cards. The card you use to pay doesn't need to be in your own name, but of course you'll require the consent of the cardholder.

What happens next?

On receipt of your application, UCAS will (usually within 48 hours) send out a welcome email containing your Personal ID and a copy of the list of your higher education course choices in random order. You should check this thoroughly and contact UCAS immediately if anything is incorrect.

You can log in to your application to follow its progress. Later in the application cycle you'll receive instructions from UCAS to help you conclude a successful higher education application. For more information on this and on offers, see Part II of this book.

26| Troubleshooting

Some common problems

I can't log in ...

If your buzzword or password does not work, check the following.

- Have you entered the password correctly? Login details are case sensitive, so check that you have all the characters exactly right.
- Are you in the student area (not the staff area)?
- Is your computer properly connected to the internet?
- Are you able to connect to other websites?

If the answer to all of these questions is 'Yes', you may have a problem with your network or internet service provider. Try connecting to the main UCAS site, www.ucas.com – if you can, there may be a problem with the application system and you should call UCAS's Customer Experience Centre on 0371 4680 468.

I've forgotten my password ...

If you forget your password, click on 'Forgot your password' and enter the email address you provided on your application. UCAS will send you a reminder of your username and a link to reset your password.

Once you have successfully logged in, you can change your password.

> **TIP!**
>
> If you leave your UCAS application open without touching it, it will time out for security reasons and you'll have to log in again.

I've pasted my statement into my application and it's all gone wrong ...

The default character size for statements in your UCAS application is 12 point. If you've written your personal statement in Word and used a larger font size, it might not fit when you try to paste it into your application.

You may lose formatting when you paste your personal statement into your application – you should edit your statement very carefully. You won't be able to use bold or italicised fonts. Plus the character and line count may be different from those in your word-processing package. This is because formatting characters, such as paragraphs, are counted in the application but may not be counted in Word or Pages.

Need help?

Once you start completing your application, you can find help on each screen of your application. Most difficulties can be sorted out quickly by clicking on the question mark icon and following the instructions.

And finally ...

If you'd like more information on the application process, find out more at ucas.com.

If you decide to go ahead with your application, good luck! And get in touch with UCAS if you have any questions.

Further information

Trotman guides (trotman.co.uk)

- *Getting into* **series:** gives advice on securing a place at university for courses leading to professional careers (such as medicine, law, psychology, physiotherapy, engineering, pharmacy, veterinary school, and business and management courses), and on gaining places on courses at Oxford and Cambridge.
- *A Guide to Uni Life*, Lucy Tobin
- *Heap 2025: University Degree Course Offers*, Brian Heap
- *Is Going to Uni Worth It?*, Michael Tefula
- *The University Choice Journal*, Barbara Bassot
- *University Interviews*, Ian Stannard & Godfrey Cooper

Money matters

Official organisations

- **England:** www.gov.uk/student-finance
- **Scotland:** www.saas.gov.uk
- **Wales:** www.studentfinancewales.co.uk.
- **Northern Ireland:** www.studentfinanceni.co.uk

Useful information

- **www.gov.uk/contact-student-finance-england**
- **www.gov.uk/education/student-grants-bursaries-scholarships**
- **www.gov.uk/extra-money-pay-university:** for information on bursaries and scholarships
- **www.gov.uk/student-finance-calculator:** helps you to estimate which loans and other sources of funding you might be able to get

General student support

- **www.becomecharity.org.uk:** for young care leavers
- **www.moneysavingexpert.com/students:** the site of money expert Martin Lewis, which gives helpful advice on student budgeting
- **https://nationalcareers.service.gov.uk/find-a-course/the-skills-toolkit**
- **www.nhsbsa.nhs.uk/nhs-bursary-students:** information on NHS student bursaries
- **www.nus.org.uk:** the National Union of Students
- **www.propel.org.uk:** a specialist website for prospective students leaving care
- **www.slc.co.uk:** the Student Loans Company
- **www.studying-in-uk.org**
- **www.studyinternational.com**
- **www.thescholarshiphub.org.uk:** information on possible bursaries, scholarships, sponsors and degree apprenticeships
- **www.ucas.com/money:** you can also contact UCAS through Facebook and X (formerly Twitter)
- **www.which.co.uk/reviews/student-finance/article/guides**

Part-time and temporary jobs

- **www.e4s.co.uk**
- **www.fish4.co.uk**
- **www.indeed.co.uk**
- **www.student-jobs.co.uk**
- **www.timewisejobs.co.uk**
- **www.uktemps.co.uk**

Careers advice

- **If Only I'd Known:** Making the most of higher education, a guide for students and parents, Association of Graduate Recruiters, www.qualityresearchinternational.com/esecttools/esectpubs/agrif.pdf. Contains tips on making the most of higher education and how to gain the skills that will increase your employability.
- **What do graduates do?**, Jisc and Association of Graduate Careers Advisory Services (AGCAS), https://luminate.prospects.ac.uk/what-do-graduates-do.

Online tools

- **Careerscape:** A website that can help students to choose higher education courses and careers (www.cascaid.co.uk)
- **eCLIPS:** allows users to search for careers against criteria such as work skills or school subjects, and also has a linked interest guide and information on over 1,200 jobs and careers (www.eclips-online.co.uk)
- **https://indigo.careers:** extensive subscription-based careers advice site that may be available at your school, college, careers centre or library
- **Job Explorer Database (Jed):** an interactive, multimedia careers information resource where you can explore over 800 jobs in depth (2,500 individual career titles), with pictures and case studies of people at work. The section 'Higher ideas' shows which higher education courses connect with interests and subject choices (https://jed.ckcareers.org.uk/docs)
- **Kudos:** information on careers and higher education courses, together with case studies and articles. This may be available in your school or college, at your local careers service or library (CASCAiD, www.cascaid.co.uk).
- **The Morrisby Profile:** assesses aptitudes, personality and interests to provide a highly reliable predictor of career matches and resources to help research further and higher education options. Online activity only. Details at www.morrisby.com
- **UCAS Careers Quiz:** find your ideal job matched to your personality and a list of courses previous students studied in order to get there (www.ucas.com/careers-quiz)
- **MyUniChoices:** a preference-based questionnaire which gives recommended university subjects to explore (www.myunichoices.com)
- **www.unifrog.org:** extensive subscription-based careers and university-based website that may be available at your school, college, careers centre or library

Websites

- **www.agcas.org.uk:** Association of Graduate Careers Advisory Services
- **www.doit.life:** a national database of volunteering opportunities where you can search by postcode and interests for opportunities in your local area
- **https://nationalcareersservice.direct.gov.uk:** search under 'job profiles'; the site contains over 800 listings. The site also offers guidance on the employability of various degree subjects and suggests different skills that specific degrees can add to your CV
- **www.prospects.ac.uk:** useful detailed information on graduate careers

- **www.thestudentroom.co.uk:** a site where students can share experiences on all sorts of education-based topics, including tips on writing the personal statement.

Making study and university choices

Websites

- www.thecompleteuniversityguide.co.uk/student-advice/where-to-study/choosing-a-university
- www.gov.uk/government/publications/higher-and-degree-apprenticeships
- https://uk.indeed.com/jobs?q=degree+apprenticeships&l=uk&vjk= 71099e6938e64ff5
- www.push.co.uk
- www.telegraph.co.uk/education/universities-colleges
- www.theguardian.com/education/universityguide
- www.thetimes.co.uk/article/good-university-guide-in-full-tp-6dzs7wn
- www.timeshighereducation.com
- www.turing-scheme.org.uk
- **www.ucas.com:** explore the different course options

For students with disabilities

- **www.rnid.org.uk:** Royal National Institute for Deaf People
- **www.disabilityrightsuk.org**
- **www.rnib.org.uk:** Royal National Institute of Blind People

Interviews and selection

Websites

- www.ox.ac.uk/admissions/undergraduate/applying-to-oxford/guide/admissions-tests
- www.undergraduate.study.cam.ac.uk/apply/how/admission-tests
- www.lnat.ac.uk (LNAT)
- www.ucat.ac.uk (UCAT)

NB: All the test websites offer free practice tests

Glossary

Clearing
A service run by UCAS in the summer which you can use to look for alternative courses. If you didn't get a place on a course – whether you didn't receive offers, declined your offers or firm place, or didn't get the grades you needed – Clearing allows you to apply for courses that still have vacancies.

Your Clearing matches
An additional tool designed to help you find your perfect course. To speed things up, UCAS takes what they know about you, and what they know about the types of students unis are looking for, to suggest some courses you might like. You can express interest in courses, and the university or college can contact you.

CV
Curriculum vitae: a document detailing your qualifications and experience.

Extra
A chance to make further applications from February until July for applicants who don't get any offers of places or don't accept any offers from their initial applications.

Indigo
Indigo is a digital platform that enables students to explore university and career choices, and includes a wide database and a variety of resources.

LNAT
A test used by some universities in selecting applicants for law.

Morrisby Profile
An online careers assessment that gives job recommendations and also A level and higher education suggestions: www.morrisby.com/morrisby-profile.

MyUniChoices
An interactive program that gives higher education course and institution recommendations based on answers to preference-based questions: www.myunichoices.com.

Postgraduate
Someone studying on an advanced degree course after undergraduate study, or as an extension of their undergraduate degree, e.g. MA, MSc, PhD.

Sandwich course
A degree or diploma course that includes work experience.

Seminar
A discussion in a small group of students, often, but not always, following a lecture on the same topic.

Tariff
The UCAS Tariff is used to allocate points to Level 3 qualifications, such as A levels, Highers, BTEC qualifications and others, making it easier for universities and colleges to compare applicants. Universities and colleges may use it when making offers to applicants.

T Levels
A group of vocational qualifications equivalent to three A levels, introduced in September 2020.

Turing Scheme
The Turing scheme is a global study and work abroad programme, which replaced Erasmus+ from September 2021.

Tutorial
A discussion between a much smaller group of students than in a seminar (sometimes just one student) and a lecturer.

UCAS Hub
A personalised online space students can register for to explore post-18 options and make their application to higher education.

UCAT
A test used by some universities in selecting applicants for medicine and dentistry.

Undergraduate
A student on a first degree course, e.g. BA, BSc.

Unifrog
A one-stop website encompassing universities, work-related learning and further education colleges in the UK and beyond.

Appendix: A note for staff on becoming a UCAS centre

Schools, educational advisers, and agents who assist students with UCAS Undergraduate applications to UK higher education can register to become a UCAS centre. It's completely free and means students can make their UCAS Undergraduate applications through you.

Not only will you be provided with a suite of tools to help manage your students' applications, you'll have access to the latest information and advice services, covering everything you need to know to support them through the application process.

To find out more about becoming a UCAS centre, visit ucas.com/becomeacentre.

Notes for UCAS centres

UCAS centres use the adviser portal, which gives a complete oversight of your students' applications and access to real-time data in one system. More information can be found at ucas.com/advisers.

COMPARING GOVERNMENT ACTIVITY

Comparing Government Activity

Edited by

Louis M. Imbeau
Professor of Political Science
Laval University, Quebec

and

Robert D. McKinlay
Professor of International Studies
Lancaster University

First published in Great Britain 1996 by
MACMILLAN PRESS LTD
Houndmills, Basingstoke, Hampshire RG21 6XS
and London
Companies and representatives
throughout the world

A catalogue record for this book is available
from the British Library.

ISBN 0–333–64412–3

 First published in the United States of America 1996 by
ST. MARTIN'S PRESS, INC.,
Scholarly and Reference Division,
175 Fifth Avenue,
New York, N.Y. 10010

ISBN 0–312–15846–7

Library of Congress Cataloging-in-Publication Data
Comparing government activity / edited by Louis M. Imbeau and Robert
D. McKinlay.
p.   cm.
Papers that originated in a conference organized by the Groupe de
recherche sur les interventions gouvernementales of the Dept. of
Political Science at Laval University.
Includes bibliographical references and index.
ISBN 0–312–15846–7 (cloth)
1. Comparative government—Congresses.   2. Policy sciences–
–Congresses.   3. Expenditures, Public—Congresses.   4. Government
spending policy—Congresses.   I. Imbeau, Louis M., 1951–   .
II. McKinlay, Robert D.   III. Université Laval.   Groupe de recherche
sur les interventions gouvernementales.
JF51.C6215   1996
320.3—dc20
                                    95–39113
                                      CIP

10   9   8   7   6   5   4   3   2   1
05   04   03   02   01   00   99   98   97   96

Printed and bound in Great Britain by
Antony Rowe Ltd, Chippenham, Wiltshire

Contents

List of Tables   vii

List of Figures   viii

Notes on the Contributors   ix

Preface   xii

1   Introduction: The Comparative Observation of Government
    Activity   1
    Louis M. Imbeau

2   Throwing Money and Heaving Bodies: Heuristic
    Callisthenics for Comparative Policy Buffs   13
    Arnold J. Heidenheimer

3   Patterns of Post-War Expenditure Priorities in Ten
    Democracies   26
    Richard I. Hofferbert and Ian Budge

4   Case Interdependence and Non-Activity in Response to
    Pressures for Activity   48
    Klaus Armingeon

5   Laws and the Distribution of Power in Society   70
    Vincent Lemieux

6   Comparative Textual Analyses of Government and Party
    Activity: The Work of the Manifesto Research Group   82
    Ian Budge and Richard I. Hofferbert

7   The Suitability of Several Models for Comparative
    Analysis of the Policy Process   101
    Paul A. Sabatier

8   Methodological Individualism and the U-Shaped Curve:
    Some Theoretical Guidelines for the Comparative
    Analysis of Public Policy   118
    Henry Milner

v

9   Politico-Economic Models and the Economic Theory of
     Government Behaviour: Some Problems and Results   139
     Jean-Dominique Lafay

10   The Developmental State: Governance, Comparison and
     Culture in the 'Third World'   159
     Christopher Clapham

11   Accumulation, Aggregation and Eclecticism in Political
     Science: A Case Study of Foreign Policy Analysis   179
     Robert D. McKinlay

Index   198

List of Tables

2.1   West German Private Expenditure for Vocational
Education by Accounting Method, 1991 in DM billion   19

3.1   Summary of General Trends in Expenditure Priorities in
Ten Post-War Democracies   36

4.1   Year of First Introduction of the Right of Association and
the Right to Combine   51

4.2   Population Size in Millions and Strength of Resistance at
the Year of First Introduction of the Right to Combine   54

4.3   Major Regulations of Collective Labour Relations, 1945–90   55

4.4   Truth Table for Distribution of Power Resources and for
Vulnerability Hypotheses   57

4.5   Truth Table of Labour Reforms by Transition of Political
System, World War, International Economic Crisis,
Change of Government, Industrial Conflict and Incumbency
of Socialist Party   61

4.6   Major Reforms after the Historical Basic Decisions   66

5.1   Rates of Presence of Actors as Controllers and as Controllees
in the Laws of the Last Legislatures of the Five Governments
in Quebec and over the Entire Period 1944–85   77

6.1   Mean Party Election Programme Emphases in Illustrative
Issue Areas: Great Britain (1945–92) and the United States
(1948–92)   86

6.2   Consolidation of Party Programme Categories   92

List of Figures

3.1 Trends in Expenditure Priorities: Percentage of Central Government Expenditures for Various Functions for Selected Countries and Ten Country Mean, 1950–85   34

3.2 Left–Right Policy Priority in Ten Post-War Democracies   38

6.1 Left–Right Emphases in Post-War British and German Party Election Programmes   88

7.1 General Model of Policy Evolution Focusing on Competing Advocacy Coalitions within Policy Subsystems   112

8.1 The U-Shaped Curve (1)   126

8.2 The Lorenz Curve (1)   129

8.3 The Lorenz Curve (2)   130

8.4 The U-Shaped Curve (2)   131

9.1 Policy Outcomes in Cooperative and Non-Cooperative Games   144

9.2 A Scheme of Politico-Economic Interactions   150

9.3 Adjustment with or without IMF Intervention (Franc Zone)   154

9.4 Adjustment with or without IMF Intervention (Non-Franc Zone)   155

Notes on the Contributors

Klaus Armingeon is professor of political science at the University of Bern. He is author of a comparative book on neo-corporatist incomes policies (1983), a monograph on the development of West German trade unions (1988), and a comparative study of the political regulation of collective labour relations *Staat und Arbeitsbeziehungen: Ein internationaler Vergleich* (1994). He has contributed to several edited works and his articles have appeared in the *Journal of Public Policy, European Sociological Review, Österreichische Zeitschrift für Politikwissenschaft* and other German journals.

Ian Budge is professor of government at the University of Essex. He is the author or the co-author of *Party Policy and Government Coalitions in Western Europe and Israel* (1992), *Parties and Democracy: Coalition Formation and Government Functioning in 22 Democracies* (1990), *Ideology, Strategy and Party Movement* (1987), *The Changing British Political System* (1983, 1987), *Explaining and Predicting Elections* (1983), *Voting and Party Competition* (1977), *Party Identification and Beyond* (1976), *Belfast: Approach to Crisis* (1973), *Political Stratification and Democracy* (1972), *Agreement and the Stability of Democracy* (1970) and *Scottish Political Behaviour* (1966). His articles have appeared in many journals including *Electoral Studies, Quality and Quantity, British Journal of Political Science, Legislative Science Quarterly, European Journal of Political Research* and *Political Studies.*

Christopher Clapham is professor of politics and international relations at Lancaster University. He is the author of *Haile-Selassie's Government* (1969), *Liberia and Sierra Leone: An Essay on Comparative Politics* (1976), *Third World Politics* (1985) and *Transformation and Continuity in Revolutionary Ethiopia* (1990). Among his edited books are: *Foreign Policy Making in Developing States* (1977), *Private Patronage and Public Power* (1982) and *The Political Dilemmas of Military Regimes* (1984). His articles have appeared in many journals including *Journal of Modern African Studies, African Affairs* and *Third World Quarterly.*

Arnold J. Heidenheimer is professor of political science at Washington University, St Louis. He is co-author of *Comparative Public Policy* (3rd edn 1990), has co-edited *The Shaping of the Swedish Health System*

(1980), *The Development of Welfare States in Europe and America* (1981) and *Political Corruption* (1989). He has written extensively on European education policies and is author of a forthcoming study of secondary and higher education in Germany, Switzerland and Japan.

Richard I. Hofferbert is professor of political science at the State University of New York in Binghamton. He is the author of *The Reach and Grasp of Policy Analysis: Comparative Views of the Craft* (1990) and *The Study of Public Policy* (1974). He is the co-editor of *Data Archives in the Social Sciences* (1977) and *State and Urban Politics: Readings in Public Policy* (1971). His articles have appeared in several journals including *British Journal of Political Science, Policy Studies Journal, European Journal of Political Research, American Political Science Review, Policy Studies Review, Journal of Public Policy, International Journal of General Systems, Policy and Politics, American Behavioral Scientist* and *Comparative Political Studies.*

Louis M. Imbeau is professor of political science at Laval University. He is the author of *Donor Aid: The Determinants of Development Allocations to Third World Countries* (1989), co-author of *Comprendre et communiquer la science* (1994) and co-editor of *Politiques provinciales comparées* (1994). His articles have appeared in several journals including *European Journal of Political Research, International Journal of Conflict Management, Québec Studies, Journal of Commonwealth and Comparative Politics, Revue québécoise de science politique* and *History of European Ideas.*

Jean-Dominique Lafay is professor of economics and director of the Laboratory of Public Economics at the University of Paris. Among his most recent books as author or co-author are: *L'économie mixte* (1992), *Analyse macroéconomique* (1993), *The Political Dimension of Economic Adjustment* (1993) and *The Political Feasibility of Adjustment in Developing Countries* (1995). He is co-editor of *Economics and Politics: The Calculus of Support* (1991). His articles, mainly on the modelling of the interaction of economics and politics in developed, less-developed and former communist countries, have appeared in several journals and edited volumes.

Vincent Lemieux is professor of political science at Laval University. He is the author of over 17 books among which are: *L'étude des politiques publiques: les acteurs et le pouvoir* (1995), *Le Parti libéral du Québec:*

alliances, rivalités et neutralités (1993), *Les relations de pouvoir dans les lois* (1991), *Systèmes partisans et partis politiques* (1985). He has published extensively in several journals including: *L'Homme, Revue canadienne de science politique, Analyse des politiques, Administration publique du Canada, Recherches sociographiques, Cahiers internationaux de sociologie, Etudes internationales, Revue européenne des sciences sociales* and *Revue québécoise de science politique.*

Robert D. McKinlay is professor of international studies at Lancaster University. He is the author of *Third World Military Expenditure* (1989), the co-author of *Global Problems and World Order* (1986) and *Aid and Arms to the Third World* (1984) and the co-editor of *The Recalcitrant Rich: An Analysis of Northern Responses to the Demands for a New International Economic Order.* His articles have appeared in several journals, including *Comparative Politics, American Political Science Review, British Journal of Political Science, World Politics, Economic Development and Cultural Change, European Journal of Political Studies, British Journal of International Studies* and *Comparative Political Studies.*

Henry Milner is adjunct professor of political science at Vanier College (Montréal). He is the author of *Social Democracy and Rational Choice* (1994), *Sweden: Social Democracy in Practice* (1989), *The Long Road to Reform: Restructuring Public Education in Québec* (1986) and *Politics in the New Québec* (1978).

Paul A. Sabatier is professor of environmental studies at the University of California, Davis. He is the co-author of *Great Expectations and Mixed Performance: Implementation of European Higher Education Reforms* (1986), *Can Regulation Work? The Implementation of the 1972 California Coastal Initiative* (1983) and *Implementation and Public Policy* (1983) and the co-editor of *Policy Change and Learning: An Advocacy Coalition Approach* (1993) and *Effective Policy Implementation* (1981). His articles have appeared in several journals, including: *Journal of Politics, Western Political Quarterly, Policy Sciences, Administration and Society, Journal of Public Policy, Legislative Studies Quarterly* and *American Journal of Political Science.*

Preface

The basic subject matter of this book scarcely needs any justification. Government activity is of central concern for political science and as such has been a major focus of research common to many sub-fields of the discipline.

The large volume of research on government activity can be categorised in various ways. One such categorisation rests on the distinction between the process and form of analysis on the one hand and the product of analysis on the other. Since most researchers are concerned at the end of the day to produce a body of empirical or substantive findings, most research in the subject area of government activity has, eminently understandably, been devoted to attempts to describe or explain such topics as the determinants, forms or impact of governments across a range of policy fields. An extensive empirical literature has developed in each of these fields.

The product of analysis is, however, reliant on the process or form of analysis. In other words, substantive or empirical findings are of necessity influenced by epistemological, theoretical and methodological considerations. Political science enquiry, consequently, has for a very long time been self-consciously preoccupied with the examination of the rules and logic of enquiry. As such a very substantial literature has developed ranging at the most general level from the philosophy of social science to issues concerned with theory construction to rather more specific issues connected to particular research methodologies or techniques.

Though this book is certainly preoccupied with substantive findings, such findings do not constitute its immediate or main goal. Equally this book is not a survey or treatise on epistemological, theoretical, or methodological issues. Rather, one hallmark of this book is the attempt to bridge the gap between two literatures, which are often kept quite separate – the nature and form of analysis on the one hand and the product of analysis on the other. Standing at the crossroads of these two literatures, the book has its rationale principally in epistemological, theoretical and methodological issues. It is, however, concerned with these issues not as ends in themselves but as they have a direct bearing on substantive findings. In other words, though rooted in issues concerned with the nature and form of analysis, the papers constituting this book look at problems of analysis with a very specific practical or substantive intent.

A second hallmark, and perhaps more striking novelty, of this book is found in its structure and content. This book originated in a conference organised by the *Groupe de recherche sur les interventions gouvernementales* of the Department of Political Science at Laval University. The conference organisers considered two formats. One option was to construct a dirigist or commissioned work. In other words, the organisers of the conference would have delineated a set of epistemological, theoretical and methodological issues and specifically solicited chapters on each of these issues. This is a perfectly legitimate and commonly used approach to edited works. The novelty in this case, while giving some clear indication of the focus of the conference, was to leave very deliberately some substantial latitude to the authors. Instead of authors being directed to write on designated topics, they were asked to reflect, from an epistemological, theoretical or methodological perspective, on what they took to be a major problem or problems confronting comparative research on government activity.

In our view, this strategy has worked rather well. The final product is not only a set of original papers which are of interest in their own right, but also a set of papers which, as they point up some related and also some very different issues, are of interest as a collectivity. Though we do not contend that the range of problems addressed in these papers or the sample of researchers who contributed these papers perfectly represent the discipline, we think that they are certainly representative of the degree of advancement of our collective reflections on our research practices.

From the planning of the conference to the final editing of the text, many persons contributed to making this undertaking possible. In addition to the contributors to this volume, we would like to thank several participants at the conference: André Blais (Université de Montréal), Frank Castles (Australian National University), Jean Crête (Université Laval), Pierre-Gerlier Forest (Université Laval), Ingrid Kissling-Naef (Université de Lausanne), Peter Knoepfel (Université de Lausanne), Réjean Landry (Université Laval), François Pétry (Université Laval), Richard Simeon (University of Toronto) and Carolyn Hughes Tuohy (University of Toronto). We would also like to thank the secretarial staff of both of our departments and in particular Trish Demery, Solange Guy and Renée Hamel. The conference and the preparation of this volume were made possible in part by grants from the Fonds FCAR (Québec Government), the Social Science and Humanities Research Council (Canadian Government), the Québec Delegation in Chicago, the British Council in Montréal, and both our Universities.

L.M.I. and R.D.M.

1 Introduction: The Comparative Observation of Government Activity

Louis M. Imbeau

When they discuss their research findings or practices, policy analysts, like their colleagues in the other social sciences, disagree most of the time. These disagreements may spring from divergent conceptions of knowledge but also from divergent conceptions of what the actual object of observation is. In other words, apparent disagreements on how to go about doing research or on what is important in a set of findings often are not really disagreements but merely parallel monologues – contenders simply do not talk about the same thing. Hence the importance of the definition of the object of analysis and of its status in a research design. In this introduction, I want to do two things. First, I want to propose a definition of government activity that will allow for the development of a typology of the forms government activity may take – a typology that will transcend the fields of government intervention and particularly the foreign/domestic divide. Second, I want to argue that, according to the methodological status government activity has in a given research, the issues of validity and of conceptualisation will have different bearings. I will then introduce each of the contributions to this volume and show how they relate to these two issues.

A DEFINITION OF GOVERNMENT ACTIVITY

It may be interesting to note that, during the conference on which this volume is based, an important part of the debate focused on the definition of policy or government activity. What should an analyst concentrate on in order to understand governments? It may be discouraging to realise that, after so many decades, or arguably centuries, of analysis of government activity, we are still discussing the definition of our research object. But, at the same time, this may be an indication that we are getting closer to a consensus. Indeed, things are clearer when we discuss the definition of government policy or activity than when we try to find common grounds in the realm of theories or in the substantive importance of any issue. Hence the proclivity to be more prolific when addressing definitional issues than theoretical or substantive issues. In their search for a useful

1

definition of 'policy', policy analysts have traditionally tried to distinguish various dimensions of the phenomenon. Thus, they argue that a distinction should be made between policy outputs and policy outcomes, between decisions and policy, or between policy as pronounced and policy as implemented (Nadel 1975). Despite these efforts, the confusion of these dimensions continues to blur our discussion about government intervention, particularly regarding the distinction between intention and behaviour in a definition of policy.

Indeed, the concept of 'policy' is often defined in terms of both intention and behaviour – both as what a government intends to do or says it will do and as what a government actually does.[1] The foreign policy of a country, for example, will be both the declaration of intention of its government and what this government does in diplomatic or military terms. This practice is an error for several reasons. First, on methodological grounds, such a definition confuses in the same concept two phenomena, behaviour and attitude, that should be kept apart. It is indeed common to hypothesise a relationship between these two phenomena. But if they are embedded in the same concept, this relationship cannot be tested. The second reason why we should not force intention in a definition of policy is a theoretical one. In doing so, we assume *a priori* intentional, if not rational, behaviour. In other words, we determine a theoretical perspective by the definition itself of the research object. As much as possible, a definition of a research object should be theoretically neutral for the simple reason that one of the things we want to do as analysts is to compare the explanatory power of different theories. To do so we need a common definition of the dependent variable, separate from the theory. This problem has been around for quite a long time but it seems that we have not yet learned the lesson.[2] Finally, it is tempting to define policy in terms of intentional behaviour because policy-makers think of themselves in that way – they choose to do or not to do this or that. But in the context of scientific research, a concept must correspond with what the analyst is looking for and not with what actors, in this case government officials, perceive themselves as doing.

Still another question must be posed. Whose behaviour are we talking about? Nadel (1975) once argued that actions or interventions by private organisations, such as corporations or non-profit organisations, enter the realm of public policy. But, following Edwards and Sharkansky (1978), we prefer to focus our attention on the activity of governments, or, to be more precise, of government agents. Thus Dye's famous definition should be amended to read: 'public policy is whatever government agents do or choose not to do'.[3] In order to emphasise this focus on behaviour, as opposed to attitudes, and on government, rather than private organisations, we refrain from talking about 'policy' and use instead the term 'government activity'.

Thus conceived, government activity is observable behaviour. Consequently, the analysis of government actions is limited by what we can actually observe. In order to find out the various types of activity in which governments get involved, the best way is to ask ourselves: What do government agents actually do? They do many things: they collect and spend money; they formulate, promulgate and enforce laws and regulations at the domestic level and they enter into more or less binding agreements at the international level; they write papers, pronounce discourses and publish analyses and other statements; they create, expand, shrink or eliminate administrative bodies; they send soldiers or policemen to force people to do (or prevent them from doing) what they would not do (or what they would) otherwise; they hold press conferences, dissolve parliament, send missions abroad and perform other such acts that have political importance. All these actions can be classified into six types of government activity: financial activity (spending and revenues), regulatory activity (laws, regulations and international agreements), discursive activity (speech and writing), administrative activity (changes in the structures of public organisations), coercive activity (policing and war) and 'event' activity (other sorts of activity).[4]

Comparative public policy analyses have been mostly concerned so far with financial activity mainly because of the availability of data. Financial data are accessible for a large number of governments, both national and sub-national, and for relatively long periods of time. Furthermore, despite important differences from one government to another, they are standardised in such a way as to make possible the comparison of a large number of governments. This reliance on financial activity is apparent in the standard comparative public policy textbook by Heidenheimer *et al.* (1990), where budgetary data appear in more than half of the tables. Event activity, as developed in foreign policy analysis (Azar 1972; Hermann *et al.* 1974), has been the object of a less extended but still important treatment because of its seemingly special importance in foreign relations. But it has not been used at the domestic level, despite the fact that it constitutes an important part of what governments do at that level. Regulatory activity 'implies the imposition of rules and controls which are designed to direct, restrict, or change the ... behaviour of individuals' (Strick 1990:1). Though this type of activity has been the object of comparative analysis from various perspectives in a number of countries, it is much less developed than the previous ones. The works of Rose (1984), Pomper

(1970) or Ginsberg (1976) give an idea of the potential importance of the analysis of government regulations and laws in the understanding of government behaviour. Coercive activity has been the object of an extended treatment by scholars, at both the domestic and the international levels. Singer's contribution (Singer and Small 1972), for example, is a landmark in international relations research in this regard. His comparisons of conflicts on a variety of dimensions can be viewed, in a public policy perspective, as a comparative analysis of government coercive behaviour. At the domestic level, an effort has also been made to compare the policing activity of governments (Skogan 1977). Finally, discursive activity can be said to be the *parent pauvre* of the comparative analysis of government activity since it has been almost completely ignored. Most studies in this domain are case studies pertaining to communication studies and social psychology. What we can see then is that some forms of government activity have been the object of more attention than others. Our typology may give us indications as to the areas of government activity that need special attention given their relative neglect in the field of comparative public policy.

THE METHODOLOGICAL STATUS OF GOVERNMENT ACTIVITY

As we defined it, government activity can have two methodological statuses, depending on the way it is conceptualised: it can be considered as the phenomenon of interest, or it can be considered as the indicator of another phenomenon.[5] Government activity is considered as a phenomenon when the researcher is interested directly with what is the object of systematic observation rather than with something that would lie behind it – much like a technician who would observe a thermometer to compare its efficiency with that of another one whereas a meteorologist would observe a thermometer while being interested in another phenomenon, temperature. Government activity is the phenomenon under study when no assumption is made about other phenomena, of which such activity would be indicative. Economists, for example, often study government financial activity in order to identify the most efficient allocation of public resources to deal with a specific problem. Legal experts often compare government regulations and their relationship to delinquent behaviour in order to find which type of regulation contributes better to peace and order. Specialists in public administration do the same with administrative activity, students of journalism with event activity, strategists with coercive activity, or linguists with discursive activity. In general, applied and atheoretical researchers on government activity consider it as the phenomenon. However, much of the work done by neo-institutionalists (Landry 1984) is examples of theoretically informed analyses where government activity is considered as the phenomenon under study. These analysts see government activity as the outcome of rules or routines. Allison (1971) proposed a compelling illustration of the usefulness of this perspective in his 'Model III'.

Though this is not always the case, comparative public policy studies often consider government activity as an indicator of the 'real' phenomenon of interest. In this case, it may be a difficult task to uncover which phenomenon government activity is supposed to indicate, especially when the theoretical bases are not fully explicit.

There are several ways to conceptualise government activity. At least four types of conceptualisation can be identified in the contributions to this volume. First, government activity may be viewed as an indication of the priorities of government agents, partisans or bureaucrats, taken collectively. Second, government activity may be conceptualised as the response of an organisation to pressures or needs emanating from its environment. Here the familiar input–output illustration of systems theory or the stimulus–response analogy provided by biology come to mind. This conceptualisation is most frequent in studies on the socio-economic determinants of policy and in evaluation studies where policy outcomes are compared with the needs that originally gave rise to the policy. Third, government activity is often conceptualised as the aggregated behaviour of individuals. This is especially the case with rational choice theorists who explain this aggregate of individual behaviour by individual preferences, interests and resources. Finally, a fourth type of conceptualisation views government activity as an indication of a macro-sociological phenomenon, like the growth of the welfare state or the role of the state in a capitalist economy or the distribution of power in society. This is typical of those students of public policy who go a step higher in abstraction in search of underlying structures such as the 'state', or the 'economy' or 'social classes'.

Even though theories will give indications as to which type of phenomenon is being considered, they are not linked in any essential way to one type or another. The public choice approach, for example, can be used to show how government activity responds to various pressures in society, as well as to illuminate the priorities of governments, or an institutional phenomenon like the inefficiency in resource allocation as an effect of corporatist arrangements in the decision-making process, or a macro-sociological one (the growth of the state in industrialised societies). The same phenomena can be explained within a Marxist frame of reference. However, the way the phenomenon is conceptualised can suggest that one indicator is more valid than another. As Lemieux argues in his chapter, regulatory activity is better than financial activity to measure the impact of governments on the distribution of power in a society. This issue of the validity of one type of government activity as compared with another is illuminated by the distinction between government activity as a phenomenon and government activity as an indicator.

Indeed, validity will be a more important criterion when government activity is regarded as an indicator since studies, following such a focus, are based on a phenomenon that is not directly observed. Thus, the issue of the validity of government spending is relevant in a study where spending is an indicator rather than the phenomenon: are expenditures a valid measure of government priorities or of government response or of the growth of the state, for example? The question, however, has a different relevance in studies where government activity is considered as the phenomenon under study since it is limited in that case to the issue of the completeness of a description: are expenditures enough to take into account the vastness and complexity of government interventions in a given field? Therefore, any evaluation of the use of one type of government activity in comparative research must be informed by this distinction.

CONTRIBUTIONS

The contributors to this collection either discuss one or more of the issues raised above or provide illustrations of them. Opening the debate on the definitional issue, Heidenheimer poses three questions: 'Do expenditures reflect national efforts more uniformly on a cross-national basis in some policy areas than in others? How conscious should we be of definitional changes applied by international agencies who produce the comparative data and indicator bases? Or, when turning to non-financial measures of policy sector activities, what are some problems encountered there in coping with structural differences among national systems?'His answers suggest that the validity and reliability of expenditure data vary from one policy sector to the other. More specifically, Heidenheimer shows that there have been changes of definition in OECD publications which have had dramatic impacts on the ranking of cross-national education expenditures. He also argues that, in comparing government activity in the education sector, 'it is essential to utilise indicators which keep tabs on what happens to bodies and minds'. In making his point, Heidenheimer emphasises the importance of taking into account outcomes as well as outputs in comparing education policies. Drawing examples from three education systems (Germany, Switzerland and the United States), he shows that this strategy highlights important differences in the academic mobility (from secondary to higher education) and variation in qualitative differences and prestige hierarchies in higher education institutions. In his conclusion, he suggests that one should ask oneself when aggregate data are acceptable for comparative purposes, and when it is advisable to look at other types of indicators.

Taking an opposing view, Hofferbert and Budge present an overview of the important research project in which they have been involved for a number of years on government spending and party platform. They argue that government expenditure is the most direct, comprehensive and accessible basis for comparative analysis of policy processes, and in particular for gaining insight into government priorities. Their review addresses the major problems that in their view have plagued this area of research. Using public expenditure as a measure of priority, they present a descriptive profile of policy priorities across time, country and policy domain, showing: that policy priorities have changed dramatically over time; that these changes are similar across modern democracies; that there has been a shift from national defence to domestic programmes; and that the process of reallocation slowed and reversed slightly in the 1970s and 1980s. These observed variations are then used to test several competing theories, their basic thesis being that the party mandate theory provides the best explanation.

In three other chapters, an argument is made for other types of government activity: Armingeon and Lemieux argue for regulatory activity, Budge and Hofferbert for discursive activity.

Grounding his arguments on a comparative analysis of labour relations regulations in twenty-one countries, Armingeon contests two assumptions of the comparative literature. First, he shows that national political systems and policy-making processes are not independent of each other, contrary to the assumption of case independence. The best predictor for the time of introduction of the right of association granted to trade unions is neither the level of industrialisation, as would be suggested by modernisation theory, nor political mobilisation as suggested by democratic theory, nor class conflicts. It is the size of a country's population, a proxy, according to the author, for the level of economic vulnerability. In other words, countries with higher economic vulnerability (i.e. with a smaller domestic market) have a higher tendency to regulate capital–labour conflicts in order to avoid the detrimental effects of such conflicts on the competitive position of a country in the world market. Armingeon's second contention is that problems rarely evolve into issues and then into policies; non-decision is more frequent than activity as a response to pressures for government intervention. Referring again to labour relations legislation, he shows that most opportunities for labour relations reforms, such as a change in government or a long period of left-wing government or a period of important labour strikes or an economic crisis, are not accompanied by policy changes. Rather there seem to be other preconditions, yet to be identified, that transform these opportunities into action. Armingeon further shows that institutional inertia may impede policy change.

Lemieux argues in his chapter that the comparative analysis of government activity should not neglect the impact this activity has on the distribution of power in a society. For him, the analysis of laws is a better way to do this than government expenditures. After a review of several comparative studies of government regulatory activity, Lemieux gives a summary of the findings of a comparative analysis of the distribution of power in the laws enacted by five Québec governments over the 1945–85 period. He shows, among other things, that the laws adopted over the period consolidated the potential power of political institutions and triggered a bureaucratisation of government intervention in society. In his conclusion, he calls for a cross-national analysis of power relationships in laws as a way to highlight political dimensions of our societies which the study of public expenditure is incapable of doing.

In their chapter on comparative textual analyses of government and party activity, Budge and Hofferbert argue that the quantitative analysis of documents is a neglected approach to the study of government activity. These authors observe that most information about government activity comes in the form of documents and they argue that, even though its qualitative nature has tended 'to impart an historical, non-replicable and non-comparative bias to analyses which base themselves on it', a systematic analysis of this form of government activity is feasible and can yield information central to the observation of government activity in democracies. Budge and Hofferbert offer both a descriptive and an explanatory account of party platforms and their relationship with government activity. Their descriptive analysis shows that parties take few specific stands in election programmes, that major policy areas are discussed, that there was a general tendency toward ideological convergence over the 1945–83 period, and that there exist ideological families of parties along the familiar left–right divide. In their explanatory analysis, they test standard theories of coalition formation and find that there is a relationship between the ideological closeness of parties and coalition formation. They also study the congruence between party programmes and government declarations and legislations.

Shifting the focus from method to theory, Sabatier underlines in his chapter the necessity of a theoretical lens to understand any policy process. Sabatier starts with a critique of the 'stages heuristic' approach that has pervaded the field of policy analysis in recent decades and then turns to review four theoretical approaches: Hofferbert's funnel of causality, Kingdon's policy streams, Ostrom's institutional rational choice approach, and his own advocacy coalition framework. According to the author, all four approaches have the advantage, as compared with the stages heuristic approach, of proposing explicit causal links and causal mechanisms among the variables chosen. Sabatier reviews each model with regard to its principal components, its major applications and its strengths and weaknesses particularly for comparative analysis. In terms of the types of conceptualisations presented above, three of the approaches are of the second type – they consider government activity as a response or a reaction to pressures in the environment. Hofferbert arranges these pressures in groups of factors put in causal sequence; Kingdon speaks of parallel streams (problem, policy, politics) of needs and pressures that must combine in a 'window of opportunity' for there to be a policy innovation; Sabatier organises needs and pressures in terms of opposing coalitions, external events and stable parameters that contribute to the decisions that are taken. Ostrom's conceptualisation is of the third type. Sabatier concludes his chapter by evaluating the usefulness of each approach to the comparative study of public policies.

Milner, for his part, tries to fill the gap between the third and the fourth types of conceptualisations. He retains a macro-sociological variable, welfare, as the dependent variable and relates it to one type of institutional arrangement, corporatism. His aim is 'to set out a basic framework for CPP [comparative public policy] analysis linking institutional choices to aggregate welfare by incorporating to the neo-corporatist framework basic elements of public choice'. Indeed, Milner agrees with Sabatier on the necessity of a theoretical framework. He even goes a step further in suggesting a contribution to the development of a core theoretical framework in CPP. His chapter proposes two elements for a place in that core: methodological individualism and the neo-corporatist 'U-shaped curve'. By closely linking the explanations about determinants and effects of policies to the choices of rational individuals in a consistent way, methodological individualism imposes rigorous standards on explanations and conclusions to be drawn. Despite the fact that this assumption is at the core of the public choice approach, it is not incompatible with a preference for a strong welfare state. The main question becomes: 'what institutional choices result in lowering the costs of individuals choosing to act in such a way as to enhance welfare?' And the 'U-shaped curve' of neo-corporatism can serve to model the answer: under high levels of corporatism, policies reinforcing corporatist institutions can have a positive effect on economic performance (as shown by neo-corporatists) – but not under low levels of corporatism (as shown by liberal analysts).

Whereas all previous chapters have been exclusively concerned with government activity in industrialised societies, Lafay's chapter addresses the issue of government activity in both developed and developing countries. Furthermore, he stresses the interaction of economic and political factors as determinants of government activity and demonstrates that economists need to include political variables in their 'purely' economic analyses. More specifically, he reports that such an analysis applied to the French economy showed that decision-makers simultaneously follow four logics: an economic stabilisation logic, a fiscal equilibrium logic, an incremental logic and a political logic. His own research on twenty-three African countries over a ten-year period shows that there is the same interaction of political and economic variables in developing countries – specifically that economic policies are related to strikes and demonstrations as well as to macroeconomic disequilibria and IMF pressures.

Clapham also stresses government activity in the Third World. He shows that divergent economic policies can explain the variation in economic development among Asian states and between Asian and African states but that this explanation does not hold when comparing among African states. He argues that these puzzling findings 'have the effect, ultimately, of undermining the basis for any comparative politics of the Third World, and indeed of challenging the idea of comparative politics in a more general sense'. He reaches two main conclusions: first that the idea of the Third World as a conceptual category has now reached the end of the road; and second that cross-national comparisons of government activity should take account of 'deep-seated attitudes to government', or of cultural differences, to be valid.

Though it was not originally intended to be used as a conclusion, McKinlay's chapter actually provides us with a useful one. Indeed, the whole process of putting together this collection of papers proceeded from the assumption that there should be some effort to improve the level of aggregation in our discipline. Defining aggregation in terms of coherence and directionality, McKinlay argues that foreign policy as a field of study (and I think that his argument could be generalised to policy studies in general) has been characterised by 'a substantial accumulation though with modest accompanying aggregation'. And, in trying to understand what impedes greater aggregation, he addresses four clusters of factors: scattered research agendas, substantive complexity, the absence of an agreed set of rules of evidence and the fragmented nature of our professional environment.

It could be conceived that the scattering of the papers presented in this volume is an illustration of the strong accumulation and the weak aggregation that characterise our discipline. If this is the case, it is important that we realise it explicitly and that we gradually move toward greater aggregation. This collection of papers is presented with one main objective, on the part of the editors as well as of the contributors: to contribute at least in some ways to the 'cross-fertilization' or the gaining of 'insight from other work' that McKinlay rightly identified as a sign of progress toward more aggregation in the field of comparative public policy. All the problems identified in this book must be viewed not as mere criticism but as an appeal for new insights toward the development of a better understanding of government activity in a comparative perspective.

NOTES

1. For a list of several such definitions, see Pal (1987:3–4).
2. See, for example, Stein (1971:372–3).
3. 'Public policy is whatever governments choose to do or not to do' (Dye 1984:2).
4. Robertson and Judd propose a comparable, though less complete, typology of government activity (they use the term 'policy outcomes' to mean: 'what government does in response to policy demands'). Their list includes: laws, executive orders, court rulings, regulation, enforcement actions, budgets, taxes (Robertson and Judd 1989:5–6). Imbeau and Lachapelle (1993) use a similar typology for domestic policies at the provincial level.
5. For a similar argument about government spending, see Crête and Imbeau (1994).

REFERENCES

Allison, Graham T. 1971. *The Essence of Decision: Explaining the Cuban Missile Crisis*. Boston: Little, Brown.

Azar, Edward. 1972. *Probe for Peace: Small States Hostilities*. Minneapolis: Burgess Publishing Co.

Crête, Jean and Louis M. Imbeau. 1994. 'Dépenses publiques et activité gouvernementale dans les provinces canadiennes.' In *Politiques provinciales comparées*, eds Jean Crête, Louis M. Imbeau and Guy Lachapelle. Sainte-Foy: Les Presses de l'Université Laval.

Dye, Thomas R. 1984. *Understanding Public Policy*. Englewood Cliffs: Prentice-Hall.

Edwards, George C. and Ira Sharkansky. 1978. *The Policy Predicament. Making and Implementing Public Policy*. San Francisco: W.H. Freeman.

Ginsberg, Benjamin. 1976. 'Elections and Public Policy.' *American Political Science Review* 70: 41–9.

Heidenheimer, Arnold J., Hugh Heclo and Carolyn Teich Adams. 1990. *Comparative Public Policy*. New York: St Martin's Press.

Hermann, Charles, Maurice East, Margaret Hermann, Barbara Salmore and Steven Salmore. 1974. *CREON: A Foreign Events Data Set*. Beverly Hills: Sage.

Imbeau, Louis M. and Guy Lachapelle. 1993. 'Les déterminants des politiques provinciales au Canada: Une synthèse des études comparatives.' *Revue québécoise de science politique* 23: 107–41.

Landry, Réjean. 1984. 'La nouvelle analyse institutionnelle.' *Politique* 6: 5–32.

Nadel, Mark V. 1975. 'The Hidden Dimension of Public Policy: Private Governments and the Policy-Making Process.' *Journal of Politics* 37: 2–34.

Pal, Leslie A. 1987. *Public Policy Analysis: An Introduction*. Toronto: Methuen.

Pomper, Gerald M. 1970. *Elections in America*. New York: Dood, Mead and Co.

Robertson, David B. and Dennis R. Judd. 1989. *The Development of American Public Policy: The Structure of Policy Restraint*. Glenview: Scott, Foresman and Co.

Rose, Richard. 1984. *Understanding Big Government*. London: Sage.

Singer, J. David and Melvin Small. 1972. *The Wages of War, 1816–1965: A Statistical Handbook*. New York: Wiley.

Skogan, Wesley G. 1977. 'Public Policy and Fear of Crime in Large American Cities.' In *Public Law and Public Policy*, ed. John A. Gardiner. New York: Praeger.

Stein, Janice. 1971. 'L'analyse de la politique étrangère: à la recherche de groupes de variables dépendantes et indépendantes.' *Études internationales* 2: 371–94.

Strick, John C. 1990. *The Economics of Government Regulation: Theory and Canadian Practice*. Toronto: Thompson Educational Publishing Inc.

Wilensky, Harold. 1975. *The Welfare State and Equality*. Berkeley: University of California Press.

2 Throwing Money and Heaving Bodies: Heuristic Callisthenics for Comparative Policy Buffs

Arnold J. Heidenheimer

For some seeking to demarcate a field labelled 'governmental activity' from the larger context, it may seem good strategy to focus attention exclusively on data derived from national budgets and national accounts. But in this essay I want to raise a number of problems that are encountered by those who rely on such measures in comparisons across policy areas and nations. Do expenditures reflect national efforts more uniformly on a cross-national basis in some policy areas than in others? How conscious should we be of definitional changes adopted by international agencies who produce the comparative data and indicator bases? Or, when turning to non-financial measures of policy sector activities, what are some problems encountered there in coping with structural differences among national systems?

Financial allotments can persuasively be held to reflect priorities among the party and governmental elites who recurrently make choices among projects, programmes and policy sectors. But most public policies cannot be adequately analysed exclusively in terms of the perceptions and allocations of powerful national political actors. When my co-authors and I first wrote our volume on *Comparative Public Policy: The Politics of Social Choice in the mid-1970s*,[1] we encountered problems in the accessibility of reliable cross-national data pertaining to most of our policy areas. Both expenditure and other data were much more extensive on the activities of national-level governments than they were for sub-national governments, with reliable cross-national information about private sectors being still more limited. This was mainly due to the data-gathering proclivities of international organisations like the OECD and UNESCO. Especially for tabular and graphic presentations we had to select reliable and meaningful data, and these were just very unevenly available. This influenced the

13

results in both the first and second (1983) editions of our book in that the majority of tables involved budgetary or expenditure data.

What did this indicate about the way in which we relied on national expenditure, as distinct from other kinds of statistical data, and how did this differ by policy area? Reviewing the chapters which I had contributed to the book, I found very sharp variations among them. In the chapter on taxation policy, all the tables dealt with governmental revenue and expenditure data. In another, the one dealing with health policy, three out of eight tables did so. But in the third, the one on education policy, none of the graphs and data were drawn from expenditure of budget data.

EXPENDITURES IN HEALTH AND EDUCATION

What, I reflected, were the reasons why I had utilised expenditure data more in the health than in the education chapter? Partly it had to do with the general quality of cross-national statistics in these policy arenas. Even at the national level, statistics had become more standardised for the health than for the education sectors. In the American case this was due partly to the fact that the resources devoted to health were more than ten times larger than those devoted to education. But it was also due to the capacity of international organisations to deal judiciously with the data provided by national authorities. It seemed that, by the 1970s, the health sector had been more uniformly demarcated in administrative terms than the education sector. In some countries the education ministries and agencies were also entrusted with the supervision and regulation of churches and cultural institutions, while vocational education was often under the economics ministries. This added to the problem of distinguishing activities and expenditures which were more universally recognised as being primarily 'educational' in nature.

At the time, the comparative education statistics published by organisations like UNESCO and the OECD left much to be desired. In 1973 the OECD prepared an ambitious initiative to develop statistics that could produce a comprehensive cross-national set of educational indicators. One of the research sectors was to deal with how resources could be used effectively to further goals like meeting the needs of the economy and furthering equality of opportunity. But critical discussion about the feasibility of educational planning and the desirability of educational expansion weakened the research thrust, 'and after an initial retreat from high ambitions, the idea to develop a set of education indicators was given up entirely.... Disappointment and skepticism towards educational research became a hallmark of the times' (OECD 1994:21–2). It took fifteen years for the project to be relaunched in the late 1980s.

Another reason why I placed greater reliance on health than education expenditures was undoubtedly that the problem of controlling costs was becoming a political issue in the health sector in a way it was not for education. In most countries, education was a declining category within public spending, whereas the financial demands of the health sector were tending to crowd out allocations to other policy arenas. This was occurring to a varying extent in all countries in good part due to the fact that technological and related factors were, together with demographic ones, driving the cost explosion. These were to a large extent similar across the boundaries of the advanced western systems. The costs of cat-scanners and dialysis machines, as well as drugs and hospital equipment, were largely determined within global markets, and even personnel was more mobile internationally in the health than in the education sectors.

The outcomes of governmental activity vary according to the nature of policy outputs. Problems of achieving comparability are of a manageable sort for programmes that involve income transfers for which techniques involving purchasing power parities and the like offer accommodation. But policy areas such as health and education, which entail more the provision of discrete idiosyncratic goods, involve much lower levels of both divisibility and fungibility (Galvin and Lockhard 1990). Here one finds less clear-cut symmetry between the costs assumed by public providers and the benefits accorded clients and service users. Hence the attempts to compare the degree to which different national programmes meet criteria of need fulfilment or inequality reduction often have to probe what is contained within similarly labelled units of service provision, whether they be labelled 'one year of secondary education' or 'ten days of hospital care'.

To what extent 'baskets' of health and education services represent varying degrees of cross-national heterogeneity of basket content has to my knowledge not been systematically examined. But some evidence suggests that the range of activities included under the education rubric clusters around the basic instruction process to a rather varying extent. This is suggested by contrasts among countries as between teaching and non-teaching staffs employed in the schools and education systems. For most OECD countries the relation between the two kinds of personnel is about two to one. But the US case is quite different – the greater significance of many athletic, advising, transportation and other school-connected roles causes the non-teaching staff, as a proportion of the total labour force (2.9 per cent), to exceed that of the teaching force (2.6 per cent). In countries where many of these specialised non-teaching occupational groups are smaller, as in Japan and the Netherlands, their ratio to the teaching personnel is less than a third (OECD 1993).

REPORTING AND RANKING OF CROSS-NATIONAL EDUCATION EXPENDITURES

Some of the problems entailed in comparing public and private expenditures across countries and time will be familiar to most students of policy analysis. How to translate expenditures in a period of floating exchange rates, or how to weight formulas for how their purchasing value differs from official rates, are problems that have been addressed by international organisations. Thus the introduction of so-called purchasing power parities (PPP) by the OECD has been widely adopted in the cross-national translation of currency rates and expenditure patterns.

An opportunity for devising ways of handling problems of making education statistics both more reliable and more meaningful developed in the late 1980s as the research climate became once again more favourable for research on education at the macro-level. In countries like the United States and Switzerland, politicians, who had earlier been suspicious of the ideological thrust behind the educational indicator efforts, became more supportive of the idea of reviving such projects. In 1990 the education ministers of OECD countries authorised that organisation to put educational indicators back on their research agenda, thus paving the way for the novel and more ambitious analyses which began to be published in 1992 under the deceivingly popular title: *Education at a Glance.*

Among the important decisions affecting the reporting categories of the international education indicators were some which redefined just which kinds of activities and expenditures should be recognised as falling within the 'educational' arena. One key case in point was the apprenticeship-based programmes which, under the label 'dual systems', are particularly developed in Central Europe. Those enrolled in them typically combine training programmes in private firms with participation in classroom instruction for one or two days a week which is largely publicly financed.

For many decades up to the 1980s, those enrolled in the dual systems were regarded by the guardians of international accounting statistics as being primarily members of the labour force, who were engaged in only part-time education. But then countries like Germany and Switzerland, whose participation rates in full-time schooling appeared to be comparatively low by these statistical criteria, saw an opportunity to press for redefinitions. Because these countries had been credited with using dual systems to hold down youth unemployment in the wake of the 'oil shocks', the other OECD countries were more willing to entertain their requests that enrolment in such programmes be redefined from part-time to full-time enrolment in secondary-level education. In other words, they agreed that apprentices were to be counted as having full-time secondary status in the same way as *lycée* or *Gymnasium* students.

If the time spent learning on shop floors and offices was recognised as constituting education, should the large amount of company funds devoted to these training programmes not also be incorporated in the amounts that countries spent on education? A positive response to this challenge came to be reflected in the categories pertaining to education expenditure statistics which began to be published in the new series: *Education at a Glance: OECD Indicators*.

For that publication, the German Statistical Office supplied for the first time a figure of what was spent by West German industry, trade and handicraft enterprises for vocational education (*betriebliche Berufsausbildung*), and the total came to DM 40 billion for the year 1988.

How had that figure been arrived at? German attempts to develop statistical bases for such estimates had been under way ever since the work of the Edding Commission in the early 1970s. Expenditures for the year 1980 were examined in two parallel studies. The one run by the Research Institute of German Business, the *Institut der Deutschen Wirtschaft* (IDW), came up with somewhat lower gross expenditures but somewhat higher net expenditures than the study based on a much larger sample of firms done by the *Bundesinstitut für Berufsbildung* (BIBB). Though its study was based on only 302 firms, the IDW researchers extrapolated from their data to come up with total gross and net estimates of 27.9 and 20.2 billion marks for 1980. To provide the private expenditure data requested by OECD, the German Statistical Office relied on a further extrapolation of the 1980 IDW gross data for changes that had occurred by 1988 to come up with the figure of DM 40 billion, representing the estimate for gross expenditure by West German enterprises. By including the salary costs of part-time instructors, while minimising the value of apprentice work to the firm, it constituted an estimate based on a so-called 'full cost' model (Falk 1982; Bardeleben *et al.* 1991).

The inclusion by the OECD of the German dual system private expenditures greatly added to the amounts the Germans were recognised as spending on education, which caused Germany to be lifted from being one of the OECD laggards (4.6 per cent in 1986) to becoming positioned well up in the middle range of national education spenders.

The consequences of the increased German figures came to affect various international rankings in striking ways. First, in the proportion of total education expenditures that are devoted to secondary education, the German ratio bounded far ahead of those for other OECD countries. Germany's rate of 66 per cent became far larger than that for the next highest country, France (52 per cent), as well as that for the OECD average (44 per cent) and that for the United States (31 per cent). Secondly, in the amount spent per student, Germany became the only OECD country which claimed to spend more for each secondary school student ($6638) than it did for each student in higher education ($6322). By contrast, the differentials for OECD countries overall, and for the United States, were more than two to one in favour of higher education. Thirdly, in the overall rankings of private.sources of education financing, Germany leap-frogged over previous leaders like Japan and the United States, to become the OECD country with the highest reliance on private sector financing. Its figure of 27 per cent was higher than that for Japan (26 per cent) or the United States (21 per cent), and more than two and a half times higher than the OECD average (12 per cent). All this occurred while the number of private schools and universities in Germany remained insignificant compared with those in Japan and the United States (OECD 1993).

Whether inclusion of the private expenditures of German business warranted such drastic recasting of the expenditure rankings was illuminated by a new study by the BIBB which was carried out as the first set of OECD indicators was published. The BIBB collected data from 1370 representative West German firms for 1991. It differed from previous studies in analysing data according to four different methods of accounting. The 'partial cost', as opposed to 'full cost', principle produced much lower estimates mainly because it excluded the wage costs of trainers – which make up two-fifths of the full cost figures – on the grounds that these costs would have had to be met whether or not personnel devoted some part-time effort to supervising apprentices. The 'net cost', as opposed to 'gross cost', method of calculation deducted what the work of apprentices contributed to the value of the products of enterprise. For small artisanal shops apprentices were found almost to pay for themselves; but in larger enterprises the remaining net costs are considerable.

As Table 2.1 indicates, the estimates of the total private expenditures by German business for 1991 varied widely depending on which accounting method was applied. By one method the outcome came close to that of the IDW projection by the OECD (of DM 40 billion). But the three other methods came out with much lower estimates: two of them came out with figures that were only three-fifths as high, while the lowest estimate,

Table 2.1   West German Private Expenditure for Vocational Education by
Accounting Method, 1991 in DM billion

	Gross	*Net*
Full Cost Principle	40	24
Partial Cost Principle	24	9

Source: Bardeleben *et al.* 1994:15–17.

which the authors characterised as 'constituting a realistic magnitude for
what the training program actually costs enterprises' (Bardeleben *et al.*
1994:17), projected a total expenditure less than one-quarter of that used
by the OECD.

BODY COUNTS AND MOBILITY: LINKING SECONDARY CREDENTIALS AND UNIVERSITY ADMISSION

To ensure that students of policy remain connected to the activities occurring in the world of schools and vocational centres and universities, it is
essential to utilise indicators which keep tabs on what happens to bodies
and minds as they get shifted and transferred between the different institutions of the education system. Let us then consider problems encountered
in those kinds of exercises.

Turning from expenditures to categories like enrolments and credentials
involves turning from the throwing of money to the heaving of bodies.
But how similar are groups of secondary school graduates which are produced by the full-time academic high schools in western countries? We
will pursue this question by examining qualitative differences encountered
in efforts to compare the transition from secondary to higher education,
building on our discussion of the German case and contrasting it with
those of Switzerland and the United States.

In our three-country comparison the relative value of a typical academic
secondary school's credentials varies directly with how they bestow an
entitlement to gaining admission to a university-level institution. For one-
eighth of Swiss youth the *Matura* opens the door to a university. For one-
third of German youth the *Abitur* opens university doors but subject to a
rather extensive *numerus clausus* in many disciplines. For the youth in the
United States, a high school graduation certificate guarantees access only

to the least prestigious 'open admission' portion of higher education. The more selective majority of US institutions demand additional proof of ability, based mainly on aptitude tests that are beyond the control of the school districts and states which set the curricula of the public high schools. Through these mechanisms the entry to higher education becomes the single most important US selection point, whereas for the Swiss, and probably still for most of the Germans, it takes second rank behind the primary-secondary selection point.

One difference between the approximately 130 Swiss *Gymnasia* and *lycées* (also called *Mittelschulen*) and the roughly 30 000 US high schools is their relative number – proportional to population the latter outnumber the former by five to one. Another is that the *Matura* examinations administered by the 26 cantons are – almost uniquely within the Swiss education system – monitored for content and quality by a Federal agency. However, the various schools set their own examination questions within a framework set by the cantonal authorities. For many fields it is believed that the examinations and the grading are harder in some cantons, like Zurich, than in others, like neighbouring Berne.

Most German *Länder* operate decentralised *Abitur* examinations, similar to the prevailing Swiss practice. But in several other *Länder* the examinations are produced at the *Land* level – this so-called *Zentral-Abitur* is given in Bavaria, Baden-Württemberg and Saar. These are also *Länder* that pride themselves on maintaining high standards, which entails transferring more poorly performing *Gymnasium* students into less selective schools well before they reach the final year.

While some states in the United States also conduct uniform leaving examinations for high school graduates, these remain marginal or, as in the case of the New York Regents examination, only partly affect university entrance to institutions within one state. What distinguishes the US higher education system is, first, that 'whether' is less important than 'where' one is admitted, and, secondly, that these decisions hinge as much or more on performance on aptitude tests like the Standard Assessment Test (SAT) and the American College Test (ACT) as they do on curriculum-related school examinations.

In both Switzerland and Germany the grades achieved in classes and the related *Abitur* examinations remain much more important. But over the past twenty-five years an important difference has also developed between these two systems. The more modest expansion of Swiss *Gymnasia* has allowed the *Matura* examination to remain an unconditional entitlement, whereas in Germany the great expansion of *Gymnasium* and other school types, like the *Gesamtschule*, has caused the *Abitur* to lose

some of its magic quality. For the past twenty years, an increasing proportion of German university faculties or disciplines have become subject to
numerus clausus allocations, which are operated for the most part nationally by the Central Admissions Agency (ZVS). This was put into operation
because the great expansion of demand was not mediated by the kind of
market or residence-based allocation criteria which come into play in the
United States. This system is unlike anything found in the two other
federal systems. It allocates places mainly on the basis of the *Abitur* (300
points) and class grades of students (maximally 540 points) applying for
particular fields of study for institutions throughout Germany.

In Germany the *Land* education ministries, which appoint secondary
teachers, supervise the *Abitur* examinations which are supposed to ascertain performance quality in a uniform manner. But when admission to particularly scarce university places, like those in medicine, became highly
competitive in the late 1970s, *Länder* like Bavaria demanded that the more
rigorous nature of their curriculum and *Abitur* examinations be given due
recognition. This led the Conference of *Land* Education Ministers (KMK)
to establish a so-called Malus-Bonus system, through which the Central
Admissions Agency weighs *Abitur* class averages in relation not to the
school but to the *Land* from which they originate. Thus a Bavarian student
with a slightly inferior average than a competitor from Hamburg for a
place in the medical faculty in Hessen would none the less be awarded the
place since he is automatically awarded a half-point bonus because his
Abitur was taken in Bavaria with a smaller and more selective portion of
his age cohort.

That the quality of high school education varies hugely between and
within the states of the United States is reflected by the average SAT
scores of public universities which recruit from particular portions of these
bodies of graduates. The SAT/ACT tests, which 'can open or close doors'
(Stocking 1985:249), are taken by the two-thirds of high school graduates
who are contemplating higher education. The greater willingness in the
United States to tolerate qualitative variations is reflected in vastly varying
entrance thresholds as shown, for example in 1988, in average freshman
SAT scores of 1185 for the University of California (Berkeley), as compared with 952 at the University of Alabama (Tuscaloosa), and 656 at
Alabama State University (Montgomery).

Unlike the states in the United States and German *Länder*, two-thirds of
the smaller Swiss cantons do not operate their own university-level
institutions. Graduates from their *Gymnasia* go to study in one of the so-
called 'university cantons'. Moreover, they do so more on German than
US terms, insofar as they pay no more than the nominal fees paid by local

students. Until fifteen years ago the university cantons received no subsidy for these out-of-canton students, and even since then the non-university cantons have made annual transfer payments of only about four thousand francs, which do not come close to covering the full cost. Among the factors that have kept this system working is that the number of applicants from small cantons, which often maintain only one *Gymnasium*, has been kept limited and consequently student aid levels have remained low.

Swiss university students are enrolled mainly on the basis of passing a Federally normed *Matura* examination, an instrument that was introduced in 1906, mainly to ensure that medical students had a uniformly adequate knowledge base. Since then it has become differentiated into five types of Federal examination areas – though cantonal *Matura* examinations still remain. In the 1970s the Germans reduced the knowledge tested in *Abitur* examinations to four core subjects, and allowed more options in the last two years. Subsequently, however, requirements have been tightened. The Swiss, by retaining required testing in eleven subjects, prevented the kind of qualitative declines which some think they observed in West Germany since the 1970s. An OECD team, which gave Swiss education its first formal outside scrutiny in 1989, expressed amazement at the ability of an alliance headed by the *Gymnasium* rectors repeatedly to repulse efforts to trim and reform the curriculum in the 1970s and 1980s. Consequently it has only been in the 1990s, with the problem of adjusting to patterns in the neighbouring countries looming on the horizon, that plans to reduce the number of examination fields came to be put on the Swiss policy agenda.

Whereas the *Abitur* grade averages of Bavarian and Hessian students are made public in Germany, the equivalent Swiss data are not accessible. Thus, a century after the Swiss rejected a Federal Education Statistics Office in the famous '*Schulvogt*' referendum of 1882, Swiss cantons still retain an effective veto power against the release of many educational statistics, which might be used to cast their efforts in an invidious light. Hence Swiss educators have been inhibited from trying to compare the record and quality of cantonal schools and universities or of their students. Also inhibiting effective competition is the fact that the number of full universities among which the German-speaking Swiss students choose has not increased over the past 150 years beyond the trio of Basle, Berne and Zurich.[2]

CALLISTHENICS FOR CREDIBILITY ENHANCEMENT

The callisthenics to which the reader has been exposed in this exercise in critical data analysis should enhance abilities to make choices as to when aggregate national data are acceptable for comparative purposes, and when it is necessary to probe further within the categorical rubrics.

Our survey of educational practices and statistical reporting usages in three federal countries has illustrated how differently educational dynamics are related to categories for which aggregate and average figures are derived. That the utilisation of such data for public consumption can also vary over time was reflected in the changing stances of US and Swiss policy-makers toward the 'indicators' revival.

The German practices and decisions, from the school level all the way up to the national and international levels, are interesting both for their distinctiveness and for their timing. One distinctive aspect is that, although there are other countries that make extensive use of the dual system, only the Germans report their employers' expenditures for the OECD compilations. That other countries do not report such expenditures is only partly due to the lack of empirical bases for reliable estimates. The Austrians published the results of data collections as early as 1981, but have not utilised them for OECD purposes. The Swiss did lag in collecting such data. But another reason why they did not supply estimates may have been that their educational expenditure from public sources as a percentage of GNP for 1991 was the same (5.4 per cent) as the similar ratio reported for Germany under the combined public and private expenditure category (OECD 1994).

A further distinctive aspect is that the rate of increase of young Germans going through the academic track to universities has been of record proportions. One result of the latter trend has been that the number of Germans attending university has increased so much that, by the traditional reporting criteria, their number has gradually caught up with the number of those enrolled as trainees within the dual system. The ratio of apprentices to students changed from over four to one in 1960 toward parity in the 1980s; in 1990 the number of students began to exceed the number of dual system trainees.

With regard to timing there are two temporal coincidences to take note of in the German setting. The first is that the overtaking of the 'apprentices' by the 'students' occurred at just about the time of German reunification. Developments since then have accentuated the trend because the East German youth have been drawn more to the academic route. The other temporal coincidence lies in the fact that the bureaucratic initiative to include employer expenditures under education spending also came at about the same time as the two aforementioned occurrences.

By some conventional measures, the German educational effort had consistently appeared low. Thus, the German public expenditures for education as a proportion of total government expenditures were scarcely half those of the United States and Switzerland, partly due to heavier spending in other sectors (OECD 1993). Some German officials had long felt that the standard definitions of full-time education had blocked recognition of training investments made through the dual system. They may have accentuated pressures for definitional changes, especially in the aftermath of German unification and the ensuing heavy demands on public budgets. Including the estimates for industrial and business expenditures under the dual system makes the overall German effort look much better in the international comparisons.

The researchers who have laboured valiantly to launch more meaningful sets of international educational indicators are aware that these should not be for 'the exclusive domain of policy-makers and administrators seeking control over schools' but should serve 'diverse audiences' and educate the community (OECD 1994:46–7). To this end the 1993 version of *Education at a Glance* was given extensive coverage on the front page of the *New York Times*. However, in Germany it received relatively limited press publicity. Thus, when I subsequently discussed education funding with the head of a leading German education research institute, he was not aware that Germany had been reported as spending more per secondary student than for those in higher education. Likewise, I have yet to meet a German professor of higher education who could really explain just how the Central Admissions Agency implements its allocations.

Academic generalists on education and education policy might well be given more opportunity to participate in the discussion of new departures in reporting practices. They would be in a better position to contribute to the meaningful reception of the revised statistics if they were better enabled to develop insights and understanding of the very complex or even arcane practices which have been discussed here. It has been observed that the indicator reporting system should have a 'strong conceptual organization that captures both established means–ends relationships from social science and the best clinical expertise' (OECD 1994:46). Broader critical discussion by academics, not presently provided for, might help to test changes for credibility and consistency.

NOTES

1. By indicating that our field of observations would encompass both political and social choice, we meant to convey that the analysis of public policies

needed to embrace not only the activities of national actors but also the role of sub-national and non-governmental providers and the preferences of citizens as consumers of both public and private services.

2. The Swiss, in 1973, considered a constitutional amendment which would have increased the Federal government's financial role in higher education somewhat along the lines of the joint tasks amendment adopted in the Federal Republic in 1969. This was passed by the Swiss Parliament but failed to get support in the required majority of cantons when it was put to the voters in a referendum.

REFERENCES

Bardeleben, Richard von *et al.* 1991. *Kosten und Nutzen der betrieblichen Berufsausbildung.* Bonn: Bundesinstitut für Berufsbildung.

Bardeleben, Richard von, Ursula Beicht and Kalmam Feher. 1994. *Kosten und Nutzen der betrieblichen Berufsausbildung: Erste repräsentative Untersuchungsergebnisse.* Bonn: Bundesinstitut für Berufsbildung.

Falk, Rudiger. 1982. 'Kosten der betrieblichen Aus- und Weiterbildung, Repräsentative Erhebung fur 1980.' In *Berichte zur Bildungspolitik 1982/83 des Instituts der deutschen Wirtschaft*, eds Uwe Gobel and Winfried Schlaffke, Cologne.

Galvin, Richard F. and Charles Lockhard. 1990. 'Discrete Idiosyncratic Goods and Structural Principles of Distributive Justice.' *Journal of Politics* 52: 1182–1204.

Heidenheimer, Arnold J., Hugh Heclo and Carolyn Teich Adams. 1990. *Comparative Public Policy.* New York: St Martin's Press.

OECD. 1987. *Pathways for Learning, Education and Training from 16 to 19.* Paris.

OECD. 1988. *Education in OECD Countries 1985–86.* Paris.

OECD. 1992. *Education at a Glance.* Paris.

OECD. 1993. *Education at a Glance.* Paris.

OECD. 1994. *Making Education Count: Developing and Using International Indicators.* Paris.

Stocking, Grad. 1985. 'The United States.' In *The School and the University: An International Perspective*, ed. Burton R. Clark. Berkeley: University of California Press.

3 Patterns of Post-War Expenditure Priorities in Ten Democracies

Richard I. Hofferbert and Ian Budge

Our goal here is to sketch broad patterns of public policy activity across a set of ten modern democracies via evidence found in governmental expenditure activities. In spite of the fact that other forms of documentary analysis may yield sometimes richer evidence on the complexities of governmental activity, expenditure records are still the most direct, comprehensive and accessible basis for maximally comparative analysis of policy processes. Spending is clearly not all governments do. They tax; they regulate; and, even in providing services that do ultimately cost money, they devise means for shifting the burden to extra-governmental entities. But this does not debar us from using expenditures as a dependent variable in comparative research – rather it merely enjoins caution as to how we use that evidence.

In some of the research we have reported elsewhere in this volume, we have explicitly juxtaposed expenditure priorities against the thematic emphases of party election programmes, precisely to see to what extent parties are able to get their own priorities through the maze of government – a full report of those findings is in Klingemann, Hofferbert and Budge (1994). In this chapter, however, we want to explore the uses of expenditure data on their own, which it will be argued give a very useful insight into governmental priorities.

In general, research on governmental activity starts with too much theory and too little systematically comparative data. Our analysis here takes up that challenge by examining trends in central government expenditures on major policy areas in ten post-war democracies. We focus on central government spending as a percentage of total outlays.[1] Percentages of totals are used in order to examine the way that governments have set priorities among competing activities at different times.

The major changes that appear from around 1950 to about 1988 cast doubt on various theories that view the policy process as either chaotic and undirected, as controlled exclusively by autonomous state agencies, or as merely a response to the constraints of capitalism. Instead, our evidence favours the idea that government policy-making is a reasonably rational response to societal problems and electoral preferences, mediated by political parties.

We begin with a general justification of the use of expenditure data in comparative studies of government. We proceed then to consider the limitations on what can be inferred from them. And we finish by examining cross-nationally common tendencies in the policy priorities of post-war democracies.

THE RATIONALE FOR DATA-BASED COMPARATIVE POLICY ANALYSIS

As has been emphasised at various points elsewhere in this book, the study of government activity suffers in an extreme way from the explanatory problems that afflict political science generally. These include:

- There are enormous numbers of unrelated but detailed historical and/or institutional descriptions of particular governments or particular undertakings by them in specific countries, either with no theoretical underpinning at all or, worse, with a disorderly admixture of two or three contradictory theories brought in at intermittent points in the narrative.
- Even when case studies build on an implicit theory, they are limited in time (to one government or episode) or space (one country). Moreover, since their approach is historical-institutional, they tend not to explicate theoretical assumptions and leave unstated in the end what the findings tell us about the theory.
- Given this disjunction between theory and evidence, the temptation for the more theoretically inclined reader or investigator is to follow one of two alternatives. The first is to impose a preferred theory on the mass of confusing and contradictory evidence and to show that much of the latter can be interpreted in conformity with it. This is the technique followed by both pluralist (Dahl 1961) and elitist conspiracy interpretations of governmental activity (Mills 1956; Lindblom 1977) in the post-war politics of the United States. The second alternative is to point up the confusion in existing descriptions of the policy process and take this as evidence either for chaos and instability or for blind and partial forces moving it beyond any potential for overall democratic control (Kingdon 1984; Wildavsky 1975). Saying that government activity

seen as a whole is essentially chaotic and/or uncontrollable is, of course, a serious criticism of modern democracy.

● A further characteristic of the observation of government activity is the extent to which the field of enquiry has been influenced disproportionately by the experience of one country, the United States. Both examples and theory are drawn most commonly from experience there. Of course, the United States is the most conspicuous actor in the community of democracies, and is much imitated elsewhere, so if we had to focus on only one country, that would be the one to study. However, it is also true that, in many ways, the politics and institutions of the United States are different from those of other democracies (not always in ways, as we shall see, that commentators assume). The point is that, to assess properly both the exceptionality and the representativeness of the policy processes of the United States, we have to put them in a comparative context.

Resolution of most of the analytical difficulties discussed above requires systematic cross-national research. By putting problems in a comparative framework, we can avoid excessive dependence on the experience of only one country. We can relate case studies and historical-institutional descriptions to each other by identifying as typical or atypical the contexts to which they refer and by characterising the ways in which they differ. Comparative data collected over long time periods and for a relatively large number of democracies should give us an advantageous basis for assessment of alternative theories. Indeed, the very prospect of being confronted with such data helps to improve theories because they need to be much more precisely specified in order to stand up to any confrontation with reasonably valid evidence. For instance, questions have to be formed in the shape of relatively exact postdictions/predictions of what kind of government activity is to be expected under the varying conditions to be measured.

This is even more evident when the data to be used are quantitative in nature. For systematic comparative investigation of many countries over the whole post-war period it is almost inevitable that the data will take quantitative form. Otherwise, the vast mass of information that comparative research produces could not be handled. Even if one were to seek to systematise the vast mass of specific, qualitative studies that have been made of government activity, these would have to be coded into clearly categorised schemes to make them manageable. So it seems that if we are to undertake the comparative observation of government activity at all, it must be through quantitative techniques.[2]

Our final general methodological point is that the systematic collection and analysis of comparative data on government activity are the most urgent priority of this field. We are in the familiar situation of having too many theories and explanations, some of them contradictory, but of being fated to argue inconclusively about them because of the lack of relevant evidence on the relative superiority of the competing approaches. The difficulty is not in thinking up possible explanations but in narrowing them down by systematically confronting competing explanations with relevant evidence.

The task we undertake below is to show that such narrowing occurs as soon as one collects and then does simple analysis of relevant and relatively easily accessible data on public expenditures.

EXPENDITURES AS INDICATORS OF GOVERNMENT ACTIVITY

The activities of modern governments are almost co-extensive with their societies. Government is so vast and pervasive as not to be measured adequately by any one indicator. When activity extends, for example, from declaring war to setting when and where one can fish, to questions of capital punishment, abortion and language, the very idea of exact measurement seems out of place.

While no one type of measure can claim a definitive status in the observation of government activities, one prior necessity for most action is to have money allocated and spent on it. Money is certainly not all there is to policy, as Esping-Anderson (1990) has well emphasised. But most policy implementation will languish without it. One need watch very little of the public debate at party conventions or conferences to see that the most frequently invoked indicator of commitment to a particular problem domain is the promise to spend or reallocate money. Much previous research on public policy outputs has made progress by studying the factors that lead different governments to cut up the fiscal pie differently (Hofferbert 1966; Dye 1966; Castles 1982).

Policy alternatives may, of course, be equally costly or cost may not be a determining decision criterion. The price of rope or electricity is not relevant in the decision to employ the death penalty. Regulatory policies are more important for what they do than for what they cost. Furthermore, regulations may even substitute for spending. Civil liberties are at best only weakly linked with what is spent on police, courts and prisons. However, they may need a lot of money spent on inspection and controls to see that they are observed.

In general, the amount of money spent on an area may not indicate its relative importance vis-a-vis other areas of policy – for example, the amount spent on environmental regulation compared with that spent for national defence. Thus confusion may result from use of expenditures as the only indicators of policy, especially if one of the alternatives for governments is to force other bodies to bear the costs – for example, industries and consumers paying for anti-pollution regulations. Arguments about the utility of particular kinds of evidence cannot be made in the abstract. The value of data depends on what one wishes to find out. The difference between money spent on environmental regulation versus education hardly tells us accurately which is the more important. But the variation in spending on even a regulatory policy over time provides a good basis for comparing the relative changes and trends in priority assigned to such a policy. And that is what our investigation here is primarily about.

Of course, as mentioned initially, we have no intention to use expenditures to reflect the full array of government actions. None the less, it is true that 30 to 60 per cent of gross domestic product since the Second World War has been collected and then reallocated by the governments of the countries we study here. This has such a major impact on the social and economic lives of their citizens that the allocation of money has to be one of the most important tasks, if not the most important, of these governments. Expenditures are clearly a major as well as the most visible and accessible measure of government activities.

We use as our main measure the percentages of total central governmental annual outlays devoted to particular functions (for example, defence, agriculture, transport, social security) because these can be broadly taken as expressing the priorities each government, relative to its predecessors and successors, actually has given to different policies. Dealing with expenditures is probably more straightforward than coding qualitative material on what governments do, since published public records provide the final spending data. The figures are supplied by government financial offices and are available from national yearbooks or similar routinely published statistical sources.

As the paucity of long-term cross-national studies using them indicates, however, the enterprise has its difficulties. The major one is that categories reported in official publications are sometimes changed or inconsistent over the years. (Compare, for example, Flora and Heidenheimer 1981; Flora 1986.) This problem will diminish with time as a result of the international standardisation of public financial records led by the International Monetary Fund (IMF). The IMF system, used by virtually all nation states, has been in place, however, only since 1972, thus truncating the first generation of data in which we are here interested. We have not used the IMF system for the data presented below, as retro-fitting the pre-1972 years would have been virtually impossible. Rather, we have relied on individual national accounts publications.[3]

Our strategy has been, therefore, to maximise cross-national coverage and consistency, perhaps at the price of some cross-national variation in categories of policy activity. Even in the national sources, categories have changed over time, sometimes reflecting changed book-keeping labels, sometimes reflecting consolidation or division of functions. Our technique has been to start with the latest year of the series and then to work back carefully through the post-war years, checking the consistency of categories both by the labelling in the original language and in terms of the way numbers follow on from each other in successive years. Clearly sudden jumps in expenditure or sharp changes in the ratio of one expenditure area to another could have perfectly good substantive explanations, such as the switches in regulatory practices. However, in following these through, very often one comes across indications that the definition of the category has been altered and that it must be dropped or aggregated into a larger set.

We generally end up with six to ten broad categories, usually including welfare, health, education, housing, administration of justice (courts, police, prisons, etc.), defence, foreign affairs, transportation and agriculture. These categories reflect the way that governments keep their books and, presumably, conceive of public services, at least so far as spending goes. As we want to create statistical analogues of party and government thinking, there are strong grounds for keeping the categories more or less as we find them, subject to dropping the ones that are not consistent over the period. Those used cover, on average, about 70 to 75 per cent of all central government spending.

Four technical points need to be made with regard to the spending figures we use. One is that they are in percentages of total spending. This is because we are interested in differences and changes in relative priorities in public policy, not in the absolute figures, nor in the total size of the budget, nor in how much a government spends overall on a given function (in which case we would indeed have had to include regional, local and possibly some private spending). We are comparing not what countries spend overall on particular activities year-by-year, but rather what priority national governments give those activities in terms of spending decisions within a given institutional structure. We wish simply to track relative national government priorities over time and to observe the extent to which they follow comparable paths in different countries.

A second point is that we use actual year-end expended funds, not budgetary allocations. This is because what is really spent is more important than what is simply anticipated to be spent.

Thirdly, expenditures are expressed as percentages of total central government outlays rather than, as is common in comparative policy and political economy research, as percentages of GDP. The latter figures are much affected by considerations, such as the general level of economic activity or the tax yield, that are simply extraneous to our interests. Further, our observations of the policy process suggest that budgetary decision-making takes place in a two-stage process, the first being how much of potential resources to spend, the second being how to allocate that sum.

Fourthly, to re-emphasise what we have already stressed above, we are concerned with shares of central government expenditures because we are interested in tracking the results of decisions taken by finite and comparable groups of decision-makers working within particular institutional settings. Unlike many other analyses of spending data, we are not interested in the social outcomes of policy. Hence the question of how much one entire country's governments spend on average in a given area compared with those of another country does not concern us.

These choices, as to what to measure and how to measure it, clearly and severely circumscribe the inferences we can derive from our analyses – a consideration that is, of course, true for all measures. Our choice has been to focus on percentages of central government spending.

Now it may well be the fact that educational taxation and spending, for example, are undertaken mainly by state governments in Germany and the United States, whereas in France and Britain they are mostly budgeted at the national level. The contrast would not invalidate our comparison of trends in education spending within the central budgets in all four countries. Federalism would simply serve as a potential explanation of any differences that might show up between the countries.

The same may be said of any other differences between national governments, such as their success in legislating to shift expenditures to non-governmental entities. Unless this occurs in the middle of a time series, thus rendering earlier percentage allocations to an area non-comparable with later ones as indicators of government priorities, success in shifting financial burdens may be an explanation of why priority trends vary between national governments, but it does not vitiate the comparison of trends themselves.

There are some other possible methodological objections to our procedures that can be dealt with briefly here. One is that percentaging automatically ensures that cuts in one area are reflected as increased shares in others, thus in effect double counting the tendencies at work. For example, cuts in defence spending could be seen as automatically increasing the percentage allocations to other areas of the budget. This, however, is a misunderstanding. There is no automatic reallocation of cuts in one area into increases in others. The decision to transfer funds (as opposed, for example, to decreasing taxes and leaving relative allocations unchanged) is a reflection of government decision. Nor is it automatic that cuts in defence would go into welfare as opposed to maintenance of law and order, for example. Thus the separate time series we examine below are reasonably independent of each other and are not logically or statistically bound together.

The same might be said for the possibility that the overall government 'take' from revenue goes up and increases one area of outlay's share in percentage terms relative to others. But, of course, this again reflects a choice to give one area more than another. Once it is recognised that we are interested in decisional priorities rather than final outcomes reflected in the national resources devoted to various functions, our use of percentages of budgetary allocations as a measure becomes relatively unproblematic.

POST-WAR EXPENDITURE PRIORITY TRENDS[4]

Each of the graphs in Figure 3.1 plots over a particular policy domain both the mean annual percentage of central government expenditure and the figures for two countries, named below the graph, respectively above and below the mean. (The full set for each country is presented in Klingemann *et al.* 1994, Chapters 4 to 13.)

The time series plots of Figure 3.1 support at least four generalisations that can be made about the broad contours of policy priorities across democratic countries in the years since the Second World War:

- Policy priorities have changed dramatically over time.
- The broad contours of that change are similar across modern democracies.
- There has been a striking shift in the allocation of resources from national defence to domestic programmes and services.
- The processes of reallocation slowed and may even have reversed slightly in the 1970s and 1980s.

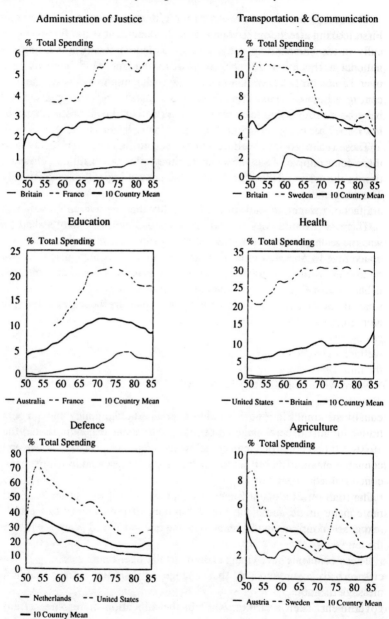

Fig. 3.1   Trends in Expenditure Priorities: Percentage of Central Government Expenditures for Various Functions for Selected Countries and Ten Country Mean, 1950–85

The common patterns are the most interesting aspect of these graphs. First, looking across all six, it is clear that policy priorities shifted dramatically in the years between 1950 and 1985. In 1953 the mean share for national defence was 35 per cent but by 1978 had bottomed out at just over 15 per cent. Education's mean rose from a post-war low of 4.3 per cent to a high of 11.6 per cent in 1971, dropping with the aging of the baby boom to 8.9 per cent in 1985. Health spending's share rose from a low of 5.3 per cent in 1953 to over 13 per cent by 1985.[5]

These reallocations took place while the general share of GDP spent by these central governments rose from around 20 per cent after demobilisation in the wake of the Second World War to over 40 per cent by 1985. The reallocation to education and other human services was not merely an artefact of reduced defence priorities, but represented real increases.

There is little question that defence during the early Cold War years was the anchoring policy. Only neutral Austria spent less than 10 per cent on average for defence. Even Sweden, likewise officially neutral, allocated on average nearly 16 per cent to defence. The post-war demobilisation that is barely visible at the left of the defence graph was rapidly reversed at the time of the Berlin Blockade and then boosted dramatically during the Korean conflict. A combination of economies of scale, some apparent easing of Cold War tension and increased demand for expansion of the welfare state encouraged a steady shift in priorities from defence between the mid-1950s and the mid-1970s.

Were we to array all ten countries, instead of the mean and two examples, the graphs would be crowded, but the similarity of patterns would be equally striking. Shares for education, health, transportation and administration of justice rise in nearly all countries, with some peaking in the 1970s. Of course, specific explanations for each policy area (and for each country's deviations, when they occur) could be presented. But here our concern is not to account for the curve in each policy area or country, but rather to draw attention to general patterns: the shift has followed comparable patterns across countries, domestic policies have gained at the 'expense' of defence and there appears to be a break in the process during the ten years between 1975 and 1985.

These conclusions are reinforced when we summarise the main tendencies verbally, over a slightly wider set of policy areas, in Table 3.1.[6] The message of Table 3.1 is the same as that implicit in the graphs: changes in government priorities across these major policy areas and across countries distinguished by very different institutional and political arrangements are surprisingly uniform. It is the uniformity of government priorities which is unexpected and overwhelming. In matters such as East–West confronta-

Table 3.1   Summary of General Trends in Expenditure Priorities in Ten
Post-War Democracies*

Policy domain	General post-war trend	Deviating countries
Defence	Peaks around 1950 and declines thereafter, with minor interruptions	Austria: peaks in mid-1960s, decline gradual; Germany: decline interrupted in 1960s, continues later
Foreign affairs	In some countries declines with defence; in others, rises in contrast with defence	[Contrasting pattern]
Agriculture	General decline	[Timing of decline varies across countries]
Administration of justice	General increase	Austria: decline; timing and rate of increase elsewhere varied
Transportation and communication	Rises to 1960s/1970s, declines thereafter	Austria: steady increase
Education	Rises to 1960s/1970s, then declines modestly	[None]
Housing	Irregular rise to early 1980s	France: general decline; US: steady; Germany: decline after 1960s
Health	Increase to 1970s, then plateau to modest decline	US: steady increase from 1960; Belgium: irregular (compounded by regionalisation)
Social security, welfare	Plateau then steady rise	Sweden and Austria: decline in later periods; irregularities in timing of increase

*The full array of graphic displays for each country is presented in Klingemann *et al.* 1994.

tion, one might expect to see a general effect for all governments in the western alliance. But common reactions extend to internal matters such as justice, education and even transportation. Exceptions can, on the whole, be readily explained with reference to particular conditions prevailing in the countries, for example the need to conclude peace treaties with Germany and Austria before they could build up their own defence forces. The general order and cross-national stability of patterns within specific policy areas can be even more dramatically illustrated if we summarise overall priorities in policy shares through a general scale. This contrasts those areas of expenditure generally favoured by the right/centre (such areas as agriculture, transportation and defence) with those favoured by the left (such as health, social security and education). While ideally we could create a cross-nationally uniform scale of rightward or leftward tendencies in government activity, we have opted to use an individualised one for each country that is at least conceptually comparable. We have chosen this route owing to the modest (but sometimes specifically unknown) differences in expenditure categories or to differences in data availability from country to country. In all cases but Austria (where we used an additive score owing to missing data), we constructed each country's 'left–right policy priority' measure by means of factor analysis and factor scores based on policy percentages over time.

Although the resulting country scales differ in detail, all broadly contrast social expenditures, on the one hand, with defence and agriculture on the other. Thus the scales are broadly comparable across countries. The trends in left–right scores for each of the ten countries are presented in Figure 3.2. One should note that a decline in right expenditure priorities does not automatically imply a rise in the leftist share of outlays, as not all categories of spending enter into the scale.

These time plots serve simply to reinforce and concentrate the finding of cross-national and cross-time uniformity in priorities which emerged already from the observation of individual expenditure areas. With only two exceptions, leftward priorities increased steadily at the expense of the right up to the 1970s, or slightly beyond. There was even a general tendency for this rise to stabilise or reverse somewhat in the 1980s. Exceptions are Austria, where left priorities declined relative to rightward ones, and Belgium, where the *Loi Unique* of 1961 produced a sharp decline followed by a steady rise in left expenditure priorities during the 1970s and 1980s.

Figure 3.2 demonstrates the triumph of the left up to the late 1970s. In spite of the attention given to the Cold War, the most striking policy development of the quarter century after 1955 was the growth and consolidation of the welfare state. In contrast to fears and theories of the 1970s predicting serious negative consequences of uncontrolled growth of various human service entitlements (Crozier *et al.* 1975; Olson 1982), the trend did begin to dip or at least flatten until around 1980.

38

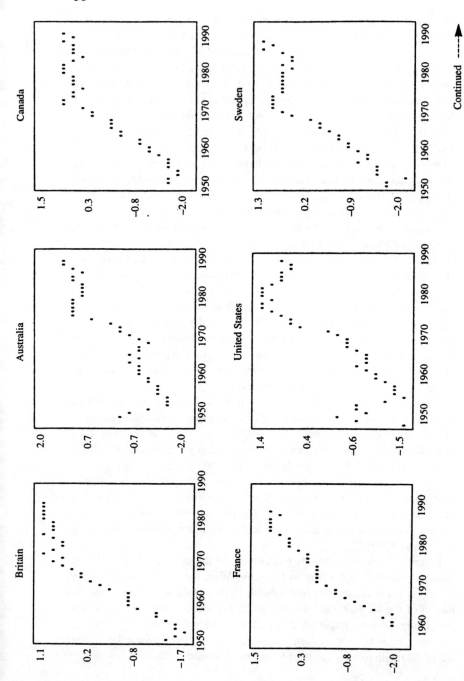

Continued ----->

39

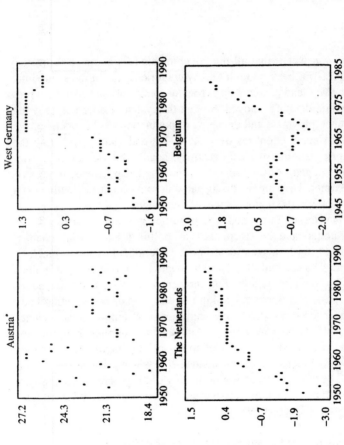

* Scores based on factor analysis of individual country expenditure percentages, arraying such domains as human services and education on the left and defence and agriculture on the right. Due to more than average missing data, Austria's score is based on adding 'left' and 'right' priorities and subtracting the latter from the former. See individual country chapters in Klingemann *et al.* 1994.

Fig. 3.2   Left–Right Policy Priority in Ten Post-War Democracies*

EXPLANATIONS AND THEORETICAL IMPLICATIONS

Our descriptive findings, though interesting in their own right, also call for explanation. Why should very different national governments set substantially the same priorities when, with the exception perhaps of defence, there was no common authority or apparently shared threat pushing them along the same path?

Chaos or Order

One obvious answer is that all the governments face common problems. Thus, the post-war baby boom hit many countries at about the same time, owing to the war, and powered an expansion in schools and education programmes while the bulge moved through the system. Recession, growing structural unemployment and the aging of population has been a recurrent experience of many countries over the 1970s and 1980s, triggering the sustained prioritisation of social security, health and welfare in central government budgets. At the same time, farming has decreased in importance, and farmers have almost disappeared in some countries, setting off a general decrease in the sector's share of the budget.

To say that trends in expenditure priorities are most plausibly interpreted as understandable responses to political and social change, however, is to imply a great deal about government action – much of which contradicts currently fashionable theories. For one thing, it implies that there is a definite pattern. For another, it suggests that this pattern reflects purposive action by some kind of directing or coordinating body rather than uncoordinated self-aggrandisement by autonomous agencies (Davis *et al.* 1966; Niskanen 1971). And, again, it implies that problems are confronted because they are seen to be socially important rather than selected merely because solutions are available which produce quick political gains. The order and seeming rationality of the processes do not seem to emerge either from the 'garbage can' (Cohen *et al.* 1972) or from 'primeval soup' (Kingdon 1984).

Incrementalism and Bureaucratic Self-Aggrandisement

The most pervasive non-Marxist theory of policy processes is probably incrementalism (Davis *et al.* 1966), to which may be linked Niskanen's (1971) theory of bureaucratic self-aggrandisement. In both cases, agencies are expected to expand steadily as they seek to extend their own power and influence by extending their functions and, along with these, their budget. While rational in a narrow self-interested way for the agency or ministry, such expansion is undertaken blindly and may be far from rational from the viewpoint of the whole structure of public policy activities. It is certainly beyond the control of the political parties, which assume power is exercised by persons dependent on the democratic process. Hence, evidence of lack of rationality feeds critiques of the state structure on the grounds that it is outside democratic control.

Incrementalism is properly a theory of expenditure aggregates rather than of government expenditure policy priorities. However, one can observe by extension that our percentaged expenditures also change gradually, on a year-by-year basis. This might support ideas about autonomous, incrementalist growth on the part of the bureaucratic entities involved. However, such a characterisation also raises the question of why the powerful defence bureaucracy did not keep changes in priorities marginal thereby preventing its steady downgrading over the period. The defence bureaucracy was surely in a more powerful and central position to enforce its priorities in the 1950s and 1960s than the relatively smaller and weaker welfare bureaucracies. But the defence agencies lost relatively, either because they themselves recognised the growth of East–West detente and responded to it, or because the top political levels of government did and were able to enforce their decisions.

It is, of course, true that most changes in expenditure priorities on a year-to-year basis are incremental (though there are examples of sudden, sharp changes as with, for example, British spending priority for housing in 1982–84). However, percentage changes over ten to twenty years are quite dramatic because the year-on-year 'incremental' changes all go in the same direction. This testifies more to a purposeful and centrally directed adjustment of policy priorities to international and internal changes than to a struggle for resources between different agencies and ministries in which victory goes, if not to the strongest, now to one side, now to another, without much effect on the overall balance.

Conservative Elites

The example of defence also brings in the question of how far government is dominated by behind-the-scenes conservative elites, who might certainly impose stability and order on policy-making but in non-democratic ways. However, shifting priorities from defence, where the military-industrial complex makes its money, to welfare, where the better-off segments pay out more than they get back, hardly comports with an interpretation of the policy process as being driven by power-brokers beyond the reach of the electorate, unless one is prepared to argue that domestic policy bureaucrats have replaced the military-industrial pluto-crats of yore as power-brokers. Furthermore, if there are such elites, subtly adjusting policy priorities to serve their desires in some very non-obvious fashion, they have to be coordinating them on a massive international scale, which is inherently implausible.

ASSESSING THEORETICAL OPTIONS

Przeworski (1990) has commented that there are three broad groupings of theory which purport to explain government activity.

The first grouping consists of theories involving some concept of state autonomy (which would cover the chaos, incrementalist and bureaucratic aggrandisement theories briefly discussed above). These seem to be con-tradicted by our descriptive finding because they do not account for the order and uniformity of the trends evident in priorities, or for their seem-ingly problem-driven nature.

The second grouping consists of theories invoking capitalist constraints on policy-making, whether these proceed from a more or less conscious conspiracy of the type invoked by Mills (1956) or from the more subtle structural framework which capitalism imposes on policy-making. Having already commented on the implausibility of an international capitalist con-spiracy directing all governments' activities, we concentrate here on the subtler idea that basically capitalist economies, with the ultimate sanction of a loss of financial confidence in government, impose much the same structure of constraints on governmental setting of priorities everywhere. This is what could account for the uniform trends we observe. Each country's governments independently would then be setting priorities within the basic set of constraints imposed by their capitalist economies.

To develop this thesis further, however, one has to ask what such con-straints would be. Certainly, on the face of it, the shift in priority from defence and agriculture to welfare and education, along with the increase in total government 'take', seem to go against capitalist interests, at any rate narrowly defined ones. It is, of course, always possible to argue that enlightened, self-interested capitalists will see a need for a stable, healthy and educated workforce. They will therefore concede to government the autonomy necessary to achieve this. But such a redefinition, in effect, makes business interests equivalent to those of society as a whole, and the theory becomes tautological. Anything governments do can be reinter-preted as permissible within the constraints of enlightened capitalistic self-interest. But, in that case, it is not telling us anything, and all sense of real constraints disappears.

Our own preferred explanation of these trends, to which our further research is directed, relates to the third group of theories identified by Przeworski – those which regard government activity as in some way responsive to the preferences of the population.

It is, of course, possible to regard policy priorities as set by purely bureaucratic responses to social problems, as might also be true for non-democracies. But it is more natural in democracies – particularly in terms of the overall consistency and stability they reveal – to attribute the patterns we find to the elected groups that control government and that are in the best position to enforce overall order and consistency. These are the political parties.

This explanatory option is particularly appropriate because parties are the only bodies to produce reasonably comprehensive medium-term plans for the whole society, in the form of the programmes they present at each election. As they use such programmes to shape the electoral debate in which they get chosen for office, their plans also have a popular endorsement and authority that no other social projects have. The programmes are also, along with and reinforcing the parties' long-standing ideology, the only general points of references which in-coming governments and the individual political appointees within them have as a basis for working out and coordinating detailed policies. (See, for an elaboration of these points, our discussion in Chapter 6.)

This body of ideas about party and governmental activity has, of course, been around at least since the late nineteenth century. And it has often been challenged, not least by the alternative theories considered above. It is the theory of the party mandate, according to which (1) electors vote for the party whose programmatic priorities they prefer (presumably in terms of the problems they think are important), and (2) parties in government set priorities among policy areas that conform to the emphases of their election programmes. Our other research has been concentrated on the second assumption of mandate theory: the assumption that there is a link between what election programmes say and what post-election governments do. This link continues to be investigated quantitatively in a growing body of research (Petry 1988; Budge and Hofferbert 1990; Hofferbert and Klingemann 1990; Hofferbert and Budge 1992; Klingemann *et al.* 1994). We find (1) that there are strong linkages but, perhaps inevitably, (2) the situation is less simple than suggested by classic mandate theory. Parties may well have dual mandates, in a presidency and a legislature; coalition and minority governments blur the distinction between being in and out of government; even in systems where boundaries are much more rigid, the opposition can have some influence (Klingemann *et al.* 1994). Nevertheless, the link between party and government policy emerges strongly in nearly all modern democracies where it has been systematically examined.

We may therefore regard this chapter's discussion of expenditure priorities as supporting theories which feature the role of parties in responding to societal problems and to electoral preferences by influencing government in these directions. While no one investigation can be regarded as the final word on this complex matter, we feel it is up to rival theories to muster equally convincing and rigorous evidence for their own ideas before these can be regarded as equally plausible.

FUTURE RESEARCH INTO GOVERNMENT ACTIVITIES

Commenting from our own perspective on some of the general problems in observing government activity, it is obvious from what has been said that we feel many or most of these analytical difficulties stem from scientific underdevelopment rather than inherent structural difficulties. Nor does the problem of comprehension and explanation lie basically in the development of theory, but rather it results from the state of comparative data collection and analysis. This is perhaps an unfashionable view, given the current elevation of theoretical over other types of research and the view that theoretical development comes first and evidence to check it a poor second. However, as we have pointed out, theory will rarely be satisfactorily specified at an adequate level of detail unless it is prepared for the confrontation with a relevant body of evidence. Given the number of theories we have on hand at the moment, comparative data are unlikely to be collected without some theoretical considerations in mind. So it seems to us that the most urgent tasks are indeed the collection of such data, the testing of theories about them and the development of rigorous and ultimately predictive models using the data.

Expenditures, for reasons of importance, accessibility and ease of analysis, seem to be the most obvious data to gather first for most countries and perhaps for more extended time periods and levels of government than we have done. Three other areas associated with outputs need also to be subjected to standardised quantification: legislation, the traditional output of governments and parliaments, administrative actions and, perhaps, judicial decisions. All of these involve complex problems of coding and classification, which might, however, be guided by the way governments choose to structure departments and ministries.

As soon as such data are collected and organised, the same need for explanations that we identified with expenditure data will come to the fore. Initially, at any rate, the same approach adopted here seems the most obvious one to take. That is to relate the indicators of government activity to party priorities in election programmes and beyond these to indicators of societal problems and public preferences.

It is interesting that the research we propose as needing to be done (which might be presented abstractly as: Problems → Party Programmes → Government Action) bears a strong resemblance to Sabatier's General Model of Policy Evolution (Chapter 7). The indicators listed in his upper left-hand box correspond to our problems; his policy coalitions at the top of the policy subsystem box centre on parties; and his policy outputs can probably be most directly measured by expenditures. There is a real convergence in approaches to the study of government activity here which might well link qualitative and quantitative approaches. For both, a question rarely posed systematically will become increasingly relevant in coming years: How effective is government activity in confronting and possibly solving the problems it confronts? Much has been made recently of the greater efficiency of democratic governments in contrast with the collapsed communist regimes, but there is little or no research that establishes how effective either has been. That question seems likely to assume increasing importance as evidence capable of answering it accumulates.

Our answer to most of the problems of comparative observation of government activity is, therefore, to collect more good data and to analyse them in the light of well-specified theories. We hope our own research helps to demonstrate how doing so enables some nagging theoretical questions to be confronted, and how those questions can be given at least the promise of ever more satisfactory, if never final, answers.

NOTES

1.   The countries included are the same as those analysed in Klingemann *et al.* (1994): Australia, Austria, Belgium, Britain, Canada, France, Germany (West), the Netherlands, Sweden and the United States. The reason for focusing on central governments, rather than the total of central and sub-national entities, is that our broader objective is the analysis of decision processes and not the levels of services provided *in toto* throughout a set of societies.

2.   We argue, in fact, that there is no ultimate distinction between quantitative and qualitative observation, and that the latter, to be done properly, must

consider most of the problems of quantitative observation. But these are philosophical points of too much complexity to be gone into here.

3. Among them, those of Federal Germany and of the United States stand out. These two countries publish a cumulative time series which is coded to maintain consistent categories for nearly the entire period covered in the present analysis. The sources we have compiled both for classification and for the actual figures are given in Klingemann *et al.* (1994).

4. We present here the graphs generated by time series of expenditure priorities in ten democracies. We do this before going on to consider the theoretical and methodological questions which these figures raise. This is purely a matter of presentation and certainly not a denial of the fact that data collection and preparation require theoretical assumptions that carry quite far-reaching substantive implications. Our decision, for example, to look at expenditures as percentages implies that what is important to policy is the setting of priorities for one area compared with another. If relatively more is spent on social services, we assume this is to enhance and extend social services rather than to cut them down, and that the government which spends more on such an area of policy is indeed more committed to the goals served by such policy.

5. There is naturally some irregularity in the classification from one country to another. As pointed out above, some policies, such as education and law enforcement, vary widely from country to country in regard to the relative role of the central government compared with provincial or local authorities. Our general research is focused on the role of national parties, expressed in national elections, so sub-national expenditures are excluded. Furthermore, cross-national statistical differences are not of major consequence for our analysis since our principal interest is in relative variations over time rather than in comparison of absolute numbers from one country to another. We have made special efforts to ensure that each country's data are indeed comparable across time. (See Klingemann *et al.* 1994, Chapter 3 for more detailed discussion of the methodology.)

6. We are able to extend the comparisons by taking some policy areas on which we do not have information for all ten countries, for example, and in the case of welfare and social security by assimilating these distinct but related categories.

REFERENCES

Budge, Ian and Richard I. Hofferbert. 1990. 'Mandates and Policy Outputs: US Party Platforms and Federal Expenditures.' *American Political Science Review* 84: 111–31.

Castles, Francis. 1982. 'The Impact of Parties on Public Expenditures.' In *The Impact of Parties: Politics and Policies in Democratic Capitalist States*, ed. Francis Castles. Beverly Hills: Sage.

Cohen, Michael, James March and John P. Olson. 1972. 'A Garbage Can Model of Organisational Choice.' *Administrative Science Quarterly* 17: 1–25.

Crozier, Michel, Samuel Huntington and Joji Watanuke. 1975. *The Crisis of Democracy*. New York: New York University Press.

Dahl, Robert A. 1961. *Who Governs*. New Haven: Yale University Press.

Dahl, Robert A. 1967. *Pluralist Democracy in the United States*. Chicago: Rand McNally.

Davis, Otto A., M.A. Dempster and Aaron Wildavsky. 1966. 'A Theory of the Budgeting Process.' *American Political Science Review* 60: 529–47.

Dye, Thomas. 1966. *Politics, Economics, and the Public*. Chicago: Rand McNally.

Esping-Anderson, Gosta. 1990. *The Three Worlds of Welfare Capitalism*. Princeton: Princeton University Press.

Flora, Peter, ed. 1986. *Growth to Limits: The Western European Welfare States Since World War II*. Berlin: de Gruyter.

Flora, Peter and Arnold Heidenheimer, eds. 1981. *The Development of the Welfare State in Europe and North America*. New Brunswick, NJ: Transaction Books.

Hofferbert, Richard I. 1966. 'The Relation Between Public Policy and Some Structural and Environmental Variables in the American States.' *American Political Science Review* 60: 73–82.

Hofferbert, Richard I. and Hans-Dieter Klingemann. 1990. 'The Policy Impact of Party Programs and Government Declarations in the Federal Republic of Germany.' *European Journal of Political Science* 18: 277–304.

Hofferbert, Richard I. and Ian Budge. 1992. 'The Party Mandate and the Westminster Model: Election Programmes and Government Spending in Britain 1948–1985.' *British Journal of Political Science* 22: 151–82.

Kingdon, John W. 1984. *Agendas, Alternatives, and Public Policy*. Boston: Little, Brown.

Klingemann, Hans-Dieter, Richard I. Hofferbert and Ian Budge. 1994. *Parties, Policies, and Democracy*. Boulder: Westview Press.

Lindblom, Charles E. 1977. *Politics and Markets*. New York: Basic Books.

Mills, C. Wright. 1956. *The Power Elite*. New York: Oxford University Press.

Niskanen, William. 1971. *Bureaucracy and Representative Governments*. Chicago: Aldine.

Olson, Mancur. 1982. *The Rise and Decline of Nations: Economic Growth, Stagflation, and Social Rigidities*. New Haven: Yale University Press.

Petry, Francois. 1988. 'The Policy Impact of Canadian Party Programmes: Public Expenditure Growth and Contagion from the Left.' *Canadian Public Policy* 14: 376–89.

Przeworski, Adam. 1990. *The State and the Economy Under Capitalism*. Chicago: Charwood.

Wildavsky, Aaron. 1975. *Budgeting: A Comparative Theory of the Budgetary Process*. Boston: Little, Brown.

4 Case Interdependence and Non-Activity in Response to Pressures for Activity
Klaus Armingeon

INTRODUCTION

The purpose of this paper is to draw attention to two substantial problems in the comparative analysis of government activities which are frequently ignored in most international comparisons of public policy. Most comparative analyses are based implicitly or explicitly on one or the other of the following assumptions: that the cases being compared, national political systems and national policy-making, are independent; or that governments, when pressured to produce policies, typically respond. Drawing on a comparative study of procedural regulation of collective labour relations (Armingeon 1994), it will be argued that cases are not independent and that pressure for government activity is a necessary but not sufficient condition for government activity.

CASE INTERDEPENDENCE

Research Question and Hypotheses

Research on the determinants of the structure of labour relations has focused on domestic problems and structures: the level of economic development, the strength of antagonistic social classes and their confrontation, or the distribution of power resources among political parties (Dabscheck 1989; Giles 1989; Schmidt 1993). However, for a long time the thesis has been put forward that a country's position in the international system determines, or at least has some influence on, its domestic policies and institutions (Almond 1990; Gourevitch 1978; Kohler-Koch 1991). More specifically, several recent analyses have demonstrated a strong impact of the international economic system on domestic industrial relations

(Cameron 1978, 1985; Castles 1988; Czada 1988; Gourevitch 1986; Katzenstein 1985).

Our main research question focuses on the extent to which a country's economic vulnerability, due to its integration in the world market, determines its regulation of collective labour relations. Drawing on the analyses of Katzenstein and Castles, the central hypothesis posits that countries with higher levels of economic vulnerability are more likely to develop regulations of collective labour relations which are least detrimental to the competitive position of their national industry in the world market. In this context one of the most important sources of danger, on which the present analysis focuses, is the regulation of the conflicts between organised labour and capital.

The economic vulnerability of a country is largely a function of the size of the domestic market. Small countries are more dependent on external trade. There is an inverse relation between population size and external trade as measured as a share of the gross domestic product. Even when small countries pursue a protectionist policy, thereby restricting their volume of external trade (as have Australia and New Zealand for example for most of this century), they remain vulnerable since their economic fate is dependent on the price relations between a small number of resource-intensive exports and vital raw materials that must be imported (Castles 1988). Small nations, furthermore, are less able to influence developments in the world market. Additionally, their export industries are often highly concentrated and specialised. It is commonly difficult for the industries producing for the domestic market to compensate for the effects originating in the world market, which are imported and reinforced by the large, specialised and concentrated export sector (Czada 1988).

In principle there seem to be two ways in which capital–labour relations may be regulated so as to reduce the dangers of decreasing international competitiveness. The first way is repression. However, this is incompatible with the values of pluralistic democracies, though it has been justified under early liberal values, such as those underlying the French *Loi Le Chapelier* of 1791 (Reynaud 1975) or the British Combination Acts of 1799/1800 (Orth 1991). In addition to such normative reasons, complete repression rarely succeeds, and the social and political disadvantages usually outweigh the economic benefits (see Jacobs 1986).

The second way is through inclusion. In this case trade unions are incorporated into economic policy-making. The aim here is to regulate distributional conflicts in such a way that there will be neither wage-push inflation, costly strikes and lock-outs, nor rigidities in adapting to new production requirements. A typical means of such inclusion is the creation of corporatist structures. In countries in which corporatism is not feasible owing to organisational or other conditions, a second-best solution exists in the form of compulsory arbitration schemes, as in Australia and New Zealand. The price to be paid for such types of regulation of class conflict is high for those who, for economic or political reasons, are adversaries of the labour movement. The price is an encompassing and institutional support of trade union organisation and policies.

In accordance with the hypothesis, the likelihood of regulation supporting trade unions decreases with the size of the home market. The hypothesis is tested from an international and historical perspective. The regulation of labour relations is examined in twenty-one countries. Totalitarian and dictatorial regimes are excluded in which the collective representation of labour independently of the state is constitutionally not permitted – for example, the Nazi regime in Germany, the Fascist regime in Italy, Spain under Franco and Portugal under Salazar.

The dependent variables are the forms of regulation of collective labour relations. The central indicators are the (generally written) collective agreements and the laws establishing formal procedures. The regulation of labour relations by means of procedural rules is intended to lead to institutions that are stable over time. It is therefore reasonable to examine the political decisions regarding procedural rules which retain their fundamental character over a longer period, and which substantially influence the nature of the system.

We concentrate in particular on two such decisions. The first concerns the demand on the part of labour for the freedom to organise. In all countries included here this demand was answered with rights – not only the right of association, i.e. to form trade unions, but also the right to combine, i.e. to exert legal collective pressure on employers in the attempt to win concessions from them.

The second type of decision examined is that which led to establishing the basic rules of collective labour relations as they existed for most of the time in the period 1945–90.

Competing perspectives see no systematic relationship between these variables, but instead trace international decisions regarding systems of collective labour relations to three clusters of determinants. The first, cast in terms of the level of economic and technological modernisation of a country, argues that modernisation causes varying systems of labour relations to converge – this is the position of systems-theoretical analysts such as Dunlop and Kerr (Kerr *et al.* 1962; Kerr 1983). The second, defined in terms of class conflicts, posits that the regulation of labour relations reflects the relative strength of the adversaries (Korsch 1972). The third, the 'democratic class conflict' (Lipset 1985), focuses on the relative strength and conflict between bourgeois and working-class parties in parliament (Korpi 1983).

Institutional Responses to Union Organisation of the Labour Force

The right of workers to organise into independent trade unions and exert pressure, generally through strikes, on employers belongs to the institutional core of modern pluralist democracies (Dahl 1971). Table 4.1 shows for each country the year in which the right of association was introduced (and after which it was maintained for at least ten years). In many countries this original introduction of the right of association came only after a long period during which trade unions were merely tolerated. Although the formation of trade unions was in principle permitted, they were prevented in a number of ways from actually confronting employers. It was

Table 4.1   Year of First Introduction of the Right of Association and the Right to Combine

Country	Right of association	Right to combine
Australia	1876	1876
Austria	1870	1918
Belgium	1866	1921
Canada	1872	1934
Denmark	1849	1849
Finland	1879	1919
France	1884	1884
Germany	1871	1918
Great Britain	1824	1875
Greece	1864	1982
Italy	1890	1890
Japan	1926	1945
Netherlands	1848	1872
New Zealand	1878	1878
Norway	1839	1839
Portugal	1891	1910
Spain	1887	1909
Sweden	1846	1864
Switzerland	1848	1848
USA	1842	1932

Source: Armingeon 1994.

only at the time indicated in Table 4.1 that the freedom to pursue collective interests by the workers was extended to include the use of legal means for applying pressure.

Why did the time vary so widely for the introduction of the right of association? In terms of modernisation theory (Kerr *et al.* 1962) the answer lies in differences regarding the process of industrialisation in the various countries: the recognition of trade union rights became unavoidable at a certain level of industrialisation. This would mean that the differences which are so evident in Table 4.1 would disappear if one were to substitute indicators of the level of industrialisation for year. However, using the relative level of occupation in the secondary and tertiary sectors as an indicator for economic modernisation at the time of introduction of the right to combine, the differences even grow larger (Armingeon 1994: Table 3.2) .

Similar views are often expressed regarding political mobilisation (Hepple 1986) – the nearer a country approaches democracy, the more likely it is to introduce the right of association. Data on indicators for the level of democratisation (at the time of introduction of the right to combine) demonstrate that this view is also without empirical basis (Armingeon 1994: Table 3.3).

The timing of the introduction also cannot be explained in terms of the status of class conflict. Regarding the introduction of tolerance for trade unions in England in 1825, Marx observed: 'The terrible laws against association fell before the threatening stance of the proletariat.... Only grudgingly and under pressure from the masses did the English Parliament dispense with the laws against strikes and trade unions, although it had, itself, for five centuries represented with shameless egoism a permanent trade union of capitalists against the workers' (1974: 768–9). If we transfer this hypothesis to the introduction of the right of association, there are three possible operationalisations for 'pressure of the masses': great industrial conflict, trade union mobilisation of the labour force and political mobilisation of the labour force. The database for frequency and scale of strike activity is too modest for the period of early industrialisation and the introduction of the right of association to permit a systematic analysis. However, there is substantial evidence against the view that a strike movement forced the introduction; genuinely powerful trade unions were uncommon, and participation in strikes was associated with considerable personal risks owing to statutory penalties and the threatened loss of employment. Data on trade union and political mobilisation (at the time of the introduction of the right to combine) show that the introduction of the right of association cannot consistently be seen as the result of worker mobilisation. In only 60 per cent of cases was there a nationally organised workers' party at the time that free collective labour relations were introduced; in only 50 per cent was there an organised trade union movement; and in only one-third was there a workers' party represented in parliament at the time that the reform was passed (Armingeon 1994: Table 3.4).

The fact that the socialist left was represented in parliament in only one-third of the countries at the time of the introduction of the right of association is also inconsistent with the thesis of democratic class conflict. In only a small minority of countries (Belgium, Germany, Austria, and Greece in 1982) was the reform the product of a government in which socialist parties participated.

On the other hand, the vulnerability thesis does possess some explanatory power regarding differences in the timing of the reform. There is a strong correlation between the year of the reform and the nation's population size in that year ($r = .52$ with population size in logarithmic form). The explanatory power increases even further when one considers additionally certain relationships between the political distribution of power and state policies – or, more specifically, various forms of resistance on the part of the ruling elites against the associational demands of the workers. Four groups of countries are distinguished below, in descending order in terms of the respective power of the resistance. In the first group are countries in which trade unions were seen as a threat to the political order, for example Germany, Austria and Japan. In the second are countries in which trade unions were seen not as a threat to the political order but merely as, in an early liberal sense, a threat to free markets. The resistance to workers' demands for the right to association were expressed less by administrative elites than by political parties representing the interests of the bourgeoisie. The third group consists of countries in which, as in the second group, the proscription of trade unions was based upon a liberal-economic rationale, but in which the bourgeoisie was politically not well organised. (In contrast to the second group, more than two bourgeois political parties received over 5 per cent of the national parliamentary seats.) The final group of countries are those in which the right of association was enacted before the bourgeoisie had organised itself into political parties which could have ensured that trade unions be proscribed.

Table 4.2 presents data on population size and the strength of the resistance to lifting the ban on workers' associations. There is a strong relationship between this resistance and the independent variable (Kendall's tau-b −0.61). These two factors, national economic vulnerability and bourgeois resistance to trade unions, can explain a substantial amount of the variance

Table 4.2   Population Size in Millions and Strength of Resistance at the Year of First Introduction of the Right to Combine

Country	Population size	Strength of resistance
Australia	2.7	4
Austria	6.4	1
Belgium	7.6	2
Canada	11.4	2
Denmark	1.4	4
Finland	3.1	1
France	37.5	2
Germany	59.9	1
Great Britain	29.2	2
Greece	10.0	1
Italy	30.2	4
Japan	83.7	1
Netherlands	3.6	3
New Zealand	0.4	4
Norway	1.4	4
Portugal	5.9	2
Spain	20.0	3
Sweden	4.0	4
Switzerland	4.0	3
USA	122.2	2

(over 50 per cent) in the timing of the introduction of the right of association.

The Decision on the Structure of Collective Labour Relations

In this section we consider the question of which variables explain the different types of regulation of collective labour relations in the period since the Second World War. The categories are based on the procedural rules which existed for at least half of the period, and which were of a fundamental nature for the system of labour relations. Table 4.3 shows the year of their establishment, a short description of the type of regulation and the assignment to one of the three types.

In type 3, trade unions have substantial power and a strong institutional base. Ideal-typically, this results from either centralist-corporatist structures or state-mandated compulsory arbitration. In both cases the trade

Table 4.3 Major Regulations of Collective Labour Relations, 1945–90

Country	Type	Rule(s)
Australia	3	1904 Commonwealth Conciliation and Arbitration Act.
Austria	3	since 1945 partial restitution of rules of first republic with regard to chambers, works councillors and collective agreements. Foundation of economic commission and parity commission.
Belgium	3	implemented since 1945: Pact of Social Solidarity.
Canada	1	since 1945 transfer of core elements of the National Labor Relations Act of the USA; initially on federal and later on province level.
Denmark	3	1899 September Agreement/1936 Standard rules for negotiating collective agreements.
Finland	3	1940/44 January Agreement and follow ups.
France	2	since 1945 partial restitution of rules of Third Republic/since 1950 encompassing restitutions of rules of Third Republic.
Germany	2	1949 Act on collective agreements/1951 Act on Co-Determination in certain industries/1952 Works Constitution Act.
Great Britain	1	1871/75 Trade Union/Conspirations and Protection of Property Act.
Ireland	2	1941/42 Trade Unions Acts/1946 Industrial Relations Act.
Italy	2	1947 Constitution.
Japan	1	since 1945 transfer of core elements of the National Labor Relations Act of the USA.
Netherlands	3	implemented since 1945: Foundation of Labour; Social-Economic Council.
New Zealand	3	1894 Industrial Conciliation and Arbitration Act.
Norway	3	1935 Main agreement.
Sweden	3	1938 Agreement of Saltsjöbaden.
Switzerland	3	1937 Peace Agreement, solidarity constitutions, 1941 possibility of declaration of collective agreements as generally binding.
USA	1	1935/47 National Labor Relations Act/Labor–Management Relations Act.

unions are able to determine in principle the working conditions for the great majority of workers without having to mobilise their members. In corporatist systems this operates by the threat of strike or the possibility of withdrawal of the general rejection of strikes (Switzerland). In compulsory arbitration systems, arbiters, after hearing the arguments of both sides, must arrive at a judgement that is considered fair by both sides (this ruling then applies not only to trade union members but to all workers).

Type 1 represents the model of 'voluntarism', in which the trade unions are neither protected by statute nor comprehensively supervised. The political clout of the trade union is a function almost exclusively of its ability to mobilise in the face of resistance from its adversaries. The ability to mobilise depends strongly upon general economic conditions.

The system represented by type 2 can be referred to as one of paternalism. It differs from voluntarism in that there is the extensive statutory regulation of labour relations, which, in contrast to type 3, does not lead to especially strong support for the trade unions.

The class-conflict view regards the form of regulation as a consequence of the extraparliamentary balance of power between capital and labour. That of the democratic class conflict looks, rather, to the balance of power in parliament and government to explain differences in the dependent variable. And finally, proponents of the vulnerability thesis maintain that the probability of rules being enacted that are favourable to labour decreases with the size of the country. As an indicator for the extraparliamentary balance of power, we took the approach of Korpi (1983) and examined the percentage of non-agricultural workers who were trade union members. Data for the average proportion of votes obtained by left-wing parties were taken, as proposed by Crouch (1990) and Korpi (1983), to assess the parliamentary balance of power. And finally, the political composition of the government was measured using an ordinal scale developed by Schmidt (1982); this extends from bourgeois hegemony and bourgeois dominance to stalemate in the middle to socialist dominance and socialist hegemony.

The results of correlation analyses can be summarised as follows. With the exception of trade union membership, there was a strong relationship in the expected direction between the dependent and independent variables. This was especially the case with government composition and size of the country. The hypotheses have also been tested in a configurative analysis, using each case of a decision and comparing it for compatibility against each of the hypotheses. Table 4.4 presents the comparison in the form of a truth table. Here the value '1' represents compatibility with the hypothesis, '0' incompatibility, and a question mark indicates strong

Table 4.4   Truth Table for Distribution of Power Resources and for Vulnerability Hypotheses

Country	Distribution of power hypothesis	Vulnerability hypothesis
Australia	?	1
Austria	1	1
Belgium	?	1
Canada	1	1
Denmark	?	1
Finland	0	1
France	1	1
Germany	1	1
Great Britain	1	1
Ireland	1	0
Italy	1	1
Japan	1	1
Netherlands	0	1
New Zealand	0	1
Norway	?	1
Sweden	?	1
Switzerland	0	1
USA	1	1

doubts about compatibility. The figures in Table 4.4 demonstrate the greater explanatory power in general of the vulnerability hypothesis regarding decisions taken in labour relations during the post-war period, in comparison with the hypothesis on political balance of power.

POOR RESPONSIVENESS

Research Questions and Hypotheses

In comparative analyses of public policies two competing explanations for policy change are usually proposed. According to the first, found in both Marxist and pluralist writings, public policy is a result of the specific distribution of political power. The second explanation, which may be called the functionalist approach, focuses on constraints and pressing problems. Functional requirements narrow the room of manoeuvre for political actors to such a degree that no substantial policy alternatives are left. For example, Wilensky (1975) holds that an increase in the proportion of elderly in a society forces an expansion in welfare state expenditures.

Although the two approaches are mutually antagonistic in many respects, they share one basic assumption. This states that changing problems, constraints or power distributions transform a theme into an issue, which then appears on the agenda of politics and afterwards becomes transformed into an appropriate policy. This assumption will be challenged in the following on the basis of the larger study on the procedural rules of labour relations.

The theoretical arguments for the central hypotheses of this section come from rational choice theory and neo-institutionalism. Elster (1979) has proposed a two-step model of (political) action, involving two filters in sequence. The first consists of structural constraints allowing only a limited number of options. The second is the mechanism that singles out which options of the feasible set shall be realised. In most or in the most important cases this filtering process is based on rational choice. Though there are often cases in which rationality is unimportant, absent or unstable, Elster argues that there is a hard core of important cases where the rational choice model is indispensable.

Even in this model, the basic assumption is that something happens as soon as the alternatives are defined. Recent research based on neo-institutionalist thinking casts some doubt on this (March and Olsen 1989; Kingdon 1984). Several characteristics of political systems can, however, impede the modification or creation of policy.

First, desirable rule changes may be associated with disadvantages and considerable risks. Therefore there may be good reason for supporting a second- or third-best policy, because pursuit of the 'best' policy has associated risks and disadvantages which outweigh the possible advantages.

Second, if a single actor wants to change a policy and if a consensual solution is not feasible, the actor must be able to force it through against other actors. In industrial relations there are at least three structural aspects which might impede reform: (1) If the legislative competence in collective labour relations is divided between federal and state institutions, the chance to bring about successful reforms at the federal level depends on state policies which do not offset federal reforms. (2) If interest organisations and political parties are integrated into institutions of cooperative decision-making, as in the case of corporatist systems, enacting a reform against the will of the other actors is not compatible with that particular form of decision-making. (3) If the party system is highly fragmented, and there is no major anti-labour party, these chances for major reforms of labour relations in the interest of either capital or labour are severely restricted.

Third, even if an actor could succeed in changing policy through conflictual politics, he must evaluate whether the gains of the new policy outweigh the costs, such as the distortion of previously cooperative politics. For example, there often have been majorities for radical policies for one or the other side of industries, which have not been pursued because actors do not wish to endanger the long-term benefits of cooperation for the short-term gains of majority decisions.

Owing to the institutional characteristics of the political system, it may be rare in many circumstances for a problem to become an issue and to be solved, even if it is pressing and obvious, and even if, according to the majority of rational observers, it needs solutions. Empirical evidence for the central hypothesis of this section is provided in two steps. In the first step it will be demonstrated that pressing and obvious problems or changing political power distributions rarely lead to successful political attempts to solve these problems. In the second step it will be shown that policy change is most likely if political power is centralised, and if decision-making does not follow a cooperative mode.

Pressing Problems, Severe Restrictions and Changing Power Distributions

Apart from national catastrophes, such as a collapse of the whole political system or war, the literature on policy change in industrial relations lists at least four conditions held to be conducive to major changes of the set of procedural rules of labour relations: a major change in the political complexion of an in-coming government; the long-lasting incumbency of a political party; extensive industrial conflict; and major economic crises.

The first pair of hypotheses stems from the research on party differences and public policies (Castles 1982; Schmidt 1982; Korpi 1983; Powell 1982). The hypothesis about major industrial unrest and policy changes has been put forward in two different theoretical contexts. On the one hand, strikes can be seen as an indicator of worker mobilisation which forces bourgeois elites to concessions (Goldfield 1989) – a view corresponding to the idea that policies result from organised and conflicting social and political interests. On the other hand, in a functionalist vein, labour unrest can be seen as 'symptomatic of a malfunctioning industrial relations system and as a sign of the need of reform' (Doeringer 1981). There are two alternative interpretations of the relationship between economic crises and policy change in labour relations. According to

Gourevitch (1986), crises open the system of relationships among societal and political actors, making politics and policies more fluid. In this new constellation of actors an institutional resolution is reached, closing the system for a time, until the next crisis. From a functionalist perspective, in major economic crises there is urgent need for change, to which the system of labour relations must adapt (Dunlop 1958).

The main results from tests of these hypotheses, detailed in Armingeon (1994), are:

- Most of the changes of governments were not accompanied by reform of the rules of industrial relations. In some exceptional cases, however, there is strong evidence that a change in the partisan composition of government does cause reform.
- Most of the time of socialist office-holding elapsed without pro-labour reforms. Certain reforms are, however, clearly linked to socialist governments – this applies in particular to co-determination laws.
- Most of the periods in which there were large strikes were not followed by major reforms of the rules of industrial relations. However, some of the reforms were caused by great strikes and lock-outs.
- In most countries economic crises did not give rise to reforms in labour relations. However, in some countries reforms occurred owing to the hard economic times.

The simple and obvious conclusion from these findings is that all such events are not determinants but opportunities for reform. In most cases, these chances either are not or cannot be used. If they are used, there must be some additional preconditions which transform the opportunities into action.

One objection that could be raised to this conclusion concerns the conditions of reform. There could be several paths to policy change, with each dependent on a particular combination of favourable conditions. This multiple conjunctural causation (Ragin 1987) might explain the rare occurrence of reform given a change of government, a major strike or a major economic crisis. For this reason a truth table was constructed listing all the reforms under consideration and examining each to identify which event caused or contributed to the reform (Table 4.5). In addition to the four independent variables (change of government, imprint of incumbency, industrial unrest, economic crisis) this analysis was complemented by the test of whether a policy change was a result of a change of the entire political system (from democracy to non-democracy or vice versa) or of world wars.

Table 4.5 demonstrates that in some cases reform was the result of the combination of conditions while in other cases one condition was

Table 4.5 Truth Table of Labour Reforms by Transition of Political System, World War, International Economic Crisis, Change of Government, Industrial Conflict and Incumbency of Socialist Party

Country	Year of reform	Tran- sition of political system	World war	Intern. econ- omic crisis	Changing composi- tion of government	Great indust. conflict	Incumbency of socialist party
Aa	1917	0	1	0	0	0	0
Aa	1918–20	1	1	0	0	1	1
Aa	1934	1	0	0	0	0	0
Aa	1945	1	0	0	0	0	1
Aa	1947–57	0	0	0	0	0	1
Aa	1973	0	0	0	0	0	1
Aus	1890–04	0	0	0	0	1	0
Aus	1930	0	0	0	1	1	1
Aus	1988	0	0	1	0	0	1
B	1921	0	1	0	1	1	1
B	1936	0	0	1	0	1	1
B	1940	1	0	0	0	0	0
B	1945ff.	1	1	0	0	0	0
B	1960	0	0	0	0	0	0
B	1968	0	0	0	0	0	1
B	1970ff.	0	0	0	0	1	1
B	1975ff.	0	0	1	0	0	0
C	1944	0	1	0	0	1	0
D	1899	0	0	0	0	1	0
D	1908–10	0	0	0	0	1	0
D	1936	0	0	0	0	0	1
D	1936	0	0	0	0	0	1
D	1940	1	0	0	0	0	0
D	1945	1	0	0	0	0	1
D	1947	0	0	0	0	0	0
D	1970	0	0	0	0	0	0
D	1973	0	0	0	1	1	1
Fn	1922	1	0	0	0	0	0
Fn	1924	1	0	0	0	0	0
Fn	1925	1	0	0	0	0	0
Fn	1931	0	0	0	0	0	0
Fn	1940–46	0	1	0	0	0	1
Fn	1968	0	0	0	0	0	1
Fn	1969	0	0	0	0	0	1
Fn	1978	0	0	0	0	0	1
Fr	1892	0	0	0	0	1	0
Fr	1919–20	0	0	0	0	1	0
Fr	1936	0	0	1	1	1	1

Table 4.5   Continued

Country	Year of reform	Transition of political system	World war	Intern. economic crisis	Changing composition of government	Great indust. conflict	Incumbency of socialist party
Fr	1940	1	0	0	0	0	0
Fr	1945	1	0	0	0	0	1
Fr	1950	1	0	0	0	0	1
Fr	1968	0	0	0	0	1	0
Fr	1971	0	0	0	0	1	0
Fr	1982	0	0	1	1	0	1
Gm	1916–20	1	1	0	0	1	1
Gm	1923	0	0	0	0	0	1
Gm	1924	0	0	0	0	0	0
Gm	1933ff.	1	0	0	0	0	0
Gm	1945–52	1	0	0	0	0	0
Gm	1972–76	0	0	0	1	0	1
GB	1906	0	0	0	0	0	0
GB	1913	0	0	0	0	0	1
GB	1918–19	0	1	0	0	0	0
GB	1927	0	0	0	0	1	0
GB	1945	0	0	0	1	0	1
GB	1971	0	0	0	1	0	0
GB	1974	0	0	0	1	0	1
GB	1975	0	0	0	0	0	1
GB	1980–88	0	0	1	1	0	0
Gr	1982	1	0	0	1	0	1
Gr	1988	0	0	0	0	0	1
It	1893	0	0	0	0	1	0
It	1922	1	0	0	0	0	0
It	1946–47	1	0	0	0	0	1
It	1962	0	0	0	0	0	0
It	1970	0	0	0	0	1	1
Ir	1922–37	1	0	0	0	0	0
Ir	1941–42	0	0	0	0	1	0
Ir	1942–46	0	1	0	0	0	0
J	1945–49	1	0	0	0	0	0
Ne	1914	0	1	0	0	0	0
Ne	1919	0	1	0	0	0	0
Ne	1923	0	0	0	0	0	0
Ne	1927	0	0	0	0	0	0
Ne	1933	0	0	1	0	0	0
Ne	1937	0	0	1	0	0	0
Ne	1940	1	0	0	0	0	0

Table 4.5 Continued

Country	Year of reform	Transition of political system	World war	Intern. economic crisis	Changing composition of government	Great indust. conflict	Incumbency of socialist party
Ne	1945–50	1	1	0	0	0	1
Ne	1970	0	0	0	0	0	0
Ne	1971	0	0	0	0	0	0
NZ	1894	0	0	0	0	1	0
NZ	1913	0	0	0	0	1	0
NZ	1932	0	0	1	0	0	0
NZ	1936	0	0	0	1	0	1
NZ	1937	0	0	0	0	0	1
NZ	1973	0	0	0	0	1	1
NZ	1983	0	0	1	0	0	0
NZ	1984	0	0	1	1	0	1
NZ	1985	0	0	0	1	0	1
NZ	1987	0	0	1	1	0	1
Nr	1902	0	0	0	0	1	0
Nr	1915	0	0	0	0	1	0
Nr	1916	0	1	0	0	1	0
Nr	1922	0	0	0	0	1	0
Nr	1923	0	0	0	0	0	0
Nr	1927	0	0	0	0	0	0
Nr	1929	0	0	0	0	0	0
Nr	1935	0	0	1	1	1	1
Nr	1940	1	0	0	0	0	0
Nr	1945	1	0	0	0	0	1
Nr	1952	0	0	0	0	0	0
Nr	1972	0	0	0	0	0	0
P	1976	1	0	0	0	0	1
P	1977	1	0	0	0	0	1
P	1979	1	0	0	0	0	0
P	1984	0	0	0	0	0	1
Sp	1923	1	0	0	0	0	0
Sp	1931	1	0	0	0	0	1
Sp	1936	1	0	0	0	0	0
Sp	1962ff.	0	0	0	0	0	0
Sp	1977–78	1	0	0	0	0	1
Sp	1980	1	0	0	0	0	0
Sp	1985	1	0	0	0	0	1
Sn	1906	0	0	0	0	1	0
Sn	1920	0	0	0	1	0	1
Sn	1928	0	0	0	0	0	0

Table 4.5   Continued

Country	Year of reform	Tran- sition of political system	World war	Intern. econ- omic crisis	Changing composi- tion of government	Great indust. conflict	Incumbency of socialist party
Sn	1936	0	0	1	1	0	1
Sn	1938	0	0	1	1	0	1
Sn	1946	0	0	0	0	0	1
Sn	1972–76	0	0	0	0	1	1
Sn	1983	0	0	0	1	0	1
Sw	1911	0	0	0	0	0	0
Sw	1937	0	0	1	0	0	0
Sw	1941	0	1	0	0	0	0
Sw	1956	0	1	0	0	0	1
Sw	1956	0	0	0	0	0	1
USA	1933–35	0	0	1	0	1	0
USA	1947	0	0	0	0	0	0
USA	1959	0	0	0	0	0	0
Total		34	15	17	20·	31	56

Source: Armingeon 1994
Aa = Austria, Aus = Australia, B = Belgium, C = Canada, D = Denmark, Fn = Finland, Fr = France, Gm = Germany, GB = Great Britain, Gr = Greece, It = Italy, Ir = Ireland, J = Japan, Ne = Netherlands, NZ = New Zealand, Nr = Norway, P = Portugal, Sp = Spain, Sn = Sweden, Sw = Switzerland, USA = United States.

sufficient for the resulting reform. Hence the question arises under what conditions the likelihood of the use of one of these opportunities increases.

Institutional Inertia and Structural Opportunities for Reform

The development of the system of procedural rules of industrial relations in each of the countries under consideration was shaped by basic decisions that were taken at critical junctures and that here remained stable for a long time afterwards. Examples include the basic decisions at the end of the German Empire and at the beginning of the Weimar Republic which were reinstated after the Second World War and which have remained in effect. Other examples are the Wagner Act in the United States and its counterpart in Canada, or the historical compromises in Denmark (1899),

Norway (1935), Sweden (1938) and Switzerland (1937). Though there have been more or less important reforms after these basic decisions, in most cases these have changed the route of development but not the general direction.

These observations are in accordance with the hypothesis of institutional inertia. The large public and private organisations of the labour market have over time invested considerable human, organisational and financial resources in a given set of rules and are therefore very reluctant to support a complete break with the past system of rules – even if this has long constituted a part of their programme. For example, the German trade unions bitterly fought the Works Constitution Act of 1952. When they had the chance to bring about a break with the old system of rules, when the first Social Democratic led government came to power in 1972, they were content with reforms which maintained the basis of that law. Or again, a Christian-Democratic government extended a law on co-determination (inaugurated in 1951) in the coal and steel industry even though the governing parties were critical towards co-determination and neither of the two supporting organisations, the trade unions and the Social Democratic Party, had the power to mobilise effectively in favour of the law. Moreover, in cases when governments eventually have been able to break with the past, as in Great Britain in 1979–90, the laws were barely used by the employers for whom they were made (Marsh 1992).

Although there has been a remarkable stability in the system of procedural rules of industrial relations in all the countries under consideration, countries differ with regard to the frequency and impact of 'second-order' reforms after the historical basic decisions. These reforms may be induced by pressing problems (for example France and Italy 1968–69), or they may represent merely codifications of long-standing practices or advancement of previous rules (for example Switzerland 1956). A third type of reform can occur owing to changed competition in the party system. With respect to this type of reform the guiding proposition of this paper is that changes occur particularly when the actors are not interlocked through federal structures, corporatism or party systems, in which class cleavage is accompanied or superseded by other cleavages.

Table 4.6 contains data on the number and type of reforms after the historical basic decisions by country. These data are in accordance with the predictions. There are only two countries, Great Britain and New Zealand, which have a substantial number of reforms related to political competition. Both countries are unitary, non-corporatist, and have party systems exclusively structured by class cleavage. In the other countries one or more of these conditions is absent.

Table 4.6   Major Reforms after the Historical Basic Decisions

Country	Total no. of reforms	Reforms due to party competition	Reforms due to pressing problems	Reforms as codification of custom or advancement of previous legislation
Australia	2	1	1	0
Austria	1	0	0	1
Belgium	4	0	2	2
Canada	0	0	0	0
Denmark	3	0	1	2
Finland	3	1	0	2
France	3	1	2	0
Germany, FR	1	1	0	0
Great Britain	9	6	2	1
Greece	1	0	0	1
Ireland	0	0	0	0
Italy	2	0	1	1
Japan	1	0	0	1
Netherlands	2	0	2	0
New Zealand	9	5	3	0
Norway	2	0	1	1
Portugal	1	0	0	1
Spain	2	0	0	2
Sweden	3	1	1	1
Switzerland	3	0	1	2
USA	2	0	0	2

Source: Armingeon 1994.

CONCLUSION

The main results of this analysis are that national political systems are not independent in domestic policy-making and that functional requirements or shifting distributions of political power are necessary but not sufficient conditions for government activity. These results, though based on a comparative study of the political regulation of collective labour relations, can be generalised to other policy areas provided the political and socio-economic framework of policy-making is similar. This seems to apply in various policy areas, such as industrial policy or social security.

Two remedies for the methodological problems emphasised by this paper are obvious but hardly sufficient: statistical control of exogenous factors and additional variables for constellations of actors. In the case of exogenous factors the major problem is the operationalisation of the theoretical variable. National societies make up and are actors in an international system which in turn has an impact on the options available to national political systems in domestic policy-making. In the case of labour relations it was argued that the most important aspect of this international integration was economic vulnerability. This was measured as the size of the domestic market, which in turn was measured as size of population. The number of people living in one country, however, is a crude and simplified proxy for vulnerability. As soon as the theoretical variable becomes more complex, such auxiliary operationalisations become entirely inappropriate. Hence a better theoretical understanding of the nature and impact of the exogenous factors on domestic policy-making is needed. This would allow more satisfactory, and probably more complex, operationalisations.

Institutions are an intervening variable between pressures for change and policy-making. Hence it is inappropriate to add indicators for institutional arrangements as independent variables on the same theoretical plane as the other independent variables. Rather we are forced to differentiate between sub-groups (for example between consociational, corporatist, majoritarian and pure pluralist democracies) and to analyse policy-making by group. This, however, would shift the methodological approach in comparative policy analysis from a variable-oriented to a case-oriented approach (Ragin 1987).

REFERENCES

Almond, Gabriel A. 1990. 'The International–National Connection.' In *A Discipline Divided. Schools and Sects in Political Science*, ed. Gabriel A. Almond. London: Sage.

Armingeon, Klaus. 1994. *Staat und Arbeitsbeziehungen. Ein internationaler Vergleich*. Opladen: Westdeutscher Verlag.

Cameron, David R. 1978. 'The Expansion of the Public Economy: A Comparative Analysis.' *American Political Science Review* 72: 1243–61.

Cameron, David R. 1985. 'Does Government Cause Inflation? Taxes, Spending, and Deficits.' In *The Politics of Inflation and Economic Stagnation. Theoretical Approach and International Case Studies*, eds Leon N. Lindberg and Charles S. Maier. Washington DC: Brookings.

Castles, F., ed. 1982. *The Impact of Parties*. London: Sage.

Castles, Francis G. 1988. 'Social Protection by Other Means: Australia's Strategy of Coping with External Vulnerability.' In *The Comparative History of Public Policy*, ed. Francis G. Castles. Cambridge: Basil Blackwell.

Crouch, Colin. 1990. 'Generalized Political Exchange in Industrial Relations in Europe during the Twentieth Century.' In *Governance and Generalized*

Exchange. Self-Organizing Policy Networks in Action, ed. Bernd Marin. Boulder: Westview.

Czada, Roland. 1988. 'Bestimmungsfaktoren und Genese politischer Gewerkschaftseinbindung.' In *Staatstätigkeit. International und historisch vergleichende Analysen*, ed. Manfred G. Schmidt. Opladen: Westdeutscher Verlag.

Dabscheck, Braham. 1989. 'A Survey of Theories of Industrial Relations.' In *Theories and Concepts in Comparative Industrial Relations*, eds Jack Barbash and Kate Barbash. Columbia: University of South Carolina Press.

Dahl, Robert A. 1971. *Poliarchy: Participation and Opposition*. New Haven: Yale University Press.

Doeringer, Peter B. 1981. 'Industrial Relations Research in International Perspective.' In *International Relations in International Perspective: Essays on Research and Policy*, ed. Peter B. Doeringer. London: Macmillan.

Dunlop, John T. 1958. *Industrial Relations Systems*. New York: Holt.

Elster, Jon. 1979. *Ulysses and the Sirens: Studies in Rationality and Irrationality*. Cambridge: Cambridge University Press.

Giles, Anthony. 1989. 'Industrial Relations Theory, the State, and Politics.' In *Theories and Concepts in Comparative Industrial Relations*, eds Jack Barbash and Kate Barbash. Columbia: University of South Carolina Press.

Goldfield, Michael. 1989. 'Worker Insurgency, Radical Organization, and New Deal Labor Legislation.' *American Political Science Review* 83: 1257–82.

Gourevitch, Peter. 1978. 'The Second Image Reversed: the International Sources of Domestic Politics.' *International Organization* 32: 881–912.

Gourevitch, Peter. 1986. *Politics in Hard Times. Comparative Responses to International Economic Crises*. Ithaca: Cornell University Press.

Hepple, Bob. 1986. 'Introduction.' In *The Making of Labour Law in Europe: A Comparative Study of Nine Countries up to 1945*, ed. Bob Hepple. London: Mansell.

Jacobs, Antoine. 1986. 'Collective Self-Regulation.' In *The Making of Labour Law in Europe. A Comparative Study of Nine Countries up to 1945*, ed. Bob Hepple. London: Mansell.

Katzenstein, Peter J. 1985. *Small States in World Markets: Industrial Policy in Europe*. Ithaca: Cornell University Press.

Katzenstein, Peter J. 1987. *Policy and Politics in West Germany: The Growth of a Semisovereign State*. Philadelphia: Temple.

Kerr, Clark. 1983. *The Future of Industrial Societies: Convergence or Continuing Diversity?* Cambridge, MA: Harvard University Press.

Kerr, Clark, John Dunlop, Frederick H. Harbison and Charles A. Myers. 1962. *Industrialism and Industrial Man: The Problems of Labor and Management in Economic Growth*. London: Heinemann.

Kingdon, John W. 1984. *Agendas, Alternatives, and Public Policies*. Boston: Little, Brown.

Kohler-Koch, Beate. 1991. 'Inselillusion und Interdependenz: Nationales Regieren unter den Bedingungen von "international governance".' In *Die alte Bundesrepublik. Kontinuität und Wandel*, eds Bernhard Blanke and Hellmut Wollmann. Opladen: Westdeutscher Verlag.

Korpi, Walter. 1983. *The Democratic Class Struggle*. London: Routledge & Kegan Paul.

Korsch, Karl. 1972. 'Jus belli ac pacis im Arbeitsrecht (1923).' *Kritische Justiz* 5: 142–9.

Lipset, Seymour M. 1985. *Political Man: The Social Bases of Politics.* Baltimore: Johns Hopkins University Press.

March, James G. and Johan P. Olsen. 1989. *Rediscovering Institutions: The Organizational Basis of Politics.* New York: The Free Press.

Marsh, David. 1992. *The New Politics of British Trade Unionism: Unions' Power and the Thatcher Legacy.* London: Macmillan.

Marx, Karl. 1974. *Das Kapital. Kritik der politischen Ökonomie.* Erster Band (1867), Marx-Engels Werke Bd. 23. Berlin: Dietz.

Orth, John V. 1991. *Combination and Conspiracy. A Legal History of Trade Unionism 1721–1906.* Oxford: Clarendon.

Powell, G. Bingham. 1982. *Contemporary Democracies: Participation, Stability, and Violence.* Cambridge: Harvard University Press.

Ragin, Charles C. 1987. *The Comparative Method: Moving Beyond Qualitative and Quantitative Strategies.* Berkeley: University of California Press.

Reynaud, Jean-Daniel. 1975. *Les syndicats en France.* Paris: Seuil.

Schmidt, Manfred G. 1982. *Wohlfahrtsstaatliche Politik unter bürgerlichen und sozialdemokratischen Regierungen. Ein internationaler Vergleich.* Frankfurt: Campus.

Schmidt, Manfred G. 1993. 'Theorien in der international vergleichenden Staatstätigkeitsforschung.' In *Policy-Analyse. Kritik und Neuorientierung,* ed. Adrienne Héritier. Opladen: Westdeutscher Verlag.

Wilensky, Harold L. 1975. *The Welfare State and Equality. Structural and Ideological Roots of Public Expenditures.* Berkeley: University of California Press.

5 Laws and the Distribution of Power in Society

Vincent Lemieux

INTRODUCTION

Though power has traditionally been considered to be the central concept of political science, it has come to be relatively neglected in the 'new' political science, strongly influenced by economics and more generally by theories of rational choice.

This relative neglect has led some critical questions about government activity to be overlooked. One of the main ones, which will form the focus of this chapter, is the effect of government activity on the structuring and distribution of power in society. Pursuit of this question can usefully be made through the study of laws and other regulatory activities of government.

This approach to the examination of the impact of government activity on the distribution of power through the analysis of laws begs the question of what is power. There is no consensus among social scientists on the definition of power, or influence or control. None of the most widely accepted definitions of these concepts adequately describes the power situation created by the enactment of a law. Take, for example, the well-known definition of influence given by Dahl (1970: 17): 'influence is a relation among actors in which one actor induces other actors to act in some way they would not otherwise act'. Such a definition may be useful for studying the practice of influence on the basis of law, but it is of very limited usefulness for analysing the potential power relationships which are built into laws.

We thus need a more general definition of power, one which is able to encompass the potential as well as the actual power of an actor. In our theoretical and empirical works (Lemieux 1989, 1995), the definition we have used is the following: the power of an actor consists in his capacity, potential or actual, to control the decisions which concern his own resources or those of other actors. Laws can be seen as a set of potential power relations in that laws define 'controllers' and 'controllees' –

70

controllers being those actors who have the capacity to affect resources in their relations with other actors, and controllees being those who do not have this capacity or who are subjected to the operations of control.

Before turning to concrete examples of this power approach to the study of laws, let us first consider the present state of the literature in the field of the legislative activity of government.

THE PRESENT STATE OF THE COMPARATIVE ANALYSIS OF LAWS

Generally speaking, the study of laws as a form of government intervention has received little attention. The field is much less developed than the study of government expenditures, which are more susceptible to standardisation and quantification. In contrast the use of laws for the purpose of comparative analysis often requires lengthy and costly processing and their quantification of content is difficult.

Rose (1984), however, identifies four different aspects of laws which can be submitted to comparative analysis. First, laws regulate government action, or the relationship between government and individuals, or relations between individuals themselves. Second, laws can be meant to control behaviour in a very strict fashion, to authorise or to prohibit certain actions, or to be more permissive. Third, laws can benefit certain groups or grant them certain rights. Finally, the impact of laws on government resources is variable. Some laws require little money and very few material resources whereas other laws, such as those in the fields of education and health services, require enormous amounts of human and financial resources.

Rose's study of the laws adopted by western countries between 1945 and 1975 shows a tendency toward the decline of the annual number of laws. There is no significant difference between the annual average for 'Roman law' and 'Common law' countries. However, within each of these two categories, the annual average varies to some extent from one country to another. (The average is approximately 20 in Switzerland and 50 in Canada at the Federal level, whereas the average is approximately 450 in the United States and nearly 600 in Italy.) Rose also notes the cumulative character of laws in all the countries under study – new laws are added to existing laws, very few of which are ever repealed.

The few comparative analyses which are sketched out in Rose's book are of a very general nature – they deal with laws as a whole, and involve a very high level of aggregation. This high level of aggregation, typical of

most of the comparative analyses which have been done to date, characterises also the work of Pomper (1970) and of Ginsberg (1976), who look
at election platforms and public statutes in order to assess the reliability of
party pledges.

According to Pomper, there are four ways to fulfil the promises made
in election platforms. First there is 'full action' when a law entirely corresponds to one of the elements contained in the election platform.
Second, the fulfilment of a promise can take the form of an action by the
executive, whether it be by the president personally or by other organisations. Third, short of having complete fulfilment, 'similar actions'
related to one of the elements of the platform can be adopted by
Congress or by the executive. Finally, the realisation of an element of the
platform can involve the preservation of the status quo. Pomper identifies
nine major sectors at which laws or government actions can be aimed:
foreign affairs, defence, economics, labour, agriculture, resources,
welfare, government and civil rights. He shows that the correspondence
between election platforms and the actions taken by Congress or by the
executive varies across sectors. Pomper's study has led to similar studies
at the state level. Elling (1979) shows that parties holding a majority at
the state level are less faithful to their election platform than are parties
at the national level, but that loyalty increases with the extent of the
majority.

Ginsberg pays particular attention to critical elections during which
significant reorientation of party options occurs. These reorientations often
arise in response to generational change which leads to voter realignment.
The categories that were used for the analysis of election platforms and
laws are: capitalism, internal sovereignty, redistribution, international
cooperation, universalism (equality of rights and privileges), labour and
ruralism. Like Pomper, Ginsberg wonders if there is a correlation between
election commitments and the actions of a political party after an election.
Unlike Pomper, he restricts his study to laws only. Some 60,000 laws were
enacted by Congress over the 180 years under review from 1729 to 1968.
The analysis shows that, in periods of voter realignment, changes in electoral choices translate into major changes in the content of laws; it also
shows that these changes are more obvious in certain sectors than in
others.

Ginsberg rightly notes that some laws are more important than others,
but it remains very difficult to assess their relative importance – the
methods used by Ginsberg and by Pomper, who restrict themselves to
classifying laws by sector, do not allow one to classify laws according to
their importance.

Influenced by an economic model of politics based on the concepts of cost and benefit, Landry (1990) presents a more disaggregated analysis of laws, based on a content analysis of the abstracts of all public statutes enacted by the Quebec National Assembly between 1960 and 1985, under the governments of three different political parties: the Liberal Party, the *Union nationale* and the *Parti québécois.*

The abstracts, which have an average of thirty lines each, were first divided into propositions of a standard form containing four components: those responsible for the intervention, the connecting verb, the nature of the intervention (cost or benefit), and its target. Take the example of a proposition which states that the Ministry of Health and Social Services may authorise continued benefits from the Quebec health insurance plan for a maximum four-month period for a person who moves to another province where such a plan does not exist. The organisation responsible is the *Ministry*, the connecting verb is *authorise*, the nature of the intervention consists of the *benefits related to health insurance* and the target is the *person who meets the stated requirements.*

Landry is more concerned with the costs and benefits and with the target of the intervention than with those responsible or with the connecting verb. A distinction is made between divisible and indivisible benefits and between excludable and nonexcludable benefits. Thus there are four types of goods: private goods provide divisible and excludable benefits; public goods provide indivisible and nonexcludable benefits; club goods provide indivisible and excludable benefits; and common pool goods carry divisible and nonexcludable benefits. A fifth category comprises undetermined goods, meaning those goods for which the proposition does not provide sufficient information.

Costs are also categorised as being divisible or indivisible and as being excludable or nonexcludable. Targets are divided into five subcategories: entrepreneurs, workers, owners of other types of production factors, consumers and undetermined. In the example presented above, the people who leave Quebec for another province but remain covered by the Quebec health insurance plan are considered to be consumers. The benefits received are common pool goods, as they are divisible and nonexcludable. The costs are undetermined, since the proposition does not provide any information in that regard.

One of the limitations of such an economic analysis of politics lies in the high proportion of costs and benefits which must be relegated to a residual category because they do not fit any of the other categories.[1] The model of political analysis which we have developed is partly intended to circumvent this problem.

A POWER ANALYSIS OF LAWS

The political analysis we have developed (Lemieux 1991) is different from Landry's model of economic analysis in three important respects. First, it deals with laws in their complete form, not with abstracts provided by the government. Second, it postulates that the outcome of any legislative intervention cannot be restricted to its costs and benefits but refers to a more complex set of issues. A complete typology of these issues, which excludes any residual category, is presented. Third, the analysis takes into account both those who have the capacity to exercise power and those who are submitted to this capacity – in other words, the controllers and the controllees relative to the issues dealt with by laws.

The Approach

As noted earlier, a law can be defined as a web of power relationships in which controllers have the capacity to dominate the controllees on certain issues. These issues, defined in terms of resources, have been divided into six categories. There are: functions, or purposive resources, which refer to specific responsibilities ascribed to an organisation or to an authority by a law; posts, or positional resources, which include organisations as well as the position to which one is appointed; levers, or actional resources, which refer to one's capacity to act; human resources, which are involved, for example, when a law states that an organisation may recruit its own personnel; informational resources, which refer to everything relating to information; and material resources, which include financial resources, and refer, in some respects, to the costs and benefits in the economic analysis of laws.

The actors, who are either controllers or controllees regarding the specific issues involved, were divided into ten categories (and subcategories): political institutions (Parliament, Cabinet); administrative institutions (including the police); autonomous bodies (including the judiciary); subgovernments (municipalities and school boards); public establishments (such as those in the health and welfare sector); trade and professional associations; businesses; voluntary organisations; aggregate groups (such as the electorate, students, beneficiaries); and primary groups (married couples, families).

Our analysis of public laws compared the legislative record of all the governments in Quebec from 1944 to 1985 by examining the power relationship in each of the laws passed by these governments. We were mainly interested in the resources, which are the issues of the relationships, and in the actors, who are the controller or the controllee. If, for example, it is written in a law that the chief electoral officer has to make an annual report to the National Assembly, then information is the issue, a political institution is the controller, and an autonomous body is the controllee. The number of power relationships in a law can vary from zero to many hundreds. For example, there is no power relationship in a very short law which makes an amendment to a former law, but there are a great number of power relationships in a general law bearing on the health and social services in Quebec.

Some General Results

The comparative analysis of the legislative activities of the five governments in Quebec from 1944 to 1985 reveals some permanent features as well as some significant variations.

One element of consistency is the number of laws adopted on an annual basis. The annual averages both of the first *Union nationale* government, from 1944 to 1960, and of the Liberal government, from 1960 to 1966, were 65. When the *Union nationale* returned to power, from 1966 to 1970, the figure was 64. It rose as high as 75 under the second Liberal government, from 1970 to 1976, but reduced to 63 when the *Parti québécois* formed the government, from 1976 to 1985. As opposed to Rose's results, there is no downward trend in the average annual number of laws.

If the number of laws does not change significantly, except for the 1970–76 period, the laws themselves do tend to become increasingly complex over time. Various indicators illustrate this. For example, the percentage of statutes having fewer than ten articles progressively reduces from 80 per cent (1944–60) to 65 per cent (1960–66) to 60 per cent (1966–70) to 50 per cent (1970–76) to 35 per cent (1976–85). A similar analysis can be made of the number of power relationships in each law, the number of issues dealt with, and the variety of actors involved. The rise in complexity is steady from one period to another. For example, the proportion of laws with ten or more power relationships increases from 9 per cent (1944–60) to 20 per cent (1960–65) to 26 per cent (1966–70) to 37 per cent (1970–76) to 50 per cent (1976–85) – the greatest increases coming under the two most reform-minded governments of the period, that of the Liberal Party (1960–66) and that of the *Parti québécois* (1976–85).

Even though every administration has to some extent contributed to this rise in the complexity of laws, the five governments under study differ in other respects. Concerning the major policy areas, the two Liberal governments (1960–66 and 1970–76) attached the most importance to the economic area, to the point of making it their top priority, and to social affairs.[2] The first *Union nationale* government (1944–60) was more preoccupied by governmental matters. The *Parti québécois* government (1976–85), whose aim was to establish a new sovereign state in Quebec, was more concerned by governmental affairs than were the administrations that preceded it since 1960. Finally, during the so-called 'Quiet Revolution' of the 1960s, the Liberal government showed the greatest concern of all governments for education and cultural affairs, which still ended up being the most neglected of the four areas during the 1944–85 period as a whole.

Regarding the resources being controlled, a comparative analysis of the legislative records of the five governments reveals once again a steady increase in the rate of state presence. For example, during the 1944–60 period, under the *Union nationale* government, only 4 per cent of laws implied a control of purposive resources, whereas during the 1976–85 period, under the *Parti québécois*, this figure reached 30 per cent.

The Distribution of Power

Table 5.1 presents a set of figures pertinent to the analysis of the distribution of power. What is defined as the 'rate of presence' is the percentage of laws in which each of the ten categories of actors is involved either as controller or as controllee. Results are presented both for the last legislature dominated by each of the five governments and for the entire period (1944–85). The last legislature has been chosen to illustrate the distribution of power of each government on the grounds that the last legislature generally bears the mark of a government better than the first one. (In the case of the second *Union nationale* government, the first legislature was also the last.)

The first of four observations that can be drawn from Table 5.1 is that there is a general trend over the period to an increase in the complexity of laws. The ten categories of actors have a greater rate of presence in the laws, as controller and as controllee, at the end of the period than they do at the beginning of the period. In other words, over time laws become more diversified in that they progressively involve a greater number of categories of actors both as controllers and as controllees.

Second, only one category of actors, that of political institutions, consistently has a greater rate of presence as controller than as controllee throughout the period. Moreover, the rates of presence for this category are always greater than those for any of the other categories. The next highest rates are those for autonomous bodies. In their case, there are vari-

Table 5.1   Rates of Presence of Actors as Controllers and as Controllees in the Laws of the Last Legislatures of the Five Governments in Quebec and over the Entire Period 1944–85*

	Union nationale 1956–60 per cent	Liberal Party 1963–66 per cent	Union nationale 1966–70 per cent	Liberal Party 1973–76 per cent	Parti québécois 1981–85 per cent	Entire period 1944–85 per cent
Political institutions	58.1 (41.9)	72.0 (47.5)	72.8 (56.8)	77.0 (59.0)	89.9 (70.2)	69.9 (51.8)
Administrative institutions	11.6 (19.1)	13.6 (29.7)	22.2 (32.7)	22.1 (31.1)	39.9 (52.8)	18.8 (38.5)
Autonomous bodies	25.1 (29.2)	39.0 (39.0)	45.9 (47.5)	53.6 (54.5)	68.1 (67.7)	44.4 (44.8)
Subgovernment	10.9 (20.2)	8.9 (11.0)	12.8 (20.6)	18.9 (20.7)	31.0 (34.7)	14.6 (19.2)
Public establishments	5.6 (8.6)	3.8 (12.3)	2.7 (10.1)	4.5 (9.9)	16.1 (25.8)	6.6 (12.4)
Trade and professional associations	5.2 (5.2)	8.9 (20.2)	8.2 (7.8)	12.6 (16.2)	22.6 (31.5)	10.7 (13.4)
Business	9.0 (24.3)	15.3 (31.8)	14.0 (32.7)	25.2 (41.0)	36.3 (55.6)	18.2 (34.1)
Voluntary associations	1.1 (3.4)	6.4 (11.4)	7.8 (10.9)	9.5 (14.0)	20.6 (25.8)	7.9 (11.0)
Aggregate groups	12.0 (22.1)	19.1 (29.2)	20.2 (24.5)	30.6 (40.1)	50.0 (58.0)	23.4 (33.4)
Primary groups	1.5 (3.4)	5.1 (7.6)	3.1 (4.3)	8.2 (12.2)	15.7 (15.7)	6.0 (8.3)
Average proportion	14.0 (17.7)	19.2 (24.0)	21.0 (24.8)	26.2 (29.9)	39.0 (43.8)	22.0 (26.7)
Total number of laws	267	238	256	222	248	2 746

*Rates of presence of controllees are in parentheses.

ations in the ratios of controller to controllee but these variations over the entire period are small. The eight other categories can be subdivided into four groups. Administrative institutions and businesses have quite high rates of presence, but their ratios of controller to controllee are rather unfavourable. This is not the case for subgovernments and aggregate groups, whose ratios are somewhat more favourable. Two groups of actors have lower rates of presence. The first group, consisting of the trade and professional associations, the voluntary associations and the primary groups, has ratios of controller to controllee which are moderately unfavourable. For their part, public establishments have the most unfavourable ratio after administrative institutions.

Third, there are some significant variations within these general trends in the distribution of power. Under the first Liberal government, at the beginning of the 1960s, the rate for political institutions increased considerably. As Table 5.1 shows, the rate increased from 58.1 to 72.0 per cent as controller, but only from 41.9 to 47.5 per cent as controllee. The 'Quiet Revolution' initiated by the Liberal Party can definitely be said to have allowed the government to play a more important role in society. There was also a significant increase in the role played by autonomous bodies. The same is true of administrative institutions as controllees, the rate for this unfavourable status increasing from 19.1 to 29.7 per cent, while the rate as controller increased only from 11.6 to 13.6 per cent. As a counterpart to these increases, the rate of presence of subgovernments decreased as did that of establishments as controllers. The main innovation of the second *Union nationale* government (1966–70) was the rise of administrative institutions. Their rate of presence increased from 13.6 to 22.2 per cent as controller, and from 29.7 to 32.7 per cent as controllee – a positive change from their position of 1963–66. Therefore, at the end of the 1960s, the legacy of the 'Quiet Revolution' initiated by the Liberals consisted mainly of a higher level of bureaucratisation as provided for through statutes. The changes were not as significant under the second Liberal government, in the 1970s, other than the significant increase in the controls given to business actors, whose rate of presence as controllers increased from 14.0 to 25.2 per cent – an increase quite consistent with the ideology of the government. There was also quite a significant increase in the rates of presence of trade and professional associations and of aggregate groups, the increase being greater in their roles as controllees. In the 1980s, the *Parti québécois* government was very interventionist. There was a general increase, the largest observed from one government to another, in the rates of presence for all ten categories of actors.

Finally, there was a significant evolution in the distribution of potential power provided by laws over the period 1944 to 1985. More and more the statutes were designed as a means to assure the potential power of the various actors, but some categories of actors seem to have profited more than others from such 'empowerment'. From this viewpoint, five groups of actors can be singled out. First, political institutions appear to be the dominant actors throughout the period, which is hardly surprising – statutes being initiated and adopted by them. With the arrival of the 'Quiet Revolution', the domination by political institutions was strengthened and this increase in empowerment was maintained for the rest of the period. Second, a similar evolution began for administrative institutions toward the end of the 1960s. The rate of presence in laws was below average for this group under the first two governments, but above average under the three later governments. Such an increase also occurred for aggregate groups, but it began only in the 1970s, under the second Liberal government. Third, business actors experienced a similar increase later in the 1970s under the second Liberal government. As was the case for administrative institutions, however, their rates of presence as controllee were significantly greater than their rates as controller, unlike the case for political institutions. Fourth, the changes for trade and professional associations, voluntary associations, primary groups and autonomous bodies were generally similar to the average experience for all groups as a whole. These four groups were neither clear winners nor clear losers in their evolution, but the ratios of controller to controllee were slightly better for autonomous bodies than for the other three categories and the ratios were slightly worse for voluntary associations. Fifth, if we have to identify losers, subgovernments and public establishments are the best candidates. If we ignore their eventual increase under the *Parti québécois* government, their rates of presence in laws increase rather modestly as compared with the rates for administrative institutions.

To put this complex evolution in a nutshell, one can say that the enactment of laws in Quebec during the 1944–85 period consolidated the potential power of political institutions and triggered a bureaucratisation of government intervention in society. This bureaucratisation is shown by a greater presence of administrative institutions and aggregate groups in laws. Later, business groups became a rather important recipient of potential power. This general evolution occurred at the expense of subgovernments and public establishments, which are a kind of intermediate public stratum between central government and society. The other categories of actors were less affected.

CONCLUSION

Considerable work is still needed to develop further the comparative analysis of laws and to bring it to the level of analytical refinement reached by the study of government spending, which it complements. A more complete view of all government activities will not be conceivable until these advances have been achieved. In particular, it is our contention that the comparative analysis of laws and of other public policies, if it pays special attention to power relationships, will have the advantage of enlightening us on some political dimensions of our societies which the study of government expenditures is unable to address. We have given an example of this in our power analysis of the laws enacted in Quebec from 1944 to 1985. Such a power analysis could be made more incisive, and thus more revealing, if it were developed along the following lines.

First, we will have to devise a structural model of power analysis which is more sophisticated than the statistical model presented in this chapter. The rates of presence of actors, as controller and controllee, give us a first approximation of the respective potential power of actors, but such measures do not permit us to disentangle the web of power relationships between actors. For example, if administrative institutions gain more power as controllers, for all the governments under study, at whose expense is this greater power acquired? If business actors have a greater rate of presence as controllees, which actors are gaining greater power over them as controllers? We are concerned here with the difference between the structuring of potential power as provided by laws, and the mere distribution of potential power which can be observed in Table 5.1. In future studies on the production of potential power by government activity it will be important to make this distinction clear, and to pay greater attention to the structuring of power, even if it requires more sophisticated methods of analysis.

Second, some of our research findings which are not presented in this chapter seem to indicate that there are significant differences in the distribution of power if we consider the various fields of the legislative activity of governments. For example, the rate of presence of non-governmental actors as controller and as controllee is always greater, for all governments under study, in the social field than in the economic field. This suggests that the centralisation of power is more significant in economic matters than in social matters. It would be interesting to know if the situation is the same in other societies.

Last, but not least, the future development of the power approach suggested here will have to tackle the effects on power distribution or structuring produced by forms of government intervention other than laws and other regulatory activities. There are many public policies which are not shaped entirely by laws or by other regulatory activities associated with laws. This is the case with economic policies. Some other government activities not considered to be public policies also have a significant impact on the distribution of power in society. Such is the case for the diffusion of information involved in many government activities. Even if we must first perform a more thorough comparative analysis of the potential power relationships built into government regulatory activities, this analysis of power will not be complete without its extension to other fields of government intervention in society.

NOTES

1. This is the case with, say, the creation or the dismantling of a ministry, which is hardly a commonplace event. Or, for example, in testing the hypothesis that wealth transfers benefit owners of production factors at the expense of consumers and taxpayers, Landry finds that 75 per cent of the propositions do not provide any information regarding the costs, compared with only 27 per cent that do not provide information about the benefits. In all, only 25 per cent of the propositions provide information about both costs and benefits.

2. The four major policy areas, following the standard classification used in Quebec public administration, are: economic, social, governmental, and educational and cultural.

REFERENCES

Dahl, Robert A. 1970. *Modern Political Analysis*. Englewood Cliffs: Prentice-Hall.

Elling, Richard C. 1979. 'State Party Platforms and State Legislative Performance: A Comparative Analysis.' *American Journal of Political Science* 23: 282–405.

Ginsberg, Benjamin. 1976. 'Elections and Public Policy.' *American Political Science Review* 70: 41–9.

Landry, Réjean. 1990. 'Biases in the Supply of Public Policies to Organized Interest: Some Empirical Evidence.' In *Policy Communities and Public Policy*, eds William D. Coleman and G. Skogstad. Mississauga: Copp Clark Pittman.

Lemieux, Vincent. 1989. *La structuration du pouvoir dans les systèmes politiques*. Sainte-Foy: Les Presses de l'Université Laval.

Lemieux, Vincent. 1991. *Les relations de pouvoir dans les lois. Comparaison entre les gouvernements du Québec, de 1944 à 1985*. Sainte-Foy: Les Presses de l'Université Laval.

Lemieux, Vincent. 1995. *L'étude des politiques publiques. Les acteurs et leur pouvoir*. Sainte-Foy: Les Presses de l'Université Laval.

Pomper, Gerald M. 1970. *Elections in America*. New York: Dood, Mead and Co.

Rose, Richard. 1984. *Understanding Big Government*. London: Sage.

6 Comparative Textual Analyses of Government and Party Activity: The Work of the Manifesto Research Group

Ian Budge and Richard I. Hofferbert

COMPARATIVE USE OF DOCUMENTARY EVIDENCE IN OBSERVING GOVERNMENT ACTIVITY

Most information about government activity comes in the form of reports and documents of various kinds, whether these are produced by cabinets or executive agencies, or by journalists and scholars commenting on what government has done. Such information is archetypically qualitative in nature, focused on the activity of one government in a particular place and time, thus tending to impart an historical, non-replicable and non-comparative bias to analyses which base themselves on it. This chapter seeks to show that this consequence, though common, does not necessarily follow from the use of documentary evidence. We illustrate this argument through the example of the Manifesto Research Group of the European Consortium for Political Research (ECPR), which over the past fifteen years has carried through perhaps the largest comparative investigation of party and governmental behaviour using texts ever done up to this point.[1]

Before going into details and drawing conclusions about this project, several preliminary points should be addressed. Obvious concerns may well be: Why, when there is so much under-utilised and ever more accessible quantitative data being produced by governments, should we have bothered with the laborious task of transforming qualitative data into systematic comparative form? Is the major strategic priority not the analysis of existing data sets (such as census or expenditure figures) which are already tailor-made for comparative analysis of government activity? If two questions are of equal theoretical potential, one of which requires expensive and cumbersome data while the other requires cheap and access-ible data, why not focus on the latter? As we argue in Chapter 3, there can be no doubt about the scholarly neglect of even the most accessible and easily analysed information about government activity, namely expendi-ture. However, this needs to be set in context. Governments may accom-plish the same ends, such as social welfare or unemployment insurance, by regulation or by other legislative and administrative measures, as well as, or as an alternative to, direct expenditure. Such policy tactics need to be examined on the basis of additional information, usually documentary, about the nature of overall government activity. (Armingeon's analysis of labour legislation, in Chapter 4, provides a pioneering example of how this may be done comparatively.)

A further observation to make about the merits of directly quantitative, compared with document-based, research is that the two are not mutually exclusive. Indeed, a point we shall make below is that the information we can get is often richest and most revealing when we can put both together. We shall give a specific example of this when we discuss below the rela-tionship between parties' programmatic priorities and government policy priorities.

This consideration cautions us against legislating *a priori* about what kind of evidence should be given priority and what kind should be ignored. In any case, documentary evidence is so indispensable to researchers that to neglect its comparative uses is really to cede the field to non-replicable and unsystematic investigation, since texts will be used one way or another in any case.

The comparative use of documents in anything other than a limited number of case studies imposes a need for their systematisation and, prob-ably, quantification. One needs to be sure exactly how documents emanat-ing from a variety of places and periods concur with or differ from each other. And for that they need to be placed within some common frame of reference. A practical reason for doing this is that the number of docu-ments to be handled is potentially very large (in the case of the current manifesto collection, now approaching 1500). Thus, categorisation and quantification become the only possible ways of making sense of them.

All treatment of documents within a unified framework is a form of content analysis. However, this term has often become associated with forms of relatively mechanistic counting (the number of times key terms, such as democracy, are mentioned, or counts of the length of column space taken up by particular topics in newspapers) deriving from early techniques applied to texts in the 1940s or 1950s. Such counts clearly have their uses. But other techniques more sensitive to textual nuances may be employed advantageously without abating the systematic nature of the comparison.

For many historians and other investigators, habituated to thinking of events as idiosyncratic and non-recurring, the idea of putting the 1945 Canadian election programme into the same framework as a Belgian government declaration in 1981 may seem to violate the uniqueness of place and time to such an extent as even to be morally repugnant. It is worthwhile pointing out, however, that no matter how much discussion is focused on one place and time such discussion still depends on implicit hypotheses and assumptions. These assumptions are rarely evaluated and checked systematically and may often, as a result, be wrong. Even a simple characterisation of Clinton as interventionist begs such questions as how interventionism is defined (which areas and actions) or with what the current government is being compared (the previous one or all western governments).

Putting the documentary evidence in an explicitly comparative frame makes such assumptions explicit and testable. In this sense, there is a continuum rather than a sharp disjunction between quantitative and qualitative approaches. Again, we should be wary of philosophical attempts to prescribe in advance what can and cannot be done with texts. It is ironic that discourse analysis, for example, is associated with a radically relativist position on the construction of meaning within each text and the lack of fixity of signifiers (Bouchard 1977). Generally, the philosophical position assumed by our analyses below concurs with that of Gardiner (1953), who points out that any object or event can be regarded either as unique or as a member of a class.

In our party manifesto research we have chosen to locate the documents within a fixed comparative classification scheme, without implying, however, that any one classification or statistical analysis is capable of squeezing all of the meaning out of the references in the original texts from which the data came. Analysing texts one way does not preclude investigation from other points of view. One would hope that it would even facilitate methodological pluralism.

GENESIS AND ACTIVITIES OF THE MANIFESTO RESEARCH GROUP

The Manifesto Research Group (MRG) was constituted as a Research Group of the ECPR in 1979, primarily to analyse party election programmes – that is, the documents setting out political parties' medium-term programmes for government, issued as part of campaigns for election or re-election. The ideal-type of such documents is the British manifestos and party platforms in the United States. In cases of parties that do not issue such comprehensive and relatively well-defined documents, the nearest equivalent was taken. In some cases this might be a collection of relatively more specialised documents, sometimes one appealing to particular electoral groups (such as women or youth in some Scandinavian elections). In other cases it might be the transcript of a television address by the party leader (New Zealand) or an authoritative newspaper interview by the Party Secretary (Japan). What all of these have in common is that they are statements of the party position in regard to current conditions, made by someone or some body authorised to do so on behalf of the party as a whole and addressed to the general public. The initial collection of such documents covered nineteen democracies and it now extends to all OECD countries and to most of those in post-communist Eastern Europe.

The initial agenda of the MRG was set by research done by its founders, David Robertson (1976) and Ian Budge (Budge and Farlie 1977) on American platforms and British manifestos from 1922 to 1976. Their interest lay in tracing movements in parties' policy positions within a Downsian frame of reference (Downs 1957). The MRG's intention was to extend this work to a much larger group of countries, covering multi-party as well as two-party systems. Tracing policy movement involved establishing the main dimensions of party policy competition in each country, so that appropriate spaces could be delineated and the location of programmes at each election determined, relative to other parties, time and countries.

The initial research focus was thus very much on political parties – the major policy divisions that separated them and how they changed in relation to these. While later research moved more to the question of governmental activity, we would argue that party policy is far from extraneous to this. Indeed, as democratic government is party government in the mass societies of today, we would argue that looking at party behaviour is largely synonymous with examining government behaviour, at least in its controlling and directing aspects. There is, of course, considerable scepticism as to how far the positions parties publicise for electoral consumption actually get carried over into government policy. Thus the assumption that there is a link needs empirical checking, which we have subsequently carried through (Laver and Budge 1992; Klingemann *et al.* 1994).

The initial research on the 'internal' analysis of the programmes established several important findings (Budge *et al.* 1987). First, parties take relatively few specific policy stands in their election programmes. The specific pledges made by parties are in peripheral policy matters (though a high proportion are actually carried out by the party that gets into government) – very few or no specific policy pledges are made in major policy areas.

A second finding is that major policy areas are identified and are discussed selectively in terms of their importance to the people affected by them and in terms of the party's past successes in dealing with them. This kind of discussion typically fills 90 per cent or more of the space in the typical programme. Unless we are to assume that most of the programme is wasted space, the parties must have a purpose in doing this.

A third finding is that the proportions of text devoted to different policy areas by different parties is a good clue as to party purposes. Typically, socialist or left-wing parties emphasise welfare, social services, government economic intervention and peaceful internationalism; conservative and right-wing parties generally emphasise freedom and individual incentives, law and order and military strength. (These contrasts are illustrated for British and American parties in Table 6.1.) In other words, each party emphasises the kind of issues that would induce voters to vote for it. The reasoning behind the emphasis on particular issues by a particular party, such as welfare by a socialist party, seems to be that if electors are convinced that issue is a priority they will vote for that party in light of its

Table 6.1   Mean Party Election Programme Emphases in Illustrative Issue Areas: Great Britain (1945–92) and the United States (1948–92)

Issue area	Britain		United States	
	Conservative	Labour	Republican	Democrat
Military: positive	2.20	1.09	8.60	2.68
Peace	1.98	3.21	2.40	4.03
Internationalism	3.07	3.88	5.35	6.41
Gov't effectiveness	1.36	0.56	1.50	0.96
Free enterprise	3.68	0.40	4.11	3.18
Economic orthodoxy	3.70	0.97	4.61	0.88
Economic planning	1.57	3.27	0.15	0.51
Controlled economy	0.41	2.75	0.00	0.15
Social justice	2.11	5.17	1.27	3.13
Labour groups	0.77	2.96	4.33	4.01
Law and order	3.48	1.36	3.17	3.05

known proclivity and past record. Rival parties seem to view election struggles from the point of view of imposing their own issue stands over those of the opponents, rather than overtly endorsing opposed stands on the same issues. The electoral programmes are means to this end, since their selective emphases set the agenda of election debate, especially as reflected in media discussion and comment during the campaign.

A fourth finding is that it is analytically fruitful to employ a scheme whereby these selective emphases are uniformly coded across time, parties and countries. We will deal below with the details of how selective emphases in policy areas are measured by counting sentences into different categories. The percentages of sentences derived from this coding can be analysed statistically, however, to show which groupings are mentioned together by the parties and which are opposed by one party to the characteristic emphases of the others. Factor analysis is about as close as one can get statistically to a purely inductive approach, which allows the parties to speak for themselves on the internal structure of their issue positions. Applied in each of twenty countries, it shows that there is a generalisable dimension of party competition, opposing the emphases on welfare and peace to those on freedom and defence – a dimension that can readily be interpreted as a left–right continuum. All countries have more idiosyncratic policy dimensions, however, that are not to be found in most places or, sometimes, anywhere else and which reflect the peculiarities of their own politics and party systems. (These confirm the point, made above, that documents have both a general and a unique content, allowing for comparative analysis of some but not all of their aspects.)

A fifth finding is that in general, in most countries, parties seem to be converging ideologically, in the sense that they were closer to each other in policy terms in the 1980s than they were immediately after the Second World War. Important exceptions to this are Britain and the United States. There does not, however, seem to be a necessary and irreversible trend to convergence, as parties in general approach and pull away from each other at different times and they seem perfectly capable of doing so now as well as earlier in the post-war period. This divergence can be illustrated with the cases of Britain and Germany, in Figure 6.1, on a scale much along the lines discussed by Laver and Budge (1992). In Germany, the much publicised shift of the Social Democrats to the right in and after the Bad Godesburg Conference of 1959 is overtaken by a shift to the left that, by 1987, had taken the party almost as far left as it was in 1949.

A final finding is that the preliminary analyses confirm the existence of ideological families of parties (for example, socialist, liberal and conservative), members of which have more in common with their fellow family

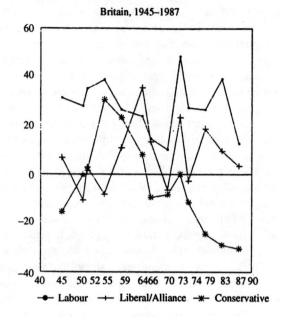

Britain, 1945–1987

●— Labour ＋— Liberal/Alliance ✳— Conservative

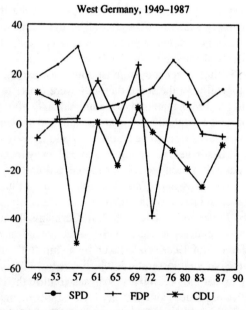

West Germany, 1949–1987

●— SPD ＋— FDP ✳— CDU

Fig. 6.1 Left–Right Emphases in Post-War British and German Party Election Programmes

members in other countries than with competing parties in their own countries.

All these findings were made on the basis of the 'internal' analyses of election programmes reported in the project's original volume (Budge *et al.* 1987). Before moving on to a discussion of subsequent research that related emphases and movements in the party programmes to government formation and policy products, it is well to consider the coding and analytical procedures used in dealing with these documents. Such procedures inevitably colour the substantive results of research. Questions of the validity and reliability of the information obtained from the documents can also be considered at this stage, as these may be more open to question than figures abstracted more or less directly from government publications (though perhaps they should not be!).

CODING PROCEDURES AND CHECKS

The coding procedures applied by the MRG cross-nationally had already been tried and tested in the United Kingdom and United States during the 1970s. The pioneering work was done by David Robertson in his analysis of British party manifestos from 1922 to 1970 (Robertson 1976). His work was replicated for Britain and extended to American party platforms by Budge and Farlie (1977).

The theoretical interest during these investigations was a concern with Downsian theories of party competition and party interaction – theories involving discovering the most suitable space within which to represent party movements. This concern contrasts with certain other investigations carried out specifically on party programmes over time. These latter studies have been concerned with identifying the concrete policy promises made by parties and with seeing whether or not these were carried out by post-election governments (Finer 1975; Kuhnle and Solheim 1981; Page 1978; Rose 1980). The conclusions of such studies have already been summarised – specific pledges, which are generally implemented, constitute a relatively peripheral part of the election programme.[2] Generally, it is only where relative emphases, rather than specific pledges, are taken into account, however, that programmes can be examined as a whole and as relatively coherent policy statements (Borg 1966; Ginsberg 1976).

With a view to covering the implicit as well as the explicit intentions of the programme and priorities, as well as specific policies, Robertson devised a twenty-one-category classification, based on intensive reading of the British manifestos. This worked successfully in the sense of producing maps of British party movement. Robertson's factor analyses corresponded to what would have been expected from the historical record. The original twenty-one-item scheme also proved to be quite adaptable to American party platforms, with the addition of a few more categories (Budge and Farlie 1977). Formal checks were instituted for this extension: Robertson replicated his initial exercise independently of his original coding, producing a 93 per cent correspondence on categories that could be matched, while a 10 per cent check coding on American platforms produced an 84 per cent correspondence.

Grammatical sentences were the coding units. Robertson chose this as the natural unit of sense in modern prose. The data which emerged from the coding thus consisted of the number of sentences in each document falling into each of the policy areas differentiated in the coding. For comparisons over time, these counts were converted to percentages of the total number of sentences in each document. (For the end result of this coding, see the percentages in Table 6.1, above.)

The introductory meetings of the MRG, which brought together comparativists and country specialists interested in extending this type of investigation into a large number of countries outside the Anglo-Saxon democracies, had a body of well-defined and tested procedures with which to begin. The major debates about coding sprang from the doubts of country specialists that 'their' countries could be adequately covered by a highly generalised coding scheme, particularly one developed for Anglo-Saxon political cultures. Good examples are 'corporatism' and 'communalism', central concepts for analysis of particular countries. As a result, the categories of the original coding scheme were doubled in number to accommodate such seeming peculiarities. Other doubts emerged in relation to the original coding of all references to a topic under one category (for example social services), without differentiating between support for or opposition to expansion of the policy target. This seemingly technical point related to a much wider theoretical debate. Are there real differences between positional issues, on which parties take opposed stands, and style issues, where there is only one stand which can be endorsed (Stokes 1963)? Or do parties always compete through selective emphases on their own proprietary issues, de-emphasising or ignoring those where they have low commitment or opposition, as Robertson's original approach implied? This pair of contrasting questions was accommodated by inserting positive and negative references for certain topics in the coding.

While most investigators accepted the sentence as the natural unit of analysis, in some languages the tendency is to list different substantive points, separated by colons within comprehensive 'periods'. This led to use of the *quasi-sentence* rather than invariably coding the sentence, allowing changes of sense within 'periods'. Furthermore, the German investigators insisted that the paragraph rather than the sentence was the natural unit of sense in their documents. Subsequent comparisons with sentence-based coding in German revealed that the choice of a different unit of analysis made little difference to substantive results.

This relative robustness of results, regardless of variations in the detailed procedures used, extends also to the different classification systems. In point of fact, the subdivision of categories insisted on by country specialists proved unnecessary, as many of the new categories attracted few entrants, even in the countries to which they were originally designed to apply. The same is true for various sub-classifications employed by some country specialists to fine-tune the categories of the cross-nationally agreed scheme.

The differentiation between support and opposition for policies such as social services, education, defence and protectionism is instructive in its general irrelevance. Only two of the categories were ever well populated, one in a positive and one in a negative way (defence and protectionism, respectively). This irrelevance of issue valence supports the idea that party hostility to a particular policy priority or direction is evinced by that party not mentioning the policy at all rather than by expressing its direct opposition.

From the actual experience of coding documents, one can say that a classification scheme of around twenty to twenty-five policy areas is adequate. Later analyses have, on occasion, reduced the fifty-four themes used in the original cross-national investigations to a more limited number of categories (the fifty-four category schedule is fully detailed in Budge *et al.* 1987, Appendix B). An example for the investigation of coalition formation and policy-making is given in Table 6.2.

Because of the need for comparability over time and with earlier studies, the fifty-four-category schedule has been retained for all subsequent investigations and additions to the data archive. It has proved remarkably robust in a number of different substantive applications; it has satisfied country specialists that it does not unduly distort party communication in 'their' country; and, above all, it has produced spatial maps of party movement that distinguish parties in ways consistent with their overall ideologies and with the historical record. Individual country investigators have, in addition, checked out the procedures in a variety of ways suitable for their own cases – some through formal checking of coding procedures and others through replication. In some cases, whole sets of documents have been re-coded, with substantive results that have proved remarkably invariant (see the individual chapters of Budge *et al.* 1987; see

Table 6.2 Consolidation of Party Programme Categories*

New category	Old category
State intervention	Regulation of capitalism
	Economic planning
	Protectionism (positive)
	Controlled economy
	Nationalisation
Quality of life	Environmental protection
	Art, sport, leisure, media
Peace and cooperation	Decolonisation
	Military (negative)
	Peace
	Internationalism (positive)
Anti-establishment views	Constitutionalism (negative)
	Government corruption
	Defence of national way of life (negative)
Capitalist economics	Free enterprise
	Incentives
	Protectionism (negative)
	Economic orthodoxy and efficiency
	Social services (negative)
Social conservatism	Constitutionalism (positive)
	Government effectiveness and authority
	National way of life (positive)
	Traditional morality (positive)
	Law and order
	National effort, social harmony
Productivity and technology	Productivity
	Technology and infrastructure

Coding categories retained intact

Military (positive)	Decentralisation (positive)
European Community (positive)	Education (positive)
European Community (negative)	Labour groups (positive)
Freedom, domestic human rights	Agriculture and farmers
Democracy	Underprivileged minorities

Coding categories omitted from consolidated set

Foreign special relationships (positive)	Keynesian demand management
Foreign special relationships (negative)	Education (anti-expansion)
	Communalism, pluralism (positive or negative)
Internationalism (negative)	Labour groups (negative)
Decentralisation (negative)	Other economic groups
Economic goals	Non-economic demographic groups

*For a full description of coding procedures and detailed description of coding categories, see Budge *et al*. 1987, Appendix B.

also the working documents written and edited by Andrea Volkens of the Science Center-Berlin, 1991 to 1993; see also Laver and Budge 1992, Chapter 2).

These questions of coding assume more importance as they have been extended to measure the activity of governments. A major set of documents brought into later investigations has been the declarations of policy made by coalition governments before investiture debates (or the formal coalition agreement between parties, if such is available). While these declarations are statements of intentions rather than a record of what has actually been legislated, the intentions are stated by those in a position both to implement them and to impose sanctions on recalcitrant parliamentarians. Thus the government declaration can function, in some sense, as a surrogate measure of actual government policy output. The general manifesto coding scheme has been adequate for analysis and quantification of these documents, without apparent distortion. Use of an identical categorisation enables the relation between electoral programmes and government projections to be examined empirically.

A more direct measure of governmental output is available from expenditure figures. While the expenditures permit very interesting inferences to be made on their own, they can also be used to track the extent to which the priorities put by parties to the electorate are actually carried through by post-election governments.

The codings and methods of analysis which we have devised for party documents thus have wide implications for the observation of government activity. By relating these observations to the priorities publicly stated by parties, we can begin to investigate systematically and comparatively some central questions of democratic theory. Among the most important of these is the extent to which the political parties actually do control government. We report our findings on this, based on the analysis of the documents and expenditure priorities, in the following section.

PARTY PROGRAMMES AND GOVERNMENT ACTIVITY: MANDATES AND AGENDA-SETTING

The election programmes of political parties are important not only for what they tell us about the bases of party competition but also for what they tell us about the intentions of the parties for government and society. Election programmes are the only medium-term plans which any organisation makes for the whole of a democratic society. They are also, because of constraints of time and resources, the only framework which parties have for directing and coordinating their activities once they are in government. These factors reinforce the standing which election programmes derive from the endorsement that the winning parties' priorities are deemed to have received from the electorate.

Quite apart from legitimation by an electoral mandate, even non-government parties may raise new matters for debate or suggest new priorities in their programmes which can be later reflected in policy. Thus programmes may serve to set an agenda as well as to provide a mandate.

Generally speaking, the behaviour of parties in government has been neglected, compared with their electoral activities. The role of election programmes in linking the two levels gives them a general relevance that we did not anticipate in our initial investigations. This, combined with the general robustness of the coding, made it possible to relate programmatic priorities to the activities of party government in two areas: that of coalition formation and that of the congruence of party programmes with legislative products.

As far as the former area is concerned, most standard theories of coalition formation predict that parties closest to each other within a policy space will form a government coalition. Most also add that the party with the median legislator within such a space will be a member of all coalitions.

One methodological question that arises immediately, prior to any empirical check, regards the space that is relevant for a test of these propositions. Conventionally, they have been investigated using a single left–right continuum. Though this must be recognised as a simplified representation that does not capture the full significance of the policy documents, it clearly did emerge as the leading dimension of our initial factor analyses (Budge *et al.* 1987). In the investigation of coalitions, 'directed' factor analyses were used to create a left–right dimension common to all countries where it made sense. This scale was created by subtracting all (percentaged) references to left-wing topics such as state intervention, peace and cooperation, democracy, and support for social services, education and labour groups from right-wing topics such as capitalist economics, social conservatism, freedom and domestic human rights, and support for the military. (See Table 6.2 for these categories.) This gave a standardised array of party positions for each party at each election in each country. This array could then be used to check postdictions of resulting governments in terms of the various coalition theories. An example of this space, and party positions within it, is given for Germany and Britain in Figure 6.1.

However, it was clear that this left–right dimension was a severely reduced summary of the policy priorities expressed in election programmes. No alternative representation of election programmes, however, appeared more informative, short of a twenty-dimensional space using all of the reduced categories in Table 6.2. Though it could not be directly pictured, distances within such a multi-dimensional space could be measured and hence predictions about the closest parties forming government could be tested within it. After much experimentation, it turned out that the most appropriate way of finding out which were the closest parties within the twenty dimensions was by adding up the distances between them within the full twenty-dimensional space. In technical terms these policy dimensions were thus separable from each other, as distances between parties could be found separately on each dimension, without taking the others into account, and then added up later. This, in turn, implied that there was always a median party around which coalitions and policy agreements could cohere, which would not have been the case had we had to calculate party distances on all twenty dimensions. This finding about the separability of policy dimensions, though technical, is very important in the context of the ongoing debate about the stability and fairness of democratic decision processes (McKelvey 1979; Ordeshook 1986). The substantive finding from using these two spatial representations of policy closeness was that some models of coalition formation were very successful in postdicting what governments would form on the basis of closeness – the most successful being the model predicting coalitions with the smallest aggregate policy distance separating them on one dimension (Laver and Budge 1992). Models predicting that the median party would be in the coalition were also notably successful.

The trouble is that such models do not usually designate a unique government that will form, but predict instead that many different coalitions might emerge. Hence their efficiency (number of governments successfully predicted divided by number of predictions made) is much less impressive than their predictive success (number of governments successfully predicted over total number of governments formed). The conclusion is that other factors need to be taken into account in order to narrow down predictions to the actual governments that form. The most likely additional factors seem to be long-standing patterns of cleavages, notably the left–right cleavage and the relative size of parties. Cleavages need to be included because right–centre parties, for example, will enter coalitions with parties of a similar ideological persuasion, even if they agree more with the left, and vice versa. Size comes in because a large party, even if it does not have a majority, can often form a government on its own.

The results of the analysis of coalition formation are thus mixed. There is no doubt, however, that the programme data on policy priorities of the parties provide the most comprehensive information currently available on where the parties are located in issue space. Hence it makes possible the most rigorous check so far imposed on policy-based theories on coalition formation.

The further information, provided by the concurrent coding of election programmes and government declarations, relates to what parties get out of coalition participation in policy terms. If parties join coalitions for policy reasons, this must be because the governments in which they participate favour the member parties' policies more than they do those of non-participating parties. Looking at distances between the position taken by parties in their election programmes and those taken by the government in its declaration tells us whether this is actually so in practice. If the distance is small, the government declaration is close to the party programme; if it is large, one does not reflect the other to any great extent.

It turns out that distances do seem to narrow with party participation if the coalition system works like a two-party alternation. Thus in Scandinavia, where a socialist bloc competes with a bourgeois bloc, and these alternate in government, policy distances in general narrow where a party is in government and widen when it is not. Thus all parties in the government get a pay-off in policy terms. Something of this can also be seen in Germany and in the Low Countries. In the latter case a Christian centre party remains in government practically all the time, but right-wing liberals and socialists alternate as coalition partners, narrowing the gap between their positions and government policy as they do so. Socialist parties, however, gain less in policy terms than do the liberals from this arrangement. However, policy pay-offs (as measured by government declarations) from being in government seem quite absent where government composition does not change very much and where the coalition process is dominated by a single party – the extreme case being Italy under the Christian Democrats.

The substantive implications of these findings are quite striking, leading to the tentative conclusion that perhaps two-party alternation and single-party majority governments are the best arrangement for ensuring party accountability after all. In the present context, however, the important thing to note is the power of the tests that these data make possible and that put them as the centre of the comparative observation of governments at the present time.

A second major area of interest concerns the congruence of party programmes with actual legislative products. It may be objected, quite justifiably, that declarations of intent to carry through certain priorities are not in themselves an implementation of them. The link between electoral programmes and legislative action requires empirical investigation.

This was one reason for the focus on expenditure priorities, described in Chapter 3. Though expenditures are obviously not the whole of government policy, they are central to many areas of it and they clearly relate to what the government has done rather than to what incumbent officials say they intend to do. Expenditures can be coded into categories that match some of the central ones in electoral programmes (Klingemann *et al.* 1994). Time series regressions can control for the independent influences of long-standing ideology, as opposed to current programmatic emphases, as well as for the differences in programme to policy congruence for parties in, as contrasted to parties out of, government. We view congruence of programmes and outlays by parties in governments as evidence of the mandate. We refer to evidence of an agenda effect coming from the more diffuse political debate whereby policies reflect programmes regardless of whether parties get into government.

Two major conclusions emerge from a series of analyses conducted for a variety of governments from single-party to multi-party coalitions. First, there is in almost every country of the ten examined a link between the priorities enunciated in programmes and those put into effect by governments for most policy areas. Programmes do relate to government action. Second, the link is often of a diffuse agenda-setting one, from which opposition parties are not excluded. Being in government is a decided advantage in getting priorities adopted, but being out of government is not a total disbarment. While this finding goes somewhat against extreme ideas of majoritarian democracy, it does strengthen our picture of democratic discussion as a persuasive and deliberative process, in which ideas certified in the process of public disputation can make their way through to policy even without the backing of political power.

A further line of research from this point of view would be to see how good parties are at identifying problems and solutions to them. After all, one justification of democracy, particularly after the collapse of communist regimes in 1989–91, was in terms of its greater efficiency. Collecting time series of problem indicators (a good example would be rising birth rate as relevant to educational resource allocation) that could be related through regressions to programmatic emphases would be a practical way of researching party responsiveness. This would complement the party programme to public spending priority links we have been studying. It would also show whether the whole democratic process in which parties play a central link does serve to alert governments to problems and to prompt useful reactions to those problems.

THE QUANTITATIVE ANALYSIS OF DOCUMENTS: A NEGLECTED APPROACH?

In the context of the present discussion, the substantive findings reported in this chapter are of less importance in themselves than as evidence that a systematic comparative analysis of documents is feasible and can yield information central to the observation of government activity in democracies.

The process of research into the ramifications of electoral programmes has in large measure also been an educational experience for the investigators. Our research started off with the idea that the formal statements of party policy were more important than the sceptics maintained but we did not realise how important they actually are, both from a practical and from a research point of view.

The initial investigation was thus narrowly limited to party competition at the electoral level. It rapidly became apparent that the ability to plot party policy positions in space made our information vital to the most highly developed body of theory about government behaviour – coalition theory. The ability to extend this investigation to what parties got out of coalition participation in policy terms – and, more broadly, to the extent and means by which party priorities get translated into government action – meant that the data themselves stimulated new research questions, refined existing theory and even supported the development of new models of the interaction between parties and government.

Some scholars, particularly those in the economics tradition, tend to belittle data collection and the testing of hypotheses against evidence. They assume that models, developed out of mainstream rational choice assumptions and formulated mathematically, have an in-built validity that overrides any mismatch with available evidence.

Few would dispute that data collection needs to be guided by theoretical consideration. It is our contention, however, from our experience with this research that theory becomes not only irrelevant but impoverished if it does not seek to meet available evidence. This is because the new considerations thrown into prominence by the attempt to organise data in a theoretically relevant way prompt new theoretical developments, even before any explicit testing of existing models takes place.[3]

Documentary analysis of government and party activity goes straight to the heart of debates about what democratic government can do. Documents are too important to be left to qualitative, often vague and generally atheoretical analyses. They should be used systematically in comparative quantitative analysis to address the great questions of our time.

NOTES

1. The Manifesto Research Group now works in cooperation with the Research Unit in Institutions and Social Change of the Science Centre-Berlin (Wissenschaftszentrum–Berlin für Sozialforschung, GmbH) to keep the data current. Data for the first phase of the project, covering 1018 election programmes in 20 countries, and the period roughly from 1945 to 1983, are available through the ESRC Data Archive, University of Essex (Colchester, England). The subsequent data are part of a number of substantive projects on parties and party systems in democratic regimes. As these reach publication, the more recent data in the collection will be made available to the academic community by the Zentralarchiv für Empirische Sozialforschung, University of Cologne.

2. For an exception, on which pledges were made by the Greek PASOK party in central policy areas with an impressive record of success, see, however, Kalogeropoulou (1989).

3. To take just one example, the focus on the whole of electoral programmes rather than on a small number of explicit pledges leads to a reconceptualisation of party competition as mainly selective emphasis on different issues, rather than direct confrontation of the same issues (see Budge and Farlie 1983). This has major implications for our view of the coalitions, as upgrading and downgrading priorities (or even pursuing them simultaneously) are easier than giving up entrenched specific policies.

REFERENCES

Borg, Olari. 1966. 'Basic Dimensions of Finnish Party Ideologies: A Factor Analytical Study.' *Scandinavian Political Studies* 1: 106–32.

Bouchard, D.F., ed. 1977. *Michel Foucault: Language, Counter Memory, Practice*. New York: Cornell University Press.

Budge, Ian and Dennis Farlie. 1977. *Voting and Party Competition*. London and New York: Wiley.

Budge, Ian and Dennis Farlie. 1983. 'Party Competition: Selected Emphases or Direct Confrontation.' In *Western European Party Systems*, eds Hans Daalder and Peter Maier. London: Sage.

Budge, Ian, David D. Robertson and Derek J. Hearl, eds. 1987. *Ideology, Strategy and Party Change*. Cambridge: Cambridge University Press.

Downs, Anthony. 1957. *An Economic Theory of Democracy*. New York: Harper.

Finer, Samuel. 1975. 'Manifesto Moonshine.' *New Society*, 13 (November).

Gardiner, Patrick L. 1953. *The Nature of Historical Explanation*. Oxford: Oxford University Press.

Ginsberg, Benjamin. 1976. 'Elections and Public Policy.' *American Political Science Review* 70: 41–9.

Kalogeropoulou, Efthalia. 1989. 'Do Parties Do What They Say They Will? Pledge Fulfilment Under the First PASOK Government in Greece 1981–5.' *European Journal of Political Research* 17: 289–311.

Klingemann, Hans-Dieter, Richard I. Hofferbert and Ian Budge. 1994. *Parties, Policies, and Democracy*. Boulder: Westview Press.

Kuhnle, Stein and Lars Solheim. 1981. 'Party Programs and the Welfare State.' *Skrifter* No.3, Oslo.

Laver, Michael J. and Ian Budge, eds. 1992. *Party Policy and Coalition Government*. London: Macmillan.

McKelvey, Richard D. 1979. 'General Conditions for Global Intransitivities in Formal Voting Models.' *Econometrica* 47: 1085–111.

Ordeshook, Peter. 1986. *Game Theory and Political Theory*. Cambridge: Cambridge University Press.

Page, Benjamin I. 1978. *Choices and Echoes in Presidential Elections*. Chicago: University of Chicago Press.

Robertson, David. 1976. *A Theory of Party Competition*. London and New York: Wiley.

Rose, Richard. 1980. *Do Parties Make a Difference?* London: Macmillan.

Stokes, Donald E. 1963. 'Spatial Models of Party Competition.' *American Political Science Review* 57: 368–77.

Volkens, Andrea. 1991–93. *Election Programmes of Parliamentary Parties: Documentation*. Berlin: Science Center-Berlin.

7 The Suitability of Several Models for Comparative Analysis of the Policy Process
Paul A. Sabatier

This chapter analyses the ability of several models (or conceptual frameworks) of the policy process to serve as guides for comparing features of that process across different units of government – whether those be nations or subunits of nations – and/or different periods of time. By policy process is meant the manner in which problems such as crime, unemployment and air pollution get defined as political problems, the remedies government devises for dealing with them, the implementation of those solutions, the impact of those supposed remedies on the problem and the subsequent revision of the remedies.

The first part of this chapter argues that the dominant contemporary theory of the policy process – the 'stages heuristic' of Jones (1987), Anderson (1975), Peters (1986) and many others – contains serious logical and empirical deficiencies. It then examines four more promising conceptual frameworks: the 'funnel of causality' approach developed by Richard Hofferbert; John Kingdon's 'policy streams' framework; an 'institutional rational choice' approach developed by Elinor Ostrom and her colleagues; and the 'advocacy coalition framework' of the author and Hank Jenkins-Smith.

THE STAGES HEURISTIC AND ITS LIMITS

Policy researchers, practitioners and teachers in the United States and elsewhere have broadly accepted a 'stages heuristic' to public policy (Nakamura 1987). Briefly put, the familiar stages model breaks the policy process into functionally and temporally distinct sub-processes. Easton (1965) elaborated a 'systems model' of politics, which specified the functioning of input, throughput, output and feedback mechanisms operating within broader 'environments' (for example ecological, biological, social and personality). Lasswell (1951) developed a more policy-specific set of stages, including intelligence, recommendation, prescription, invocation, application, appraisal and termination.

The functions and stages set out by Easton and Lasswell have been diffused throughout the literature of public policy, although the specification and content of the stages vary considerably. Among the most authoritative statements of the stages heuristic are Jones (1987) and Anderson *et al.* (1984). Both of these works, leaning heavily on Lasswell and Easton, distinguish among the stages of problem identification, agenda setting, adoption, implementation and policy evaluation. Both cast these stages within a broader environment characterised by political institutions, public opinion, political culture and other constraints. Each of the functional stages in the process involves distinct periods of time, political institutions and policy actors.

The widespread acceptance of the stages model results from important contributions. As it evolved from the works of Easton and others, the concept of a process of policy-making, operating across the various institutions of government, has provided an alternative to the institutional approach of traditional political science that emphasised analysis of specific institutions – such as cabinets, legislatures and administrative agencies – or of public opinion. By shifting attention to the 'policy process', the stages model has encouraged analysis of phenomena that transcend any given institution. Implementation of national legislation in the United States, for example, typically involves one or more national agencies, Congressional policy and appropriations committees, several court decisions, a multitude of state and local agencies and the intervention of interest groups at multiple levels of government.

The reconceptualisation accomplished by the stages heuristic has also permitted useful analysis of questions that were less readily perceived from within the institutionalist framework. Perhaps the most important of these has been its focus on the impact of policy – the ability of governmental institutions to accomplish policy objectives in the real world, such as improving air quality or assuring secure energy supplies. Traditional institutional approaches tended to stop at the output of that particular institution – whether it be a legislative law, a court decision or an administrative agency rule – without specific attention to the ultimate outcome or impact of the policy.

Finally, the stages model has provided a useful conceptual disaggregation of the complex and varied policy process into manageable segments. The result has been an array of very useful 'stage focused' research, particularly regarding agenda-setting (for example Nelson 1984; Kingdon 1984) and policy implementation (for example Bardach 1977; Barrett and Fudge 1981).

In addition to the ready division of scholarly labour, scholars find the stages heuristic congenial because it fits the self-consciously rational method of the policy science disciplines. Bureaucrats find it attractive because it portrays a rational division of labour between the executive and legislative institutions of government, thereby legitimising the role of the bureaucracy within representative systems. For policy-makers the stages model provides a view of the policy process that is in accord with democratic theory – the decision-maker draws on the inputs of the broader society to make policy that is, in turn, handed over to other governmental institutions for implementation.

Despite its conceptual strengths and broad acceptance, the stages metaphor has serious limitations as a basis for research and teaching. First and most importantly, the stages model is not a causal model. It lacks an identifiable force or forces that drive the policy process from one stage to another and that generate activity within any given stage. While it has heuristic value in dividing the policy process into manageable units for analysis, it does not specify the linkages, drives and influences that form the essential core of theoretical models. Furthermore, because it lacks causal mechanisms, the stages heuristic does not provide a clear basis for empirical hypothesis testing. This lack of a crucial component of causal models is why we prefer to refer to it as 'the stages heuristic'.[1]

Second, the stages heuristic suffers from descriptive inaccuracy in positing a sequence of stages starting with agenda-setting and then passing through policy formulation, implementation and evaluation. Although proponents often acknowledge deviations from the sequential stages in practice (for example Jones 1987), a great deal of recent empirical study suggests that deviations may be quite frequent – evaluations of existing programmes often affect agenda-setting, and policy-making occurs as bureaucrats attempt to implement vague legislation (Barrett and Fudge 1981; Kingdon 1984).

Third, the stages heuristic suffers from a built-in legalistic, top–down focus. It draws attention to a specific cycle of problem identification, major policy decision and implementation of that decision that focuses attention on the intentions of legislators and on the fate of a particular policy initiative. Such a top–down view results in a tendency to neglect other important players, such as street-level bureaucrats, restricts the view of 'policy' to a specific piece of legislation, and may be entirely inapplicable when 'policy' stems from a multitude of overlapping directives and actors, none of which is dominant.

Fourth, the stages metaphor inappropriately emphasises the policy cycle as the temporal unit of analysis. Examination of a range of policy areas demonstrates that policy evolution often involves multiple cycles initiated by actors at different levels of government, as various formulations of problems and solutions are conceived, partially tested and reformulated by a range of competing policy elites against a background of change in exogenous events and related policy issue areas (Heclo 1974; Nelson 1984). Thus, rather than focus on a single cycle initiated at a given (usually federal) governmental level, a more appropriate model would focus on multiple, interacting cycles involving multiple levels of government.

Fifth, the stages heuristic fails to provide a good vehicle for integrating the role of policy analysis and the role of policy-oriented learning throughout the public policy process. It tends to confine analysis to the evaluation stage and to post-hoc assessments of the impacts of a given policy initiative. This is much too simple. Analysis clearly plays a large role in policy adoption (Jenkins-Smith and Weimer 1985) and agenda-setting (Kingdon 1984; Nelson 1984). The practical result, in policy studies, has been to 'ghettoise' the perceived role of analysis and learning, as evidenced by the development of two distinct literatures: one that focuses on the interplay of self-interested policy actors pursuing rational strategies in pursuit of predetermined goals (Riker 1962; Moe 1984) and another that suggests some of the processes by which analysis and learning are integrated into policy-making (Caplan *et al.* 1975).

In general, then, while the stages heuristic served a useful purpose in the 1970s and early 1980s – particularly in its delineation of a 'policy process' involving problem definition(s), major decision(s), implementation of those decisions and policy impacts – it has outlived that usefulness as a basic guide to policy research and needs to be replaced.

FOUR THEORIES OF THE POLICY PROCESS

Political scientists and policy scholars share a common interest in developing better theories of the policy process than the stages heuristic. Such theories should integrate many of the contributions of policy scholars – in terms of the importance of intergovernmental policy communities, substantive policy information and policy elites (Sabatier 1991) – with political scientists' traditional focus on the preferences, interests and resources of various actors, institutional rules and background socio-economic conditions. Four efforts which do this are: the 'funnel of causality' framework of Hofferbert; Kingdon's 'policy streams' framework; an approach involving rational actors within institutions developed by Ostrom and her colleagues; and the 'advocacy coalition' framework developed by Sabatier and Jenkins-Smith.

All but the first were developed during the 1980s, suggesting that alternatives to the stages heuristic are finally emerging. Other approaches have also proved useful. They include Ripley's (1985) synthesis of the stages heuristic with a modified version of Lowi's arenas of power and Wildavsky's 'cultural' explanations of policy change (Wildavsky, 1982, 1987; Thompson *et al.* 1990).

In the sections that follow, the basic elements of each approach will first be presented; one or more attempts to apply the framework to comparative public policy will then be discussed; and finally the strengths and limitations of each approach will be addressed.

Hofferbert's Funnel of Causality Approach

Two decades ago, Hofferbert (1970, 1974) developed a conceptual framework of the policy process. It represented a synthesis of the literature seeking to explain interstate variation in governmental decisions, with decisions usually operationalised as expenditures for various categories of programmes, such as education or health. Governmental decisions were seen as a direct and indirect function of historical-geographic conditions, socio-economic conditions, mass political behaviour, governmental institutions and elite behaviour. Hofferbert borrowed from Easton's (1965) open-systems framework of the policy process, but dispensed with Easton's aggregated support and demand variables and disaggregated both the political system and the external environment into a few more variables.

Hofferbert's 'funnel of causality' formalised a set of assumptions prevalent among American political scientists in the late 1960s and early 1970s that guided an enormous amount of research involving cross-sectional comparisons of policy outputs across states and localities (Sharkansky 1970; Eulau and Prewitt 1973). It has also guided, usually more implicitly than explicitly, a great deal of cross-national policy research, including: Leichter's (1979) analysis of health care policy in four nations; comparisons of regulatory policy in the United States and Sweden by Lundqvist (1980); and Vogel's (1986) analysis of environmental policy in Great Britain and the United States; and it underlies a monumental analysis of political party manifestos (Klingemann *et al.* 1994).

The distinctive features of this approach are, first, that it involves five sets of independent variables arranged in a causal sequence consistent with democratic theory. The two sets of exogenous variables, historical/ geographical conditions and socio-economic conditions, affect mass political behaviour; that, in turn, helps establish political institutions; those institutions constrain elite behaviour; and elites directly affect policy outputs, the dependent variable. Second, there is very little attention to the precise causal process within any variable set or between variable sets; each set is essentially a 'black box' with arrows going in and out. Finally, the dominant mode of analysis tends to be either qualitative case studies of a specific policy sector in several political systems (for example Lunqvist or Vogel) or regression/correlational analyses of budgetary expenditures across numerous polities (for example Sharkansky or Hofferbert).

The strengths of this approach are twofold. First, the variable sets constitute a very convenient check-list of possibly important variables and the causal ordering is intuitively plausible. The focus on exogenous historical-geographical and socio-economic conditions as the basic drivers of the policy process certainly helps explain why automotive pollution control first arose as a policy issue in Los Angeles and why welfare expenditures are much lower in Mississippi than in New York. Second, the very parsimony of the approach and the aggregated nature of the variables mean it is well suited to data sets involving large numbers of political systems. None of the other models discussed in this paper could deal with the Klingemann *et al.* (1994) data set involving party manifestos and budgetary expenditures in ten countries over thirty years. Because of their greater attention to the process by which, in this instance, party manifestos get translated into budgetary expenditures, the other models would have been overwhelmed by the scope of the manifesto research project.

On the other hand, the Hofferbert 'funnel of causality' approach has some serious limitations. First and foremost, the fact that it is basically a black-box open-systems model means that it never seeks to model individual behaviour and, therefore, cannot deal with the details of the causal process (Rose 1973; Eyestone 1977). This is particularly true at the level of elite behaviour, where individual actors or sets of actors are important. It is also a potentially important deficiency at prior stages: ascertaining the impact of income and unemployment on mass political behaviour requires some assumptions about people's values and information processing capabilities, but the Hofferbert approach never makes any assumptions about the drivers of individual behaviour. Second, because it neglects individuals, the Hofferbert approach cannot readily deal with the importance of substantive policy information in the policy process, the topic of policy-oriented learning, or the interactions within policy communities. Third, the original versions of the framework were extremely vague concerning the aspects of elite behaviour which should be of interest to policy scholars. In a study of agency decision-making utilising the Hofferbert approach, Mazmanian and Sabatier (1980) helped fill this black box by pointing to the values and beliefs of agency decision-makers, the information processing work of staff and the intervention of external interest groups at public hearings as three important, and measurable, aspects of elite behaviour. Fourth, the original version of the Hofferbert approach was completely silent about intergovernmental relations, but he has subsequently made some effort to rectify this omission (Hofferbert and Urice 1982). Fifth, Hofferbert assumed that socio-economic conditions and mass political behaviour, as mediated by governmental institutions and elite behaviour, drove policy decisions – a view that runs counter to a fair amount of research concerning the ability of governmental elites to manipulate public opinion (Dye and Ziegler 1975). Finally, the original version of the Hofferbert model lacked feedback loops and thus could not deal with policy change over time, but that is a defect which is easily fixed.

The Policy Streams Approach

Drawing upon the 'garbage can model' of decision-making within organisations (Cohen *et al.* 1972), John Kingdon (1984) has developed an interesting approach to agenda-setting and policy formulation which may be expandable to the entire policy process. In his view, policy-making can be conceptualised as three largely unrelated 'streams': a problem stream consisting of information about real world problems and the effects of past governmental interventions; a policy stream composed of researchers, advocates and other specialists who analyse problems and formulate possible alternatives; and a political stream consisting of elections, legislative leadership contests, etc. According to Kingdon, major policy reforms result when a 'window of opportunity' joins the three streams in response to a recognised problem, the policy community develops a proposal that is technically feasible and has wide value acceptability, and politicians find it advantageous to approve it.

The Kingdon approach has many praiseworthy features. It incorporates an enlarged view of policy communities which goes beyond the traditional 'iron triangles' of US politics (Fritschler 1975) to incorporate policy analysts in a variety of institutions. It gives a prominent role to substantive policy information about real world problems and the impacts of previous governmental interventions. It gets beyond the rigid institutionalism in which many political scientists confine themselves. And it acknowledges the role of serendipity in the policy process.

On the other hand, several aspects need further development. First, the conditions creating windows of opportunity need further analysis. Both Jones (1987) and Zahariadis (1994) have suggested that a change in the ruling party at the national level often gives rise to such a 'window of opportunity', although neither is clear whether they view this as a necessary and/or a sufficient condition for such a window. Second, Sabatier (1988) would contend that Kingdon views policy analysts and researchers as being too apolitical, thus neglecting the role of advocacy analysis and putting too much distance between the 'policy' and the 'political' streams. Third, if the framework is to be expanded to include the entire policy process, more attention needs to be given to bureaucracies and courts in implementing those reforms and more recognition needs to be accorded to the intergovernmental dimension in both formulation and implementation.

Finally, if Kingdon is to be useful in comparative policy analysis, particularly across nations, his framework needs to be modified to give more attention to the historical and/or institutional differences across countries. For example, Kingdon argues that a proposed policy alternative arising out of the policy stream must have 'value acceptability' if it is to stand any chance of being adopted. But the necessary level of value acceptability (or consensus) varies with the institutional rules regarding policy adoption in different countries. Britain is a clear example of minority rule: the Conservative Party completely dominated national policy-making during the Thatcher era even though it obtained only about 35 to 40 per cent of the popular vote. The reasons were institutional rules calling for single member districts with plurality winners, a single important legislative body involving basically a single veto point and a tradition of very strong party loyalty. In the United States, by contrast, one needs at least 60 to 75 per cent consensus among the relevant elites at the national level to pass most major pieces of legislation through both houses of Congress and the President. Most other western countries are probably somewhere between these two extremes. Similarly, the analysis by Klingemann *et al.* (1994) of the relationship between priorities expressed in political party manifestos and the budgetary priorities of subsequent governments demonstrates that in some countries (such as Sweden or France) party manifestos have an impact irrespective of whether or not the party is a member of the subsequent governmental coalition; in most other countries, becoming a member of the subsequent government enhances the relationship between spending priorities in a party's manifestos and the budgetary priorities of subsequent governments. Clearly, what constitutes a necessary degree of 'value acceptability/consensus' varies across countries and Kingdon's analysis needs to be modified to take this into account.

Institutional Rational Choice

In direct contrast to the systems appoach of Hofferbert, a large group of 'rational choice' scholars over the past twenty years have started with self-interested individual actors – their preferences, interests and resources – as the basic unit of analysis and then have examined how institutional rules affect their behaviour (for example Buchanan and Tullock 1962; Miller 1992; Moe 1984). From a policy perspective, the most useful body of work within this tradition has been that of Elinor Ostrom and her colleagues because it combines an actor-based perspective with attention to institutional rules, intergovernmental relations and policy decisions.

The basic approach, found in Kiser and Ostrom (1982), views individual actions as a function of both the attributes (values and resources) of the individual and the attributes of the decision situation. The latter is, in turn, a product of institutional rules, the nature of the relevant good and the attributes of the community (which would include Hofferbert's socioeconomic conditions and community opinion). The principal insight of this approach is that the same individual will behave differently in different decision situations. The theoretical focus has been on developing a classification of institutional rules that delineate entry and exit to various positions, the scope of authority for each position, permissible communication among actors in various roles and the aggregation of individual actions into a collective decision (Ostrom 1986, 1990; Ostrom *et al.* 1994).

This approach to institutional analysis defines three levels of institutions: the operational level (for example agency permit decisions), the collective choice (for example the statute governing the agency) and the constitutional (the constitution governing the legislature). There are two fundamental insights. First, the decisions of a given level basically set the institutional rules of the next lower level. Thus a constitution sets the basic institutional rules for a legislature, while a legislative statute sets the basic rules governing agency permit decisions. Second, it is primarily decisions at the operational level that directly affect citizens; the decisions of higher levels are instructions to lower levels. This is consistent with findings from a decade of implementation research: what happens in Washington or London is little more than words on paper until it affects the behaviour of 'street level bureaucrats' and, ultimately, target groups (Barrett and Fudge 1981).

The institutional rational choice approach has been employed in a wide variety of settings, including the management of fisheries, groundwater basins and other 'common pool' resources in a wide variety of countries (Ostrom 1990; Bromley 1992); the problematic maintenance of irrigation and road systems in underdeveloped countries (Ostrom *et al.* 1993); and the efficacy of public versus private schools in the United States (Chubb and Moe 1990). All of these studies involve situations in which self-interested, rational behaviour by individuals can result in socially undesirable outcomes. Their common theme is that such 'tragedies of the commons' (Hardin 1968) can be avoided by designing institutions in which local individuals are given a prominent role in designing and enforcing rules which often take the form of a contingent contract: 'I commit myself to follow the set of rules we have devised in all instances except dire emergencies if the rest of those affected make a similar commitment and act accordingly' (Ostrom 1990:99–100). The basic rationale for local autonomy is that local individuals are more knowledgeable than central government officials about the local situation and will put forth the extra effort to produce socially efficient results only if they have substantial control of the situation (see also Chubb and Moe 1990).

This is a superb framework for thinking about the effects of individuals and institutions on governmental policy decisions and for designing governmental institutions in such a way that individually rational decisions produce socially efficient results. It has, of course, some limitations. First, while 'community characteristics' are mentioned as one of the three sets of factors affecting a decision situation, they have largely been neglected in the work to date of Ostrom and her colleagues. Second, a framework which tends to resolve tragedies of the commons by resort to mutually applicable rules enforced by the individuals involved tends to have limitations when there are significant negative externalities on third parties, when the communities involved do not share common norms or when the resources involved extend beyond the local level, such as regional or national road networks. Finally, the focus on individual behaviour within specific institutions renders this framework a little unwieldy for dealing with the dozens (if not hundreds) of institutions in most national policy communities.

The Advocacy Coalition Framework (ACF)

Sabatier (1988) has recently developed a conceptual framework of the policy process that synthesises many of the features discussed in this paper. It views policy change over periods of a decade or more within a specific policy domain, such as air pollution or transportation, as a function of three sets of factors.

The first is the interaction of competing advocacy coalitions within a policy subsystem/community. An advocacy coalition consists of actors from interest groups, governmental agencies, legislatures and research institutions at all levels of government who share a set of basic beliefs (policy goals plus causal and other perceptions) and who seek to manipulate the rules of various governmental institutions to achieve those goals over time. Conflict among coalitions is mediated by 'policy brokers', i.e. actors more concerned with system stability than with achieving policy goals. The second set is changes external to the subsystem in socioeconomic conditions, system-wide governing coalitions and decisions from other policy subsystems. Since 1970, for example, US air pollution policy has been affected by changes in petroleum prices, by Republican electoral victories in 1980 and by decisions from the tax and energy subsystems. The third set is the effects of stable system parameters – such as basic social structure and constitutional rules – on the constraints and resources of various actors. The strategies available to advocacy coalitions in US air pollution policy are, for example, obviously constrained by federalism.

With respect to both belief systems and public policies, the framework distinguishes 'policy core' from 'secondary' elements. Coalitions are assumed to organise around common policy core beliefs – such as the proper scope of governmental versus market activity, the relative priority of different values and the proper distribution of authority among levels of government – that apply across that policy domain. Since these policy core beliefs are hypothesised to be relatively stable over periods of a decade or more, so too is coalition composition. Coalitions seek to learn about how the world operates and the effects of various governmental interventions in order to realise their goals over time. Because of resistance to changing policy core beliefs, policy-oriented learning is usually confined to the secondary aspects of belief systems, such as the health effects of particular air quality standards or the severity of air pollution problems in different locales.[2] Changes in the core aspects of public policies require the replacement of a dominant coalition by another, which is hypothesised to result primarily from changes external to the subsystem (i.e. from the second set of factors listed above).

The advocacy coalition framework has been applied to a number of policy areas, primarily in the United States but also in Canada and the Netherlands (Sabatier and Jenkins-Smith 1988, 1993; Jenkins-Smith 1991; van Muijen 1993). While none of the work thus far has been explicitly

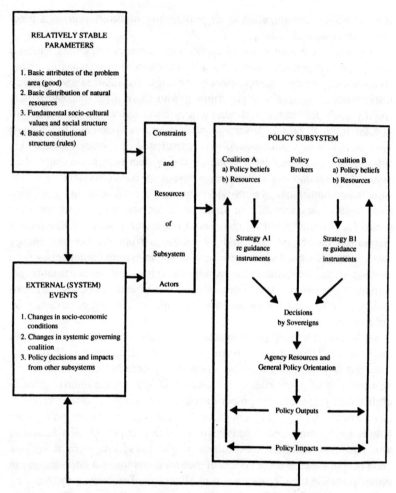

Fig. 7.1 General Model of Policy Evolution Focusing on Competing Advocacy Coalitions within Policy Subsystems

comparative, the framework is well suited to analyse policy change in a specific policy domain across a few political systems.[3] First, the set of 'relatively stable parameters' – constitutional structure, social structure, distribution of natural resources – are likely to vary across political systems and thus be among the critical variables in any controlled comparison or quasi-experimental design. Second the focus on advocacy coalitions – composed of actors from different institutions who share most elements of a belief system – and policy-oriented learning suggests a comparison of the beliefs of similar coalitions in different political systems. For example, why have environmentalists in the United States insisted on technology-forcing legal standards while those in Britain and Sweden have been much more willing to give great discretion to agency inspectors (Lundqvist 1980; Vogel 1986)? It also points to the diffusion of ideas, for example the use of economic incentives in pollution control, among members of similar (or the same) coalition operating in different political systems; such diffusion of policy innovations is likely to be increasingly important because of the work of the OECD, the UN and other international institutions.[4] Finally, the focus on exogenous shocks suggests comparisons about how different political systems respond to the same exogenous shock, for example the 1973–74 Arab oil embargo.

At any rate, the work thus far on the advocacy coalition framework within specific countries tends to support its emphasis on advocacy coalitions, policy-oriented learning and the role of exogenous shocks. Amendments have been suggested concerning the hierarchical structure of elite belief systems and the role of subsystem actors in interpreting exogenous events (Sabatier and Jenkins-Smith 1993). The very fact that the ACF proposes specific, testable hypotheses should encourage further empirical research and, quite likely, additional amendments.

CONCLUSION

The theories of the policy process discussed in this paper represent the sort of 'middle-range' theories which seem to be most prevalent in the field of comparative politics. They do not seek to explain all major differences across political systems, but instead seek to compare significant aspects of those systems – in this case, the factors affecting policy outputs and impacts. The four theories of the policy process discussed in the preceding section are superior to the stages heuristic because they are all causal theories with explicit assumptions and hypotheses about what is driving the policy process. For Hofferbert, it is primarily background socio-economic conditions; for institutional rational choice theorists, it is individual values and information, as well as rules at the constitutional level; for the ACF, it is individual/coalition values and exogenous shocks; for Kingdon, it is a combination of information concerning the problem, the values and interests of those in the policy and political streams and the presence of windows of opportunity. They all make some effort to propose testable hypotheses and all except Hofferbert try to deal seriously with substantive policy information and the interaction of policy elites. Each of the four theories probably has some advantages vis-a-vis the others. The great advantage of Hofferbert is that its parsimony and 'black box' character make it ideally suited to comparative policy research across large numbers of political systems and, even more so, to cross-sectional, longitudinal designs. The Kingdon, Ostrom and Sabatier approaches, however, are likely to be superior to Hofferbert in comparing developments in the same policy domain, such as transportation or health policy, across a few political systems because they give more attention to the strategies, learning and interaction of policy elites.

If Kingdon has an advantage, it is in understanding major policy innovations – particularly from the standpoint of policy practitioners. Most practitioners I know readily identify with Kingdon's view of multiple, poorly interconnected streams which may, on occasion, be joined by a 'window of opportunity'. On the other hand, the policy streams approach needs to be expanded to include background socio-economic and institutional variables, as well as the actors involved in policy implementation, before it will be able to compete successfully with the other three.

The greatest advantage of the institutional rational choice approach is its strong connections to a well-developed body of theory in microeconomics and to other rational actor models which are now permeating the social sciences. At the same time, there is an impressive array of evidence that most people are neither as self-interested nor as rational as these models assume (Cook and Levi 1990). While the Ostrom approach is superb for analysing specific institutional contexts, its focus on institutional rules tends to neglect background socio-economic conditions and to present difficulties when dealing with the dozens, if not hundreds, of different institutions involved in most policy subsystems.

The advocacy coalition framework, on the other hand, is well suited to deal with large numbers of institutions in policy subsystems. It also focuses on changes in socio-economic conditions and the belief systems of policy elites – the strengths of the Hofferbert and Kingdon models, respectively. Finally, it is relatively easy to 'nest' Ostrom's institutional rational choice approach into the ACF (Jenkins-Smith 1991; Schlager 1994).[5] In short, the ACF may well do the best job of synthesising the strengths of the other three approaches. On the other hand, its tendency toward highly aggregated analysis means that thus far it has neglected a number of critical topics, such as the interaction of elites within a coalition (Schlager 1994).

In sum, while I certainly have a bias towards the ACF, all four of the approaches discussed here are superior to the stages heuristic. They all need further theoretical development and testing in a variety of settings to assess their relative strengths and weaknesses.

NOTES

1. *Webster's Unabridged Dictionary* defines 'heuristic' as 'helping to discover or learn'. Thus the 'stages heuristic' is a conceptual tool which helped us to learn about certain features of the policy process which were hidden by the institutionalist approach. It has accomplished that purpose and now needs to be replaced by more explicit causal models.
2. Sabatier (1988) hypothesises that policy-oriented learning is more likely to occur between coalitions when the issues are technically tractable, when they deal with important secondary aspects of belief systems and when coalitions are forced to confront each other in professionalised forums. See Jenkins-Smith (1988) for very similar arguments developed independently.
3. The ACF is currently being applied in two cross-national policy studies: Jan Eberg's analysis of hazardous waste policy in the Netherlands and Bavaria and Rinie van Est's study of wind power in the Netherlands, Denmark and, possibly, California. Both are at the Department of Public Administration, University of Amsterdam, working with Robert Hoppe.
4. The ACF is, in many respects, an elaboration of some of Heclo's (1974) basic ideas in his analysis of social welfare policy in Britain and Sweden during this century; as will be recalled, the diffusion of policy ideas across countries was an important feature of his analysis.
5. For example, it would be easy for the ACF researcher to assume that coalitions use Ostrom's categories of institutional rules and of levels of institutional analysis in determining their strategies for institutional design.

REFERENCES

Anderson, James. 1975. *Public Policy-Making*. New York: Praeger.

Anderson, James, David Brady, Charles Bullock and Joseph Stewart. 1984. *Public Policy and Politics in America*, 2nd edn. Monterey: Brooks/Cole.

Bardach, Eugene. 1977. *The Implementation Game: What Happens After a Bill Becomes a Law?* Cambridge, MA: MIT Press.

Barrett, Susan and Colin Fudge. 1981. *Policy and Action*. London: Methuen.

Bromley, Daniel. 1992. *Making the Commons Work*. San Francisco: Institute of Contemporary Studies.

Buchanan, James and Gordon Tullock. 1962. *The Calculus of Consent*. Ann Arbor: University of Michigan Press.

Caplan, Nathan *et al*. 1975. *The Use of Social Science Knowledge in Policy Decisions at the National Level*. Ann Arbor: Institute for Social Research, University of Michigan.

Chubb, John and Terry Moe. 1990. *Politics, Markets and America's Schools.* Washington, DC: Brookings Institution.

Cohen, Michael, James March and John Olsen. 1972. 'A Garbage Can Model of Organizational Choice.' *Administrative Science Quarterly* 17: 1–25.

Cook, Karen and Margaret Levi. 1990. *The Limits of Rationality.* Chicago: University of Chicago Press.

Dye, Thomas and Harmon Ziegler. 1975. *The Irony of Democracy,* 3rd edn. North Scituate: Duxbury Press.

Easton, David. 1965. *A Systems Analysis of Political Life.* New York: John Wiley.

Eulau, Heinz and Kenneth Prewitt. 1973. *Labyrinths of Democracy.* Indianapolis: Bobbs-Merrill.

Eyestone, Robert. 1977. 'Confusion, Diffusion and Innovation.' *American Political Science Review* 71: 441–7.

Fritschler, A. Lee. 1975. *Smoking and Politics,* 2nd edn. Englewood Cliffs: Prentice Hall.

Hardin, Garrett. 1968. 'The Tragedy of the Commons.' *Science* 162: 1243–8.

Heclo, Hugh. 1974. *Social Policy in Britain and Sweden.* New Haven: Yale University Press.

Hofferbert, Richard. 1970. 'Elite Influence in State Policy Formation: A Model for Comparative Inquiry.' *Polity* 2: 316–44.

Hofferbert, Richard. 1974. *The Study of Public Policy.* Indianapolis: Bobbs-Merrill.

Hofferbert, Richard and John Urice. 1985. 'Small Scale Policy: The Federal Stimulus versus Competing Explanations for State Funding of the Arts.' *American Journal of Political Science* 29: 308–29.

Jenkins-Smith, Hank. 1988. 'Analytical Debates and Policy Learning: Analysis and Change in the Federal Bureaucracy.' *Policy Sciences* 21: 169–212.

Jenkins-Smith, Hank. 1991. 'Alternative Theories of the Policy Process: Reflections on a Research Strategy for the Study of Nuclear Waste Policy.' *PS: Political Science and Politics* 24: 157–66.

Jenkins-Smith, Hank and David Weimer. 1985. 'Analysis as Retrograde Action.' *Public Administration Review* 45: 485–94.

Jones, Charles. 1987. *An Introduction to the Study of Public Policy,* 2nd edn. Belmont: Wadsworth.

Kingdon, John. 1984. *Agendas, Alternatives and Public Policies.* Boston: Little, Brown.

Kiser, Larry and Elinor Ostrom. 1982. 'The Three Worlds of Action.' In *Strategies of Political Inquiry,* ed. E. Ostrom. Beverly Hills: Sage.

Klingemann, Hans-Dieter, Richard Hofferbert and Ian Budge. 1994. *Parties, Policies and Democracy.* Boulder: Westview Press.

Lasswell, Harold. 1951. 'The Policy Orientation.' In *The Policy Sciences,* eds D. Lerner and H. Lasswell. Stanford: Stanford University Press.

Leichter, Howard. 1979. *A Comparative Approach to Policy Analysis.* London: Cambridge University Press.

Lundqvist, Lennart. 1980. *The Hare and the Tortoise: Clean Air Policies in the U.S. and Sweden.* Ann Arbor: University of Michigan Press.

Mazmanian, Daniel and Paul Sabatier. 1980. 'A Multivariate Model of Public Policy-Making.' *American Journal of Political Science* 24: 439–68.

Miller, Gary. 1992. *Managerial Dilemmas: The Political Economy of Hierarchy.* Cambridge: Cambridge University Press.

Moe, Terry. 1984. 'The New Economics of Organization.' *American Journal of Political Science* 28: 739–77.

Nakamura, Robert. 1987. 'The Textbook Policy Process and Implementation Research.' *Policy Studies Review* 7(1): 142–54.

Nelson, Barbara. 1984. *Making an Issue of Child Abuse.* Chicago: University of Chicago Press.

Ostrom, Elinor. 1986. 'A Method of Institutional Analysis.' In *Guidance, Control and Evaluation in the Public Sector*, eds F.X. Kaufmann, G. Majone and E. Ostrom. Berlin: de Gruyter.

Ostrom, Elinor. 1990. *Governing the Commons.* Cambridge: Cambridge University Press.

Ostrom, Elinor, Larry Schroeder and Susan Wynne. 1993. *Institutional Incentives and Sustainable Development: Infrastructure Policies in Perspective.* Boulder: Westview Press.

Ostrom, Elinor, Roy Gardner and James Walder. 1994. *Rules, Games and Common Pool Resources.* Ann Arbor: University of Michigan Press.

Peters, Guy. 1986. *American Public Policy: Promise and Performance*, 2nd edn. Chatham: Chatham House.

Riker, William. 1962. *The Theory of Political Coalitions.* New Haven: Yale University Press.

Ripley, Randal. 1985. *Policy Analysis in Political Science.* Chicago: Nelson Hall.

Rose, Douglas. 1973. 'National and Local Forces in State Politics.' *American Political Science Review* 67: 1162–73.

Sabatier, Paul. 1988. 'An Advocacy Coalition Framework of Policy Change and the Role of Policy-Oriented Learning Therein.' *Policy Sciences* 21: 129–68.

Sabatier, Paul. 1991. 'Toward Better Theories of the Policy Process.' *PS: Political Science and Politics* 24: 147–56.

Sabatier, Paul and Hank Jenkins-Smith, eds. 1988. 'Policy Change and Policy-Oriented Learning.' *Policy Sciences* 21: 123–277.

Sabatier, Paul and Hank Jenkins-Smith, eds. 1993. *Policy Change and Learning: An Advocacy Coalition Approach.* Boulder: Westview.

Schlager, Edella. 1994. 'Policy Making and Collective Action: Defining Coalitions with the Advocacy Coalition Framework.' Tucson: School of Public Administration, University of Arizona.

Sharkansky, Ira, ed. 1970. *Policy Analysis in Political Science.* Chicago: Markham.

Thompson, Michael, Richard Ellis and Aaron Wildavsky. 1990. *Cultural Theory.* Boulder: Westview Press.

van Muijen, Marie-Louise. 1993. *Better Safe than Provocative.* Amsterdam: VU University Press.

Vogel, David. 1986. *National Styles of Regulation: Environmental Policy in Great Britain and the US.* Ithaca: Cornell University Press.

Wildavsky, Aaron. 1982. 'The Three Cultures: Explaining Anomalies in the American Welfare State.' *The Public Interest* 69: 45–58.

Wildavsky, Aaron. 1987. 'Choosing Preferences by Constructing Institutions: A Cultural Theory of Preference Formation.' *American Political Science Review* 81: 3–22.

Zahariadis, Nikolaos. 1994. *Selling the Family Silver: Privatization in the UK and France.* Ann Arbor: University of Michigan Press.

8 Methodological Individualism and the U-Shaped Curve: Some Theoretical Guidelines for the Comparative Analysis of Public Policy
Henry Milner

INTRODUCTION

The purpose of this collection is to stimulate thinking about what it means to observe government activity from a comparative perspective. Government activities are concerned with (public) policy, and, like the other contributors to this volume, I am interested in making sense of these activities. We are engaged in what is thus best identified as comparative public policy (CPP) analysis, a field in the continual process of defining itself. In this paper, I seek to make a contribution to that process. While other contributions focus on the validity of certain common practices, I am more interested in the conceptualisation underlying these practices and its theoretical foundations.

Thinking about what it means to do comparative public policy analysis is especially pertinent at this point in time as every year thousands of scholars publish articles in hundreds of journals and collections. The quantitative surge is even greater than revealed by the number of publications owing to the revolution in data collection, processing and transmission. A project requiring comparative data of a magnitude that a generation ago could be aspired to only by teams of researchers at the richest institutions is today within the reach of students working alone.

The researcher today can instantaneously electronically 'access' longitudinal data from all over the world comparing voting results, government expenditures, GDP growth, unemployment, years of schooling, strikes and lock-outs, criminal behaviour – the list goes on and on. The numbers can be 'crunched' at a speed so high and a cost so low as to have been inconceivable twenty years ago. The CPP investigator thus finds him/herself with virtually unrestricted choices as to dependent and independent variables to be tested from which to derive hypotheses concerning the relationship between institutional arrangements and public policy outcomes. While hypotheses investigated are typically cast in relation to the conclusions of existing work of senior members of the profession, the resulting appearance of cumulativeness is misleading. Each tree is portrayed in the setting of a particular grove, but the view of the entire forest is missing – a state of events compounded by the blurring of traditional disciplinary distinctions in the social sciences and the fall of Marxist-based ideological barriers.

As a result, there is no widely accepted criterion for judging whether a given study makes a contribution to the overall advance of CPP analysis. Appearances here are deceiving. CPP papers increasingly resemble those in economics in their highly technical language and formal presentation. But the similarity stops there. Reputable work in economics operates in some identifiable relationship to the basic competitive model in product, labour and capital markets that forms the central theoretical core of the discipline. The groves, at least in principle, can be seen in the context of the forest: the relationships among the various sub-fields are set out in standard textbooks in macro- and microeconomics, of which there are no real equivalents in CPP. In the absence of such a disciplinary core in and around which research agendas find their niches, the claim to scientific status for CPP is unjustifiable. The increasing use of stylised mathematical formulations in fact conceals its failure to develop the cumulative process of information gathering and theory building that constitutes science.

This is not intended as criticism. Students of public policy can hardly be blamed for taking advantage of new techniques, or for the absence of an acknowledged theoretical core in their field of research. Indeed, some reject the very idea of a single theoretical core – and not without reason. A case can be made for reverting to an earlier conceptualisation when the study of politics was that of statecraft: informed, systematic explanation leading to reasoned policy recommendations in a language accessible to the educated generalist – something precluded by the use of stylised mathematical formulations. In this conceptualisation, instead of aspiring to the status of a cumulative scientific discipline like economics, CPP is content to take its place with applied fields like law, journalism and social work.

But the genie is out of the bottle. Only if it is demonstrated that aspiring to develop the core theoretical framework for a science of comparative public policy analysis is futile can we reasonably limit our aspirations to CPP as statecraft. Such an effort can hardly be proved futile if it has not really been attempted. In this paper, I seek to contribute toward such an attempt, following the direction taken in my recent work (Milner 1994). I propose two elements for a place at the theoretical core of comparative public policy: methodological individualism, as prescribed by rational choice theory, and the neo-corporatist 'U-shaped curve'.

THE STARTING POINT: METHODOLOGICAL INDIVIDUALISM

If there is one day to be a cumulative science of comparative policy analysis, it must be based on methodological individualism, premised on individual rational choice. As North argues (1990:5): 'The choice theoretic approach is essential because a logically consistent, potentially testable set of hypotheses must be built on a theory of human behavior.' In making this assertion, I am explicitly arguing that political science must share certain fundamental theoretical premises with economics. We can choose to reject methodological individualism, but only on the condition that we acknowledge that in so doing we are taking the road of the second-best option, that of statecraft, abandoning the possibility of a cumulative science of public policy.

Methodological individualism does not mean we are interested in the behaviour of individuals as individuals, rather, it means that assumptions and explanations about determinants and effects of policies must be consistent with the choices of rational individuals. Hypotheses identifying variables to be tested and accounting for the relationship between them must be cast in terms taking into account and making sense of the choices of affected individuals. Methodological individualism does not rule out any particular area of concern or topic of research and analysis. It does, however, impose rigorous standards on explanations and conclusions to be drawn. In order to argue that a policy goal is feasible, one must show that at every practical stage in the implementation of the policy it is compatible with the requisite individual behaviour by rational actors.

Rational behaviour – by definition – can always be expressed in cost–benefit terms: expected action by affected individuals entails higher benefits and/or lower costs to them than known alternatives. Individuals are thus understood to act as if they compare expected benefits and costs of action prior to adopting strategies for action (Ostrom 1991). The benefits need not be selfish or material ones; moreover, choices can be mistaken since relevant knowledge about the relationship between choices and preferred outcomes may be absent. Rational choice leaves to psychologists the realm of unconscious factors causing individuals to act against what they themselves express to be their interests.

Application of the theory is necessarily imprecise. Preferences are not always clear or people can be uncertain, especially when emotions are at play. Moreover, they cannot always compare all expected costs and benefits before acting because circumstances are such as not to permit it – that is, the information costs are too high. Assuming that under similar circumstances, and with the same relevant knowledge, individuals with the same preferences will make the same choices, rational choice theory allows for culturally based differences in preferences and knowledge, but it starts from the only possible common ground from which one can transcend relativism. Similarly, looked at from a different angle, the rational choice approach also breaks down the barrier between the producer and consumer of knowledge.

Thus conceived, comparative policy analysis, like other work in the social sciences based on rational choice, is interested in aggregates. It shares with economics its stress on human choices taken 'at the margin'. In economics, the world is taken as it is, and then the effects of policy change or institutional innovation are modelled on the basis of altered costs and benefits: what would be the effect on behaviour of higher interest rates, a weaker exchange rate, a lower tariff, a change in the price of energy...? Except for the greater difficulty in quantifying costs and benefits, there is no intrinsic distinction between the effect of these measures and those of more direct concern to CPP such as changes in laws affecting labour force training or collective bargaining rights. The model treats the aggregate of marginal individual responses to these changes as explained by the altered cost–benefit situation in which individuals find themselves, without entering into the motivations of any particular individual.

By taking an institutionalist approach, as set out below, rational choice is in a position to overcome any bias favouring individual/market as opposed to collective/public policy alternatives. Methodological collectivism proved to be the fatal flaw in Marxist theory. The unexamined notion of an objective working-class interest assumed away the central question to be explored: namely the circumstances under which individual workers will support their organisational leaders in their actions. Residues of this methodological collectivism found their way into the programmes of even the most pragmatic social democratic parties in and outside Scandinavia (Milner 1989), and unfortunately, from the point of view presented here, affected much of the analysis of the European welfare state.

A case in point is the influential work of Esping-Andersen (1985) who analyses the emergence of the welfare state in terms of the strategic interests of the working class. Working-class victories result in the 'decommodification' of labour (Kolberg and Esping-Andersen 1992) which is assumed to be intrinsically in the interests of the workers and opposed to those of business. In fact, the individual knows that though she benefits by being freed of market-driven imperatives in her working life, she loses from the reduced productivity when workers in general are so freed. Methodological individualism teaches that not only business but also labour benefits from the existence of 'commodifying' labour market institutions that inhibit employees from staying at home when capable of working and otherwise abusing the regulations designed to protect them.

Let there be no misunderstanding: methodological individualism means paying attention to incentives; it need not mean that rational choice is incompatible with the welfare state. For a rational individual, a well-functioning welfare state can be compared to a comprehensive insurance policy. When we buy insurance, we give up consumption when resources are greater in order to have them available when needed at another time; the same, we shall see, can be true of efficient redistributive policies. But not all insurance is efficient; in many cases, co-insurance is required to achieve the desired effect. In general, methodological individualism entails incorporating appropriate disincentives to free riding into welfare state redistributive policies.

We can now turn to applying the cost–benefit approach to the subject matter of comparative public policy analysis, the relationship between institutional choices and policy outcomes.

THE COSTS AND BENEFITS OF INSTITUTIONAL CHOICES

In the perfect market of the classical microeconomic model, choices are entirely free. The consumer depends only on herself for information, and the outcome of the action is not affected by the actions of other consumers. Once the choices of other individuals enter into consideration, the analysis enters a new dimension, that of institutions. In rational choice analysis this dimension is captured through game theory. Consider two neighbours and their choice of where to shop. Each wants access to the cheaper products and larger selection of the supermarket, but each would like the local corner store to stay in business because of its convenience and its contribution to the vitality of the neighbourhood. When A shops at the supermarket, she is, in effect, 'free riding' on B patronising the corner store – an inherently unstable situation. Institutional solutions in this simple two-person game may take the contractual form of 'side-payments', in which A subsidises part of B's extra cost, or in their agreeing to alternate shopping at the corner store.

In reality, of course, many shoppers are involved, in effect ruling out such solutions. A solution to this 'n-person' game must be found in wider institutional arrangements, for example, a law barring supermarkets from selling beer and wine, or from being open on evenings or Sundays. Institutional or policy choices of this kind serve to alter the cost–benefit calculations of individuals in ways that have desirable aggregate consequences. In these economic examples, institutional interventions can alter either the relative costs or benefits of alternate choices. The former become more salient once we broaden our application to public policy in general. It is difficult to aggregate choices based on benefits provided, since individuals seek different benefits from public policies and evaluate them differently. On the other hand, costs are less affected by such subjective considerations, since their reduction affects all individuals in a similar manner.

Consider the decision of whether to vote or to join a party or interest group – acts considered desirable in a democracy – as opposed to not doing so. The benefits derived from such a choice vary: some individuals (X) place greater emphasis on furthering their own narrow interests; others (Y) are more concerned with the betterment of society (Whiteley and Seyd 1994). If, say, by reforming the electoral system, we give parties an incentive to move from a more ideological to a more pragmatic stance, we cannot easily know whether the resulting reduced benefits and thus participation levels of Y will exceed the enhanced benefits and participation of X. On the other hand, a change in electoral rules reducing the costs of participation, say by simplifying the registration process or keeping the polling booths open longer, is certain to increase political participation.

There is a parallel indirect argument to be made, one related to the fact that political participation is higher among more informed voters. I have argued elsewhere (Milner 1993) that the more a form of election produces a legislature accurately reflecting the make-up and sentiments of the population the more political parties have an interest in informing the population about the consequences of existing and alternative policies. This adds a cost-based explanation of higher participation under proportional representation (Blais and Carty 1990) to the usual one based on benefits – namely that in a proportional system there are fewer wasted votes and hence greater aggregate benefits from voting (Powell 1980).

Applied to electoral systems, methodological individualism thus invokes a principle similar to that of economics in relation to taxation: they should not institutionally distort the signals expressed in each vote (just as taxes should not distort the signals in each consumer's purchase). In terms of the wider concerns addressed here, methodological individualism converts into the following operating principle: CPP analysis should be concerned with policy alternatives that reduce the costs of the requisite behaviour by rational individuals.

In what follows, I apply this logic to political economy, that is that wide range of CPP analysis that takes the dependent variable to be social and economic well-being or welfare. We thus rephrase the central question posed by political economy – that of which institutions promote greater welfare – in the terms of our initial operating principle: what institutional choices result in lowering the costs of individuals choosing to act in such a way as to enhance welfare? In contemporary western political economy – now that Marxism has proved to be an empty shell – two schools of thought dominate the field: public choice – which is here identified as the application of the classical microeconomic model to public policy issues – and neo-corporatism. If our question is indeed the right one, then it should enable us to address the concerns and incorporate the insights of both schools of thought.

NEO-CORPORATISM AND THE U-SHAPED CURVE

The task is thus an ambitious one: to set out a basic framework for CPP analysis linking institutional choices to aggregate welfare by incorporating to the neo-corporatist framework basic elements of public choice. In taking it on, we look especially to the recent work of a number of economists who have sought to adapt neo-corporatist analysis to their own concerns and priorities.

At its best, neo-corporatism has managed to reconcile analysis of organisational action with methodological individualism. For neo-corporatist students of European interest groups, the most important characteristic of these organisations was that they cooperated among themselves and were incorporated by government directly into the decision-making process (Rokkan 1966), creating a 'negotiated economy' (Nielsen and Pedersen 1988). Public policy could be interpreted as the outcome of a 'social partnership' between 'peak' or 'encompassing' representative organisations (Schmitter 1981, 1985), especially the trade unions and the business-interest organisations, which take each others' differing interests into account in tri-partite bargaining (Korpi 1991). For Katzenstein (1985), a culturally based belief in the value of social partnership is a third fundamental characteristic of corporatist societies along with centralised and concentrated interest groups and a voluntary system of policy coordination. Albert (1991) develops a parallel interpretation of what he calls the 'Rhenish' model, in which ownership in business and commerce is understood to carry with it social responsibility, expressed through cooperative long-term relationships.

Neo-corporatist studies published in the 1970s and 1980s proved fruitful in explaining choices pertaining to economic, social and labour market policies and their outcomes especially in Nordic and Germanic Europe in the post-war decades. Though focusing on organisational actors, neo-corporatists, unlike neo-Marxists, made use of advances in the application of game theory in economics (see, for example, Scharpf 1991). In such game-theory based conceptualisations, institutional arrangements are usually modelled as potential cooperative solutions to a Prisoners' Dilemma which take the form of a macroeconomic trade-off: labour restrains demands for money-wage increases and collaborates on industrial adjustment in return for a 'social wage' in the form of social security and full-employment policies.

In the 1980s, this rather crude analysis was refined by economists who applied the techniques of economic analysis to corporatist relationships. The best-known work was by two Swedes, Lars Calmfors and E.J. Driffill (1988), who showed how, under corporatist centralised bargaining, shared knowledge that real wage gains are dissipated in higher prices leads actors to take advantage of the structures to restrain wages. 'Because of their individual power and small number ... agents have the incentive to behave strategically, taking explicit account of how their actions will affect others – and what the resulting feedback to themselves will be.... As the theory of repeated games shows, such [ongoing and repeated interactions] are conducive to compromise and to forms of cooperative behaviour which are to the mutual benefit of all concerned' (Rowthorn 1992:84–5; see also Freeman 1988).

With the high-employment Nordic and Northern European economies performing reasonably well in overall economic performance in the post-war decades, a positive correlation between such economic performance and the level of corporatism, as indicated by high unionisation and centralised bargaining, could be discerned. Wage restraint under corporatism allowed these countries to implement successfully a 'neo-corporatist strategy for economic growth' (Paloheimo 1984; see also Keman 1984; Keman and Whiteley 1987).

But much was left out of this conceptualisation. In order to get a significant correlation between the level of corporatism and economic performance, Japan had to be excluded or cast as corporatist.[1] Yet even then much depended on one's measure of economic performance. Corporatist institutional arrangements were indeed positively associated with the level of employment but, when economic growth and inflation were included as measures of performance, the picture became blurred (Scharpf 1987). A better fit, it began to emerge, was that of a curvilinear relationship (see Steinmo 1988; Lehner 1988). This argument was developed in the work of Finnish political scientist Heikki Paloheimo and was taken up by economists. Paloheimo (1984) insisted that, apart from the neo-corporatist strategy, there was also a '*laissez-faire* strategy for economic growth, which could succeed in certain countries with dominant neo-conservative parties where there were weak and fragmented trade unions'. In effect, the curve changes directions: the relationship between corporatism and economic performance is U-shaped (see Figure 8.1). This means that, under high levels of cor-

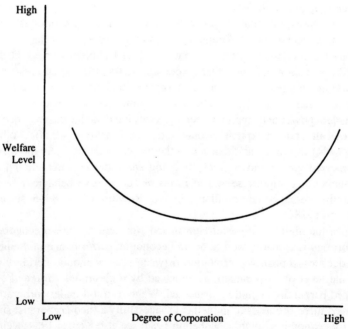

Fig. 8.1   The U-Shaped Curve (1)

poratism, policies reinforcing corporatist institutions can have a positive effect on economic performance – but not under low levels of corporatism.

In the economist's terms, corporations in the non-corporatist (*laissez-faire*) countries keep down wages because they cannot raise prices without weakening themselves in the product market. It is among nations in the middle, with labour markets dominated by medium-size institutions with enough market power to win concessions, but small enough to pass most of the cost on to others, that the restraining forces are inadequate. Thus economic performance can be expected to be lowest under a medium level of corporatism, accounting for the U shape of the curve.

Paloheimo (1990) finds that only in the highly unionised countries does more centralised bargaining correlate with lower rates of inflation and unemployment. In this he adds weight to Calmfors and Driffill's and the other economists' emphasis on the importance and concentration of trade unions in their operationalisation of corporatism. But other work, using different criteria for rating the level of corporatism,[2] arrives at the same U-shaped relationship. I suggest that the U-shaped curve thus derived can potentially serve CPP analysis in a manner similar to that of the supply and demand curves in the classical macroeconomic model. Because neo-corporatist logic applies at one pole, and that of public choice at the other, placing the level of corporatism in institutional arrangements on one axis allows for a potential detente between neo-corporatists and public choice scholars when it comes to interpreting outcomes on the other axis, that of economic performance or welfare. As Paloheimo puts it: 'we should henceforth see liberal-pluralism and corporatism ... as complementary sub-theories of a more general political and economic theory' (1990:404).

Evidently, unlike price and quantity in the supply and demand curves of the classical macroeconomic model, placing on one axis a measure of the level of corporatism in institutional arrangements and, on the other axis, the level of welfare raises conceptual problems. It is not a question of lack of data: hundreds of recently published studies correlate the level of corporatism of western societies with one or more economic, political or social dependent variables. The problem appears less acute when it comes to locating societies on the corporatist–non-corporatist axis. Though different criteria are used, it is possible to discern a gradual process of refinement of the criteria proposed, bringing with it a greater, if incomplete, consensus over where given societies are to be placed (Lijphart and Crepaz 1991).

AGGREGATE WELFARE: COMBINING ECONOMIC PERFORMANCE AND REDISTRIBUTIVENESS

It is likely, however, to prove more difficult to arrive at a criterion for locating societies based on their level of (aggregate) welfare acceptable to both neo-corporatist and public choice oriented scholars. The latter place greater emphasis on comparative wealth indicators like level and growth in GNP per capita, while the former look to rates of employment and unemployment as indicators of fair distribution of resources. One useful composite measure for the latter has been developed by Rowthorn (1992) who subtracts wage dispersion (the inter-industry coefficient of variation in earnings) from employment (the average proportion of the population aged 15–64 employed from 1973 to 1985, with a part-time job tabulated as half a unit). On this scale, the mean for industrial democracies is 44, with the Nordic countries occupying the top four places, with rates of 51 to 61. High employment usually translates into low rates of unemployment, but not necessarily, as high unemployment levels in Denmark, and recently Finland and Sweden, show.

Efforts such as this are promising, though, admittedly, outside the mainstream of contemporary political economy. Still, the prospects for progress toward consensus around a U-shaped-curve-based analysis are encouraging since, at the theoretical level, the convergence of neo-corporatism and public choice has been facilitated by the decline of methodological collectivism. In what follows I attempt to cast the argument for the existence of a curvilinear relationship between corporatism and welfare in terms of individual calculations compatible with rational choice analysis. We start from the following proposition: if people in a democratic industrial society are given the opportunity to choose between living in one of two roughly equally rich societies, most would choose the one where wealth is distributed more equally and poverty is less extensive than the one with greater extremes between rich and poor. This choice is visualised in the Lorenz curves drawn below in Figures 8.2 and 8.3.

The Lorenz curve displays the share of total income received by the bottom X per cent of income units (individuals or households). Figure 8.2 shows two curves. From curve A it can be seen that the bottom 50 per cent of income units receive 28 per cent of total income; curve B shows a greater degree of inequality than curve A, especially at the lowest income levels. It is plausible to assume that for most individuals the marginal utility of a given unit of income decreases as overall wealth increases. Though some individuals are risk-takers for themselves, of these, most will seek to reduce risk once the well-being of dependants and descendants is at stake. As a consequence, since they cannot be certain of their future position or that of their children, they will prefer distribution A to B – an assumption strengthened by the degree of altruism among the better off toward the worse off.

Public choice oriented political economists, it is fair to assume, would question the choice depicted in Figure 8.2 as unrealistic, suggesting the real choice lies (as depicted in the stylised Figure 8.3) between curve A´ (rather than curve A) and curve B. Such a view is based on the assumption that, beyond a certain minimum, there is a trade-off between efficiency and equality: the more equally the pie is shared, the smaller it gets. If that assumption is correct, and the choice comes down to that depicted in Figure 8.3, as between B and A´, then outcome B will be the result and the more egalitarian distribution precluded. This is because, once a certain threshold is crossed, people perceive the redistributive measures as

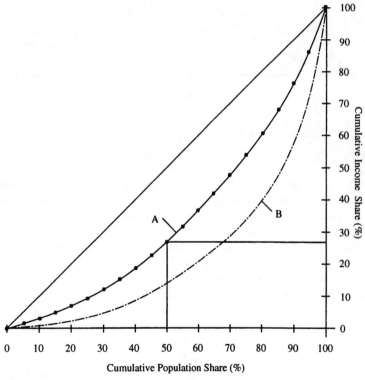

Fig. 8.2   The Lorenz Curve (1)

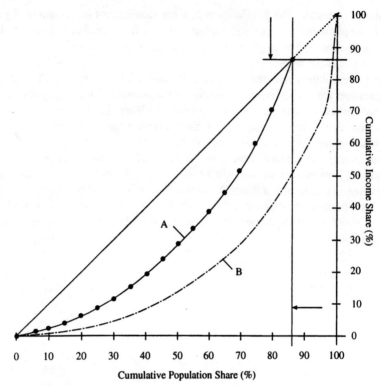

Fig. 8.3   The Lorenz Curve (2)

necessarily entailing falling economically behind a comparable neighbouring society. Armed with this perception, they will vote against these measures first with their feet (by moving resources to the neighbouring society)
and then with their hands.

But this is where the corporatist dimension enters. Can we not suppose
that the above public choice logic applies inevitably only under the set of
institutional arrangements to be found on the *laissez-faire* side, while at
the corporatist end institutional arrangements allow for the choice facing
individuals to be that depicted in Figure 8.2 rather than in Figure 8.3?
While most public choice theorists are naturally sceptical of this possibility, it has been taken seriously in the work of Mancur Olson[3] and in a
fairly extensive literature his ideas have spawned. In such a characterisation, the citizen in the United States, a country with non-corporatist institutional arrangements, by keeping taxes and levels of redistribution low,

attains outcome B, while the highly taxed Scandinavian attains something close enough to outcome A. Both are making rational choices within their own institutional framework.

We can incorporate this understanding into our U-shaped curve by refining our conceptualization of the outcomes at either end of the curve, disaggregating welfare into its constituent elements. The U-shaped curve (S) in Figure 8.4 is derived by summing up the values set out in curve (T), which depicts wealth and economic performance, and those in curve (V), which depicts redistributiveness. T is here conceived as a combined measure of economic performance (say GDP growth and current account balance) and comparative wealth (say GDP per capita in purchasing power parities). V could be a measure of the data in the Rowthorn composite scale of employment level and wage dispersion combined with the level of income inequality as revealed by post-tax Gini coefficients. (Gini coefficients are derived by dividing the area between the Lorenz curve and the diagonal by the total area under the diagonal.)

Fundamental to the argument being made is the fact that T contributes to S disproportionately on the non-corporatist side, while V does so on the

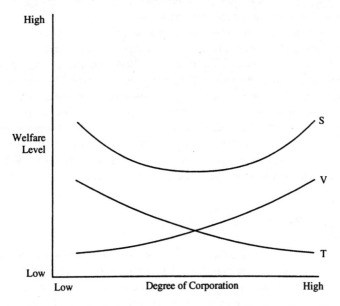

V = Level of redistributiveness; T = Aggregate wealth; S = Sum of V and T.

Fig. 8.4   The U-Shaped Curve (2)

corporatist side. This is our central working hypothesis. While I have not attempted to operationalise it empirically by placing the different countries, the literature strongly suggests that doing so would produce the correlations depicted in Figure 8.4, namely that V correlates positively with corporatism, while T correlates negatively with corporatism until a point roughly in the middle and then remains more or less steady. The United States, universally characterised as located at the non-corporatist end among the OECD countries, owes its high welfare rating to its comparative wealth (its score on the T scale) – especially when calculated in purchasing power parities; the same is true, though more moderately, of Canada and Switzerland. The Scandinavians take up positions at the other extreme, their high welfare levels owing more to redistributiveness, as captured by their V score.[4]

If our working hypothesis is correct, then, given the choice to do so, individuals as voters, but also as consumers and members of unions and other organisations, are acting rationally in supporting policies that maintain and reinforce existing institutional arrangements. This is so despite the fact that it entails in many cases quite different policy choices in countries at the *laissez-faire* end and in those at the corporatist end, since a given policy choice could be expected to have a different effect on welfare in a corporatist than in a non-corporatist society.

Consider, for example, differences in attitudes toward immigration and foreign aid in North America and the Scandinavian countries. In the context of pluralist (non-corporatist) institutional arrangements, a policy of open immigration not only increases the welfare of the new immigrants but also adds to the overall wealth of the society. On the other hand, providing existing services to a large number of newcomers insensitive to the trade-offs these entail can place great stress on institutional arrangements in corporatist societies. The citizens in such societies thus find it more appropriate to aid the needy in other countries through high levels of foreign aid than through opening the doors to immigration.

SOME PATHS FOR FUTURE RESEARCH

While rational choices differ in the context of differing institutional arrangements, the conceptualisation based on methodological individualism of what constitutes such choices is the same. For example, an explanation for a given society having a level of welfare which is lower (falling below S in Figure 8.4) than its (high or low) level of corporatism would lead one to expect is likely to be found in policies which place perverse incentives upon individuals. Perverse incentives are those that make it rational to act to undermine rather than reinforce the capacity of existing (corporatist or non-corporatist) institutional arrangements to optimise welfare. While the analogy should not be pushed too far, there is a parallel here with the development in economics of various explanations for 'market imperfections', including strategic behaviour and imperfect information.

In the *laissez-faire* context, there is wide literature on policies required to reduce the ability of groups to draw unproductive rents. For example, Gordon Tullock (1975) argues in favour of the continental European 'inquisitorial' court system and against the adversarial one in the United States, which promotes rent seeking on the part of lawyers to the tune of billions of dollars. In the corporatist context, explanations for lower than expected attained levels of welfare are sought in policies which place incentives upon individuals to undermine rather than reinforce existing corporatist institutional arrangements. An example, as noted above, was Swedish sick-leave and long-term disability policy in the 1980s which replaced pay at 100 per cent and failed to monitor employees' actions while removing from employers all financial incentives to do so.

Neo-corporatist research is primarily concerned with factors related to the existence and functioning of encompassing organisations in collective bargaining and collaboration in policy setting and implementation (see Scharpf 1991). But, while central, this is only one dimension of corporatist institutional arrangements. Two others are elaborated in recent work by this author. The first, mentioned above, concerns electoral and other specifically political institutional arrangements (Milner 1994: Chapter 8). The second is cultural: the mechanisms for the dissemination of the knowledge on the basis of which individuals decide whether and how to act as voters, consumers and members of organisations (Milner 1994: Chapter 6).

While neo-corporatists are generally open to a U-shaped relationship, most mainstream political economists, at least in North America, are more likely to regard corporatist institutional arrangements as short-lived, especially now, though this may be about to change, that there is no call for a middle ground between state socialism and *laissez-faire* capitalism in the wake of the demise of the former. A crucial testing ground for the validity of this approach is thus provided by developments in the corporatist/social democratic countries (see Bergounioux and Manin 1989). The recent economic difficulties of Sweden, most prominent of the countries generally placed at the neo-corporatist pole of the U-shaped curve, seemed to furnish the evidence to this effect.[5]

The analysis herein would look for poor policy choices at the root of Swedish economic problems and expect that individuals and organisations would seek to reinforce rather than undermine existing institutional arrangements when it came to addressing the problems. Let me summarise briefly from my analysis of recent developments in Sweden and the other Nordic countries (Milner 1994: Part 3) in this regard. Swedish sick-leave policy exacerbated labour shortages which, combined with poorly timed deregulation of financial markets, led to a massive outflow of capital in the late 1980s. On the surface, these developments threatened corporatist institutional arrangements as manifested in the rejection of participation in corporatist bodies by the Swedish Employers' Federation (SAF) in the late 1980s and its demands for a more flexible, decentralised form of contractual negotiations (Swenson 1991).

How profound are these developments? The change in the employers' attitudes is less perceptible in the other Nordic countries. Moreover, a second glance at Sweden reveals a somewhat different picture. Sick-leave policy has been changed, and the Social Democrats have regained their traditional support in the electorate. At the local level, cooperation among business, labour and public agencies dealing with employment, training and research, and development has remained very much alive, while sectorial bargaining combined with coordination of demands, especially on the labour side, has meant that labour market outcomes were not all that different from those under centralised bargaining (see Agell and Lundborg 1993). And when the economy worsened, Swedish business was prepared to look to corporatist solutions. In the 'crisis deal' of September 1992, the political allies of business and labour reached a wide-ranging agreement on economic and social policies to overcome financial problems – as they did on a complete overhaul of the pension system in January 1994.

With high unemployment and high debt, Sweden faces major difficulties in maintaining the welfare state programmes people have come to expect. But, on balance, facing them seems more likely to reinforce than undermine corporatist institutional arrangements. In the long run, the pronouncements of organisational leaders matter less than the everyday choices of individuals, who, if they continue to see value in preserving long-standing institutional arrangements will find ways of doing so. It is only if the new conditions, and the policy changes initiated by government to accommodate them, are such that rational individual choices undermine existing arrangements that we can conceive of a society significantly altering its location on the corporatist–*laissez-faire* axis. Short of such exceptional developments, corporatist arrangements should prove resilient, leaving the U-shaped curve as a potent conceptual tool for comparative public policy analysis.[6]

NOTES

1. Lange and Garrett (1985) describe the system in Japan (and Switzerland) as 'corporatism without labour'. Tarantelli (1986), identifying corporatism with the degree of consensus of interest groups and their interaction in the economic and political machinery of the government, places Japan at the top along with the Nordic countries, Germany and Austria.

2. Apart from the various measures related to trade union strength and centralisation, other criteria include the scope of collective bargaining (Cameron 1984; Lange and Garrett 1985), the scope of government activity (Martin 1988), the political strength of labour parties (Muller 1986), the extent to which business operates in a cohesive and coordinated manner (Dore 1990) and whether the economy is a small and open one (Cameron 1978; Katzenstein 1985).

3. Olson, unlike most public choice inspired political economists, draws widely on European experience, and is keenly interested in understanding efficient institutions of redistribution. While suspicious of the neo-corporatists counting on powerful groups to act in the interests of the weak in society (expecting them rather to siphon the benefits of redistributive policies to unions and cartels of professionals), he remains open to the possibility of very large organizations working together for the common good, something he discovers in the institutions of egalitarian Sweden which manage to stand up to cartels seeking hand-outs and tariff protection (Olson 1983, 1990).

4. One confirmation of our working hypothesis lies in comparative Gini data. The Luxembourg Income Study (LIS) has carried out the most thorough and genuinely comparable studies of income inequality in western countries. Using households as units and assigning members of the family, and including transfers and excluding taxes, LIS studies reveal a sharp contrast between the United States and Canada on one side, and Sweden, Norway and Finland on the other, with Gini levels of 32.6 and 29.9 versus 20.5, 22.5 and 24.3, respectively (Uusitalo 1989:80).

5. Generally speaking, this was the position taken by the Commission set up in 1992 to investigate Swedish economic policies and political institutions chaired by leading economist, Assar Lindbeck. The Commissioners, though seeking to preserve the welfare state and reduce unemployment, were not kind to the Swedish corporatist model. In the name of flexibility they called for even more decentralisation of collective bargaining and further dismantling of corporatist institutions.

6. This resilience, or 'path dependency', is a theme of a developing literature sometimes identified as new institutionalism or historical institutionalism and identified with such divergent observers as Skocpol (1985) and March and Olsen (1989).

REFERENCES

Agell, Jonas and Per Lundborg. 1993. *Theories of Unemployment: Survey Evidence from Swedish Manufacturing Firms.* Stockholm: IUI.

Albert, Michel. 1991. *Capitalisme contre capitalisme*. Paris: Seuil.

Bergounioux, A. and B. Manin. 1989. *Le Regime Social-Democrate*. Paris: Presses Universitaires de France.

Blais, A. and R.K. Carty. 1990. 'Does Proportional Representation Foster Voter Turnout?' *European Journal of Political Research* 18: 167–81.

Calmfors, L. and E.J. Driffill. 1988. 'Bargaining Structure, Corporatism and Macroeconomic Performance.' *Economic Policy* 6: 13–47.

Cameron, David. 1978. 'The Expansion of the Public Economy: A Comparative Analysis.' *American Political Science Review* 72: 1243–61.

Cameron, David. 1984. 'Social Democracy, Corporatism, Labour Quiescence and the Representation of Economic Interest in Advanced Capitalist Society.' In *Order and Conflict in Contemporary Capitalism*, ed. John H. Goldthorpe. Oxford: Oxford University Press.

Dore, Ronald. 1990. 'Japan: A Nation Made for Corporatism.' In *Corporatism and Accountability*, eds Colin Crouch and Ronald Dore. Oxford: Clarendon Press.

Esping-Andersen, Gosta. 1985. *Politics Against Markets*. Princeton: Princeton University Press.

Freeman, Richard. 1988. 'Labour Market Institutions and Economic Performance.' *Economic Policy* 6: 64–80.

Katzenstein, Peter. 1985. *Small States in World Markets: Industrial Policy in Europe*. Ithaca: Cornell University Press.

Keman, Hans. 1984. 'Politics, Policies and Consequences: A Cross-national Analysis of Public Policy-Formation in Advanced Capitalist Democracies (1967–1981).' *European Journal of Political Research* 12: 147–69.

Keman, Hans and Paul F. Whiteley. 1987. 'Coping with Crisis: Divergent Strategies and Outcomes.' In *Coping with the Economic Crisis: Alternative Responses to Economic Recession in Advanced Industrial Societies*, eds Hans Keman, Heikki Paloheimo and Paul F. Whiteley. London: Sage.

Kolberg, Jon E. and G. Esping-Andersen. 1992. 'Welfare States and Employment Regimes.' In *Between Work and Social Citizenship*, ed. J.E. Kolberg. Armonk: M.E. Sharpe.

Korpi, Walter. 1991. 'Political and Economic Explanations for Unemployment: A Cross-national and Longterm Analysis.' Presented at the SASE/IAREP Conference. Stockholm.

Lange, Peter and G. Garrett. 1985. 'The Politics of Growth: Strategic Interaction and Economic Performance in the Advanced Industrial Democracies.' *Journal of Politics* 47: 792–827.

Lehner, F. 1988. 'The Political Economy of Distributive Conflict.' In *Managing Mixed Economies*, eds F. Castles, F. Lehner and M. Schmidt. Berlin: Walter de Gruyter.

Lijphart, Arend and M.L. Crepaz. 1991. 'Corporatism and Consensus Democracy in Eighteen Countries: Conceptual and Empirical Linkages.' *British Journal of Political Science* 21: 235–56.

March, James G. and Johan P. Olsen. 1989. *Rediscovering Institutions: The Organizational Basis of Politics*. New York: The Free Press.

Martin, Andrew. 1988. 'Labor, Politics and Changing International Political Economy.' Presented at the International Political Science Association Congress of Washington DC.

Milner, Henry. 1989. *Sweden: Social Democracy in Practice.* Oxford: Oxford University Press.

Milner, Henry. 1993. 'In Defense of the European Model.' Presented at the Joint Workshops of the European Consortium for Political Research, Leiden (Netherlands).

Milner, Henry. 1994. *Social Democracy and Rational Choice: The Scandinavian Experience and Beyond.* London: Routledge.

Muller, Edward N. 1986. 'Distributions of Income in Advanced Capitalist Societies: Political Parties, Labour Unions, and the Industrial Economy.' Presented at annual meeting of the American Political Science Association, Washington DC.

Nielsen, Klaus and Ove K. Pedersen. 1988. 'The Negotiated Economy: Ideal and History.' *Scandinavian Political Studies* 11: 79–101.

North, Douglas C. 1990. *Institutions, Institutional Change and Economic Performance.* New York: Cambridge University Press.

Olson, Mancur. 1983. *An Approach to Public Policy that Transcends Outdated Ideologies.* Berlin: Wissenschaftszentrum.

Olson, Mancur. 1990. *How Bright are the Northern Lights? Some Questions about Sweden.* Lund: Lund University Press.

Ostrom, Elinor. 1991. 'Rational Choice Theory and Institutions.' *American Political Science Review* 85: 237–43.

Paloheimo, Heikki. 1984. 'Distributive Struggle and Economic Development in Developed Capitalist Countries.' *European Journal of Political Research* 12: 171–89.

Paloheimo, Heikki. 1990. 'Micro Foundations and Macro Practices of Centralized Industrial Relations.' *European Journal of Political Research* 18: 389–406.

Powell, G. Bingham. 1980. 'Voting Turnout in Thirty Democracies.' In *Electoral Participation: A Comparative Analysis*, ed. Richard Rose. London: Sage.

Rokkan, Stein. 1966. 'Norway: Numerical Democracy and Corporate Pluralism.' In *Political Oppositions in Western Democracies*, ed. Robert A. Dahl. New Haven: Yale University Press.

Rowthorn, B. 1992. 'Corporatism and Labour Market Performance.' In *Social Corporatism: A Superior Economic System?* eds J. Pekkarinen, M. Pohjola and B. Rowthorn. Oxford: Clarendon Press.

Scharpf, Fritz. 1987. 'Interpretation of Inflation and Unemployment in Western Europe.' *Journal of Public Policy* 7: 227–57.

Scharpf, Fritz. 1991. *Crisis and Choice in European Social Democracy.* Ithaca: Cornell University Press.

Schmitter, Philippe C. 1981. 'Interest Intermediations and Regime Governability in Contemporary Western Europe and North America.' In *Organizing Interests in Western Europe*, ed. Suzanne Berger. Cambridge: Cambridge University Press.

Schmitter, Philippe C. 1985. 'Neo-Corporatism and the State.' In *The Political Economy of Corporatism*, ed. Wyn Grant. London: Macmillan.

Skocpol, Theda. 1985. 'Bringing the State Back In: Strategies of Analysis in Current Research.' In *Bringing the State Back In*, eds P. Evans and T. Skocpol. Cambridge: Cambridge University Press.

Steinmo, Sven. 1988. 'Social Democracy versus Socialism: Goal Adaptation in Social Democratic Sweden.' *Politics and Society* 16: 403–46.

Swenson, Peter. 1991. 'Managing the Managers: On the Swedish Employers' Association and the Fall and Rise of Labour Market Dualism.' Presented at the SASE/IAREP Conference, Stockholm.

Tarantelli, E. 1986. 'The Regulation of Inflation and Unemployment.' *Industrial Relations* 25: 1–15.

Tullock, Gordon. 1975. 'On the Efficient Organization of Trials.' *Kyklos* 28: 745–62.

Uusitalo, Hannu. 1989. *Income Distribution in Finland.* Helsinki: Central Statistical Office of Finland.

Whiteley, Paul F. and Patrick Seyd. 1994. 'Rationality and Party Activism – Encompassing Tests of Alternative Models of Political Participation.' Presented at the Joint Workshops of the European Consortium for Political Research, Madrid (Spain).

9 Politico-Economic Models and the Economic Theory of Government Behaviour: Some Problems and Results

Jean-Dominique Lafay

This paper presents an appraisal of the politico-economic modelling of government behaviour, based on the author's own French/European experience. The first main section outlines briefly the normative/positive problem in public economics and its analytical consequences; the second deals with politico-economic models in industrialised democracies; the third surveys results for less developed countries (LDCs) and non-democratic cases.

PUBLIC ECONOMICS AND THE NORMATIVE/POSITIVE DEBATE

More than 80 per cent of economic policy problems are discussed in normative/prescriptive terms with the exclusive aim of defining 'optimal policies'. More than thirty years after the emergence of public choice and associated theories, the economics profession largely continues to ignore the problem of positive government behaviour. It has difficulties understanding that public policy could also be something to explain or to predict rather than dictate.

Several papers with a positive approach have indeed been published during the last ten years in the major professional journals, but these papers still represent a very small proportion of the total of those devoted to public economics in general, and the trend is not increasing significantly. Monetary policy is a very relevant case. This branch of economic theory has progressed much during the last twenty years. However, the assumption that monetary authorities are benevolent welfarists is seldom really questioned.[1]

This bias toward normative/prescriptive approaches is all the more surprising given that the situation is very different in the other areas of economics. Positive aims are, for example, very important if not dominant in the microeconomics of the private sector. There are four main reasons for the bias of public economics against positive analysis. First, economists have historically encountered great difficulties in having their discipline accepted as a 'science', i.e. to change its status from 'political economy' to 'economic science' – hence their taste for 'neutrality' in analysis and broad 'consensus' in social goals. To explain government behaviour means making assumptions about the political and bureaucratic aims of public decision-makers, i.e. to speak about politics. The fear here is that to speak about politics means, more or less, to engage in politics. Secondly, the demand for policy prescriptions is much greater in public economics. Supplying these prescriptions is generally easier and more immediately rewarding than providing pure positive analysis, especially when it is grounded in empirical research. Scholars therefore have incentives to overproduce normative theory. Thirdly, public economics attracts a higher proportion of scholars with a strong normative interest in social affairs. A similar selective mechanism is found, for example, in development economics. Finally, normative economics has become an important 'industry', with numerous public and private firms or independent workers producing policy advice, for example, to governments, social institutions or international organisations (Cairncross 1985; Stein 1986). There is a basic inconsistency between predicting what government will do (positive view) and saying what it has to do (normative/prescriptive view). For example, if the public sector is totally endogenous, as in politico-economic models, there is nothing more to be said about optimal policy, except for long-term institutional changes.

Other factors, however, have recently pushed in the opposite direction, creating strong incentives for economists to understand better the real behaviour of the public sector. First, modern welfare states have been built on many generous ideas but also on a surprisingly light analytical basis. Their present malfunctioning fully reveals this analytical deficit and creates a compensating demand for positive public economics. Secondly, there is a growing awareness, due to historical events, of the interaction between economics and politics in industrialised democracies, as well as in LDCs or in the former communist countries. Thirdly, the growing share of the public sector in the economy raises technical problems in macro-economic models. It is increasingly difficult to continue considering this sector as being exogenous, because this is a growing source of specification biases (Blinder and Solow 1974), and because the predictions for the endogenous private variables become conditional to variables of increasing importance (the exogenous public sector often representing more than 40 per cent of the total gross national product to predict). Finally, the development of statistical information on economic and political variables, which now covers a large period of time and a large number of countries, allows the use of econometric methods for more sound empirical studies (although the statistics produced by governments are still less clear and are published with more delay than the statistics those same governments demand of their own private sectors).

GOVERNMENT BEHAVIOUR AND POLITICO-ECONOMIC MODELS IN INDUSTRIALISED DEMOCRACIES

It is not possible to explain government behaviour without introducing politics. First, the government utility function clearly contains both political and economic variables and, second, the constraints to which it is submitted are also both economic and political. However, unlike the case for political scientists, the interest of economists in politics is limited to the explanation and prediction of public decisions (and more particularly of those with direct economic consequences). Economists have no direct interest in who wins elections, who governs or how specific coalitions are formed. Hence, the political block in their politico-economic models remains intentionally oversimplified.

In this section, the consequences of the introduction of political factors will first be analysed. The main conclusions obtained from the empirical estimates of politico-economic models based on French data will then be examined.

Political Factors and the Government Sector in Macromodels

1: Political Variables in Structural Constraints
For structural constraints, the introduction of politics in economic analysis and macromodels had to include, first, political variables in previously well-documented functions, such as investment functions, because they may have a direct effect on private expectations and, second, new functions explaining key political variables, hence the extended interest in vote or popularity functions.

As far as the first point is concerned, research on the influence of political variables on private economic choices is surprisingly little developed. The experience of many LDCs demonstrates, however, the strong influence of political stability variables on economic variables such as foreign financial flows, direct investment or national capital flight. Moreover, political troubles in these countries disorganise economic exchanges. Regarding industrialised countries, some research has been done on the influence of electoral cycles on stock exchange indices or on private investment (Aubin and Goyeau 1986). From a theoretical point of view, it is clear that: if individuals and firms are rational in their expectations, they will use all the available economic and political information (a point generally ignored by economists); and uncertainty about electoral results is associated with uncertainty about future policy choices. A deeper awareness of these problems has been the source of a renewed interest in partisan models of macroeconomic cycles (Alesina and Sachs 1988; Hibbs 1991).

Research on the second point (new functions explaining key political variables) is now, on the contrary, voluminous. The recent survey of vote and popularity functions by Nannestad and Paldam (1992) mentions 'almost 200 titles', a figure which is a highly conservative estimate. The studies concerning France have found results similar to those obtained in other countries (Lewis-Beck 1988). A significant link appears to exist between popularity indices for the President or Prime Minister and the major macroeconomic variables (real income growth, inflation and unemployment). However, two distinctive institutional features have to be taken into account. First, the executive branch is divided between a president and a prime minister, and their respective popularities react differently to the macroeconomic indicators. Second, in periods of 'cohabitation' when the president and the prime minister belong to different parties, the popularity functions change significantly. This raises interesting and complex problems regarding the responsibility which public opinion imputes for the economic and political situation. The empirical analysis confirms that institutions are very significant at this level (Lafay 1991).

Empirical work is much less developed for vote than for popularity functions. The main reason for this is the lack of data – unlike popularity indices, elections do not take place monthly. Consequently, the estimates are much less robust. An often used strategy is to estimate popularity in a first step (using a popularity function) and to introduce it as an explanatory variable in a vote function. Because popularity and votes have many similar determinants, this approach limits the number of explanatory variables in vote functions, i.e. it reduces the degrees of freedom. Another, and not exclusive, alternative is to increase the number of observations by using pooled data and to predict the vote at a regional level. Recent experience with vote functions estimated on such a basis shows that they give good predictions, even when electoral preferences reveal significant changes.[2]

The extended interest in popularity functions is explained by the idea that popularity is an indicator of the re-election prospects of a government. However, there is here an often overlooked consistency problem with the traditional (spatial and deterministic) theory of voting. The relevant information for the government (and for politicians in general) is either the preferences of the median voter or the preferences of the minorities expected to form a winning coalition at election time. The link between these specific preferences and popularity indices is certainly very weak, because the latter measure is a sum of the preferences of the whole electorate.

This problem becomes much less serious, however, if the recently developed probabilistic voting theory is used as the theoretical framework (Coughlin 1991; Lafay 1993). The reason for this is that rational parties are then no longer interested in the median voter; instead, they maximise a weighted sum of individual preferences. Of course, the weights are not equal, as in the popularity indices (they depend on the degree to which each individual sticks to his or her vote), but the link between popularity indices and the politically relevant information tends to be much stronger. Hence, the common procedure receives a much better ex-post justification with probabilistic voting theory.

2: Politico-Economic Reaction Functions

Government behaviour is modelled by a set of reaction (or policy) functions, linking policy instruments to deviations of an array of objective variables from their respective bliss values. These functions can be deduced from the maximisation of a utility function under the constraints of the politico-economic system discussed above (Aubin 1983). Some authors (Frey 1978) think that the government is more likely to adopt satisficing rather than maximising behaviour. The main practical consequence of this limited rationality assumption is that it introduces discontinuities in governmental objectives. When some thresholds are reached, the motives of public policy change radically, switching for example from ideological to electoral motives.

The theory and the first estimates of reaction functions appeared during the 1960s. These functions were assumed to be purely economic. Political elements were excluded both from the government utility function and from the constraints. However, the empirical estimates appeared to be highly unstable over time, and were thus a poor ex-ante predictive tool for government behaviour. The introduction of dummy variables, representing each specific administration or president or prime minister, resulted in a noticeable improvement. Similarly, it was shown that variables representing electoral cycles, the length of time before the next elections or popularity indices had a significant impact. All this research, based on the experience of several countries, demonstrates that political elements are a central feature in reaction functions.

Nevertheless, the instability of the first, purely economic, reaction functions cannot be explained only by the neglect of political factors. The assumption of a unique utility function for an aggregate named 'the state' must also be questioned. At least two groups need to be distinguished: the government and the bureaucracy. Public policy results from bargaining between these two groups regarding their respective preferred policies (Aubin 1983; Andersen and Schneider 1985). This situation is well illustrated by a graphical analysis of a simplified monetary policy problem, based on simple game theory.

It is assumed that the policy model contains two objectives, inflation (p) and unemployment (u), and two instruments, fiscal deficit (d), controlled by the government, and money supply (m), controlled by the specific bureaucracy known as the central bank. In the space of instruments, each institution has a preferred policy point, i.e. preferred reactions for given values of p and u. These bliss points are respectively G and B. They are the centre of a family of indifference curves (Figure 9.1).

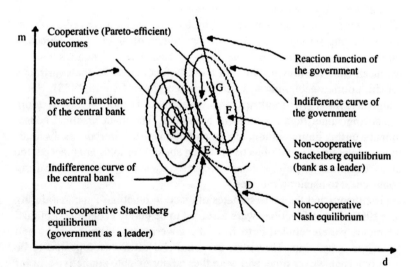

Fig. 9.1   Policy Outcomes in Cooperative and Non-Cooperative Games
Source: Andersen and Schneider 1985

Cournot-Nash reaction curves can then be drawn for each institution. They correspond to the tangency points with the higher indifference curves for given values of the instrument controlled by the other institution. Three types of equilibrium are then possible. One is an equilibrium on the contract curve (a Pareto-efficient outcome) when the two institutions play cooperatively – the exact point on the curve depends on the relative 'bargaining power' of the players. A second is a non-cooperative Nash equilibrium at the intersection of the two reaction curves. A final one is a non-cooperative Stackelberg equilibrium – on the reaction curve of the bank if the government is the leader, and on the reaction curve of the government in the opposite case.

Reaction functions are supposed to explain changes in the equilibrium point. These changes have three main sources. One is a change in p or u, which moves the bliss points G and B, and hence leads to a new equilibrium point. A second is a change in the basic conditions of the game, which may result in sharp and discontinuous movement – the equilibrium may jump from a cooperative to a non-cooperative point, from a Nash to a Stackelberg equilibrium, or, when the respective identities of the leader and the follower switch, from one Stackelberg point to the other. A third is a change in the relative bargaining power in the cooperative case, which corresponds to movement on the contract curve.

Reaction functions contain variables that essentially reflect the first kind of change. The discontinuous movement corresponding to the second kind of change (a jump from one type of equilibrium to another) happens when some critical thresholds are overcome. However, the values of these thresholds are very difficult to estimate, owing to the low number of relevant observations. For this reason, reaction functions will certainly remain subject to unpredictable, significant displacements in the non-cooperative cases.

The third type of change is limited to cooperative games, but, in the monetary policy game case, it certainly concerns many countries, at least those where the central bank is not formally independent (as in France to date). Unlike the previous type of change, this can be taken into account to some extent in empirical reaction functions. If the contract curve is approximately linear, the effective monetary policy is a weighted average of the policies desired by the government and by the bank:

$$m = (1 - \mu).mG(p,u) + \mu.mB(p,u),$$

In this equation, μ measures the relative bargaining power of the bank. On *a priori* grounds, its value is certainly closely linked to the political climate. If the government is sure to be re-elected, the costs of narrowly controlling the bank outweigh the expected advantages – the bank has more freedom to implement its preferred monetary policy. Conversely, the worse the electoral prospects are for the government, the greater its pressure on the bank to implement the government's preferred policy (mG).

Empirical values for μ can be computed easily by assuming that they are proportional to the 'expectation of political life' of the government (Lafay 1988). It is then possible to estimate reaction functions which smoothly shift from mG(p,u), when $\mu = 1$, to mB(p,u), when $\mu = 0$.

Very stable and empirically satisfactory politico-economic reaction functions of this type have been obtained for monetary policy (Aubin and Lafay 1990) and for different types of public expenditures (Lecaillon and Lafay 1988).

Lessons from the Estimates

A politico-economic model usually consists of the addition of an endogenously explained public sector to a 'pure' economic model (see Schneider 1992 for a recent survey). This additional sector contains both politico-economic reaction functions and evaluation (i.e. vote and popularity) functions. However, these models usually suffer from several limitations.

Owing to the influence of the political business cycle theory, they concentrate on a small number of macroeconomic variables (inflation, unemployment and economic growth). In so doing, they risk hiding an essential part of what political control of the economy is trying to achieve, namely to produce redistributive effects in order to gain the support of specific groups. A minimal level of disaggregation is then required. Furthermore, even if political or bureaucratic goals play a crucial role in determining economic policy, they are not necessarily the only goals. Intertemporal calculus, combined or not with imperfect information or limited rationality, prompts politicians and bureaucrats to disregard their short-term interest. A sort of Becker's 'rotten kid theorem' may apply here (Becker 1981), so that it is in their personal interest to simulate a 'public interest' behaviour. It is also possible that at least some politicians and bureaucrats have an altruistic desire to serve the collectivity. Moreover, government can control bureaucracy more than is generally assumed (Breton 1991) and compel it to follow governmental objectives relatively faithfully. For all these reasons, the utility functions of political and bureaucratic decision-makers cannot be restricted to variables corresponding to their narrow, short-term personal interest. In general, politico-economic models only explain political influences on public sector behaviour. As mentioned earlier, private persons also use political information when their expectations contain a minimum of rationality. Thus, private investment and consumption decisions depend on the political situation, at least as a leading indicator of future economic policies.

The quarterly politico-economic model for the French economy built and estimated by Aubin *et al.* (1985a, 1985b) tries to take all the above considerations into account. The sixty independent equations of the model allow a minimum level of disaggregation, with three main agents (general government, households and private firms) and three main subsets of equations. The public sector subset is devoted to the analysis of public sector behaviour with respect to taxation, social transfers, public consumption and public investment. The private sector subset explains large aggregates (consumption, investment and imports), with a distinction between firms and households, and a few minor items. The third subset concerns indicators of the economic and political situation. Indicators of the economic situation highlight the government role regarding employment (public and private), prices (the general price index and the public sector price index) and wages (private, public and minimum wage rates). The basic political indicator is the popularity of the head of state, explained by traditional macroeconomic variables, plus the exchange rate and direct household taxation. All the public reaction functions include political and bureaucratic variables as well as traditional economic variables. Their mathematical structure corresponds to the switching logic described above. The sample period is 1966–81 and 1982–84.[3]

The empirical estimates clearly confirm that governmental economic policy can be explained in a systematic way. It is not the result of an unpredictable, abstract and sovereign 'will'. Furthermore, the estimates for the endogenous variables in the public sector are roughly as accurate as those obtained for the private sector.

Political factors, mainly political popularity and electoral imminence, shape in a highly significant way the public sector reaction to the economic situation. However, this question is more complex than is generally supposed in simple politico-economic models, because economic policy cannot be explained solely on the basis of political objectives. Other factors are clearly at work, even if their respective weight can fluctuate according to the electoral cycle or current levels of popularity. At least four different logics are simultaneously taken into account by governmental decision-makers.

First, there is an economic stabilisation logic. The major macroeconomic aggregates have a significant impact in the reaction functions concerning fiscal policy, public employment and price and wage changes controlled by the government. Indeed, these variables also influence popularity, but, in some circumstances, policy changes clearly involve the search for an economic equilibrium, the accepted canons of 'optimal' economic policy, and not short-term, narrow political goals.

Second, there is a fiscal equilibrium logic. The ratio of public expenditures to public receipts, of for example social security payments to contributions, are systematically significant as explanatory variables. As far as the French case is concerned, the government does not escape entirely from its financial as well as its economic responsibility, even if such behaviour contradicts its immediate political interest. The pressures of the central bank or of the Treasury, which are bureaucracies directly interested in economic and fiscal equilibrium, also play a significant role.

Third, there is an incremental logic. Public expenditures have a well-known tendency to grow at a continuous rate (Alt and Chrystal 1983) so that lagged endogenous variables often present a highly significant coefficient. This corresponds to bureaucrats' preference for stable growth in their budgets and to an adaptive structure in the expectation process of political decision-makers.

Finally, there is a political logic. Ideology, popularity and electoral calendars are the key variables here. The sample period (1966–81 and 1982–84) does not contain a sufficient number of observations of left-wing governments to study the role of ideological variables. However, later research has shown that a significant but moderated left-wing bias is present for transfer payments (Lecaillon and Lafay 1988). On the other hand, no significant ideological difference in monetary policy is observed (Aubin and Lafay 1990). The influence of popularity and of the length of time before the next elections is much more significant for disaggregated than for global variables. Governments try to reconcile political logic with financial and economic responsibility by resorting to selective actions. For example, taxes levied on households tend to decrease in the year preceding an election but taxes on companies tend to increase simultaneously, so that no clear electoral cycle appears when taxes are considered globally. These trade-offs sometimes give counter-intuitive results. For example, governments tend to increase public prices in periods of low popularity, although this decision is clearly unpopular, both directly and indirectly, owing to its short-term positive influence on the general inflation rate. However, given the desire for a balanced budget, the corresponding political costs are lower than those of alternative policies, notably tax increases.

POLITICO-ECONOMIC INTERACTIONS IN LDCs

Most of the politico-economic models concern developed countries. However, strong interactions between economics and politics exist in LDCs, and they may have much more tragic consequences. For example, some adjustment programmes, chosen by the government alone or under International Monetary Fund (IMF) pressure, have brought about severe political trouble, with hundreds or even thousands of casualties. The series of financial crises which hit many LDCs in the 1980s also had their origin in debt problems, the political basis of which cannot be ignored (Lafay and Lecaillon 1993).

Public choice theory has been developed in the context of industrialised, democratic countries, but its potential applications to development problems are very significant. The extensive malfunctioning of the public sector clearly necessitates a better positive understanding of state behaviour in these countries. The question of the 'political feasibility' of adjustment programmes is also a growing source of interest concerning politico-economic interactions. The fact that most LDCs are autocratic or quasi-autocratic has stimulated new analytical developments (Tullock 1987; Wintrobe 1989). In such an institutional context, the main problem for the government is no longer the risk of losing elections but rather the risk of being illegally overthrown by a coup, a guerilla war, or social unrest and riots.

Building a politico-economic model for a developing country requires the integration of corresponding governmental behaviour with group reactions, international pressures and aid. This was done recently in the pioneering study by Frey and Eichenberger (1992). However, the question of whether it would be possible to estimate such a model remained. Despite the great weakness of the statistical information in the countries concerned, the answer seems to be positive, according to the study by Morrisson, Lafay and Dessus (1993), henceforth referred to as the MLD model.

Theoretical Framework of the MLD Model

The MLD model contains fifteen independent equations and distinguishes between four main actors: economic actors (the 'economy'), social groups, the government, and foreign public institutions (international organisations, essentially the IMF and the World Bank, and public aid donors). Figure 9.2 gives an overview of the various politico-economic interactions between these four groups.

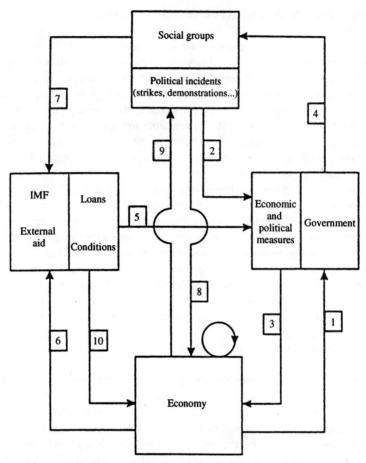

Fig. 9.2   A Scheme of Politico-Economic Interactions
Source: Morrisson *et al.* 1993

The economy corresponds to six equations explaining gross national product, inflation, exports, imports, the balance of payments (before public transfers) and external debt. The economic situation influences group reactions (social unrest functions – arrow 9), government policy (reaction functions – arrow 1) and foreign public institutions (aid function – arrow 6). It is influenced by the level of aid (arrow 10), the economic consequences of social troubles (arrow 8) and government economic policy (popular expansionary measures, unpopular stabilisation measures, and monetary and exchange rate control – arrow 3).

Owing to the chosen level of aggregation and to informational limits, the action of social groups is not detailed. It is represented only by strikes, demonstrations and coups (this last variable being assumed to be exogenous). The two equations corresponding to strikes and demonstrations depend on the economic situation (arrow 9), on governmental economic measures and on political measures, i.e. repression and political liberalisation (arrow 4). Strikes and demonstrations influence the economy (arrow 8), international aid policy (arrow 7) and government policy (economic policy and political measures – arrow 2).

The foreign public institutions correspond to international public aid and to IMF interventions. For simplicity's sake, these last interventions are assumed to be exogenous, so that there is only one equation explaining total aid. It depends on domestic economic and political situations (arrows 6 and 7). The IMF gives conditional aid, i.e. aid in exchange for adjustment measures (arrow 5). To sign an agreement with the IMF, i.e. to accept unpopular adjustment measures, is crucial for a country because it is the starting point for several other important decisions (international debt rescheduling and further lending by other international institutions, foreign countries and private banks). One dollar of IMF lending corresponds to approximately four dollars of total financial aid.

The governmental block is central in the model. The basic behavioural assumption is that it seeks to minimise suppression provided that its probability of political survival is above a given threshold. This assumption is suited to the autocratic or quasi-autocratic nature of a large majority of LDC regimes. The idea is that suppression is costly, because it consumes discretionary resources and because it causes negative international reactions. Six reaction functions are deduced on this basis. Two functions concern political measures – unpopular political measures, suppression, and popular political measures, political liberalisation. These depend on the domestic political situation (arrow 2). Two economic instruments, unpopular stabilisation measures and popular expansionary measures, correspond to general indices, such as fiscal decisions, subsidies, regulation or privatisation. The two other instruments are the quantity of money and the exchange rate (provided, in the latter case, that the country does not belong to a monetary zone such as the franc zone in Africa). These four economic policy instruments depend on the economic situation (arrow 1), the political situation (arrow 2) and IMF interventions (arrow 5). All these governmental measures, political and economic, have economic and political impacts (arrows 3 and 4).

Solving the Data Problems

The model contains dynamic interactions which require time series data for estimation. However, the necessary series are not available for a sufficiently long period. For this reason, the estimates have been performed on pooled data. Twenty-three African countries have been chosen for a ten-year period (1981–90), so that the number of observations is 230 per variable.

The main statistical sources for the economic data are World Bank tables and OECD statistics on public development aid. In order to avoid heteroscedasticity problems, all the variables are either normalised (generally deflated by the gross domestic product) or computed as growth rates.

Eight crucial variables in the model were not directly available. Indices for them have been constructed on the basis of the summary information published weekly by the magazine *Marchés tropicaux*. The IMF index is measured by the yearly number of IMF interventions in a given country. The seven other indices concern strikes, demonstrations, coups and attempted coups, popular economic measures, unpopular economic measures, unpopular political measures (suppression) and popular political measures (political liberalisation). These indices are annual aggregates of qualitative measures of the intensity of basic events (none, weak, medium, high). While it is true that this method uses only approximate information, this is not necessarily a limitation – such information corresponds well to what the governments had at their disposal when they needed to make decisions.

Results and Simulations

The empirical results confirm the numerous and important politico-economic interactions in LDCs.[4] Examples of some of most interesting results include:

- Real income growth depends significantly on economic policies, aid and strikes (but not on demonstrations).
- The inflation rate is closely linked to monetary growth, indebtedness and the exchange rate.
- Strikes and demonstrations respond strongly to the inflation rate, price increases being very costly politically, and to unpopular economic measures. Income growth tends to reduce strikes while aid helps to limit demonstrations.
- Unpopular economic measures are a clear reaction to macroeconomic disequilibria and IMF pressure.

- Popular economic measures are chosen to alleviate strike pressures, or in periods of political liberalisation or sustained growth.
- Monetary policy is eased when the strike variable is high. Monetary growth in countries belonging to the franc zone is significantly lower.
- In countries belonging to the franc zone, the rate of exchange with the dollar reflects, by definition, fluctuations in the French franc. For other countries, the inflation differential, IMF interventions and domestic demonstrations are the main significant determinants.
- The equations concerning suppression and political liberalisation give interesting information on the choices of African governments. Attempted coups or demonstrations give rise to immediate suppression. Because political crises cannot be solved by resorting to elections, they necessarily become regime crises. On the other hand, strikes are not a significant determinant of suppression. Governments seem to consider them as being purely material claims, which do not threaten political stability. The equation for political liberalisation shows that it depends only on previous suppression. This indirectly confirms the high costs of suppression for autocratic or quasi-autocratic African regimes.
- The main characteristic of the aid equation is its rigidity, reflected by the high, significant value of the coefficient of the lagged endogenous variable (.8). At the margin, however, aid-giving seems to respond rationally to a country's economic situation (decreasing when the situation improves). The significant value for the IMF variable also confirms that an IMF agreement is the starting point for much greater international aid.

Another interesting feature of the MLD model is its capacity to explore, by simulation, the economic and political consequences of different situations (compared with a reference solution). A first simulation compares adjustments with or without IMF intervention. The results, summarised in Figures 9.3 and 9.4, indicate that IMF intervention is economically and politically beneficial for countries belonging to the franc zone. For the other countries, the economic advantage of intervention is significant, but intervention has a political cost. More social unrest is observed during the second and third years because the IMF package generally includes a devaluation, which is the source of higher inflation up to at least year three.

Other simulations concern the effects of increased growth in Europe, political shocks, an increase in international aid, different monetary policies and changes in the exchange rate. An example from the last case may be noted as it illustrates perfectly what politico-economic models can contribute to policy debates.

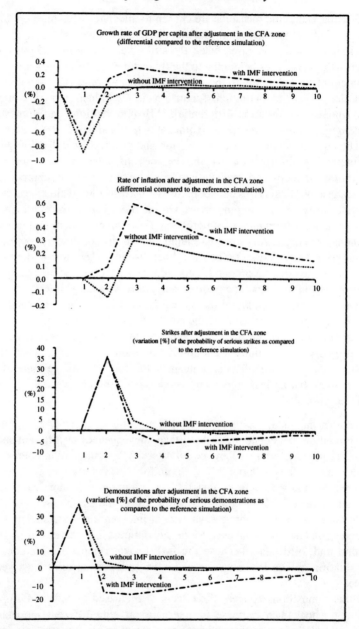

Fig. 9.3   Adjustment with or without IMF Intervention (Franc Zone)
Source: Morrisson *et al.* 1993

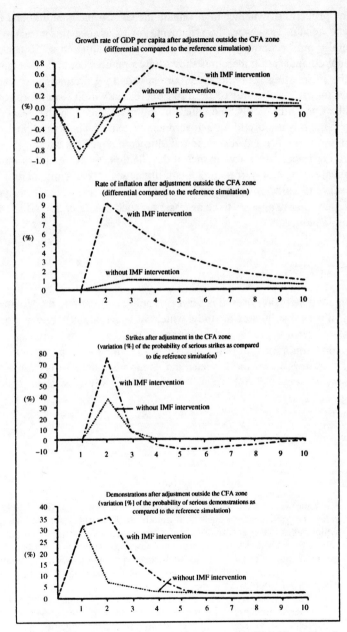

Fig. 9.4 Adjustment with or without IMF Intervention (Non-Franc Zone)
Source: Morrisson *et al.* 1993

The problem of whether to devaluate the CFA franc is an old and passionate debate. However, the arguments for or against this measure are generally only economic. The simulation of a devaluation of 50 per cent without compensating measures shows how a purely economic assessment can be misleading. This measure corresponds to a dramatic increase in social unrest, as a result of the price increases which usually follow a devaluation. Admittedly, the situation improves much in the years that follow, but it is not useful for a government to expect a better political situation tomorrow if it expects to be overthrown today. That several African rulers are reluctant to accept such a devaluation, whatever its economic justification, is not surprising. A simultaneous, significant increase in international aid, to alleviate social pressures resulting from price increases, clearly appears to be necessary if such a devaluation policy is to be implemented.[5]

CONCLUSION

The main conclusion from this survey of politico-economic models is that this is a very worthy area of study, which raises particularly relevant questions concerning both industrialised democracies and LDCs. The enormous importance of political goals and politico-economic interaction clearly appears in all the models, and economists need to take this into account if they do not want to mis-specify severely their 'purely economic' analyses.

NOTES

1. Even the words are misused. For example, when Barro and Gordon (1983) refer to a 'positive' monetary policy analysis, they simply mean an analysis which takes better account of the positive reactions of individuals (i.e. the rationality of individuals' expectations) rather than the positive reactions of governments, with the resulting problems regarding credibility, reputation, time, consistency and rules versus discretion (see Blackburn and Christensen 1989 for a survey).
2. A model built by Jérôme, Lafay and Lewis-Beck (1993) gave very satisfactory ex-ante predictions for the French general elections of March 1993. The prediction for right-wing parties was 453 seats, a huge increase of 196 seats over the previous vote – the actual figure was 470 seats in metropolitan France. Moreover, predictions were given for each of the twenty-two

French regions, sixteen of which had a prediction error of two seats or fewer.

3. The first sixty-one quarters of the period concern conservative governments (under de Gaulle, Pompidou and Giscard d'Estaing), while the seven last quarters correspond to a socialist government (under Mitterrand). The number of observations then available was too small to study accurately potential partisan biases.

4. For a discussion of the test procedures see Morrisson *et al.* (1993).

5. The CFA franc was actually devalued by 50 per cent on 12 January 1994, exactly as had been simulated in Morrisson *et al.* (1993) several months before. However, the aid-compensating programme which was announced simultaneously seemed to be less extensive than would be necessary in order to eliminate all the expected negative political consequences of the devaluation.

REFERENCES

Alesina, A. and J. Sachs. 1988. 'Political Parties and the Business Cycle in the US, 1948–1984.' *Journal of Money, Credit, and Banking* 20: 63–82.

Alt, J.E. and K.A. Chrystal. 1983. *Political Economics.* Brighton: Wheatsheaf Books.

Andersen, T.M. and F. Schneider. 1985. *Public Decision Process in Fiscal and Monetary Policies Under Different Institutional Arrangements.* Aarhus: Institute of Economics, University of Aarhus, mimeographed.

Aubin, C. 1983. *Intégration du comportement de la Banque centrale dans une analyse positive de la politique monétaire.* Thèse de doctorat d'Etat. Poitiers: Université de Poitiers.

Aubin, C. and D. Goyeau. 1986. *Les influences politiques sur les comportements économiques privés: l'investissement des entreprises en France.* Poitiers: IRAPE, Université de Poitiers, mimeographed.

Aubin, C. and J.D. Lafay. 1990. *L'analyse positive de la politique monétaire et son application au cas français (1974.01–1986.03).* Poitiers and Paris: Université de Poitiers and LAEP, Université de Paris I, mimeographed.

Aubin, C., J.P. Berdot, D. Goyeau and J.D. Lafay. 1985a. *Un modèle politico-économique de la France (1966–1982).* Poitiers: IRAPE, Université de Poitiers, mimeographed.

Aubin, C., J.P. Berdot, D. Goyeau and J.D. Lafay. 1985b. *A Complete Politico-Economic Model of the French Economy (1966–1982).* Poitiers: CEDS, University of Poitiers, mimeographed.

Barro, R.J. and D.B. Gordon. 1983. 'A Positive Theory of Monetary Policy in a Natural-Rate Model.' *Journal of Political Economy* 91.

Becker, G.S. 1981. *A Treatise on the Family.* Cambridge: Cambridge University Press.

Blackburn, K. and M. Christensen. 1989. 'Monetary Policy and Policy Credibility: Theories and Evidence.' *Journal of Economic Literature* 27: 1–45.

Blinder, A.S. and R.M. Solow. 1974. 'Analytical Foundations of Fiscal Policy.' In *The Economics of Public Finance*, eds A.S. Blinder, R.M. Solow, G.F. Break, P.O. Steiner and D. Netzer. Washington DC: The Brookings Institution.

Breton, A. 1991. *Organizational Hierarchies and Bureaucracies: An Integrative Essay*. Toronto: University of Toronto, mimeographed.

Cairncross, A. 1985. 'Economics in Theory and Practice.' *American Economic Review* 75: 1–14.

Coughlin, P.J. 1991. *Probabilistic Voting Theory*. Cambridge: Cambridge University Press.

Frey, B.S. 1978. *Modern Political Economy*. Oxford: Martin Robertson.

Frey, B.S. and R. Eichenberger. 1992. *Economic Analysis of Stabilization Programmes in Developing Countries*. Paris: OECD Development Centre.

Hibbs, D. 1991. *The Partisan Model of Macroeconomic Cycles: More Theory and Evidence for the United States*. Stockholm: Trade Union Institute for Economic Research.

Jérôme, B., J.D. Lafay and M.S. Lewis-Beck. 1993. *Elections législatives de mars 1993: Prévisions politico-économiques par région. Document technique*. Paris: LAEP, Université de Paris I, mimeographed.

Lafay, J.D. 1988. 'Bureaucracy in the Macro-Theory of Public Sector Behavior.' *European Journal of Political Economy* 4: 77–94.

Lafay, J.D. 1991. 'Political Dyarchy and Popularity Functions: Lessons from the 1986 French Experience.' In *Economics and Politics: The Calculus of Support*, eds H. Norpoth, M.S. Lewis-Beck and J.D. Lafay. Ann Arbor: The University of Michigan Press.

Lafay, J.D. 1993. 'The Silent Revolution of Probabilistic Voting.' In *Preferences and Democracies*, eds A. Breton, G. Galeotti, P. Salmon and R. Wintrobe. Dordrecht: Kluwer Academic Press.

Lafay, J.D. and J. Lecaillon. 1993. *The Political Dimension of Economic Adjustment*. Paris: OECD.

Lecaillon, J. and J.D. Lafay. 1988. 'Idéologie politique et comportement des gouvernements: étude économétrique du cas français.' In *L'impact du libéralisme sur les institutions et les politiques économiques*, eds J.P. Betbèze, G. Gallais-Hamonno, J.D. Lafay, P. Llau and G. Terny. Paris: Nathan.

Lewis-Beck, M.S. 1988. *Economics and Elections, The Major Western Democracies*. Ann Arbor: The University of Michigan Press.

Morrisson, C., J.D. Lafay and S. Dessus. 1993. *La faisabilité politique de l'ajustement en Afrique (1980–1990)*. Paris: OECD Development Centre.

Nannestad, P. and M. Paldam. 1992. *The VP-Function: A Survey of the Literature on Vote and Popularity Functions*. Aarhus: University of Aarhus, mimeographed.

Schneider, F. 1992. *Public Choice–Economic Theory of Politics: A Survey of Selected Areas*. Linz: Johannes Kepler Universitat.

Stein, H. 1986. 'The Washington Economics Industry.' *American Economic Review* 76: 1–9.

Tullock, G. 1987. *Autocracy*. Dordrecht: Martinus Nijhof.

Wintrobe, R. 1989. *The Tinpot and the Totalitarian: A Simple Economic Theory of Dictatorship*. London: University of Western Ontario, mimeographed.

10 The Developmental State: Governance, Comparison and Culture in the 'Third World'

Christopher Clapham

GOVERNMENT ACTIVITY IN THE 'THIRD WORLD': PROBLEMS OF COMPARISON

The comparative analysis of government activity in that large part of the globe which has been lumped together under the title of the 'Third World' raises serious conceptual problems. Comprising the whole of Africa, almost all of Asia (normally excluding only Japan and Russia), South and Central America, and the oceanic islands, this vast swathe of territory exhibits a massive range of variation across almost every indicator that might be taken to define a population of states for comparative purposes. In population size, geographical location, social structure, historical origins, wealth and political institutions, these states appear to defy any attempt to devise the structure of similarity within which any meaningful comparison can be undertaken.

'Third World' states have none the less provided the subject matter for numerous attempts at comparison.[1] Their eruption on to the global scene with the ending of European colonialism, from the late 1940s onwards, is indeed frequently regarded as having given a major impetus to the development of comparative political science. Their sheer number, more than trebling the existing world population of sovereign states, readily lent itself to comparative approaches, while the problems of coming to grips with so many new subjects of study could be made more manageable by grouping them into categories, such as socialist, military or single-party states, which could then be made the subjects for comparative analysis.

The underlying problem of comparability was characteristically dealt with (or perhaps merely glossed over) by comparing them, not by reference to the common characteristics which they possessed, but instead by reference to the characteristics which they lacked. They were not developed industrial, western capitalist, liberal democratic states; and all the terms by which they were generically described – whether as 'developing' states, 'underdeveloped' states, 'non-western' states or the Third World – implicitly or explicitly reflected this element of exclusion. They could likewise be excluded from the other main universe of states available for comparison, the Marxist-Leninist or communist world.

This negative comparability could in turn be activated as a basis for comparison in either of two main ways. On the one hand, the group of scholars lumped together as 'modernisation theorists' could compare them in terms of the ways in which, and the extent to which, these states were able to approach the condition of the existing relatively wealthy, stable and democratic (or, in a word, 'developed') states which were taken as a norm. Inherently teleological, this approach assumed that other societies could become 'more developed', even though they might approach this ideal at different speeds and in different ways; it viewed development as a pilgrimage, on which different states could be compared by reference to their starting places, and the routes by which they sought to attain a common goal. On the other hand, a rival group, lumped together as 'dependency theorists', took the subordination of Third World or under-developed states to the developed industrial capitalist world as their defining characteristic, which in turn imposed a considerable element of commonality over all of the states and societies which were subjected to it, regardless of the original differences in their social structures. These states could then be compared according to the extent to which, and the ways in which, they had been incorporated into (and in the process exploited by) the capitalist world system. In each case, though in very different ways, the nature of the First World imposed a basis for comparison on the Third.

These bases for constructing a structure for Third World political comparison, however oversimplified this brief description of them may be, have however been severely challenged by recent developments in the global economy. The most evident empirical basis for this challenge is the extraordinary divergence in economic performance between groups of states within the would-be Third World. At its most dramatic, this is expressed by the difference between an average annual increase in gross national product (GNP) per capita of 6.1 per cent in the East Asia and Pacific zone over the 1980–91 period, and an average annual decrease of 1.2 per cent in Sub-Saharan Africa (World Bank 1993, Table 1). This difference in GNP per capita corresponds, moreover, to high levels of variance across the whole range of indicators which have been used to measure 'development', including social and political variables as well as structural indicators of economic change, such as industrialisation. It is not limited to simple output indicators, such as GNP per capita, which may be the result of chance factors like the fluctuation in oil revenues in a low-population oil-exporting state.

Gross comparative indicators of this kind must obviously be subject to a certain level of scepticism. It can certainly be pointed out that the collection of economic and social statistics, especially for many African states, is subject to a wide margin of uncertainty and may often amount to little more than guesswork. In economies where much economic activity has escaped from the supervision of state authorities, levels of decline may well have been exaggerated because significant transactions do not show up on the official record: a high proportion of external trade, for example, is in parts of Africa conducted by smuggling. Statisticians have also encountered considerable difficulties in estimating the value of non-monetised parts of the economy, notably subsistence agriculture, which may well therefore have been underestimated. It has likewise been demonstrated that cross-national comparisons of GNP per capita which depend on converting national currencies into a common denominator (normally the US dollar) at current market rates seriously underestimate standards of living in Third World states if these are measured in terms of purchasing power parities. None of these necessary statistical caveats can, however, alter the fact that we are observing a massive divergence in living standards and levels of economic development between groups of states which can broadly be demarcated in geographical terms. Both in terms of statistical indicators which are relatively free from bias, such as levels of direct foreign investment or exports of manufactured goods, and in terms of the visible observation of living standards in states such as Malaysia or South Korea, by comparison, say, with Ghana or Ethiopia, the differences are so dramatic that problems of precise measurement should not be allowed to obscure them.

These differences have in turn undermined both of the competing (though equally western-oriented) bases for comparison on which the analysis of state performance in the Third World has characteristically depended. The remarkably rapid development of eastern Asian states, including notably their breakthrough into the large-scale export of manufactures, has effectively destroyed those dependency theories which postulated that such states were permanently subjected to a subordinate position within the global political economy.[2] Modernisation theories find it almost equally difficult to deal with states whose populations are demonstrably less well-off than they were thirty years ago. In either case, the idea of a comparative politics of the Third World has been severely damaged. The purpose of this paper is to explore the explanations for the divergence between the extreme cases, of East and South-East Asia on the one hand, and Sub-Saharan Africa on the other, in terms of the comparative analysis of government performance in the two regions. It will conclude that, while such explanations can plausibly be put forward, they have the effect, ultimately, of undermining the basis for any comparative politics of the Third World, and indeed of challenging the idea of comparative politics in a more general sense.

THE ASIAN 'DEVELOPMENTAL STATE'

The economic development of eastern Asia was first demonstrated, and is still obviously led, by Japan, which as the second largest economy in the world (after the United States), and the second wealthiest in GNP per capita (after Switzerland), has now attained a position not merely of parity but of leadership within the global economy. It was followed by the 'four tigers' – South Korea, Taiwan, Singapore, Hong Kong – which have now reached GNP per capita levels equivalent to those of the poorer members of the European Union. These four all achieved annual average growth rates in export volume of 10 per cent or more over the 1980–93 period, as did the People's Republic of China, Thailand and Malaysia. This level of success has understandably attracted widespread attention, and has led to attempts at explanation which have broadly coalesced around the idea of the 'developmental state' (Koo and Kim 1992; White 1984).

As the phrase implies, the developmental state hypothesis ascribes a central role in economic success to government activity (see Appelbaum and Henderson 1992). This success may in turn, however, be ascribed to the combination of two distinct elements: the first may be described as having the 'right kind of state', distinguishable in terms of its autonomy from societal forces, and its capacity to implement government policies; the second may be described as using the state to do 'the right kind of thing', in terms of the specific policies which it follows. At this second level, some states within the eastern Asia region have been able to achieve startling success, whereas others have not, and this difference can be directly accounted for by the policies followed by the government of each; in these terms, the differences between regions outlined in the previous section can readily be explained by the number of states pursuing the correct policies within each region. The most striking comparison, between two adjacent states of similar size with an identical cultural background, separates South Korea from North Korea; the first has enjoyed the fastest rate of GNP per capita growth in the world, whereas the second, though reliable economic data are unavailable, is apparently unable even to feed its own population. The economic performance of the People's Republic of China, before and after the instituting of market reforms by the Deng government, provides an equally remarkable comparison.

If successful economic development is then simply a matter of having governments that do the right thing, what are the things that they have to do? These may broadly be divided into the maintenance of certain basic economic conditions on the one hand, and the provision of a number of broader social and political services on the other. The basic economic conditions are those conducive to export-led growth, especially in manufactures. They notably include an undervalued exchange rate, designed to make export earnings relatively profitable by comparison with earnings from the domestic market, while simultaneously discouraging imports by making these relatively expensive; measures designed to encourage a high level of domestic saving, through which to finance investment; and the maintenance of a disciplined and relatively lowly paid domestic labour force, through which both to produce cheaply for the export market and to encourage the inflow of foreign direct investment. The governments of newly industrialising countries differ quite markedly in the extent to which they seek to intervene in the productive process, in order to encourage industries in which the country is deemed to have an international comparative advantage; in Hong Kong, for example, such intervention is virtually non-existent, whereas in South Korea and Singapore it is relatively high. In every successful state, however, direct government management of the productive sector, through nationalised industries or parastatal corporations, is slight; only the People's Republic of China and to a lesser extent Indonesia retain large state sectors, and in each case these constitute a drain on the resources and productivity of the national economy.

The provision of broader social and political conditions may be related to the need to enable the 'supply side' of the economy to respond to the incentives provided by economic policy. A striking feature of almost all the successful eastern Asian economies is a relatively high level of social equality, expressed notably in terms of low rates of infant mortality and high rates of female participation in education. The early stages of rapid economic growth in agrarian societies (obviously excluding the city states of Hong Kong and Singapore) have been associated with increases in agricultural production, resulting from land reform in Taiwan and from the freeing of the peasant sector from state controls in China; as well as generating food surpluses to feed an increasing urban labour force, this has spread the benefits of economic growth very widely through the national population. A high level of investment in education has been identified as another critical variable. In political terms, many if not most of these regimes have been authoritarian; the two states which have maintained regularly elected governments over a long period, Malaysia and Singapore, have been governed by the same party since independence, while the governing parties of both China and Taiwan have each been in power for over forty years. Other economically successful regional states such as South Korea, Thailand and Indonesia have – despite political instability in both South Korea and Thailand – been able to maintain a broad consistency in economic policy. Hong Kong, with a GNP per capita higher than that of four member states of the European Union, and a GNP greater than that of Pakistan and Bangladesh combined, has remained under British colonial administration. Only the Philippines, with a negative GNP per capita growth rate over 1980–91 precisely equal (at –1.2 per cent per annum) to the Sub-Saharan African average, has been unable to benefit from the correlation between stable if authoritarian government and economic growth.

THE POLITICS OF AFRICA'S ECONOMIC STAGNATION

The shift from eastern Asia to Sub-Saharan Africa appears to provide ample confirmation of the 'government performance' explanation of successful economic development. The sources of Africa's all too obvious economic failure have been extensively analysed, and a consensus based in orthodox liberal economics has ascribed it to government measures which almost precisely mirror the policy successes of eastern Asia (Bates 1981; Sandbrook 1985). These policies have consistently had the effect of draining surpluses out of the productive sectors of the economy, and notably the export sector, and using them to sustain inflated and inefficient state sectors. Agricultural export crops, which traditionally provided the largest share of Africa's export earnings, and continue to account for almost all the earnings of a number of African states, were marketed through state-controlled boards which characteristically purchased the produce from smallholders at well below the international market price, and used the profits to help sustain the state apparatus. Large areas of production outside the agricultural sector were brought under the control of parastatal organisations, which were almost invariably run as patronage operations for the benefit of those with political connections. The mineral sector, which has now displaced agricultural produce as the major source of African export earnings, was for the most part run by transnational corporations, which managed it with relative efficiency, but helped through royalties and profit-sharing schemes to fund a rentier state which encouraged high levels of public sector corruption. Perhaps most subversively of all, artificially overvalued exchange rates provided relatively cheap imported goods for privileged urban sectors of the population (including notably those dependent on state employment), while at the same time discouraging exporters who were paid at a correspondingly undervalued rate for their produce. Measures which actively promoted imports and discouraged exports in turn required foreign exchange controls, which provided ample opportunities for individuals with political connections to make large profits through their access to foreign exchange. In the francophone states of west and central Africa, the foreign exchange regime maintained through the franc zone (at least until the 50 per cent devaluation of January 1994) served a similar function, and in the process bound import-consuming elites to the French connection (van de Walle 1991). In contrast to the encouragement of food production in the eastern Asian states, African food producers were driven out of the market through the maintenance of low food prices, for the benefit of politically dangerous urban consumers.

The effects of such policies were readily predictable. Export producers resorted where possible to smuggling, which (since African borders are generally porous) at least assured them the best prices available in their immediate region, or else reverted to subsistence production. Food producers, whose production costs (especially when dependent on imported fertilisers) often exceeded the earnings which they could make at regulated prices, either were forced into the black market (and hence subjected to punitive measures by agents of the state) or else again reverted to subsistence. As production declined, and an increasing proportion even of that which was produced escaped from the control of the state, so government revenues were likewise reduced, and even the supposedly privileged strata for whose benefit economic policies were operated found themselves desperately pressed to survive. Government officials (including university academics) were pushed into supplementary employment as traders or even as food producers. As levels of per capita food production declined, so reliance on imported food increased, and, in states where foreign exchange earnings were inadequate to pay for it, this in turn created dependence on 'famine relief' supplied through western charities.

Subsidies for food production in virtually all western states also helped imported food to undercut the prices of local produce.

Whereas economic growth in eastern Asia might broadly be associated with stable if authoritarian regimes, however, there was no equivalent correlation in Sub-Saharan Africa between economic decline and political instability, let alone democracy. There were certainly important states, including Somalia and Zaire, whose level of government collapse was such that the World Bank was obliged to remove them from the statistical record for lack of any adequate information – even though Zaire was 'stable' in the very limited sense that it had been governed by the same head of state since 1965. However, two of the highest measurable rates of decline in GNP per capita in the entire world, at –4.6 per cent per annum over the period 1980–91 for Côte d'Ivoire and –4.2 per cent for Gabon, were recorded in states with stable regimes and reasonably effective systems of government. And though brief periods of multi-party government could sometimes be associated with high levels of mismanagement and corruption, notably in Nigeria from 1979 to 1983, no African state during the 1970s and 1980s enjoyed a system of government that was democratic in the sense that rival parties peacefully alternated in power, while only in very few were multi-party elections held at all.

Once a large number of African states were forced by virtual economic bankruptcy into the receivership of international financial institutions (IFI), as happened from the early 1980s onwards, these adopted a fairly standard set of measures which were broadly intended to restore incentives to the productive sectors of the economy, and in particular to revive export production – both because foreign exchange provided the essential motor for growth in other parts of the economy, and to enable IFIs and other creditors to collect on at least some of their debts. These measures notably included the often drastic devaluation of the currency, the removal of state control over domestic prices and agricultural marketing, the privatisation of public sector enterprises and restrictions on government spending designed to slim down the state apparatus and shift skilled labour into the commercial sector (see Mosley *et al.* 1991; Callaghy and Ravenhill 1993).

These measures, however, have had only very limited success. Since they were generally imposed against the intense opposition of the very state elites whose interests were most directly threatened by them, it is no surprise that their implementation was often half-hearted, as governments sought to gain access to the foreign exchange available as structural adjustment loans, while seeking to avoid the adjustment itself. It is understandable, too, that economic decay was often too far advanced for any swift turnaround to be possible. But even in Ghana, where structural adjustment policies have been pursued over more than a decade, with the full support of the national government, it remains open to question whether the base for any process of self-sustained growth has really been laid, or whether the detectable improvement that certainly has been achieved has been the result of external donors continuing to pump funds into the flagship economy for structural adjustment in Africa (see Herbst 1993; Toye 1991).

EXPLAINING GOVERNMENT PERFORMANCE

While, at one level, differences in economic policy may evidently go some way towards explaining differences in development performance between eastern Asian and African states, it is also clear that these are very far from providing a full or even an adequate explanation. For a start, they do nothing to explain why states which, in the mid-1950s, were very similarly placed in terms of indicators such as GNP per capita or dependence on primary produce exports, should have pursued such radically different economic policies. Nor can they account for the very different capacities of different states to pursue consistent policies over a fairly long period, when these involve the imposition of significant hardships on important sections of the population. Most puzzling of all, whereas it is possible to detect a substantial level of variance between the economic performance of governments pursuing different policies in eastern Asia, it is much harder to detect such variance in Africa. In South and North Korea, Malaysia and the Philippines, or Thailand and Burma/Myanmar, one can take pairs of broadly comparable states and show with reasonable plausibility that the policies followed by the first have been substantially more successful, in terms of achieving sustainable economic growth, than those followed by the second. In the case of China, one can likewise demonstrate a dramatic turnaround in economic performance once one set of policies were replaced by another.

In Africa, on the other hand, the economic performance even of states following apparently contrasting policies has been distressingly similar. In the early years of independence, much play was made of the 'wager' between Presidents Nkrumah of socialist Ghana and Houphouet-Boigny of capitalist Côte d'Ivoire over which policy would prove most effective, and after a decade or so the comparison was very much in favour of Côte d'Ivoire (Woronoff 1972). Analogous comparisons, again to the advantage of the more 'capitalist' state, were made between Kenya and

Tanzania. After more than thirty years, however, there is no plausible indication that even the apparently most successful states have any prospect of developing economies like those of Malaysia or South Korea, which in the mid-1950s stood at Kenyan or Ghanaian levels of development; Côte d'Ivoire, as already noted, has been regressing at almost the fastest rate of any economy in Africa. While it is certainly possible to demonstrate that really disastrous failures of government can have appalling consequences for the people of the state concerned, there is no example to demonstrate African states' capacity to escape from the cycle of underdevelopment. Even the most successful African economy, Botswana, with a GNP per capita of $2530 in 1991 and average annual GNP per capita growth of 5.6 per cent over the previous eleven years, demonstrates the advantages accruing to a relatively small number of people living in a territory with large deposits of minerals – accompanied, it is true, by peace and reasonably good government – rather than any eastern Asian trajectory.

In this context, it may be most illuminating to regard the 'right' economic policies not as an independent variable which may be used to explain the more or less successful economic development performance of different groups of states, but rather as a dependent variable which is itself to a large extent the result of other constitutive elements in their make-up. Economic policies, after all, are not cost-free decisions which governments are at liberty to take as they wish, and which can then be implemented regardless of their political consequences. They are, rather, decisions which define the nature of the governments which take them, which allocate benefits and costs between different groups and individuals within (and, indeed, outside) the state concerned, and which are of the greatest importance in determining the regime's prospects of political survival.

This in turn forces the quest for comparison back to the first of the two elements identified above as necessary to the successful developmental state. If African states as a whole do not follow the 'right' kind of economic policy, save under intense external duress and even then with at best only mixed results, then we may be justified in concluding that they are not the 'right kind of state'. At all events, it may well be in the nature of their statehood, rather than in the nature of their economic policies, that the answers are to be found.

CULTURE AND COMPARISON

African and eastern Asian states may be contrasted in terms of a number of variables, and notably the appreciably greater 'artificiality' of most

African states, resulting from the externally determined arbitrariness with which their boundaries were often drawn up, and the generally much shorter experience of shared government – whether under European colonialism or under an indigenous regime – before their emergence into the modern global system in the aftermath of the Second World War. At least thirty years after most of these states attained their independence, however, the specific legacies of their colonial and pre-colonial past, and indeed the underlying structures of their societies, have been overlaid by more recent experiences, and all of these elements together may be said to constitute the 'culture' of African and eastern Asian states, within which their specific policies have to be made and implemented. It is therefore with cultural comparison, and its role in explaining government performance, that the rest of this paper is concerned. Before going further, then, it may be helpful to sketch out something of the history of 'culturalism' in comparative political science, and to indicate some of the major reasons for its decline and recent resurgence.

At the outset of the post-1945 explosion in comparative political studies, what was then termed 'political culture' was very widely assumed to play a prominent role in comparing different political systems. Such path-breaking works as Almond and Verba (1963) sought to ascertain levels of commitment to 'civic' or democratic values in different industrial societies, a venture which could itself be traced back to the perceived prominence of national cultures (and notably the supposedly authoritarian cultures of Germany and Japan) in the origins of the Second World War, and the prospects for success of programmes for democratic reconstruction. Once political scientists started to concern themselves with the comparative politics of Asian and African societies, whose cultures appeared to be strikingly different from those of their North American or European homelands, the emphasis on culture could only be expected to increase. In addition to works such as Pye and Verba (1965), for example, Pye (1962) sought to unravel the origins of Burmese political culture in infant-rearing practices, while Apter (1965) compared the different approaches to 'modernisation' adopted by African monarchies such as Buganda and Ashanti.

While some of these studies now seem merely quaint, others well repay re-reading. All of them, however, rapidly dropped out of sight from the later 1960s onwards. The reasons for this are not difficult to discern. One of them is the profound commitment of many social scientists to the principles of methodological individualism. Taken to its furthest extent in liberal economic theory, and embodied in the various 'rational choice' approaches which were in vogue from the 1960s onwards, methodological individualism assumes as its basic tenet that human beings are rational creatures who may be expected to respond to similar circumstances in similar ways; this assumption in turn appears to provide a readily available path to a universal social science. Cultural approaches, on the other hand, draw on variables which are often vague and hard to pin down, and which implicitly subvert the whole idea of comparison: they draw on holistic models, in which different elements of the 'culture' concerned are intricately related to one another and cannot be satisfactorily disentangled, while making it difficult to take comparison far beyond the assertion that different societies are different, and that is that.

Culturalism also ran up against the profound moral commitment of virtually all western social scientists to the equality, and hence in a sense the identity, of all human beings. Once it was admitted that peoples or societies were culturally different, it became difficult to avoid the imputation that some of these cultures might be 'superior' to others and, in the context especially of studies which were necessarily concerned with massive inequalities in living standards between peoples, the potential implications of this were extremely disturbing. Both the 'modernisation' approaches to political comparison, with their assumption that all peoples could achieve 'modernity', and the 'dependency' approaches, with their assumption that the poverty of many Third World peoples could be ascribed to the exploitative consequences of western capitalism, may in this light be regarded as attempts to remove the imputations of western 'civilisation' or 'superiority' which earlier contacts with African and Asian peoples had brought forth. Given the historical experience especially of peoples of African origin, it was understandable that any supposed explanation of their level of economic development in terms of their culture should be regarded as deeply offensive.

Thirdly, insofar as social science explanations, not least in the field of development studies, were often expected to provide the basis for remedial action, cultural approaches left would-be policy-makers with very little to do. Cultures might certainly be expected to change slowly over time, and some measures such as formal education programmes might be adopted in order to guide this process in the desired direction; but cultural explanation must necessarily place a heavy emphasis on continuity, and by comparison with an individualist approach – which postulated that suitable changes in the balance of options facing individuals were all that was necessary to induce the desired response – its attractions to development practitioners were slight.

Few social phenomena, however, follow a trajectory more predictable than the cyclical nature of fashions in social science explanation, and it could perhaps only be a matter of time before culturalist approaches reasserted themselves. At one level, the resurgence of culturalism may be traced back to the gradual seepage into the consciousness of Anglo-American social science of the *annales* school of French historians led by Fernand Braudel. Braudel's studies of Mediterranean societies had emphasised the enormous importance of continuities, which were summed up in the phrase '*la longue durée*' (the long term) which became the watchword of the movement (see Braudel 1970). In this context, the task of the historian was to trace those elements which gave to each historical community its own distinctive nature. In the context of modern American social science, Putnam *et al.* (1994), who trace the effectiveness of modern Italian regions to a legacy of civic engagement dating from the early Middle Ages, may be seen as reinventing the idea of the civic culture in the Braudelian tradition.

At a more mundane level, the rediscovery of culturalism may perhaps be ascribed to the Islamic revolution which broke out in Iran in 1979, and to the astonished recognition by western social scientists of societies in which people did not behave in anything remotely resembling the manner which the rational actor model prescribed by methodological individualism would predict. The collapse of Soviet communism, and the replacement of a global system in which the major competing strands were both evidently descended from alternative western traditions by the new world disorder, gave a powerful impetus to an awareness of differing (and perhaps mutually unintelligible) cultures. When, finally, no less a bellwether than Samuel Huntington (1993) conceptualises the international system in terms of a 'clash of civilizations', we may be sure that the wheel has turned full circle, and that culturalism is once more at the centre of the agenda.

Such cultural perspectives are in turn readily applicable to east Asian and Sub-Saharan African trajectories of development. Unsurprisingly, east Asians have been happy to ascribe their economic success to features of their own societies in a way which, at the very least, provides an internalising myth which enables them to appropriate and indigenise an economic system which would otherwise have to be regarded as 'copied' demeaningly from the West. This process has notably been expressed through the idea of 'Asian values', which have been treated as providing an eastern Asian equivalent to that Protestant ethic which Weber identified in the rise of capitalism in Europe. Centred on China and the set of attributes associated with Confucianism, the east Asian cultural zone may be extended to Japan and Korea, as well as to the communities of the Chinese diaspora, and in a possibly diluted form to South-East Asia as well. In the eyes of its proponents, it is associated with discipline, hard work, a respect for knowledge, a readiness to accept deferred expectations and a strong commitment to the members of one's family. For such strident advocates as Lee Kuan Yew of Singapore, it provides a morally superior as well as economically more effective alternative to degenerate westernism (see Zakaria 1994). Methodological individualists, and notably western liberal economists, have sought to demystify the claims of Asian culturalism, ascribing the successes of Asian development merely to sound government policies (see, for example, *The Economist*, 28 May 1994); and it can certainly be very plausibly argued, from the experience of attempts at socialist development in China, North Korea and Vietnam, that such policies are a necessary condition for success. But it must at the very least be recognised that cultural factors may well contribute critically to the levels of discipline, organisation, enterprise and deferred gratification that are needed to make those policies work.

It is likewise understandable that African writers should generally have ascribed the continent's economic failures to external factors, and notably the exploitative legacies of the slave trade, European colonialism and dependent incorporation into the world capitalist economy, rather than to anything inherent in African culture. It has therefore been left to Jean-Francois Bayart (1993), a French political scientist writing explicitly in the Braudelian tradition, to develop a conception of African 'historicity' which may be counterposed to the claims of Confucianism and Asian values. For Bayart, the maintenance of political authority in Africa has been critically constrained by the paucity of the continent's economic resources, which has made it essential for would-be rulers to gain control over such resources, and to use them – notably through the medium of patronage networks of one kind or another – as a means of inducing political obedience (see Clapham 1994). Given the inadequacy of the resources available within the continent, moreover, access to the external resources made available by participation in global economic and political transactions has often been essential for domestic political survival. This use of external resources to maintain internal power, which Bayart terms 'extraversion', can in his view be traced from the slave trade through to modern economic development aid and military assistance programmes.

Though Bayart is frankly uninterested in economic development, his analysis places African states at the opposite end of the spectrum from the 'developmental states' of eastern Asia. It suggests that it is virtually impossible for African states to acquire the autonomy from societal forces necessary to implement effective development policies, since immersion in the daily struggle for subsistence (the 'politics of the belly' referred to in his sub-title) is critical to the state's own survival. It is likewise extremely difficult at best for such a state to implement policies effectively, since the process of implementation itself is subverted by the need to meet immediate political demands. Nor, perhaps most significantly of all, can such a state achieve autonomy from the international system, since it is by managing the transfer of resources between domestic and external political arenas that it acquires a critical part of its working capital. The structural adjustment programmes imposed by international financial institutions further undermine the autonomy of the state, and make it all the more necessary for desperate African rulers to divert the funds provided by such programmes into the all-important struggle for political survival.

CULTURE, STATE AND GOVERNMENT ACTIVITY

Returning to the distinction already made between having 'the right kind of state' and having states which 'do the right thing', it becomes possible to construct a rationale, not only for the relative failure of structural adjustment programmes in Africa, but more generally for the very different impact of government activity and political structure on economic development in African and eastern Asian states. The failures of structural adjustment, in these terms, may be explained as resulting from the imposition of the 'right' policies on the 'wrong' kind of state. These policies do not work, because the state through which they have to be implemented is not capable of making them work.

This is partly a matter of simple administrative capacities: though market-oriented economic development strategies of the kind promoted by the major international financial institutions make appreciably smaller demands on states than the interventionist policies which they are designed to replace, they do none the less depend on the state's ability to carry out a limited range of functions in an effective and impartial way. These functions notably include some infrastructural requirements such as education and communications, and the maintenance of a conducive political and economic environment through the assurance of public order, the stability of the currency and the legal and institutional framework necessary to encourage long-term investment. If these functions cannot be efficiently performed, as is unquestionably the case for a large number of African states, then development policies which depend on them will fail.

The IFI model of development depends, moreover, on the working of effective institutions not only within the state but beyond it. This is most clearly illustrated by the privatisation of previously state-owned enterprises, on the assumption that the profit-and-loss derived incentives of private sector management will impose efficiencies on corpulent and ill-managed parastatal corporations which previously ran according to the logic imposed by government patronage. The story of privatisation in Africa does not always, however, correspond to this rationale. Indeed, African ruling elites have been 'privatising' their national assets for decades, by using their control of the state to convert these assets into their own property, a process (often described as kleptocracy, or government by theft) most blatantly illustrated by the career of President Mobutu of Zaire (Askin and Collins 1993). IMF-induced privatisation provides the opportunity to legitimise such previously furtive activities in the name of an internationally acclaimed (and indeed imposed) ideal of capitalist development. Privatisation in Sierra Leone involved the sale by President Stevens of the most valuable state enterprises at a knock-down price to a shadow company established by himself (Reno forthcoming). In neighbouring Guinea and Côte d'Ivoire, such enterprises were sold without public scrutiny to French companies operating in close association with leading state officials (Smith and Glaser 1992). Such examples could be duplicated from much of the continent.

More general problems of an institutional kind are evident from those states, notably Ghana, in which a sincere and consistent attempt has been made to implement adjustment policies. The early stages of a structural adjustment programme, which depend on specific policy measures such as liberalising exchange rates, are relatively easily implemented, despite the political costs arising from the increase in import prices for urban consumers. The subsequent and much more fundamental task of creating the economic and political institutions which constitute 'restructuring' is much more difficult (Herbst 1993; Toye 1991). Institution-building is an enterprise which depends to a large extent on culture: on the ability to respect and delegate authority; on the capacity to conceptualise and implement a distinction between the 'public' interests of an institution and the 'private' interests of the individuals within it; on conceptions of obligation and accountability which are ultimately moral and societal in nature. Recognising these problems, proponents of structural adjustment have called for changes in political culture, characteristically by strengthening the institutions of 'civil society' (Landell-Mills 1992), an approach which may well be regarded as carrying within it the cultural assumptions of western (and especially Anglo-American) societies. As any Braudelian would recognise, however, these values are extraordinarily difficult to change.

These issues bear, finally, on the relationships between development and democracy, and on the role of the state in economic development.

Critics of structural adjustment have frequently pointed out that the liberalising policies imposed on Africa by the IFIs bear little relationship (except in the sense that they run directly counter) to the statist policies followed by successfully industrialising states in eastern Asia. They have also pointed to the discrepancy between the 'political conditionalities' imposed on Africa by donor agencies, notably in the form of multi-party democracy, and the authoritarianism of many successful regimes in Asia (Leftwich 1993). These criticisms have a certain validity: it can plausibly be argued that structural adjustment requires a measure of authoritarianism, and that the 'all good things go together' assumption that democracy necessarily aids economic reform is naive in the extreme (Jeffries 1993). However, neither authoritarianism, nor a high level of state regulation of the economy, has produced the economic benefits in Africa that they have sometimes (though not always) produced in Asia. They have been more likely to result in gross levels of brutality and corruption, and eventual political and economic collapse. If a case is to be made for either economic liberalism or multi-party democracy in Africa, it is most plausibly based not on the promotion of development, but on the prevention of harm.

CONCLUSION

Proceeding, in contrast to several of the other contributions to this volume, at the broadest macro-comparative level, this study necessarily ignores many of the factors which have contributed to the success or failure of would-be developmental states, and overlooks numerous variants within each of the vast geopolitical regions which it has ambitiously sought to compare. Even within the relatively homogeneous environment of Western Europe, after all, the attempt to run a common governmental structure in the form of the European Union has drawn attention to a fascinating range of governmental values and assumptions among officials from different member states, and a still greater spread is only to be expected within each of the much larger regions which form the subject of this paper. The massive discrepancies in development performance, and hence also in human welfare, between eastern Asian and African states do none the less demand some attempt at explanation, which in turn calls for comparison on however gross a scale. In isolating culture as a potentially critical variable, however, I certainly do not wish to overlook the problems of culturalist approaches noted earlier in this paper, still less to assume that culture can provide any all-purpose explanation for the successes and failures, or indeed the rights and wrongs, of government activity. Plentiful examples from both eastern Asia and Africa could be brought forward to attest to the difference that can be made to development and welfare both by decisions that lie within the scope of particular regimes, and by the political skills and personal values of individual leaders.

So far as the comparison of government activity is concerned, it does however seem to me that the idea of the Third World as a conceptual category has now reached the end of the road. I would likewise question the validity of cross-national or indeed cross-continental comparisons of government activity which ignore deep-seated attitudes to government – 'governmentalities', in Bayart's expressive term – among both state officials and populations, which have proved extremely resistant to change. The dangers of such comparisons are particularly great when they lead to the external imposition of common policies, derived ultimately from individualist methodologies for the explanation of human behaviour, which fail to take account of the very different cultural contexts within which they have to be implemented. More broadly still, while the comparison of government activities evidently draws attention to important and intriguing variations in the working of governments and their impact on peoples, it does not evidently lead to the articulation of any general theories or explanations of government activity. It may, rather, lead us back to an appreciation of the particularities of the social and cultural settings from which those governments have sprung.

NOTES

1. The term 'Third World', as defined in the first paragraph, is henceforth used without distinguishing quotation marks.
2. I use the term 'eastern Asia' to refer both to 'East Asia', comprising the Chinas and Koreas (and Japan, though for most purposes it may be omitted), and to 'South-East Asia', comprising the ASEAN states, Burma/Myanmar and Indochina. This paper excludes consideration of two other regions, South Asia and South and Central America, most of the comparative indicators for which fall between the two extremes represented by Sub-Saharan Africa and eastern Asia; the Middle East is also excluded, because its high dependence on oil exports precludes useful comparison.

REFERENCES

Almond, Gabriel A. and Sidney Verba. 1963. *The Civic Culture*. Princeton: Princeton University Press.

Appelbaum, Richard P. and Jeffrey Henderson, eds. 1992. *States and Development in the Asian Pacific Rim*. Beverly Hills: Sage.

Apter, David E. 1965. *The Politics of Modernization*. Chicago: Chicago University Press.

Askin, Steve and Carole Collins. 1993. 'External Collusion with Kleptocracy: Can Zaire Recover Its Stolen Wealth?' *Review of African Political Economy* 57: 72–85.

Bates, Robert H. 1981. *Markets and States in Tropical Africa*. Berkeley: University of California Press.

Bayart, Jean-Francois. 1993. *The State in Africa: The Politics of the Belly*. London: Longman.

Braudel, Fernand. 1970. 'History and Social Science: The Long Term.' *Social Science Information* 9(1): 145–74.

Callaghy, Thomas M. and John Ravenhill, eds. 1993. *Hemmed In: Responses to Africa's Economic Decline*. New York: Columbia University Press.

Clapham, Christopher. 1994. 'The *longue durée* of the African State.' *African Affairs* 93(372): 433–9.

Herbst, Jeffrey. 1993. *The Politics of Reform in Ghana*. Berkeley: University of California Press.

Huntington, Samuel. 1993. 'The Clash of Civilizations.' *Foreign Affairs* 72(3): 22–49.

Jeffries, Richard. 1993. 'The State, Structural Adjustment and Good Government in Africa.' *Journal of Commonwealth and Comparative Politics* 31(1): 20–35.

Koo, Hagen and Eun Mee Kim. 1992. 'The Developmental State and Capital Accumulation in South Korea.' In *States and Development in the Asian Pacific Rim*, eds Richard P. Appelbaum and Jeffrey Henderson. Beverly Hills: Sage.

Landell-Mills, Pierre. 1992. 'Governance, Cultural Change, and Empowerment.' *Journal of Modern African Studies* 30(4): 543–67.

Leftwich, Adrian. 1993. 'Governance, Democracy and Development in the Third World.' *Third World Quarterly* 14(3): 605–24.

Mosley, Paul *et al.* 1991. *Aid and Power: The World Bank and Policy-based Lending*. 2 vols, London: Routledge.

Putnam, Robert D. *et al.* 1994. *Making Democracy Work: Civic Traditions in Modern Italy*. Princeton: Princeton University Press.

Pye, L.W. 1962. *Politics, Personality and Nation Building: Burma's Search for Identity*. New Haven: Yale University Press.

Pye, Lucien W. and Sidney Verba. 1965. *Political Culture and Political Development*. Princeton: Princeton University Press.

Reno, William. forthcoming 1995. *The Past in Africa's Future: The Shadow State Struggle with Reform*. Cambridge: Cambridge University Press.

Sandbrook, Richard. 1985. *The Politics of Africa's Economic Stagnation*. Cambridge: Cambridge University Press.

Smith, Stephen and Antoine Glaser. 1992. *Ces Messieurs Afrique: Le Paris-Village du Continent Noir*. Paris: Calmann-Levy.

Toye, John. 1991. 'World Bank Policy-Conditioned Loans: How Did They Work in Ghana.' In *Policy Adjustment in Africa*, eds Chris Milner and A.J. Rayner. London: Macmillan.

van de Walle, Nicholas. 1991. 'The Decline of the Franc Zone: Monetary Politics in Francophone Africa.' *African Affairs* 90(360): 383–405.

White, Gordon. 1984. 'Developmental States and Socialist Industrialisation in the Third World.' *Journal of Development Studies* 21(1): 97–120.

World Bank. 1993. *World Development Report 1993.* Oxford: Oxford University Press.

Woronoff, Jon. 1972. *West African Wager: Houphouet versus Nkrumah.* Metuchen, NJ: Scarecrow Press.

Zakaria, Fareed. 1994. 'A Conversation with Lee Kuan Yew.' *Foreign Affairs* 73(2): 109–26.

11 Accumulation, Aggregation and Eclecticism in Political Science: A Case Study of Foreign Policy Analysis

Robert D. McKinlay

INTRODUCTION

Particularly with the expansion of universities and research institutes in the post-Second World War period, the volume of research in political science has grown enormously. The principal concern of this chapter is focused on an important aspect of the status of the knowledge produced by this increased volume of research. Rather than surveying the discipline as a whole, this chapter concentrates, for illustrative purposes only, on a particular sub-field of the discipline, foreign policy analysis. The chapter is not concerned to summarise the sub-field of foreign policy analysis, let alone produce an inventory of propositions or findings within foreign policy analysis – both of which arguably are dimensions of the status of our knowledge. Rather I am concerned to approach the issue of the status of our knowledge by asking the question: is a body of research being produced that progressively integrates and amplifies our understanding of foreign policy?

The thesis of the chapter, which is generalisable beyond but illustrated only within foreign policy analysis, is developed through three main arguments. The first suggests that there has been a growth of an impressively rich literature (which I will term accumulation); the second contends that this growth has taken place largely in the absence of any substantial degree of integration (which I will term aggregation); the third argument maintains that there are some major obstacles to any significant degree of aggregation.

ACCUMULATION

The claim that there is a rich literature on foreign policy, a claim I take to be largely uncontentious, can be substantiated through three straightforward arguments.

The first is that there is a focal point around which a literature can develop. Deliberately avoiding, for the moment, terms that are in any way obtuse or contentious, foreign policy would seem quite readily to provide a distinctive focal point.

Most people would readily accept that the world is divided into countries, an 'official' list of which is kept by the United Nations Organisation, which have national governments. National governments are highly visible and important, not least because they produce policies that have major impacts on our lives. These policies can be felt in a whole variety of areas, one conventional ordering of which is in terms of domestic versus foreign. Governments are doing something fundamentally domestic when they raise or lower taxes, and equally are doing something fundamentally non-domestic, or foreign, when they sign an international treaty.

The second fairly simple argument is that there is a large and growing literature which bears in some way on foreign policy. Without pretending for a moment to summarise this literature, some of its main forms can be indicated.

Certainly the easiest and also largest literature to access is that which is defined in the simple fashion above. A search under country and then under foreign policy, through a terminal connected to a good university library, would yield literally hundreds of entries.

A search could also be conducted under issue areas rather than country. Tapping into the terminal a series of well-known and simple issue areas, such as economic aid, arms sales, human rights, refugees or the environment, would again yield a voluminous literature.

It is also rather basic knowledge that governments consist of individuals and groups which interact domestically with other groups. It is not unreasonable to assume that foreign policy is 'made' by foreign policy-makers. One very distinctive literature, testimony to some degree to the importance and visibility of both foreign policy and its 'makers', consists of the memoirs of such persons. The search under country and issue area would need to be extended to include a search under names of individual decision-makers. Academic researchers are not only not in the dark about the 'memoir' literature but have also produced their own complementary literature on the role of individuals or of personality. Indeed, following this line of 'makers', academic researchers do not stop with individuals but go on to include a whole list of domestic influences, such as public opinion, the media, pressure groups, political parties or the bureaucracy.

Governments interact not simply with other governments but with a range of other international actors, principal among which are intergovernmental organisations (now numbering nearly 400), non-governmental international organisations (now numbering over 4000), multinational corporations, international banks, or 'terrorist' organisations. Searches under these headings would also prove fruitful.

Armed with some more detailed information on the study of foreign policy analysis, further searches could be made. For example, the adjective 'foreign', as applied to policy, is subject to one or two idiosyncratic conventions. Much literature could well be missed if searches were not made under the headings of foreign economic policy or security policy (which slightly confusingly is not usually preceded by the adjective foreign). Or again, there is a literature organised round what are often termed instruments or means of foreign policy. In terms of volume, searches under law, or diplomacy, or sanctions, or force, or war would again be very fruitful. Or again, foreign policy can and has been studied by a variety of approaches or analytical frameworks. Such approaches are most easily found only indirectly by locating reviews of the foreign policy literature. Assuming such reviews have been located, not many would have to be read before a relatively long list of approaches, such as cybernetics, communications, bargaining, formal models, simulation, artificial intelligence, cognitive processes, or crisis management, began to appear. Finally, foreign policy analysis is just one of the sub-fields of international relations. It would be as well therefore to check what other sub-fields of international relations had to say about foreign policy – minimally this would mean checking international relations theory and international political economy.

Turning to the third fairly simple argument, it can safely be said that the literature, which has now been identified, is of high quality. Even though quality is more awkward to assess than quantity, this literature has been produced by bright and hard-working persons often after the expenditure of much time and effort.

In sum, we have a large literature (if by large we mean publications numbering in the thousands), which does have a readily understandable point of reference, and which is of high quality. This seems a very reasonable way in which to characterise a rich literature.

By way of footnote to this section, it may seem strange that literature has not been cited. One of the several reasons for this may be seen from Gerner's thorough review, which does not pretend to be exhaustive, of what is in effect a particular sub-field of the sub-field of foreign policy analysis – this partial review has fourteen pages of citations. A further reason is that there are numerous reviews and bibliographic surveys, for examples of which see: Bull (1966), Bobrow (1972), Caporaso *et al.* (1987), Cohen and Harris (1975), East (1987), Faurby (1976a, 1976b), Ferguson and Mansbach (1988), Gerner (1991), Hermann *et al.* (1987), Hill and Light (1985), Rosenau (1966, 1976, 1984), Smith (1981, 1983, 1986, 1987).

ACCUMULATION WITH LIMITED AGGREGATION

The principal claim of this section is that the rich literature on foreign policy analysis displays a markedly greater degree of accumulation than of aggregation. This claim is developed in several stages, the first of which makes a brief excursion into the area of the philosophy of science, as it is within science that the nature and importance of the cumulative process were first and most clearly seen.

Many writers on the philosophy of science, Rudner (1968) or Nagel (1961), usefully distinguish scientific method and scientific content. The former is in essence a body of epistemological rules of investigation. It is the application of these rules of investigation which is responsible for the production of a scientific content. While the basic rules of procedure can be quite highly formalised and codified, in which respect their application is in part mechanical, it must of course be emphasised that scientists are not simple automatons that blindly execute a particular method. The development of scientific content is the product also of imagination (for an interesting discussion of which see Koestler 1961).

The application of the scientific method is conventionally held to produce both an expanding and also an integrated body of content. It achieves the former basically because it becomes a kind of dynamo or engine for the growth of content. Though the growth of scientific content is certainly influenced by factors other than the scientific method, the method itself plays an important role in identifying problems. Numerous philosophers of science, see for example Laudan (1977) or Nagel (1961), observe how the solution of one problem throws up new problems, which in turn do the same.

The claim that science is not only expanding but doing so in an integrated manner rests principally on the nature of the rules of investigation. These rules in a fundamental fashion are agreed and acceptable rules of investigation. As such the content of science is not haphazard. Acceptable knowledge is only that body of knowledge which has been produced according to the appropriate and highly specified application of agreed and acceptable rules of investigation.

Science is often and quite reasonably described as progressive. When science is so characterised, observers for the most part are not making evaluative judgements on the desirability of the content but are referring to progress as cumulation. Science is progressive or cumulative basically because the store of knowledge, manifested in the content, has over several centuries expanded in an integrated fashion.

It is equally commonly and reasonably observed that the cumulative form of science not only is one of its hallmarks but is also highly desirable. Fukuyama (1992) makes a recent and provocative statement on the importance and consequences of cumulation. Less provocatively the desirability of a cumulative store of knowledge can be seen from the benefits gained by those familiar with such a store. Such persons can communicate, they confront a well-defined body of what needs to be learned, they do not engage in unnecessary replication and different components or areas of the store stand in known and understandable relations to each other.

In even such a brief detour it would be wrong to imply that progress or cumulation in science are entirely smooth. Both scientists and philosophers of science emphasise that science is relative rather than absolute. What is acceptable knowledge at any one time can prove to be a future heresy. Furthermore, the scientific method is not quite so 'cook-book' as has been implied above. Numerous surveys, such as that of Keat and Urry (1982), point to some relatively marked differences in what are taken to be basic rules of procedure. Such issues, which bear critically on the cumulative process, become very prominent in the well-known Popper (1959, 1968) and Kuhn (1970) debate. The influential work of Lakatos and Musgrave (1970) does, however, seem to have produced some degree of consensus. Though it may well be quite erroneous to see cumulation in science as an incremental and absolute progression, science does seem, despite some fits and starts or some re-writing, to have displayed a marked degree of directionality, of growth and of integration – in short a marked degree of cumulation. Whether this will continue is of course unknown – some interesting thoughts on the future, just about comprehensible to the lay reader, can be found in Davies and Gribbin (1991) and Penrose (1989).

The second stage of the argument of this section suggests that political scientists need to distinguish between accumulation and aggregation, each of which may be represented as poles of a continuum. Accumulation lies at the weaker end of the spectrum and represents minimally collection, albeit around some common denominator or focal point. As such, accumulation certainly requires more than random gathering. (The random selection of books within a library would not constitute accumulation, though the way libraries order books by subject would meet the minimum requirement for accumulation.) Aggregation lies at the stronger end of the spectrum. It presupposes accumulation but makes the additional and more stringent requirements of coherence and directionality within an expanding literature. Directionality is manifested if studies directly and explicitly complement each other. For example, if one study triggers another which in turn triggers further studies, then directionality is being displayed. Coherence requires that the findings of any one study can be directly and explicitly connected to the findings of other studies. Directionality and coherence are not independent or autonomous dimensions but simultaneous aspects of a single process. In effect, the coterminous development of directionality and coherence defines the increase in the power of the common denominator that characterises the movement of an expanding body of literature from accumulation towards aggregation.

While the progress of science may well be assessed in terms of cumulation, the progress of political science requires a less stringent form of assessment. Similar arguments are made by Ashley (1976) and Zinnes (1976), who respectively distinguish expansive versus selective cumulation, and additive versus integrative accumulation. If we are to use aggregation, or what in science is taken to be cumulation, we would simply find no progress whatsoever. If, on the other hand, we take accumulation as the point of departure, then we not only can see progress but can begin to make some assessment of how far that progress has developed by assessing the amount of movement from accumulation to aggregation.

The third and final stage of this section attempts, in an admittedly crude way, to make such an assessment. It is argued that, from the basic and minimum accumulation of an expanding literature organised around a focal point noted above, there are a number of indications of movement towards aggregation but that these indications offer only limited evidence of aggregation.

One indication of some degree of aggregation would be the emergence of a group of scholars who identify themselves and are identified by others as foreign policy analysts. The term 'foreign policy analyst' is a concept. Concepts are simply terms which group a particular set of properties into a unique constellation which demarcates that set from other constellations. By virtue of defining unique constellations, concepts are by definition aggregative. As the component properties of a concept become more ambiguous and less easy to identify, then the aggregative power of the concept reduces (in which respect I see concepts as variable). The aggregative power of the concept 'foreign policy analyst' seems very weak.

One of three illustrative weaknesses centres on foreign policy itself, which is scarcely an unambiguous focal point. Thus, Cohen and Harris (1975) declare: 'There is a certain discomfort in writing about foreign policy for no two people seem to define it in the same way.' Or Munton (1976:258) writes:

...students of foreign policy do not have even a reasonably clear or generally agreed upon notion of the very concept of 'foreign policy'. Few have bothered to define the concept at all, and those who have done so often leave as much or more confusion in their wake as existed before. When the term appears, it is seldom clear whether it refers to actions, goals, decisions, objectives, initiatives, attitudes, plans, undertakings or whatever.

Not only does foreign policy have multiple meanings but also, as Munton points out, any one analyst often slides across these different meanings.

A second illustrative difficulty is that, while we can argue that there are scholars who identify themselves and are identified as foreign policy analysts, we certainly cannot argue that there is a community, in the sense of a coherent group, of such analysts. Northedge (1974) or Jones (1970, 1979) or East *et al.* (1978) or Wilkenfeld *et al.* (1980) may well identify themselves as foreign policy analysts. The work of the first two bears precious little resemblance to or connection with the last two.

A third illustrative difficulty is that many people study foreign policy but without calling themselves foreign policy analysts. Taking the deliberately primitive definition of foreign policy of the first section (in effect the intentions or actions of governments in responding to their external environment) then anyone studying international relations could hardly avoid foreign policy. Looking to international relations, however, brings only more confusion. For example, Waltz (1979) more or less legislates foreign policy out of existence. Or again both Strange (1986) and Ohmae (1990) have something very interesting and important to say about governments. The connection or resemblance of their work either to Northedge or to East is, to put it mildly, tenuous.

A second indication or sign of aggregation could be held to be manifested in the existence of textbooks. Boynton (1976) makes a pertinent point, in discussing 'cumulativeness as a frame of mind', when he suggests that we focus on 'what is known now that was not known before'. Textbooks are compendiums not merely of information but of large volumes of information. They could not come into existence, following Boynton's point, if we did not know now much that was not known before. There is furthermore no shortage of textbooks. Indeed there are even bibliographic essays on textbooks – see Sandole (1985).

Several factors, however, would seem to indicate that current textbooks in foreign policy or international relations profile accumulation other than aggregation. First, if textbooks were to be aggregative (which they could be) we should expect to find textbooks written by researchers for researchers. Textbooks, however, are written almost exclusively for undergraduates and indeed mostly for beginning undergraduates – without wishing to denigrate the effort that must go into writing a textbook, the information contained in textbooks is rather basic. Secondly, textbooks do not so much integrate as survey a field and as such tend to summarise and profile controversies and conflicts.

A third sign of possible aggregation could be the increasing number of conferences, journals or citations. Conferences and publications can, for example, foster aggregation by institutionalising communication; some journals are explicitly devoted to particular sub-fields and as such are testimony to a recognised body of research; or again, publications commonly use citations extensively, which again to some degree must manifest reference to or reliance on other work.

There can be no doubt that conferences and publications are staggeringly important for aggregation. However, while they are prerequisites of accumulation, they are not in themselves valid measures of aggregation. Conferences and publications would become valid measures of aggregation if and only if they displayed a high degree of both coherence and directionality, which for the most part they do not.

In the coherence context, both conferences and journals can reflect or foster a form of 'intellectual apartheid'. We generally very carefully select not only which conferences we attend but also which panels. This selectivity, often learned as part of our 'professional training', becomes even more pronounced and serious in the case of publishing in journals. Given the number of journals it is not surprising that we find specialisation. Furthermore, specialisation and aggregation are not incompatible as long as there is a connecting rationale for the specialisation. This does not seem to be the case in foreign policy analysis. Someone who may send an article to *Foreign Affairs*, or *Foreign Policy*, or *International Affairs* would most certainly not send that article to the *Journal of Conflict Resolution* or *International Studies Quarterly*. What tends to happen through both conferences and publications is that we overwhelmingly communicate with those with whom we agree. This segmentation or intellectual apartheid has been noted by numerous others with their own special terminology. Thus Singer (1975) talks of 'tribal reservations', Ferguson and Mansbach (1988) talk of 'partisan bands', or Hollis and Smith (1990) talk of 'intellectual clubs'. Hollis and Smith indeed take the argument one stage further in pointing to the largely sterile debate between 'intellectual clubs':

> ...each has its own journals, meetings, and leaders. Each knows the weaknesses in its own and in the other approaches and therefore debates between them tend to result in predictable discussions within a well-trodden terrain. (1990:61)

As far as directionality is concerned, we would expect publications to augment directly and explicitly other publications. To some degree this does happen and the convention of citation is testimony to it. However, citations can be used selectively to support or condemn particular literatures. More significantly, our quality control procedures are light-years away from being agreed impartial standards. Consequently it is very difficult to know whether a mass of supportive citations is referencing a blind alley, a fad or an emergent dominant orthodoxy.

In concluding this section, it would have to be conceded that I am making an assessment of a literature, the whole of which I most certainly have not read, along a scale from accumulation to aggregation, which is far from highly operationalised. On the other hand, accumulation and aggregation have been distinguished in a moderately clear manner. Furthermore, the foreign policy literature as a whole seems to be so distant from aggregation that any great precision of measurement, though it would be desirable, is not really required. By way of corroboration of the claim for impressive accumulation albeit with limited aggregation, I cite two very different studies which, though not using this terminology, reach effectively the same conclusion. On the basis of a micro study, Faurby (1976b:205, 210) writes:

> ...our understanding of foreign policy is small and certainly not increasing at a speed in any way comparable with that of publication output.

or again:

> There is an enormous amount of 'replication' ... not of the kind argued for in theoretical discussions but of the kind where succeeding researchers go through the same large amount of primary sources and end by reporting vague and unverifiable conclusions, unaware that a colleague has already been there with more or less the same purpose.

On the basis of a macro study, Ferguson and Mansbach (1988:163) write:

> Can we make meaningful generalisations about the relative significance of many ill-defined variables in explaining decisions, often of dubious relevance and impact, made in various national contexts by a great number of potentially influential individuals and/or groups?! The outlook for doing so is, to say the least, hardly bright.

OBSTACLES TO AGGREGATION

By virtue of having argued that we have substantial accumulation though with modest accompanying aggregation, we have immediately restricted the area of our search for explanations of this descriptive outcome. We do not need for example to contemplate lack of resources or lack of imagination or lack of research infrastructure, without which of course we could not have accumulation. Rather we need explanations which focus directly on lack of coherence and directionality. In other words, we are looking for factors which encourage diversity and in so doing stimulate incoherence and multi-dimensionality, which then by definition impede aggregation.

The first of four main clusters of factors concerns the selection of the research topic, where several factors encourage diversity.

One such factor concerns the construction of what is taken to be a problem. A researcher could select a research topic because that issue is seen as constituting a problem. The growth of non-tariff barriers to trade could for example be selected as a topic because these barriers are seen as constituting a problem. Non-tariff barriers to trade are, however, a problem only from the perspective of certain values (liberal ones); from other values (neo-mercantilist ones), non-tariff barriers to trade far from being a problem are in fact a solution. The point of some significance here is that not only can research topics be influenced by sets of values but competing sets of values will produce different topics.

A further factor, likely to be very important in an area of research such as foreign policy which has a strong applied component, is topicality. It would be rather surprising if dramatic events such as the Gulf War or the end of the Cold War did not attract substantial attention. In some respects it can be of no great surprise that bookshelves are already groaning with a literature on the end of the Cold War. This 'news' item is sufficiently topical that much of the research is highly repetitive. More importantly, this is an indication of how topics on a research agenda are driven by world events rather than by any theory.

Another factor refers to a different dimension of topicality, namely academic topicality. Ferguson and Mansbach (1988) do perhaps put the point rather strongly when they talk of 'the grip of fads that like novas light up the scholarly heavens for a brief time and then disappear'. There can, however, be little doubt that there are academic fashions. International relations has for example recently been swept by such 'cutting edge' topics as interdependence, regime analysis and hegemonic stability. These fashions produce equally fashionable counter-fashions such that the literature quickly begins to mirror the mutual veto system of interest groups.

Another very different source for the selection of research topics can lie in a researcher's methodology. Thus a researcher may choose to focus on a particular measurement problem; or, given particular data requirements for a particular methodology, a researcher may select a topic for which there are data; or the development of a new technique, such as log-linear models, may stimulate some research on a topic to which the new technique is readily applicable. The diversity in this context is not simply that topics may be selected for methodological rather than, say, topical reasons, but also that there are numerous competing methodologies.

A final illustration concerns accumulation. If foreign policy analysis is characterised by a high degree of accumulation, then a researcher, before undertaking any project, would need to make a very substantial investment in reading the literature. Since we cannot both read and write books at the same time and since writing any book presupposes a massive reading investment, then the research agenda of any one researcher may be heavily conditioned by previous research. In this respect accumulation has something of its own dynamic.

Further multiplication of the illustrations is unnecessary for the main point, namely that topic selection can be made from a host of different vantage points. Dryzek (1986), drawing on Laudan (1977), argues strongly that there is a categoric difference between political science and a discipline such as physics in that problems for the former are externally driven and 'socially mediated' whereas problems for the latter are internally or theory driven. As far as topic selection is concerned I am not convinced that there is a complete hiatus between the social and natural sciences. Thus scientists themselves, such as Watson (1968), or very different commentators on science, such as Rose and Rose (1969) or Schilts (1987), make it abundantly clear that science is far from asocial. None the less, though Dryzek makes a much stronger case in this area than I would choose, it does seem to be the case that topic selection in political science enjoys substantial latitude. Furthermore, this latitude rests upon some very different driving forces, which far from being predicated on a logic of aggregation seem to be antithetical to it. We do not consequently confront any agreed research agenda which could provide a strong directionality to our studies.

If political scientists begin by pointing in different directions, they then run into a second cluster of difficulties, which may be termed substantive complexity. The foreign policy analyst incurs two areas of enormous difficulty, both of which are related to what is commonly referred to as the bridging role of foreign policy.

The first of these relates to the domestic–foreign divide. Traditionally, international relations and comparative politics, both of which are equally mis-named fields, have thrived on what in international relations has been termed the billiard ball model. Though there is now widespread and well-founded agreement that the billiard ball model is inappropriate, there is, to put it mildly, substantial controversy on the factors that have eroded the billiard ball model and how far these factors have moved us on the state-centric to cobweb continuum. The central importance of this debate for present purposes is that the boundary between domestic and foreign has become blurred and as such foreign policy analysis has been thrust into comparative politics.

The second area of bridging difficulties concerns issue areas. Traditionally, foreign policy has concentrated on so-called high politics, which was basically the management of diplomacy and, should diplomacy break down, of war. The high politics focus of international relations was reflected in the dominant theory of international relations, that of realism, which until recently has claimed not only to explain the world but also to provide foreign policy guidance as though economic interactions, except as they bore immediately on a capacity to wage war, did not matter (see for example such leading writers as Kennedy 1987, Morgenthau 1985, Waltz 1979, but also some major exceptions, such as Strange 1988). Governments have not proved themselves to be quite so blinkered. In part the proliferation of intergovernmental organisations, by which governments have come close to replicating 'domestic' functions at an 'international' level, is testimony to this. Government leaders, as is true for an increasing number of academics, are well aware that things international do not respect the so-called high and low politics divide. Trade, investment, money, food, refugees, human rights, the environment are now, for example, readily regarded as important international issues.

The extension of foreign policy both into domestic politics and across issue areas means that we confront what Hollis and Smith (1990) refer to as 'more of an interdiscipline than a discipline'. Or again, as a consequence of these bridging developments, Caporaso *et al.* (1987:33) assert that for foreign policy analysts:

...the whole gamut of human experience falls within their purview .... Those who study foreign policy must concern themselves with politics at every level. It is in a profound sense a discipline without borders.

Exciting though an interdiscipline without borders may be, it does pose serious problems for aggregation. One way of illustrating this is to draw on the division of labour analogy. As Adam Smith noted, productivity, to give it its contemporary name, could be increased by workers specialising in a narrowly defined part of the production process. There has also been a progressive division of labour in the intellectual world. There are, however, two crucial differences between the intellectual and pin factories. First, the intellectual division of labour in the social sciences has been made not proactively to stimulate productivity but reactively because our brains are simply not large enough to absorb the volume of information that we have produced. Second, the division of labour in the pin factory could be made in a coherent manner – each discrete stage of the production process had a clear and known relation to other stages. This has not proved to be the case for the intellectual division of labour. This second cluster of problems becomes therefore a major obstacle for coherence in the aggregation process. We seemingly confront the world with an incoherent and reactive division of analysis (labour), which is not respected by the world.

The third and probably most serious obstacle concerns the manner in which research topics are analysed. Even if there were to be agreement on an agenda of topics within a clearly defined field, aggregation would be impossible as long as there was no agreed set of rules of investigation. No-one of course pretends there is such an agreed set. However, conventionally modes of investigation are divided, very misleadingly, into traditional or classical studies versus behavioural studies. Were this distinction to be accurate, we would simply have two modes of analysis. Though aggregation across the modes would be difficult, aggregation within each would be relatively straightforward. The problems and choices facing any political scientist are massively more complex than the dual choice implied in the traditional–behavioural distinction. Though it is well beyond the scope of this paper to discuss these problems and choices fully, some of them can be indicated in an ordered manner.

The first set of difficult choices begins in ontology and teleology – a good and comprehensible recent introduction is given in Hollis and Smith (1990). There can be little doubt that the subject matter of the social sciences, unlike that of the natural sciences, has attitudes and values, and uses these to endow its behaviour with meaning and purpose. Looking backwards to ontology there seems to be an intractable debate, intractable in the sense that there are multiple competing positions engendering important divisions, as to whether reality is knowable. Looking forward to the role played by meaning and purpose there is an equally intractable debate as to the relative importance of values and perception. There is an immense distance to be travelled from Winch (1970) or Eco (1989) to Marx or Waltz (1979).

Assuming a position in this area has been taken either wittingly or by default, we seemingly reach the firmer ground of concept formation. At least we can all seemingly agree that concepts are the building blocks of our analyses. This, however, is where the firm ground ends as we must now confront endless unresolved conflicts. Ontology rears its head again as we need to consider to what extent our concepts reflect reality or our abortive attempts to construct a reality we can never know. Or again we need to consider to what extent our concepts are socially or ethnocentrically mediated. Some analysts argue that concepts are fundamentally or should be fundamentally theory driven while at the other end of the spectrum others take an inductionist or empiricist position. Some analysts demand that irrespective of the level at which concepts originate they must finally have clearly specified empirical referents. There is, however, no known means of choosing between competing sets of empirical referents. Others largely ignore clearly specified empirical referents. Some analysts see key concepts, such as the state or sovereignty or the Cold War, as variable while others regard these concepts as discrete and absolute entities. Or again some choose to try to delineate dimensions of concepts, such as dimensions of bipolarity or spheres of influence, while others regard these in effect as uni-dimensional phenomena. The principal consequence of these and other difficulties is that we simply do not have an agreed lexicon or for that matter anything which even begins to approximate an agreed lexicon. Holding constant for the moment rules of evidence, it is small wonder that propositions about interdependence or hegemonic stability, for example, yield no consensus when analysts mean such different things by them.

Putting aside these difficulties, I take it to be moderately uncontentious that a store of knowledge is produced when corroborated patterns between concepts are established. Since there are few if any fully accepted rules of evidence, then what constitutes a corroborated pattern becomes yet another Pandora's Box.

Some of the main choices over which there is again serious dispute include the following. Some analysts focus on longitudinal and others on latitudinal patterns. Within each there can be serious conflict over the appropriate number of cases. Some analysts choose to focus on a clearly delimited set of concepts while others impose no restrictions. For those dealing in only limited sets there are problems of at what levels variables are to be arrayed and of whether intervening variables are to be used. For some, incorporation of causality to patterns is central; for others, reciprocal variation is adequate. Some are satisfied with corroboration as a specified relationship for which some support can be adduced. For other analysts corroboration can come only through controlled investigation (of which there are numerous forms) and the explicit testing of competing explanations. Probably most analysts would agree that change is a major difficulty not simply because of its rate but because change can bring new forms of relationship across new actors. This leads some at the idiographic end of the spectrum to argue that the search for general explanations is fundamentally fruitless. Others at the nomothetic end reject the assertion that we cannot escape from the unique, but then have to confront immense problems identifying the boundary conditions under which the search for nomothetic propositions can be made.

The above, as has been conceded, is simply a tour of some, and by no means all, of the difficulties in defining a mode of analysis. What truly hinders aggregation as far as mode of analysis is concerned is not simply that there are numerous unresolved, and likely to be unresolvable, disputes, but that a bewildering set of choices can be made down the menu. (Hence, the comment earlier on the gross oversimplification of traditional versus behavioural studies.) Fowles (1965), in the course of a wonderfully irritating game with 'reality', invites us to consider why we choose to study abnormal people when the real puzzle is why anyone is normal. Following Fowles, it is perhaps not nearly so surprising that communication across different research projects is difficult as that any communication takes place at all.

The fourth and final obstacle to aggregation concerns our professional environment, or more precisely the fragmented nature of this environment.

The fragmentation rests upon two related factors. First, overwhelmingly the basic unit is the individual researcher. Even though there is a marked tendency, particularly in the United States and increasingly in Britain, for 'better' researchers to gravitate towards 'better' departments in 'better' universities, the individual researcher constitutes the basic unit of output and evaluation. This is seen very clearly in, and hence related to, the second factor, the reward and incentive system, which is fairly explicitly tied to the individual. The more independent effect of the reward and incentive system is that it is almost exclusively based on publication. The pressure to publish and furthermore to publish within a particular time frame scarcely needs documenting.

There are undoubtedly counter pressures towards 'community'. There are professional associations, journals, exceptional examples of team research, or conferences, all of which mean that the pluralised environment is most assuredly not one of atomised individuals. None the less, these counter pressures towards 'community' rarely get beyond the 'partisan', 'tribal reservation' or 'intellectual club' levels noted above. Further 'corroboration' of where the balance between the individual versus community positions lies can be seen in a number of 'academic novels', of which some interesting and possibly telling examples are Bradbury (1976), Davies (1982), Lodge (1984) and Snow (1951).

My argument in this context is not that the structure and ideology of individualism is a major independent obstacle in its own right, which directly impedes aggregation – our environment does not for example differ substantially from that of natural scientists. Rather it is the case that the fragmented environment, defensible of course in terms of liberal claims that it encourages initiative and stimulates change, impedes aggregation indirectly by providing a base which sustains and reinforces the other more serious obstacles to aggregation.

CONCLUSION

I do not need deconstructing to be reminded that I, as much as anyone else, am a prisoner of an epistemology. It is in large part this epistemology which not only defines lack of aggregation as a problem but also influences the type of investigation that has been made. It is furthermore this epistemology which informs me that I have not done anything very novel and more importantly have made a descriptive analysis (limited aggregation) and an explanatory analysis (the four obstacles) both of which are far from exact. None the less, I do have some confidence in the overall thesis, which leads me to two final comments.

First, it seems to me that there is no easy solution to the limited aggregation. I differ from most stock-takers not in the descriptive conclusion but in the explanatory one. Virtually all stock-takers produce by way of conclusion a set of solutions. Several things are striking about these lists of solutions. First, if we sum the individual lists the total list is very long. Second, the lists divide into either technical fixes or cries of the functional equivalent of 'for England, Harry and St. George'. Third, the solutions of any one reviewer scarcely tend to be agnostic. In fact, it is often rather easy to read back from the types of suggested solutions to the form of research undertaken by the reviewer. Fourth, the aggregated list contains numerous contradictions – for instance, more data are matched by fewer data, more case studies by fewer case studies, more formal models by more substantive research, and so on. What we are seeing of course is a splendid celebration of accumulation. The error is that reviewers do not take sufficient account of the reasons why aggregation is so limited. The obstacles to aggregation are sufficiently powerful and/or interlocked that it is an absurdity to pretend that there is *a* new direction or horizon, which will yield *the* solution. Foreign policy analysis fundamentally cannot escape from the diversity of some multi-dimensionality and some incoherence.

The second and final comment concerns the movement from accumulation to aggregation. Though aggregation strikes me as a holy grail type of goal, it does seem that there is an encouraging development within what still remains a fundamentally accumulative process. This development is that of insights or cross-fertilisation. Though research does not aggregate vertically and horizontally into a kind of giant 'Lego' system, it does seem that the less automated researchers do borrow ideas, concepts, findings, approaches and test procedures, and in this respect gain insight from other work. Though we pay an immense, and arguably growing, price for the lack of aggregation, the cross-fertilisation of borrowed insight leads me to think there is progress if not to aggregation then to eclectic accumulation.

REFERENCES

Ashley, Richard K. 1976. 'Noticing Pre-Paradigmatic Progress.' In *In Search of Global Patterns*, ed. James N. Rosenau. New York: Free Press.
Bobrow, Davis B. 1972. *International Relations: New Approaches.* New York: Free Press.
Boynton, G.R. 1976. 'Cumulativeness in International Relations.' In *In Search of Global Patterns*, ed. James N. Rosenau. New York: Free Press.
Bradbury, Malcolm. 1976. *The History Man.* Boston: Houghton-Mifflin.
Bull, Hedley. 1966. 'International Theory: The Case for a Classical Approach.' *World Politics* 18: 361–77.
Caporaso, James N., Charles F. Harmann, Charles W. Kegley, James N. Rosenau and Dina A. Zinnes. 1987. 'The Comparative Study of Foreign Policy.' *International Studies Notes* 13: 32–46.
Cohen, Bernard C. and Scott Harris. 1975. 'Foreign Policy.' In *Handbook of Political Science.* Vol. 6, *Policies and Policymaking*, eds Fred I. Greenstein and Nelson Polsby. Reading, MA: Addison-Welsey.
Davies, Paul and John Gribbin. 1991. *The Matter Myth.* London: Viking.
Davies, Robertson. 1982. *The Rebel Angels.* New York: Viking Press.

Dryzek, John S. 1986. 'The Progress of Political Science.' *Journal of Politics* 48: 302–20.

East, Maurice A. 1987. 'The Comparative Study of Foreign Policy: We're Not There Yet, But...' *International Studies Notes* 13: 31.

East, Maurice A., Stephen A. Salmore and Charles F. Hermann. 1978. *Why Nations Act*. Beverly Hills: Sage.

Eco, Umberto. 1989. *Foucault's Pendulum*. San Diego: Harcourt, Brace, Jovanovich.

Faurby, Ib. 1976a. 'Premises, Promises and Problems of Comparative Foreign Policy.' *Cooperation and Conflict* 11: 139–62.

Faurby, Ib. 1976b. 'The Lack of Cumulation in Foreign Policy Studies.' *European Journal of Political Research* 4: 205–25.

Ferguson, Yale H. and Richard W. Mansbach. 1988. *The Elusive Quest*. Columbia: University of South Carolina Press.

Fowles, John. 1965. *Magus*. Boston: Little, Brown.

Fukuyama, Francis. 1992. *The End of History and the Last Man*. New York: Free Press.

Gerner, Deborah J. 1991. 'Foreign Policy Analysis: Renaissance, Routine or Rubbish.' In *Political Science: Looking to the Future*, Vol. 2, ed. William Crotty. Evanston: Northwestern University Press.

Hermann, Charles F., Charles W. Kegley and James N. Rosenau, eds. 1987. *New Directions in the Study of Foreign Policy*. Boston: Allen & Unwin.

Hill, Christopher and Margot Light. 1985. 'Foreign Policy Analysis.' In *International Relations: A Handbook of Current Theory*, eds Margot Light and A.J.R. Groom. London: Pinter.

Hollis, Martin and Steven Smith. 1990. *Explaining and Understanding International Relations*. Oxford: Clarendon Press.

Jones, Roy E. 1970. *Analyzing Foreign Policy*. London: Routledge & Kegan Paul.

Jones, Roy. E. 1979. *Principles of Foreign Policy*. Oxford: Martin Robertson.

Keat, Russell and John Urry. 1982. *Social Theory as Science*. London: Routledge & Kegan Paul.

Kennedy, Paul. 1987. *The Rise and Fall of the Great Powers*. New York: Random House.

Koestler, Arthur. 1961. *The Sleepwalkers*. New York: Macmillan.

Kuhn, Thomas S. 1970. *The Structure of Scientific Revolutions*. Chicago: University of Chicago Press.

Lakatos, Imre and Alan Musgrave, eds. 1970. *Criticism and the Growth of Knowledge*. Cambridge: Cambridge University Press.

Laudan, Larry. 1977. *Progress and Its Problems: Towards a Theory of Scientific Growth*. Berkeley: University of California Press.

Lodge, David. 1984. *Small World*. London: Secker & Warburg.

Morgenthau, Hans J. 1985. *Politics Among Nations*. New York: Alfred Knopf.

Munton, Don. 1976. 'Comparative Foreign Policy: Fads, Fantasies, Orthodoxies, Perversities.' In *In Search of Global Patterns*, ed. James N. Rosenau. New York: Free Press.

Nagel, Ernest. 1961. *The Structure of Science*. London: Routledge & Kegan Paul.

Northedge, Fred S. ed. 1974. *The Foreign Policies of the Powers*. London: Faber.

Ohmae, Kenichi. 1990. *The Borderless World*. New York: Harper.

Penrose, Roger. 1989. *The Emperor's New Mind*. Oxford: Oxford University Press.

Popper, Karl R. 1959. *The Logic of Scientific Discovery*. New York: Harper & Row.

Popper, Karl R. 1968. *Conjectures and Refutations: The Growth of Scientific Knowledge*. New York: Harper and Row.

Rose, Hilary and Steven Rose. 1969. *Science and Society*. London: Allen & Unwin.

Rosenau, James N. 1966. 'Pre-Theories and Theories of Foreign Policy.' In *Approaches to Comparative and International Politics*, ed. R. Barry Farrell. Evanston: Northwestern University Press.

Rosenau, James N., ed. 1976. *In Search of Global Patterns*. New York: Free Press.

Rosenau, James N. 1984. 'A Pre-Theory Revisited: World Politics in an Era of Cascading Interdependence.' *International Studies Quarterly* 28: 245–305.

Rudner, Richard R. 1968. *The Philosophy of the Social Sciences*. Englewood Cliffs: Prentice-Hall.

Sandole, Dennis J.D. 1985. 'Textbooks.' In *International Relations: A Handbook of Current Theory*, eds Margot Light and A.J.R. Groom. London: Pinter.

Schilts, Randy. 1987. *And the Band Played On*. New York: St Martin's Press.

Singer, J. David. 1975. 'Tribal Sins on the QIP Reservation.' In *In Search of Global Patterns*, ed. James N. Rosenau. New York: Free Press.

Smith, Steven. 1981. 'Traditionalism, Behaviouralism and Change in Foreign Policy Analysis.' In *Change and the Study of International Relations*, eds Barry Buzan and R.J. Barry Jones. London: Pinter.

Smith, Steven. 1983. 'Foreign Policy Analysis: British and American Orientations and Methodologies.' *Political Studies* 31: 556–65.

Smith, Steven. 1986. 'Theories of Foreign Policy: An Historical Overview.' *Review of International Studies* 12: 13–29.

Smith, Steven. 1987. 'CFP: A Theoretical Critique.' *International Studies Notes* 13: 47–8.

Snow, Charles P. 1951. *The Masters*. London: Macmillan.

Strange, Susan. 1986. *Casino Capitalism*. Oxford: Blackwell.

Strange, Susan. 1988. *States and Markets*. London: Pinter.

Waltz, Kenneth N. 1979. *Theory of International Politics*. Reading, MA: Addison-Wesley.

Watson, James D. 1968. *The Double Helix*. New York: Atheneum.

Wilkenfeld, Jonathon, Gerald W. Hoppoe, Paul J. Rossa and Stephen J. Andriole. 1980. *Foreign Policy Behaviour*. Beverly Hills: Sage.

Winch, Peter. 1970. *The Idea of Social Science*. London: Routledge & Kegan Paul.

Zinnes, Dina A. 1976. 'The Problems of Cumulation.' In *In Search of Global Patterns*, ed. James N. Rosenau. New York: Free Press.

Index

Page numbers in bold denote major section/chapter devoted to subject. f denotes figure. t denotes table. n denotes note.

Abitur 19, 20–1, 22
ACF *see* advocacy coalition
 framework
accumulation 179, 189, 195
 difference between aggregation
  and 183–4
 growth in literature **180–2**
 with limited aggregation **182–8**
 progress to eclectic 195
 and science 182–3, 184
advocacy coalition framework
 (ACF) **111–13**, 114, 115n
Africa 153, 168, 169
 culture and government
  activity 169, 172–3
 devaluation of CFA franc 156
 difficulties with economic statistics
  161
 divergence of economic
  performance between East Asia
  and 160–1, 167, 175
 economic stagnation due to
  government activity **164–7**,
  168, 173
 food production 165–6
 measures to help economy 166
 privatisation 173–4
 role of state in economic
  development 174–5
 similarity between states in
  economic performance
  167–8
 and structural adjustment
  programmes 167, 173, 174,
  175
agenda setting 103, 104, 107
 party programmes 93–7
aggregation 71–2, 194–5
 difference between accumulation
  and 183–4

importance of conferences and
  publications to 186–7
 with limited accumulation **182–8**
 obstacles to in analysis of foreign
  policy **188–94**, 195
 absence of agreed set of rules of
  investigation 191–3
 bridging role difficulties 190–1
 fragmented nature of
  environment 193–4
 topic selection and factors
  encouraging
  diversity 188–9
 and science 182–3
agriculture
 decline in expenditure 34f, 36t, 40
aid 153
Albert, Michel 125
Allison, Graham 5
Almond, Gabriel and Verba,
 Sidney 169
apprenticeship-based programmes
 (dual systems) 16–17, 23, 24
Apter, David 169
arbitration schemes, compulsory 50,
 54, 56
Armingeon, Klaus 60, 83
Ashley, Richard 184
Asia *see* East Asia
Aubin, C. *et al.* 147
Australia 50
 left–right policy priority 38f
Austria 23
 defence expenditure 35
 left–right policy priority 37, 39f

Barro, R.J. and Gordon, D.B. 156n
Bayart, Jean-François 172
Belgium
 left–right policy priority 37, 39f

BIBB (Bundesinstitut für
     Berufsbildung) 17, 18
Botswana 168
Boynton, G.R. 185
Braudel, Fernand 171
Britain 32, 65
   election programme emphasis
        compared to United States 86t
   example of minority rule 108
   left–right emphasis in postwar
        election programmes 87, 88f
   left–right policy priority 38f
business
   distribution of power and law 77,
        79

Calmfors, Lars and Driffill, E.J. 125,
     127
Canada
   average number of laws 71
   left–right policy priority 38f
   see also Quebec
capitalism 42–3
Caporaso, James *et al.* 191
Castles, F. 49
CFA franc
   devaluation of 156
China 162, 163, 164, 167, 171
coalitions 93
   advocacy coalition framework
        (ACF) 110–13, 114, 115n
   formation and election programmes
        analysis 94–6, 98
coercive activity
   and comparative public policy 3, 4
Cohen, Bernard and Harris, Scott 185
Cold War 37
   defence spending during 35
collectivism, methodological 121–2,
     128
communism, Soviet
   collapse of 171
comparative public policy *see* CPP
concepts 184–5, 192–3
conferences
   and aggregation 186
conservative elites 41–2
corporatism 58, 128
   characteristics 124–5

and trade unions 149–50, 54, 56,
     124, 127
and welfare **124–7**, 128, 130–1,
     132, 133, 134
Côte d'Ivoire 166, 167, 168, 174
CPP (comparative public policy)
   analysis **118–34**
   absence of theoretical core 119–20
   corporatism and welfare **124–7**,
        128, 130–1, 132, 133, 134
   institutionalist approach 121,
        122–4
   methodological individualism 5,
        120–4, 128, 132, 169–70, 172
   public choice theory and
        welfare 124, 127, 128,
        129–30, 132, 133
culturalism **168–73**
   and African development 169,
        172–3
   decline 169–70
   and East Asian
        development 171–2
   institution building dependence
        on 174
   resurgence 170–1
   used in comparative analysis of East
        Asia and Africa **168–73**

Dahl, Robert 70
defence
   expenditure 34f, 35, 36t
   shift in priority from 33, 35, 41, 42
discursive activity
   and comparative public policy 3,
        4
documents
   and merits for comparative analysis
        of government activity **82–4**
   need for quantitative analysis of 98
Dryzek, John 189
dual systems 16–17, 23, 24
Dye, Thomas 2, 11n

East Asia
   and authoritarianism 164, 166,
        175
   cultural perspectives on
        development 171–2

East Asia — *continued*
  divergence of economic
    performance between Africa
    and 160–1, 167, 175
  government activity and economic
    development **162–4**, 166
Easton, David 101–2, 105
economics 120, 121, 124, 139
  bias against positive analysis of
    public **139–40**
  game theory 125, 144–5
  incentives for economists to better
    understand public 140–1
  interaction with politics *see*
    politico-economic models
economy
  government activity and success of
    in East Asia **162–4**, 166
  stagnation of African **164–7**, 168
  vulnerability of and effect on
    regulation of labour
    relations 49, 53–4, 56, 57t, 67
ECPR (Manifesto Research Group of
    the European Consortium for
    Political Research) 82, 84
education
  apprenticeship based programmes
    (dual systems) 16–17, 23, 24
  contrasts between employment of
    teaching and non-teaching
    staff 15–16
  expenditure 32, 34f, 35, 36t
    cross-national **16–19**, 23, 24
    German 16–19t, 23–4, 32
    reasons for utilisation of health
      data rather than **14–16**
  secondary credentials and university
    admission **19–22**
election programmes **84–9**
  Britain and US emphasis
    compared 86t
  and budgetary expenditures 106,
    108
  and coalition formation 94–6, 98
  coding procedures 87, 89–93
  consolidation of categories 92t
  features 85–9
  and government activity 43–4, 45,
    89, **93–7**

left–right continuum 87, 88f, 94
  link with legislative action 72, 96,
    123
  and Manifesto Research
    Group **84–9**, 90, 99n
elections
  political participation 123
  vote function 142–3
Elling, Richard 72
Elster, Jon 58
Esping-Anderson, Gosta 29, 122
European Union 175
expenditure data **26–45**
  advantages of utilisation of in
    comparative analysis 26,
    27–9, 44, 97
  disadvantages of utilisation
    of 13–14, 16, 23, 80
  education **16–19**, 23–4
  focus on percentage of government
    spending 32–3
  as indicators of government
    activity **29–33**, 93
  priority trends in postwar **33–40**
  left–right priority 37, 38–9f
  summary 36t
  problems with comparing 16
  reasons for similarity in
    cross-national **40–2**
  utilisation of in health rather than
    education **14–16**

Faurby, Ib. 187
Ferguson, Yale and Mansbach,
    Richard 188, 189
financial activity
  and comparative public policy 3,
    4, 6
  see also expenditure data
foreign policy 2, 3, **179–95**
  analysts 184–5
  difficulty in defining 185
  expenditure trends 36t
  growth of literature in analysis
    of 180–2, 189
  literature and distance from
    aggregation **182–8**
  obstacles to aggregation in analysis
    of

absence of agreed set of rules of
investigation 191–3
bridging role difficulties 190–1
fragmented nature of
environment 193–4
topic selection and factors
encouraging diversity
188–9
weakness 185
Fowles, John 193
France
education expenditure 18, 32, 34f
left–right policy priority 38f
politico-economic model of
economy 147, 148
vote and popularity functions 142,
156–7n
franc zone 151, 153, 154f, 165
Frey, B.S. and Eichenberger, R. 149
Fukuyama, Francis 183
'funnel of causality' approach **105–7**,
113, 114

game theory 122–3, 125, 144–5
General Model of Policy
Evolution 45, 112f
Germany
education expenditure 16–19t,
23–4, 32
left–right emphasis in postwar
election programmes 87, 88f
left–right policy priority 39f
secondary credentials and university
admission 19, 20–1, 22
trade unions 65
Ghana 167, 174
Ginsberg, Benjamin 72
Gourevitch, Peter 60
government activity
considered as phenomenon 4–5, 6
defined **1–4**
future research into 44–5
methodological status **4–6**
problems with study 27–8
theory groups explaining 42–4
types of 3–4
types of conceptualisation 5–6
see also policy, government; policy
process

health
expenditure on 34f, 35, 36t, 40
reasons for utilisation of expenditure
data compared with education
14–16
Hofferbert, Richard
'funnel of causality'
approach **105–7**, 113, 114
Hollis, Martin and Smith, Steven 187
Hong Kong 163, 164
Huntingdon, Samuel 171

IDW (Institut der Deutschen
Wirtschaft) 17
IFI (international financial
institutions) 166, 173, 175
IMF (International Monetary
Fund) 152, 174
adjustment programmes 149, 151
and financial records 30–1
intervention 153, 154f–5f
immigration 132
incrementalism 40–1
individualism, methodological *see*
methodological individualism
individuals
in institutional rational choice
approach **109–10**
Indonesia 163
industrial relations *see* labour
relations
industrialisation
effect on recognition of trade
unions 52
institutional rational choice **109–10**,
113, 114, 121, 122–4
international financial institutions *see*
IFI
International Monetary Fund *see* IMF
Islamic revolution 171
Italy 71, 96

Japan 16, 18, 162

Katzenstein, Peter 49, 125
Keat, Russell and Urry, John 183
Kingdon, John
policy streams approach **107–9**,
113

Klingemann, Hans-Dieter *et al.*   106, 108
Korea   161, 163, 164

labour relations   **48–67**
  characteristics of political systems
    that impede reform   58–9
  conditions that cause policy changes
    in   57–8, 59–60, 61–4t
    economic crises   59–60
    industrial unrest   59, 60
    truth table of reforms and reasons
      for   61–4t
  determinants for decisions regarding
    regulation of
    class conflict   52–3, 56
    distribution of power,   56, 57
    economic vulnerability   49,
      53–4, 56, 57t, 67
    modernisation   50, 52
  inclusion of trade unions in
    economic policy-making
    49–50, 54, 56
  institutional inertia and reform   65,
    66t
  major regulations of collective
    (1945–90)   55t
  reasons for diversity of introduction
    of right of association/to
    combine   51f–4
  trade unions and corporatism
    49–50, 54, 56, 124, 127
laissez-faire   126, 127, 130, 132, 133
Landry, Réjean   73
Lasswell, Harold   102
Laver, Michael and Budge, Ian   87
laws   **70–81**
  comparative analysis of   4, 71–3,
    79–80
  congruence of election programmes
    with   72, 96, 123
  decline in annual number   71
  defined   70–1, 74
  Landry's economic analysis of
    Quebec laws   73
  need for development of
    comparative analysis   79–81
  power analysis of Quebec
    laws   **74–9**

approach   74–5
  distribution of power   74–5,
    76–9, 77t
  results   75–6
LDCs
  politico-economic interactions
    in   140, 141–2, **149–56**
  MLD model   **149–51**, 150f
  results   152–3, 154–5f, 156
  sources of economic data   152
left–right policy
  emphasis in post-war British and
    German party election
    campaigns   87–8f
  priority in ten postwar
    democracies   37, 38–9f
legislation *see* laws
Leichter, Howard   105
literature
  distance from aggregation   **182–8**
  growth of in foreign policy
    analysis   180–2, 189
Lorenz Curve   128–9f, 130f
Lundqvist, Lennart   105
Luxembourg Income Study
    (LIS)   135n

mandate theory *see* election
    programmes
Manifesto Research Group *see* MRG
Manifesto Research Group of the
    European Consortium for
    Political Research (ECPR)   82,
    84
manifestos *see* election programmes
Marx, Karl   52
Matura   19, 20, 22
Mazmanian, Daniel and Sabatier,
    Paul   107
methodological collectivism   121–2,
    128
methodological individualism   5,
    120–4, 128, 132, 169–70, 172
Mills, C. Wright   42
MLD model   **149–51**, 150f, 152
monetary policy   139, 145–6
MRG (Manifesto Research
    Group)   **84–9**, 90, 99n
Munton, Don   185

Nadel, Mark 2
Nannestad, P. and Paldam, M. 142
neo-corporatism *see* corporatism
Netherlands 16
  left–right policy priority 39f
New Zealand 50, 65
Niskanen, William 40
North, Douglas 120
North Korea 163

OECD 14, 16, 18
Olson, Mancur 130, 135n
ontology 191, 192
Ostrom, Elinor 109–10, 114

Paloheimo, Heikki 126, 127
parties, political *see* political parties
party mandate theory *see* election
  programmes
party policy *see* policy, party
party programmes *see* election
  programmes
People's Republic of China *see* China
policy, government
  concept 2
  definition **1–4**
  impeding of creation of by certain
    characteristics of political
    systems 58–9
  see also government activity
policy, party
  and comparative analysis of election
    programmes **84–51**
policy process **101–15**
  advocacy coalition framework
    (ACF) **111–13**, 114, 115n
  'funnel of causality'
    approach **105–7**, 113, 114
  institutional rational
    choice **109–10**, 113, 114, 121,
    122–4
  policy streams approach **107–9**,
    113, 114
  stages heuristic theory **101–4**, 113
policy streams approach **107–9**, 113,
  114
political institutions
  and distribution of power and
    law 76, 77t, 79

political parties
  and mandates *see* election
    programmes
politics
  integration into economic analysis
    see politico-economic
    models
politico-economic models **139–56**
  in industrialised democracies
    141–8
  and French economy 147
  influence of political variables on
    private economic
    choices 141–2
  limitations of 146–7
  logics taken into account by
    governmental
    decision-makers 147–8
  reaction functions **143–6**
  vote and popularity functions 141,
    142–3
  in LDCs 140, 141–2, **149–56**
  MLD model **149–51**, 150f
  results 152–3, 154–5f, 156
  sources of economic data 152
Pomper, Gerald 72
popularity function 141, 142–3
power
  definition 70
  distribution of and law **76–9**
private sector
  positive approach towards 140
privatisation
  in Africa 173–4
programmes, party *see* election
  programmes
proportional representation 123
Przeworski, Adam 42, 43
publications
  and aggregation 186–7
public choice theory 139, 149
  and welfare 124, 127, 128,
    129–30, 132, 133
public economics *see* economics
Putnam, Robert *et al.* 71
Pye, Lucien 169
qualitative data 30, 45
  reasons for utilisation of in
    comparative analysis 82–3

quantitative data   28, 45
    and documents   98
Quebec
    Landry's economic analysis of
        laws   73
    power analysis of laws   **74–9**

rational choice theory   58, 70
    institutional   **109–10**, 113, 114,
        121, 122–4
    and methodological individualism
        5, **120–2**, 128–32, 169–70
reaction functions,
    politico-economic   143–6
regulatory activity
    and comparative public
        policy   3–4, 6
    expenditure on   29, 34t, 35, 36t
Research Institute of German Business
    (IDW)   17
'Rhenish' model   125
Robertson, David   89–90
Rose, Richard   71, 75
Rowthorn, B.   128

Sabatier, Paul   107, 108
    and advocacy coalition
        framework   111–13, 114,
        115n
    General Model of Policy
        Evolution   45, 112f
Scandinavia   96, 121, 131, 132
science   198
    cumulation in   182–3, 184
    topic selection in   189–90
Sierra Leone   174
Singer, J.   4
Smith, Adam   190, 191
South Korea   163, 164
stages heuristic theory   **101–4**, 105
    limitations   103–4, 113
    strengths   101–3
state
    role of in economic development in
        Third World   174–5
statecraft   119, 120
strikes
    and MLD model in LDCs   151,
        152, 153

and policy changes   59, 60
structural adjustment
    programmes   167, 173, 174, 175
Sub-Saharan Africa *see* Africa
Sweden   133–4
    defence expenditure   35
    left–right policy priority   38f
    sick-leave policy   134
Switzerland
    annual number of laws   71
    education expenditure   16–17
    lagging in data collection   23
    secondary credentials and university
        admission   19, 20, 21–2

Taiwan   164
textbooks   185–6
Third World   **159–76**
    cultural comparison   **168–73**, 175–6
    culture, state and government
        activity   **173–5**
    divergence in economic
        performance   160–1, 167, 175
    economic development and
        government activity in East
        Asia   **162–4**, 166
    economic stagnation and
        government activity in
        Africa   **164–7**, 168, 173
    problems with comparison of
        government activity in
        159–62, 176
    reasons for differences in
        development performance
        between Africa and East
        Asia   167–8
    see also Africa; East Asia
trade unions
    and corporatism   49–50, 54, 56,
        124, 127
    inclusion in economic
        policy-making   49–50, 54, 56
    introduction of right of association
        and to combine   50, 51t, 52
    population size and strength of
        resistance   53, 54t
    see also labour relations
transportation
    expenditure on   34f, 35, 36t

Tullock, Gordon 133

UNESCO 13, 14
unions *see* trade unions
United States 130–1, 132
  air pollution policy 111
  average number of laws 71
  education expenditure 18, 32
  election programme emphasis
    compared to Britain 86t
  election promises and laws passed
    by Congress 72
  implementation of national
    legislation 102, 108
  left–right policy priority 38f
  non-teaching staff and teaching
    staff 15
  secondary credentials and university
    admission 19–20, 21
universities
  secondary credentials and admission
    to **19–22**

U-Shaped Curve 126f–27, 128, 131f,
  131–2, 133

Vogel, David 105
voting 123, 142, 143

Waltz, Kenneth N. 185
welfare
  and corporatism **124–7**, 128,
    130–1, 132, 133, 134
  and public choice theory 124, 127,
    128, 129–30, 132, 133
  Sweden 133–4
welfare state 37, 41, 42, 121–2,
  140
West Germany *see* Germany
Wilensky, Harold 58
World Bank 166

Zaire 166
Zinnes, Dina 184